UNITED NATIONS CONFERENCE ON TRADE AND DEVELOPMENT
GENEVA

TRADE AND DEVELOPMENT REPORT, 2008

Report by the secretariat of the
United Nations Conference on Trade and Development

UNITED NATIONS
New York and Geneva, 2008

Note

PER
UNI
TD
T62

- Symbols of United Nations documents are composed of capital letters combined with figures. Mention of such a symbol indicates a reference to a United Nations document.

- The designations employed and the presentation of the material in this publication do not imply the expression of any opinion whatsoever on the part of the Secretariat of the United Nations concerning the legal status of any country, territory, city or area, or of its authorities, or concerning the delimitation of its frontiers or boundaries.

- Material in this publication may be freely quoted or reprinted, but acknowledgement is requested, together with a reference to the document number. A copy of the publication containing the quotation or reprint should be sent to the UNCTAD secretariat.

UNCTAD/TDR/2008

UNITED NATIONS PUBLICATION
Sales No. E.08.II.D.21
ISBN 978-92-1-112752-2 ISSN 0255-4607

Contents

Chapter VI

CURRENT ISSUES RELATED TO THE EXTERNAL DEBT OF DEVELOPING COUNTRIES

List of tables

List of charts

List of boxes

Explanatory notes

Classification by country or commodity group

The classification of countries in this *Report* has been adopted solely for the purposes of statistical or analytical convenience and does not necessarily imply any judgement concerning the stage of development of a particular country or area.

The major country groupings used in this *Report* follow the classification by the United Nations Statistical Office (UNSO). They are distinguished as:

» Developed or industrial(ized) countries: the countries members of the OECD (other than Mexico, the Republic of Korea and Turkey) plus the new EU member countries and Israel.

» Transition economies refers to South-East Europe and the Commonwealth of Independent States (CIS).

» Developing countries: all countries, territories or areas not specified above.

The terms "country" / "economy" refer, as appropriate, also to territories or areas.

References to "Latin America" in the text or tables include the Caribbean countries unless otherwise indicated.

References to "sub-Saharan Africa" in the text or tables include South Africa unless otherwise indicated.

For statistical purposes, regional groupings and classifications by commodity group used in this *Report* follow generally those employed in the *UNCTAD Handbook of Statistics 2006–07* (United Nations publication, sales no. E/F.07.II.D.2) unless otherwise stated. The data for China do not include those for Hong Kong Special Administrative Region (Hong Kong SAR), Macao Special Administrative Region (Macao SAR) and Taiwan Province of China.

Other notes

References in the text to *TDR* are to the *Trade and Development Report* (of a particular year). For example, *TDR 2007* refers to *Trade and Development Report, 2007* (United Nations publication, sales no. E.07.II.D.11).

The term "dollar" ($) refers to United States dollars, unless otherwise stated.

The term "billion" signifies 1,000 million.

The term "tons" refers to metric tons.

Annual rates of growth and change refer to compound rates.

Exports are valued FOB and imports CIF, unless otherwise specified.

Use of a dash (–) between dates representing years, e.g. 1988–1990, signifies the full period involved, including the initial and final years.

An oblique stroke (/) between two years, e.g. 2000/01, signifies a fiscal or crop year.

A dot (.) indicates that the item is not applicable.

Two dots (..) indicate that the data are not available, or are not separately reported.

A dash (-) or a zero (0) indicates that the amount is nil or negligible.

A plus sign (+) before a figure indicates an increase; a minus sign (-) before a figure indicates a decrease.

Details and percentages do not necessarily add up to totals because of rounding.

Abbreviations

ACP	African, Caribbean and Pacific (group of States)
BIS	Bank for International Settlements
BNDES	Brazilian Development Bank (Banco Nacional de Desenvolvimento Econômico e Social)
CAC	collective action clause
CIS	Commonwealth of Independent States
CFF	Compensatory Financing Facility (of IMF)
CPI	consumer price index
CPIA	Country Policy and Institutional Assessment (of the World Bank)
DAC	Development Assistance Committee (of the OECD)
EBRD	European Bank for Reconstruction and Development
ECB	European Central Bank
EU	European Union
FAO	Food and Agriculture Organization of the United Nations
GCC	Gulf Cooperation Council
GDF	Global Development Finance (database of the World Bank)
GDP	gross domestic product
GFCF	gross fixed capital formation
GNI	gross national income
HDI	Human Development Index
HIPC	Heavily Indebted Poor Country (also HIPC Initiative)
ICA	international commodity agreement
ICT	information and communication technology
IDA	International Development Association (of the World Bank Group)
IDB	Inter-American Development Bank

IMF	International Monetary Fund
LDC	least developed country
LIFDC	low-income food-deficit country
MDG	Millennium Development Goal
MDRI	Multilateral Debt Relief Initiative
NGO	non-governmental organization
NIE	newly industrializing economy
NPV	net present value
ODA	official development assistance
OECD	Organisation for Economic Co-operation and Development
OECD-IDS	OECD - International Development Statistics
OPEC	Organization of the Petroleum Exporting Countries
PPG	public and publicly guaranteed (debt)
PPP	purchasing power parity
PRSP	Poverty Reduction Strategy Paper
REER	real effective exchange rate
RER	real exchange rate
SDR	Special Drawing Right
SDRM	Sovereign Debt Restructuring Mechanism
TDR	Trade and Development Report
TFP	total factor productivity
UNCTAD	United Nations Conference on Trade and Development
UNDP	United Nations Development Programme
UNSD	United Nations Statistics Division
USDA	United States Department of Agriculture

OVERVIEW

Since 1999, many developing countries have registered strong improvements in their external balances, and their aggregate current account has swung into surplus. As a result, as a group they have become net exporters of capital to developed countries. Many of them, particularly a number of fast growing exporters of manufactures, owe this situation to their successful global integration and to a reorientation of their macroeconomic policies towards a greater focus on competitive exchange rates. In other countries, substantially increased earnings from primary commodity exports have also led to stronger current-account positions.

But the situation is fragile: uncertainty and instability in international financial, currency and commodity markets, coupled with doubts about the direction of monetary policy in some major developed countries, are contributing to a gloomy outlook for the world economy and could present considerable risks for the developing world. Many developing countries that have seen improvements in their terms of trade in recent years remain highly vulnerable to a possible prolonged global slowdown and an end to the commodity boom. For a number of them, higher prices of their net food and energy imports have already created a heavy burden, particularly for the poorer segments of their populations, seriously jeopardizing progress towards meeting the Millennium Development Goals (MDGs) set by the United Nations in 2000.

This is why development policies need to continue to focus on diversification and sustained industrialization based on higher investment in new productive capacities, especially in agriculture and manufacturing, and on the provision of adequate, reliable and cost-effective financing of such investment. Recent experience in several fast growing developing countries has shown that, from a macroeconomic angle, this does not always require a current-account deficit – that is, a net capital inflow – provided that domestic monetary policy and the local financial system offer a favourable environment for long-term financing of private firms. In many developing countries this requires a stronger focus on improving the conditions for reinvestment of company profits and for an enhanced role of the banking sector in financing investment. However, a number of poorer countries that are unable to boost export earnings owing to structural constraints continue to rely on foreign capital inflows to finance imports of essential capital goods. This implies that official development assistance (ODA) will need to be further increased, not only with a view to filling the existing financing gap to help meet the social and human development objectives of the MDGs, but also to help generate higher per capita income growth and employment for sustained development beyond the MDG deadline of 2015.

The global outlook: a slowdown in developed countries and higher risks in financial and commodity markets

The financial turmoil that erupted in August 2007, the unprecedented oil price increases and the possibility of tighter monetary policy in a number of countries presage difficulties for the world economy in 2008 and 2009. The impact of the sub-prime crisis has spread well beyond the United States, causing a widespread squeeze in liquidity and credit. And price hikes in primary commodities, fuelled partly by speculation that has shifted from financial instruments to commodity markets, adds to the challenge for policymakers intent on avoiding a recession while at the same time keeping inflation under control. The situation could become even more difficult if large movements in the exchange rates of major currencies add to the turmoil in the financial markets, a risk that has increased in the first half of 2008.

In this highly uncertain environment, output in the world economy as a whole is expected to grow by around 3 per cent in 2008, almost one percentage point less than in 2007, and in developed countries as a group, GDP growth is likely to fall to about half this rate. By contrast, growth in developing countries as a group can be expected to remain quite robust, at more than 6 per cent, as a result of the relatively stable dynamics of domestic demand in a number of large developing economies. However, possible restrictive monetary policy responses to increasing pressure on the overall price index from higher commodity prices could well lead to a further deceleration of growth in developed and developing countries alike.

For a large number of developing countries, the outlook depends primarily on future trends in the prices of their primary commodity exports. Although several structural factors support the expectation that prices will remain at a higher level than over the past 20 years, cyclical factors and delayed supply responses could well cause a weakening of some commodity prices, especially when the impact of speculation is taken into account. Just as such speculation has amplified the upward movement of prices, it may also amplify any downward movement. This could happen, for example, if forecasts for global demand growth need to be adjusted downwards in the course of the year as a result of further turmoil in financial markets or an abrupt change in the mood of investors in response to events on financial markets, such as a rise in interest rates or a stock market recovery. Additionally, if the liquidity crisis were to spill over to the market for emerging-market debt, some developing and transition economies – mainly in Eastern Europe and Central Asia – which carry a substantial stock of external debt and have large current-account deficits, could face a sudden increase in their financing costs and debt servicing problems.

Monetary policy: divergence may encourage speculation

The meltdown in the sub-prime mortgage segment of the most sophisticated financial market in the world has exposed the fragility of today's global financial sector. Instead of reducing risk, complex financial instruments have served to spread the impact of risky investments across countries and markets. The recent crisis has shown once again that market discipline is ineffective in preventing recurrent episodes of "irrational exuberance", when financial firms attempt to extract double-digit returns out of economies that grow at much slower rates. And since financial crises can have major repercussions on the real economy, policymakers have no choice but to bail out parts of the financial sector when systemic threats loom. But such bailouts also underline the case for tighter prudential regulation.

The current international framework for monetary and exchange-rate policies offers opportunities for speculative activities that are highly profitable for a limited period of time, but ultimately destabilize the entire system. The rapid unwinding of "carry trade" activities, aimed at extracting gains from nominal interest rate differentials, presents another threat for the global financial system. The financial turbulence, the speculative forces contributing to commodity price hikes and instability, and the apparent failure of foreign-exchange markets to bring about changes in exchange rates that reflect current-account trends suggest that there is an urgent need for reviewing the institutional framework of the global economy.

The major central banks have shown considerable coherence in their response to the sub-prime crises by providing liquidity to affected banks and financial institutions. But their monetary policies are diverging more than ever. The Federal Reserve has been very aggressive in cutting policy rates, whereas other central banks have been much more timid, and some, including the European Central Bank (ECB) and the central banks of a number of emerging-market economies, have even raised their interest rates. These divergent policies may invite renewed speculation in foreign exchange markets instead of calming the system.

Global imbalances: need for coordinated international action

An adjustment of some of the current-account imbalances that have shaped the world economy over many years is now under way. But a continuation of this trend hinges almost entirely on a slowdown of the United States economy and a depreciation of the dollar, while the adjustment process can only be painless for the world economy as a whole if domestic spending and imports in the surplus economies rise.

However, not all surplus countries have the same scope for increasing domestic demand. In China, for example, this is much more difficult than elsewhere, as private consumption is already rising fast and the economy is close to overheating. The appreciation of the yuan may nevertheless contribute to the global adjustment of trade balances. On the other hand, in Western Europe (especially in Germany) and Japan there is a much greater scope for domestic demand to expand. Overall, there is a strong likelihood of a sharp and prolonged downturn of the world economy as long as policymakers do not agree on ways to tackle global imbalances through coordinated and concerted action.

Macroeconomic stabilization: the risk of anti-inflationary overkill

At more than $140 per barrel in mid-2008, the price of oil reached a new peak in nominal and real terms. Oil price hikes in recent years have been accompanied by a sharp increase in the prices of most other primary commodities, and this has prompted calls for central banks to take strong action to prevent an acceleration of inflation. However, it may well be that the risk of galloping inflation is considerably overestimated, as the probability of a wage-price spiral occurring is much smaller today than it was in the episode of rising oil prices in the 1970s. Today, trade unions in most developed countries are either too weak to push for higher wages or they have learned from past experience. Consequently, the rise in unit labour costs, a key determinant of inflation, has been low in most countries.

In the current fragile condition of the global economy, measures to tighten monetary policy would exacerbate the global slowdown. Given the need to contain the macroeconomic impact of the sub-prime crisis and to raise domestic demand in surplus countries to ensure a smooth redressment of the global trade imbalances, any policy with contractionary effects will have to be applied very cautiously. In the present environment of rising commodity prices, a cooperative approach involving trade unions, employers, governments and central banks seems to be more appropriate for preventing a wage-inflation spiral than the use of monetary policy alone.

Developing countries could consider combining a broader range of policy instruments in responding to increasing food and energy costs, which are a much heavier burden on most household budgets in these countries than in developed countries and create an understandably strong pressure for wage increases. Indeed, the dramatic social and humanitarian consequences of the surge in food prices in some countries are jeopardizing progress towards meeting the Millennium Development Goals (MDGs), especially that of halving poverty by 2015. This calls for specific income transfers targeted to the most needy households. Yet many of the concerned countries cannot afford such additional social expenditure unless they reduce spending for other purposes, including urgent infrastructure investments. This dilemma suggests the need for additional foreign assistance to overcome this distribution problem in poor countries. It also demonstrates the importance, from both a macroeconomic and social perspective, of new measures aimed at achieving greater commodity price stability and of quick-response instruments to mitigate the impact of sharp commodity price fluctuations.

Primary commodity markets: new patterns and linkages

In 2008, the prices of all commodity groups were much higher than their peaks of the mid-1990s, except for tropical beverages. This upward trend has been mainly the result of rapidly increasing demand from several fast growing developing economies. Price movements have also been influenced by the closer links between energy markets and agricultural commodity markets, particularly those for food crops, and by the closer links between primary commodity markets in general and financial markets. Thus the level and stability of commodity prices has become an important policy issue, not only from the traditional development perspective, but also from the perspective of the functioning of a highly integrated global economy.

Higher oil prices influence the final prices of other commodities, particularly food crops and vegetable oils, because they have led to increased competition for arable land to grow crops for biofuel production, as an alternative to oil. This trend has been reinforced by policy measures in the EU and the United States to accelerate the substitution of traditional fuels by biofuels. Together with extremely low inventory levels and the turbulence in financial markets, this has probably been one of the factors encouraging speculative demand for such commodities. The depreciation of the dollar is an additional factor contributing to the higher commodity prices in dollar terms. For instance, between May 2007 and May 2008 the index of non-fuel commodity prices in dollars increased by 41.9 per cent, but only by 32.7 per cent in SDRs and by 23.3 per cent in euros.

Primary commodities: unresolved problems of commodity dependence and price instability

Uncertainty about key prices generally has a negative impact on the investment and production planning of both sellers and buyers, and renders macroeconomic, fiscal and financial management more difficult. This is why, from the perspective of those developing countries whose export earnings and national income are highly dependent on commodity markets, both the long-term trend of primary commodity prices and their volatility have always been a concern. Price volatility is one of the reasons why commodity-dependent economies have lower long-term average growth rates than economies with diversified production structures.

For every country, reducing dependence on a few primary commodities through diversification and industrial development is the best strategy in the long run to reduce vulnerability to commodity price shocks and unfavourable price trends. But diversification is a complex and time-consuming process that is not possible without capital formation and skills acquisition. It also depends on stable earnings from primary commodity exports. From the perspective of consumer countries and the world economy as a whole, fluctuating commodity prices render policies aimed at macroeconomic stability more difficult. Given the problems created by unstable commodity prices, the global economic system would gain greater coherence if new efforts were made at the multilateral level to control price fluctuations on international commodity markets, while allowing smooth adjustments of relative prices that reflect market fundamentals and structural changes.

However, it is unlikely that international price stabilization mechanisms agreed multilaterally between producers and consumers, such as the various commodity agreements of the past, will again become a political option in the near future. It would therefore be useful to tackle the factors that cause large commodity price fluctuations in the first place and correct any undesired market outcomes. Stricter regulatory measures that help contain speculation on commodity markets could be one important step, since commodity market speculation typically exacerbates price trends originating from changes in fundamentals.

International compensatory finance schemes employed in the past to mitigate the impact of volatility on developing countries have proved insufficient. Such schemes would need to make more rapid disbursements and be equipped with more financial resources for balance-of-payments or income support. They should not only be able to cover shortfalls in export earnings but also higher import costs resulting from sharp increases in prices of essential commodity imports, particularly food and energy. These schemes might also include the provision of grants to be passed through to the most seriously affected producers or households in the poorest countries. In principle, it should be sufficient that the country has no control over the cause of the underlying price shock to be eligible for such assistance, and conditionality, if any, should be linked directly to the use of the financial resources provided under the scheme.

At the national level, institutional arrangements that serve as a buffer between prices on international commodity markets and earnings of domestic producers may facilitate the latter's investment decisions and the financing of measures to improve productivity. Experience with systems of income support in many developed countries could provide useful lessons, but the costs of these systems normally exceed the budgetary possibilities of developing countries. A possible solution would be for these countries to consider an institutional arrangement whereby they would retain part of the windfall gains from high commodity prices in national funds for release to domestic producers when international market conditions are unfavourable. If initiated in a phase of relatively high prices, such an arrangement would assure a smooth income stream for their producers without unduly straining budgetary resources.

The gains of developing countries from commodity exports and their impact on financing investment in support of diversification and industrialization also depend on how they are distributed. There are strong indications that in several countries a large share of the considerable gains from the higher prices of hydrocarbon and mining products have gone into profit remittances of the foreign enterprises involved in their exploitation. This means they are lost for capital accumulation in the country where they originate, unless they are reinvested by the foreign companies. But the latter may often not be in the interest of the exporting country either because, rather than contributing to diversification and industrial upgrading, such reinvestment in the same activities tends to perpetuate commodity dependence.

Current-account reversals: the roles of real exchange rates and terms of trade

Higher commodity prices and better terms of trade have greatly contributed to improving the current-account balances of some developing countries in recent years. Another factor, at least equally important, has been the fast growth of exports of manufactures of a number of developing countries based on rapid productivity growth and favourable real exchange rates. As a consequence, developing countries as a group have been net exporters of capital for several years. Following the financial crises in Asia in 1997–1998, an increasing amount of capital began flowing "uphill", from poor to rich countries, to such an extent that many observers concluded that some developing countries had created a "savings glut" for the world economy.

Improvements in the current account, and swings from deficit to surplus, were initially driven by large exchange rate devaluations in emerging-market economies that are exporters of manufactures. In most of these countries, their current-account improvements began in the aftermath of the Asian financial crisis and were sustained as governments and central banks subsequently sought to maintain a competitive real exchange rate. For most countries whose trade performance is determined primarily by world demand for primary commodities the improvement in the current account began in 2003, when prices for oil and mining products started to increase.

The macroeconomic and exchange-rate policies that have played a major role in the improvement of the current-account position of many developing countries mark a departure from past strategies. In the past, both exchange-rate pegging and flexible exchange-rate regimes often led to real currency appreciation and growing current-account deficits. Over time, a worsening of the current-account balance increased the perception among international investors of greater currency risk, and at a certain point triggered a sudden and strong capital outflow. By contrast, the new strategy of many countries has been aiming at defending favourable competitive positions created by undervalued exchange rates and avoiding dependence on the international capital markets that is associated with a current-account deficit. As this strategy often requires intervention in foreign exchange markets, it contributes to a rapid accumulation of foreign-exchange reserves and higher net capital outflows from developing countries.

This also confirms the more general finding that current-account reversals in developing countries with a high share of manufactures in their total trade are primarily driven by large real-exchange-rate changes, whereas for commodity-dependent economies, terms-of-trade shocks are the major factor. An increase in the current-account deficit as a result of an appreciation of the real exchange rate and a concomitant loss of competitiveness of domestic producers may be temporarily financed by a net capital inflow, but it will sooner or later require some form of adjustment, normally a real depreciation. Indeed, overvaluation has been the most frequent and the most "reliable" predictor of financial crises in developing countries. On the other hand, a depreciation of the real exchange rate is a necessary condition for an expansionary current-account reversal. A competitive real exchange rate is a key factor for increasing aggregate demand in the short run and achieving faster growth and higher employment in the long run.

However, there is a risk that governments will use exchange-rate manipulation in the same way as wage compression, subsidies and lower corporate taxation to artificially improve the international competitiveness of domestic producers. This kind of "new mercantilism" in the competition for higher market shares cannot achieve the desired results. This is because, while all countries can simultaneously boost productivity, wages and trade to improve their overall economic welfare, all of them cannot simultaneously increase their market shares or their current-account surpluses. Successive rounds of competitive devaluations are therefore unproductive and likely to cause considerable damage. This problem could be addressed by a framework of international rules similar to those governing the use of trade policy measures in agreements of the World Trade Organization (WTO).

Net capital flows, investment and growth: theory and reality

The fact that developing countries as a group are net capital exporters contrasts with expectations based on mainstream economic theories, that with open capital markets capital would flow from rich to poor countries, attracted by higher rates of return. What is even more surprising in light of mainstream theory is that, on average, developing countries that are net exporters of capital also tend to grow faster and to have a higher investment ratio than developing countries that receive net capital inflows.

These facts have been considered "puzzles", but they are no longer puzzling if one recognizes the limitations of the underlying theories: the savings gap model and the neoclassical growth model. These models are based on the assumption that investment is financed from a savings pool created mainly by household savings. Accordingly, entrepreneurial investment will be maximized by policies aimed at increasing household savings rates and capital imports ("foreign savings"), and improving the efficiency of financial intermediation by developing a competitive financial system and creating securities markets. Not only are the assumptions of these models far from reality, but also their predictions have been repeatedly refuted by empirical evidence. For example, many developing countries, particularly in Latin America, failed to achieve higher productive investment despite monetary and financial policies that attracted waves of capital inflows.

In an alternative view, based on the works of Schumpeter and Keynes and deriving from the experiences of post-war Western Europe and the successful catching-up experiences in East Asia, the financing of investment depends primarily on savings from corporate profits and the possibility of the banking system to create credit. Strong enterprise profits simultaneously increase the incentive of firms to invest and their capacity to finance new investments from retained earnings. This view better reflects the complexity and imperfections of the real world, where entrepreneurial profits immediately adjust to changes in demand, and entrepreneurial decisions based on profit expectations (rather than the level of savings) determine the level of investment in real productive capital. For example, a fall in the savings ratio does not lead to a fall in investment; on the contrary, since it implies an increase in consumer demand, it will increase profits and stimulate investment. By the same token, an improvement of the current account as a result of changes in relative prices in favour of domestic producers does not represent a reduction in the inflows of foreign savings that causes a fall in investment; on the contrary, it is equivalent to an increase in aggregate demand and in the profits of domestic producers, and tends to lead to higher investment. Thus, an increase in savings is not a prerequisite for either higher investment or an improvement in the current account. Rather, the causality works in the opposite direction: changes in the current account lead to changes in the level of investment and savings.

The consequences of the different theoretical approaches for economic policy could not be more different. When investment, output growth and employment are determined largely by profits of enterprises, economic policies have an important role to play in absorbing shocks and providing a stable environment for investment. By contrast, in the neoclassical model there is little room for economic policy, and where it offers economic policy options, they often point in the opposite direction to those suggested by the Keynes-Schumpeter model. Where the neoclassical model sees the need for private households "to put aside more money" or for developing countries to attract more "foreign savings" to raise investment in fixed capital, the Keynes-Schumpeter model emphasizes positive demand and profit expectations as incentives for domestic entrepreneurs, and the need for reliable and affordable financing for enterprises.

Financing of fixed investment: the role of company profits and the banking system

Empirically, from a macroeconomic perspective, domestic resources are more important for investment financing than foreign ones. However, the latter can play a critical role at certain times and for certain countries, for instance to finance imports of capital goods when there are structural impediments to increasing export earnings. From the perspective of firms, self-financing from retained earnings is the most important and most reliable source for financing investment. In addition to self-financing from profits, bank credit is empirically the most important source of external financing for enterprises, particularly for new businesses and small and medium-sized firms.

It is very important that a substantial part of firms' earnings be reinvested in productive capacity, rather than being used, for example, for luxury consumption or speculative activities. As the availability of internal funds is a key determinant of investment, measures that increase the liquidity of firms and encourage the retention of profits may help to spur investment. Possible measures include a range of fiscal incentives and disincentives, such as preferential tax treatment for reinvested or retained profits, special depreciation allowances, and high taxation of income from speculative activities.

The impact of such measures on productive investment can be amplified if banks are encouraged to make loans more easily available for investment. To the extent that investment can be financed by the banking system, which has the power to create credit depending on the amount of liquidity provided by the central bank, the prior existence of savings balances in the financial system is not a prerequisite for investment. But in order to prevent a monetary policy that focuses on the stimulation of investment from becoming inflationary, it has to be combined with institutional arrangements and additional policy instruments to maintain price stability. In particular it calls for an incomes policy that prevents excessive nominal wage increases and a flexible fiscal policy that responds to cyclical changes in aggregate demand. This has been a successful recipe in the newly industrializing economies (NIEs) of East Asia, where policy interest rates generally have been slightly higher than the rate of inflation but lower than real GDP growth rates. By contrast, they have been higher than GDP growth rates in most countries in Latin America and Africa, where monetary policy has tended to focus entirely on avoiding inflation, with the result that investment ratios and growth rates remained low. It is only since the beginning of the new millennium that an increasing number of countries in the latter regions have also adopted more expansionary monetary policies and achieved better growth performance.

Cost and availability of investment finance: policies matter

An investment-friendly monetary policy would also help to reduce the costs of bank financing. These are determined by the cost of refinancing by banks, the average amount of loan losses that banks have to bear, and the degree of competition in the banking system. When interest rates are too high, they have a negative impact on the most important sources of financing for investment: company profits and bank credit. This is probably the main reason why the financial reforms undertaken by many developing and transition economies in the 1980s and 1990s generally failed to improve investment ratios. As reforms were undertaken in the context of a restrictive monetary policy aimed at achieving and maintaining low inflation, they were generally accompanied by an increase in interest rates.

Financial deregulation undertaken since the mid-1980s in many developing countries, coupled with liberalization of the capital account, brought about an expansion of banking activity and a fast increase in net inflows of foreign capital, but it seldom led to the expected sustained increase in bank lending to private enterprises for investment purposes. Instead, it led to a boom in lending mainly for consumption and real estate acquisition. The process often ended in financial and banking crises, in the course of which governments and central banks had to rescue the banking system at considerable fiscal costs. The expectation that financial liberalization and opening up of the domestic financial sectors to foreign banks would introduce more competition, which would eventually reduce interest spreads and the cost of credit, did not materialize either. Spreads and lending rates have remained generally high, to the detriment of corporate and investment financing. Even after banking crises, commercial banks apparently find it more profitable and less risky to extend consumption and housing credits, or to purchase government securities, than to provide longer term loans for investment projects or new business activities.

Banks and other financial institutions influence the pattern of economic activity by the way in which they allocate financial resources among different types of borrowers and economic activities, according to their own objectives and strategies. However, their choices are not necessarily in the best interest of the economy as a whole. The unwillingness of banks to provide long-term investment credit, combined with high interest spreads and lending rates, often reflects a perception of high credit risk and difficulties in collateralizing such loans. Therefore, when developing countries with weak financial systems undertake domestic governance reforms, as frequently advocated, priority may need to be given to dealing with those institutional shortcomings that represent major obstacles to the provision of long-term credit for investment at reasonable interest rates. These shortcomings tend to differ from country to country but are likely to concern property rights, provision of collateral and enforcement of credit contracts, and effective competition in the banking sector.

In most countries, access to bank credit still depends heavily on the size of the firm, so that new, innovative and small enterprises, in particular, often encounter severe financing constraints even when they are able to pay high real lending rates. Financing from securities markets is usually available only to a small number of large private corporations or public entities. But access for firms to reliable, adequate and cost-effective sources for financing productive investment is precisely what matters for the success of financial policies in developing countries.

Clearly, in allocating credit, every financial system has to discriminate between borrowers and projects to be financed. But, as has been seen from various outcomes of financial reforms and numerous episodes of financial crisis, the market mechanism does not always produce optimal allocation of credit. Governments can play a role in directing credit to sectors and activities that are strategically important for the economy as a whole, for example through the direct provision of credit by public financial institutions or by intervention in financial markets, through such measures as interest subsidies, the refinancing of commercial loans, or provision of guarantees for certain types of credit.

Credit allocation can also be influenced by stricter control of lending for consumption or for speculative purposes, which could induce banks to extend longer term loans for investment purposes. In instances where high lending rates reflect perceived risks, government guarantees for loans to finance promising investment projects of firms that otherwise may have limited access to longer term bank credit (or may be able to obtain such credit only at extremely high cost that would make their investment unviable) could be envisaged. While this may entail fiscal costs when a project financed this way fails, these costs have to be weighed against the total increase in investments that can be made only because of such guarantees, and the dynamic income effects (including higher tax revenues) which these additional investments may generate. They should also be weighed against the fiscal costs of large rescue operations for the banking system, as became necessary following the uncontrolled increase in credit for consumption and speculative purposes that took place in many countries after financial liberalization.

Public banking: reconciling commercial and development objectives

Public sector banks, particularly development banks, could play an important role in ensuring access of firms to reliable sources for financing productive investment. In the light of past experience, the debate about the role of public banks has often centred on the argument that State ownership of such institutions, which are not subject to market discipline, may increase the opportunities for corruption and patronage, rather than on an assessment of their economic merits. But private banks are not immune to corruption and patronage either, especially when they are linked to conglomerates that rely on them for cheap finance. On the other hand, it is clear that public and development banks can fulfil their developmental role only if they are governed by clear mandates and strict rules of accountability, accompanied by regular performance monitoring.

It is important to remember that, from the perspective of financing for development, it is not only the microeconomic profitability of an investment project that matters, but also the external benefits the project generates for the economy as a whole. This consideration is generally accepted for infrastructure projects and their public financing from budget receipts or with the support of development banks. But it is equally rational for public financial institutions with expertise in specific sectors to contribute to the financing of private productive and innovative activities in agriculture, industry and services when those activities generate important external benefits and social returns but are unable to obtain the necessary financing from commercial sources of finance.

One way to bring both commercial and development considerations to bear on credit allocation could be through joint financing of certain investment projects by private and public banks. Whereas the commercial bank would contribute its expertise in assessing the viability of a project from a private sector perspective, the public financial institutions would make a judgement from the point of view of the project's overall developmental merits, and through its participation in the financing it could reduce the risks to the commercial bank. It might also serve to leverage public financing with private financing, and reduce the risk of patronage on the part of both the private and public financial institutions involved. This kind of arrangement has precedents in some developed countries in the 1950s and 1960s as well as in several emerging-market economies more recently.

Official development assistance: substantial rise but a shortfall persists

Another aspect of investment financing in support of diversification and structural change in developing countries is their foreign exchange requirement for imports of capital goods. This is a problem in particular for poor commodity-dependent economies, which typically rely on official loans and grants from bilateral and multilateral donors. Following the Monterrey Consensus of 2002, most bilateral donors providing official development assistance (ODA) set ambitious targets for increasing their ODA as part of efforts to meet the MDGs. But despite a substantial increase in disbursements, most donors are not on track to meet their ODA pledges. Moreover, there is still a considerable gap between actual ODA flows and the aid estimated to be necessary for implementing measures in pursuit of the MDGs.

There is broad agreement among donors and beneficiaries that it is not only the amount of ODA that matters, but also how effectively the funds from donors are being used. Improved aid effectiveness has been increasingly associated with better institutions and policies. Although views differ as to what constitutes good institutions and policies, and despite weak evidence that such a correlation actually exists, the provision of ODA has increasingly become conditional on fulfilling numerous criteria of good governance. Aid effectiveness is also often viewed in relation to procedures for implementing it. In this regard, as discussed in UNCTAD's *Least Developed Countries Report 2008*, aid management policies that enhance mutual accountability of donors and recipient governments could help reduce transaction costs and strengthen States' capacities for effective use of foreign aid. But equally important is the development effectiveness of the aid resources provided by donors. In determining a yardstick for such effectiveness, it is useful to distinguish between social and human development objectives on the one hand, and growth objectives on the other.

Social and economic aid: getting the right balance

Traditionally, the objective of ODA has been per capita income growth, with attendant effects on human development. With the Millennium Declaration, human development objectives have come to the forefront. Meanwhile growth has lost prominence as an explicit objective of development policy in an intellectual and policy environment that seems to be governed by the implicit assumption that, in a liberalized and globalizing economy, growth and structural change are generated automatically by market forces. Accordingly, aid effectiveness is increasingly viewed in terms of the contribution of ODA to the achievement of the MDGs. Consequently, a larger proportion of ODA is being spent for health, education and other social purposes.

This kind of ODA is essential and justified in its own right. However, for poverty reduction to be sustainable it cannot rely exclusively on the redistribution of a given income; it also depends on increases in domestic value added and per capita incomes. Unless ODA helps boost growth, it is unlikely to be effective in reducing poverty in the long term, beyond the MDG target year of 2015. ODA for investment projects in economic infrastructure and in the productive sectors is essential to support domestic efforts to raise levels of real income and employment and to shift income distribution in favour of the poor.

Another way to increase ODA effectiveness could be to leverage ODA with domestic financing. For example, this may be done through the creation or strengthening of institutions that would channel ODA into public and private investment projects financed jointly with domestic financial institutions. This could facilitate access of potential domestic investors to long-term financing and reduce the credit risk of domestic banks – and thus the spreads they charge. At the same time it would help to build a better functioning system of domestic financial intermediation.

In the past, the relative needs of countries, which could be measured by levels of per capita income and human development indicators, or the degree of their fiscal or foreign-exchange gap, only had a limited influence on the geographical distribution of ODA. Yet aid effectiveness could be improved by directing further increases in ODA grants to the poorest countries that have the greatest difficulty in initiating a self-sustaining process of investment and growth.

Debt relief: the need for additionality

A considerable financing gap appears to persist with respect not only to MDG-related activities, but also to investments that will be beneficial for growth and structural change beyond the MDGs, let alone for tackling new challenges for developing countries as a result of climate change. For a realistic chance of meeting the MDGs, the level of annual ODA would need to be $50–$60 billion higher than current disbursements, to complement efforts by developing countries to finance additional investment from domestic sources.

Debt relief has played an important role in ODA, particularly since 2003. However, there is no clear evidence that it has been additional to other forms of aid, as called for in the Monterrey Consensus. Such additionality is indispensable because the reduction of the debt stock has a very limited effect on the capacity of governments to increase their expenditure in the period in which it is granted. Full additionality would not only improve the chances of beneficiary countries to meet their growth and social objectives, including those set by the MDGs, but it would also increase their ability to do so without encountering an unsustainable debt situation in the future.

Past debt relief efforts have largely by-passed the considerable development needs of low-income countries that have relatively low debt levels either as a result of prudent external financing strategies or because they have not undertaken essential public sector investments. In order not to discriminate against such countries, it would be appropriate to allow other poor countries to benefit from the Multilateral Debt Relief Initiative, including those that have sustainable levels of indebtedness. Moreover, it may also be necessary to consider providing debt relief to developing countries that have an unsustainable level of debt but are not eligible under the Heavily Indebted Poor Countries debt initiative.

Debt sustainability: borrowing for the right purpose

It is often during periods of economic boom that borrowing and lending decisions are taken on the basis of overoptimistic expectations. This consideration is particularly important at the current juncture, as a large number of developing countries have strengthened their current-account positions and lowered their external debt ratios. They have been able to achieve this partly through better macroeconomic policies and debt management, but mainly as a result of a favourable external environment, characterized by high commodity prices and low interest rates, a scenario that may not last forever.

The challenge is therefore to build on recent improvements in debt indicators, and economic indicators more generally, and accelerate the process of investment, growth and structural change while maintaining a sustainable debt situation. The first step towards achieving debt sustainability is to borrow for the right reasons and not borrow too much during "good times". Debt should be used only to finance projects that generate returns that are higher than the interest cost of the loan. And foreign-currency-denominated borrowing should, in principle, be limited to projects that can either directly or indirectly generate the foreign currency necessary to service the debt. To the largest extent possible, and especially when the projects do not depend on imports, developing countries should seek to finance them from domestic sources. Therefore external debt strategies should be closely related to renewed efforts to strengthen domestic financial systems and to macroeconomic and exchange-rate policies that aim to prevent unsustainable current-account deficits.

External indebtedness: dealing with vulnerability to external shocks

A major constraint on countries that have access to international financial markets is their vulnerability to the effects of the high volatility of these markets. Shocks that may lead to a liquidity crisis in the developing world often depend on external factors that may originate from policy decisions of developed countries. The use of innovative debt instruments that reduce the vulnerability of developing countries to shocks or unfavourable developments in the international economic and financial environment could help maintain debt sustainability. Such instruments could include issuance of external debt in domestic currency, which would reduce the foreign exchange risk, and of GDP-indexed bonds that allow lower debt service payments when capacity to pay is low. The creation and dissemination of these instruments could be facilitated by support from the international community for developing uniform standards and achieving the required market size.

Implementing national policies to reduce the risk of a debt crisis is especially difficult for low-income countries. These countries often depend on external resources to finance not only projects in the productive sectors of their economies and large infrastructure projects, but also the development of their health and education sectors. Although these social sectors may yield high returns in the long run, they are unlikely to generate the cash flows necessary to service the debt in the short and medium term. This suggests that, since low-income countries cannot sustain high levels of debt, most of their external support should take the form of grants.

Finally, it must be accepted that, even with improved debt management and better and safer debt instruments, debt crises are bound to occur. Thus the international community should not abandon the idea of creating a mechanism aimed at speedy resolutions of debt crises and fair burden-sharing among creditors and debtors. The latter would also help to improve risk assessment of creditors. Because of their particular vulnerability to external shocks originating in international financial and commodity markets, developing countries should also evince a particular interest in reform of the international monetary and financial system. Such reform should aim at minimizing destabilizing speculative financial flows and at strengthening institutions and mechanisms in support of macroeconomic policy coordination.

Supachai Panitchpakdi
Secretary-General of UNCTAD

CURRENT TRENDS AND ISSUES IN THE WORLD ECONOMY

A. Global growth and trade

In mid-2008 the global economy is teetering on the brink of recession. The downturn after four years of relatively fast growth is due to a number of factors: the global fallout from the financial crisis in the United States, the bursting of the housing bubbles there and in other large economies, soaring commodity prices, increasingly restrictive monetary policies in a number of countries, and stock market volatility. Without strong and internationally coordinated action on macroeconomic policy, a fully-fledged global economic recession seems unavoidable.

Growth in developing and emerging-market economies has been fairly resilient in the first half of 2008, but there is mounting evidence that they cannot escape the global slowdown. Even under benign circumstances in the second half of the year, the pace of world output growth is expected to decline to around 3 per cent in 2008 – almost one percentage point less than in the past two years (table 1.1).

Although a number of relatively large developing countries increasingly rely on domestic demand, many other countries continue to depend on the evolution of external demand and international commodity prices. Their growth rates also depend on how they are using the higher revenues from primary commodity exports (see also chapter II). Despite a slowdown, output growth in China in 2008 can be expected to expand close to a double-digit rate. West Asia and both North Africa and sub-Saharan Africa (excluding South Africa) are the only regions where average rates of output growth are likely to rise compared to the past two years. At about 7 per cent, sub-Saharan Africa is even expected to achieve its highest annual growth rate in more than three decades. However, this acceleration of growth is largely due to higher income from exports of primary commodities, particularly oil, and therefore will be unequally distributed across countries, depending on their trade structure. Moreover, the gains from higher commodity export earnings may have only a marginal effect on the incomes of the poorer segments of the population, as the linkages between the oil and mining sector with the rest of the economy are generally weak.

World trade in 2007 expanded less in real terms than in the preceding four years, but that of developing and transition economies continued to grow unabated (table 1.2). Their exports rose by more than 9 per cent in volume terms, but there are considerable regional differences. As the supply response to higher commodity prices has generally been weak, regions that have a large share of primary commodities in their exports saw lower growth in export volumes than regions that have a large share of manufactures

Table 1.1

WORLD OUTPUT GROWTH, 1991–2008[a]

(Annual percentage change)

Region/country	1991–2001[b]	2002	2003	2004	2005	2006	2007[c]	2008[d]
World	**3.1**	**1.9**	**2.7**	**4.0**	**3.4**	**3.9**	**3.8**	**2.9**
Developed countries	**2.6**	**1.3**	**1.9**	**3.0**	**2.4**	**2.8**	**2.5**	**1.6**
of which:								
Japan	1.1	0.3	1.4	2.7	1.9	2.4	2.1	1.4
United States	3.5	1.6	2.5	3.6	3.1	2.9	2.2	1.4
European Union	2.4	1.2	1.3	2.5	1.8	3.0	2.9	1.8
of which:								
Euro area	2.2	0.9	0.8	2.0	1.5	2.7	2.6	1.6
France	2.0	1.0	1.1	2.5	1.9	2.2	2.1	1.5
Germany	1.8	0.0	-0.2	1.2	0.9	2.9	2.5	1.8
Italy	1.6	0.3	0.0	1.1	0.0	1.7	1.5	0.4
United Kingdom	2.8	2.1	2.7	3.3	1.9	2.8	3.0	1.6
South-East Europe and CIS	..	**4.9**	**7.1**	**7.6**	**6.6**	**7.5**	**8.4**	**7.4**
South-East Europe[e]	..	3.0	2.4	4.5	5.0	5.0	6.0	5.2
Commonwealth of Independent States (CIS)	..	5.2	7.6	8.0	6.8	7.7	8.6	7.6
of which:								
Russian Federation	..	4.7	7.3	7.1	6.4	6.7	8.1	7.5
Developing countries	**4.8**	**3.9**	**5.4**	**7.2**	**6.6**	**7.1**	**7.3**	**6.4**
Africa	2.9	3.7	4.9	5.4	5.7	5.6	5.8	6.0
North Africa, excl. Sudan	3.2	3.4	5.4	4.8	5.4	5.5	5.6	6.0
Sub-Saharan Africa, excl. South Africa	2.8	4.0	5.4	6.4	6.2	5.8	6.5	7.1
South Africa	2.2	3.7	3.1	4.8	5.1	5.4	5.1	3.8
Latin America and the Caribbean	3.1	-0.5	2.2	6.2	4.9	5.6	5.7	4.6
Caribbean	2.2	2.6	2.9	3.9	7.1	8.5	6.2	5.3
Central America, excl. Mexico	4.3	2.8	3.8	4.2	4.6	6.5	6.6	4.6
Mexico	3.1	0.8	1.4	4.2	3.0	4.9	3.2	2.8
South America	3.0	-1.5	2.4	7.4	5.6	5.7	6.7	5.3
of which:								
Brazil	2.8	2.7	1.1	5.7	3.2	3.7	5.4	4.8
Asia	6.1	6.0	6.8	7.9	7.5	7.9	8.1	7.2
East Asia	7.8	7.4	7.1	8.3	8.0	8.8	9.1	8.1
of which:								
China	10.3	9.1	10.0	10.1	10.4	11.1	11.4	10.0
South Asia	5.1	4.5	7.8	7.5	7.7	8.2	8.5	7.0
of which:								
India	5.9	3.6	8.3	8.5	8.8	9.2	9.7	7.6
South-East Asia	4.8	4.8	5.4	6.6	5.7	6.0	6.4	5.4
West Asia	3.6	3.2	6.0	7.9	6.8	5.7	5.1	5.7

Source: UNCTAD secretariat calculations, based on *UNCTAD Handbook of Statistics* database; and United Nations, Department of Economic and Social Affairs (UN/DESA), *LINK Global Economic Outlook 2008* (May 2008).

a Calculations for country aggregates are based on GDP at constant 2000 dollars.
b Average.
c Preliminary estimates.
d Forecast.
e Albania, Bosnia and Herzegovina, Croatia, Montenegro, Serbia, and the former Yugoslav Republic of Macedonia.

Table 1.2

EXPORT AND IMPORT VOLUMES OF GOODS, BY REGION AND ECONOMIC GROUPING, 2002–2007

(Percentage change over previous year)

Region/country	Volume indices of exports						Volume indices of imports					
	2002	2003	2004	2005	2006	2007	2002	2003	2004	2005	2006	2007
World	**4.5**	**6.3**	**11.4**	**5.2**	**8.1**	**5.5**	**4.2**	**7.7**	**12.1**	**7.0**	**7.3**	**5.8**
Developed economies	**2.3**	**3.1**	**8.4**	**4.9**	**7.7**	**2.8**	**3.0**	**5.1**	**9.0**	**5.9**	**5.8**	**2.3**
of which:												
Japan	7.7	9.2	13.4	5.1	11.8	8.2	1.1	5.9	6.3	2.0	4.5	0.6
United States	-4.0	2.9	8.7	7.4	10.5	6.8	4.4	5.5	10.8	5.6	5.7	0.8
European Union	3.4	3.3	8.8	4.9	8.3	2.2	2.8	5.5	8.7	5.7	7.0	3.3
South-East Europe and CIS	**8.8**	**9.0**	**12.9**	**-1.5**	**10.3**	**9.2**	**13.7**	**21.5**	**20.1**	**11.5**	**21.8**	**27.3**
South-East Europe	6.2	21.2	26.7	2.7	16.7	19.3	19.6	22.8	17.6	-2.5	8.6	22.2
CIS	9.0	8.3	12.2	-1.4	10.0	8.6	12.5	21.2	20.6	14.6	24.3	28.2
Developing economies	**8.8**	**12.9**	**16.7**	**6.3**	**9.2**	**9.3**	**6.6**	**12.9**	**18.4**	**8.5**	**8.9**	**10.8**
Africa	5.5	10.4	8.6	-0.2	2.4	2.2	6.3	16.0	16.4	9.8	6.5	5.9
Sub-Saharan Africa	6.3	11.5	10.9	-1.0	-2.1	1.9	6.2	22.7	15.0	10.5	8.6	2.1
Latin America and Caribbean	0.5	4.0	9.6	5.0	4.2	4.6	-7.0	1.2	14.1	10.3	13.0	14.2
East Asia	14.8	22.0	24.3	17.1	17.8	16.2	13.4	19.3	19.2	5.9	9.2	11.3
of which:												
China	24.0	35.3	33.0	26.2	24.4	23.3	22.5	35.2	25.9	7.5	11.5	16.1
South Asia	13.8	11.8	11.5	6.7	3.3	8.8	12.0	15.0	15.9	14.9	6.1	5.4
of which:												
India	17.4	13.6	19.5	14.8	10.5	12.3	10.4	18.7	19.4	20.8	6.6	13.1
South-East Asia	6.6	7.7	19.0	6.6	11.2	8.3	5.2	6.9	18.0	10.2	7.2	7.4
West Asia	6.3	7.6	10.8	-0.2	4.9	2.5	8.8	15.5	27.0	11.4	9.5	17.3

Source: UNCTAD secretariat calculations, based on *UNCTAD Handbook of Statistics* database.

in their total exports. The United States experienced a particularly sharp slowdown in import volume growth, which was associated with a significant improvement in its current-account balance owing to sluggish domestic demand and a sharp depreciation of the dollar.

Overall, the financial turmoil, the commodity price hikes and the huge exchange-rate swings are having an enormous impact on the global economy and are casting a shadow on the outlook for 2009. The fallout from the collapse of the United States mortgage market and the reversal of the housing boom in a number of countries has turned out to be more profound and persistent than was expected in 2007. The shock waves of these events have spread well beyond the countries directly involved, and have triggered widespread uncertainty in the financial

markets. A year after the outbreak of the crisis it remains unclear how long it will last.

For a large number of developing countries the outlook depends primarily on future trends in the prices of their primary commodity exports. Although several structural factors support the expectation that prices will remain higher than they have been over the past 20 years, cyclical factors, the end of speculation on higher prices and delayed supply responses could result in a weakening of some commodity prices. In particular, the mood of speculators in commodity futures markets may change abruptly in reaction to events on other markets, such as a recession in goods markets or a recovery of stock markets. Additionally, some developing and transition economies, mainly in Eastern Europe and Central Asia, that have accumulated a substantial stock of external debt and run up large current-account deficits due to overvaluation of their currencies could face a sudden increase in their financing costs and the threat of a sharp reversal of their currency valuations.

The recent experience with contagion and interdependence in the global economy should be reason enough to review the role of public policy and government intervention in influencing market outcomes at both the national and international level. One of the reasons for the current fragile state of the world economy is the shortcomings in the system of global economic governance, in particular a lack of coherence between the international trading system, which is governed by a set of internationally agreed rules and regulations, and the international monetary and financial system, which is not. The financial turbulence, the speculative forces affecting food and oil prices, and the apparent failure of foreign exchange markets to bring about changes in exchange rates that reflect shifts in the international competitiveness of countries suggest that there is an urgent need for redesigning the system of global economic governance.

B. The fallout from the sub-prime crisis

The meltdown of the sub-prime mortgage market, originating in the most sophisticated financial market in the world, has once again exposed the fragility of today's global financial sector. Instead of reducing risk, the complex financial instruments developed in recent years have served to spread the impact of risky investments across continents, institutions and markets. A financial system that every three or four years is subject to a severe crisis that not only hurts actors in financial markets but also has repercussions on the real sector must be deeply flawed. The recurrent episodes of financial volatility seem to be driven by a mix of opaque instruments and massive leverage with which financial firms attempt to extract double-digit returns out of a real economy that is growing at a much slower rate. Since the outbreak of the sub-prime crisis, the risks of securitization have become ever more evident, and there are widespread concerns over the financial industry's ability to generate large temporary profits by applying unsustainable refinancing schemes while passing part of the losses that arise

> A financial system that experiences a severe crisis every three or four years must be fundamentally flawed.

from inevitable market corrections to the public sector and the taxpayer. Indeed, since financial crises can have enormous negative effects on the real economy, policymakers have no choice but to bail out parts of the financial sector when systemic threats loom.

Until recently, it was thought that moral hazard associated with the explicit or implicit presence of a lender of last resort was a problem only for deposit-taking commercial banks. However, recent actions of the United States Federal Reserve have shown that investment banks and mortgage lenders, too, can be deemed "too big to fail" and that their liabilities are protected by implicit insurance. Given the risks for financial stability, the Federal Reserve was certainly right to provide such insurance and prevent the bankruptcy of a large investment bank and the two largest mortgage lenders in the United States; but insurance should not come for free. If the government decides that different types of financial institutions need to be bailed out because their failure could lead to a systemic crisis, these institutions should be subject to tighter prudential regulation similar to that imposed on deposit-taking banks. The recent crisis has shown once again that market discipline alone is ineffective in preventing recurrent episodes of "irrational exuberance" and that the market mechanism cannot cope with massive drops in financial asset prices.

The latest casualties of the sub-prime crisis are Fannie Mae (Federal National Mortgage Association) and Freddie Mac (Federal Home Loan Mortgage Corporation). These agencies, which have the hybrid status of government-sponsored enterprises (GSE), are the most important players in the United States housing market and hold or guarantee $5,200 billion worth of mortgages (corresponding to more than 40 per cent of all mortgage debt in the United States). Even though these agencies are not allowed to extend or guarantee sub-prime loans, they have been badly affected by the fall in housing prices that followed the sub-prime crisis. Their stock price started to decline in mid-2007 and it suddenly collapsed in early July 2008 after it became clear that they were insolvent on a mark-to-market basis. Both the United States Treasury and the Federal Reserve quickly announced their support for these two agencies and the Federal Reserve allowed them to borrow from its discount window. In response, the valuation of the debt issued by these agencies continued to be traded at normal values even after the collapse of their equity value.

As long as the United States Government backs their liabilities, the two agencies will be able to keep rolling over their debt, continue their operations, and thus prevent a further deterioration of the United States real estate market. However, this may generate perverse incentives, because the management of a company with negative or zero equity value but with guaranteed debt might be tempted to "gamble for redemption" (i.e. adopt a strategy which may lead to a high pay-off with low probability and to large losses with high probability). The rationale for adopting such a strategy is its asymmetric pay-off. If the gamble is successful, the shareholders make a profit. If it is not successful, the shareholders do not lose anything (because the equity value was zero from the start) but the public sector then has to pay an even higher cost. This would be another example of a situation where profits are privatized and losses are socialized. If the crisis persists, it would probably be better for the Government to assume temporary full ownership of the two agencies and decide later whether to liquidate them, fully privatize them, or keep them fully and permanently in the public sector.

C. Global economic imbalances and exchange rates

The current crisis not only has implications for the prudential regulation of financial institutions at the national level, but also for macroeconomic policies, especially monetary and exchange-rate policies, at both the national and global levels. The last 25 years have been characterized by limited macroeconomic volatility and low inflation in the developed world. This has led several central banks in many developed and developing countries to focus on national inflation targets and domestic short-term interest rates, while allowing other key variables, such as the exchange rate, to be determined entirely by market forces.

However, this policy approach does not take sufficient account of the fact that countries and economies are closely interlinked, and that the exchange rate plays a key role in these linkages. The recent financial turbulence and the unsustainable position of a number of countries with large current-account deficits in all parts of the world have shown that the current framework for monetary and exchange-rate policies generates temporarily profitable opportunities for speculative activities which eventually have a destabilizing effect. This experience underscores the need for more and better international economic coordination to avoid unsustainable trade and current-account imbalances in the future.

The largest of the global current-account imbalances that have shaped the world economy over the past decade, the United States trade deficit, is receding, thanks to the depreciation of the dollar and the looming recession in the United States. However, in many other countries there has been no correction of the exchange rate and neither is an end to destabilizing speculation in sight. This speculation is still pushing many exchange rates in the wrong direction despite huge and rising current-account deficits in some countries and regions (*TDR 2007*, chap. I, section B). A survey of real exchange rate developments since 2000 is given in the annex to this chapter.

A current-account deficit or surplus is not an economic problem per se. However, when a big and rising deficit coincides with a loss of competitiveness, for example caused by a currency appreciation that is triggered by speculation on short-term interest rate differentials, it is as a rule unsustainable. The disequilibrium will sooner or later have to be corrected even if the correction is very costly in terms of real income losses.

For the past decade or so developing countries as a group have registered a current-account surplus, with concomitant current-account deficits in a number of developed countries and some transition economies. Factors that have contributed to the improvements in current-account balances vary: for some fast growing exporters of manufactures, particularly in East and South-East Asia, these improvements are the result of a further increase in their international competitiveness; for some oil-exporting countries in West Asia and the Commonwealth of Independent States (CIS) they result from the rapidly rising price of oil; and for a number of countries in Africa and Latin America they

> There is a need for better economic coordination at the global level to prevent unsustainable current-account imbalances.

> An adjustment of the United States current-account deficit is now under way.

are due not only to the higher prices of oil but also of other primary commodities, in particular industrial raw materials. While developed countries as a group are in deficit, both the second and the third largest economies in the world – Japan and Germany – continue to register large current-account surpluses, combined with further improvements in their competitiveness.

A new feature of the world economy since the turn of the century is the rapidly rising current-account deficits in a number of countries in Eastern Europe. The accession of several of these countries to the European Union (EU) and their reasonably high growth rates, combined with some degree of monetary stability, raised expectations that they would be able to tackle their economic problems much better than before, which in turn encouraged massive short-term capital inflows. But in most countries the main source of growth has been buoyant domestic demand fuelled by high wage growth and easy access to consumer credit and mortgage lending. This has led to strong growth in private consumption, rising imports and a thriving housing market.

However, inflation rates and interest rates that are higher in these countries than in many other countries have led to the accumulation of a huge amount of mortgage debt in foreign currencies, in particular Swiss franc and yen. This has created an enormous currency mismatch between the earnings of the debtors and their debt service obligations. At the same time, nominal and real currency appreciation has undermined the competitiveness of these economies in the European and the world economy, and this will sooner or later require an exchange-rate depreciation.

From 1999 to 2007, the real effective exchange rate in Eastern Europe and the Russian Federation appreciated by more than 30 per cent. Their average current-account deficit in 2007 reached about 9 per cent of gross domestic product (GDP), more than twice its level in 1999 when the real appreciation started (chart 1.1). The largest current-account deficits were recorded in

Bulgaria, Estonia, Latvia, Lithuania and Romania which reached double-digit levels as a percentage of GDP. In the Russian Federation, soaring exports, particularly of energy and primary commodities, have outpaced import growth but the formerly large surplus on the current account has shrunk.

The real appreciation of the exchange rate in Eastern European countries has been exacerbated by the effect of carry-trade operations, whereby capital flows from countries with low inflation and low nominal interest rates to countries with higher inflation and higher nominal interest rates. This happens when it is expected that the exchange rate will either remain stable or move in a favourable direction, so that there is an "uncovered" interest rate differential. This can lead to the paradoxical and dangerous situation of countries with a current-account surplus (e.g. Japan or Switzerland) facing devaluation pressure on their currencies, and countries with a current-account deficit facing a similar pressure to appreciate, when in fact the opposite would be required to correct the current-account imbalance.[1]

To redress persistent imbalances, adjustment is unavoidable. Countries that have lost overall competitiveness need to restore it to avoid a permanent loss of market shares and growing indebtedness vis-à-vis other countries. As economic history shows, this adjustment can be the outcome of either a deep recession or a large devaluation in real terms. The latter has to come from a large nominal currency devaluation, which will induce a switch of domestic expenditure from more expensive foreign goods to cheaper domestic goods and also shift external demand towards the exports of the devaluating country.

Over the past 10 years, the United States has been the main deficit country. China, Germany, Japan and Switzerland have been the main surplus countries as far as the absolute size of their current-account imbalances is concerned. Although an adjustment of the United States imbalance is now under way, a further reduction of the remaining imbalances would require the surplus countries to expand their domestic demand. If the entire remaining adjustment depends on exchange-rate changes, this can have dramatic negative repercussions for those countries where large currency mismatches have built up.

However, not all surplus countries have the same capacity to increase demand. In China, for

Chart 1.1

CURRENT-ACCOUNT BALANCE AND REAL EFFECTIVE EXCHANGE RATE IN EASTERN EUROPE AND THE RUSSIAN FEDERATION, 1996–2007

(Simple average)

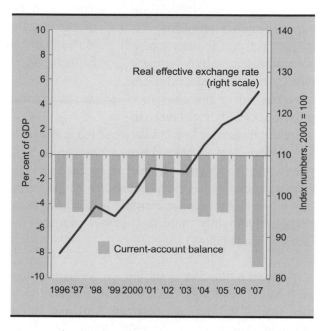

Source: UNCTAD secretariat calculations, based on IMF, *Balance of Payments*; UNCTAD database on real effective exchange rates; and national sources.

Note: Eastern Europe: Bulgaria, Czech Republic, Estonia, Hungary, Lithuania, Poland and Romania.

example, this is much more difficult than elsewhere, as domestic demand is already rising fast and the economy is close to overheating. The continued appreciation of the yuan can nevertheless contribute to a global adjustment of trade balances by slowing down export growth and stimulating import growth. However, given the rising inflow of short-term capital, attracted by government-controlled appreciation and rising foreign-exchange reserves, the Chinese authorities might consider revaluing the yuan to a target rate in one big step rather than a series of incremental steps.

The potential for a strong global expansionary stimulus is much greater in Western Europe, where domestic demand is flat but more than five times the size of China's domestic demand. Germany in particular has been experiencing an unprecedented export boom, with a current-account surplus of more than 180 billion euros in 2007; at the same time real wage growth has been very slow and there remains a large underutilized potential to stimulate domestic demand. A turnaround in its wage policy and a direct stimulation of domestic demand would help the adjustment process. Interest rate cuts of the European Central Bank (ECB) in the second half of 2008 and into 2009 would support such a stimulus. Although such policies may appear contentious in an environment where rising fuel and food prices have pushed up the consumer price index (CPI), the actual risk of inflation remains low in Europe as the increase in the consumer prices has not been accompanied by a rise in unit labour costs. Indeed, in recent years the German economy has even witnessed a stagnation in unit labour costs because nominal wages have been rising only slightly more than labour productivity (see section D below).

> The potential for a strong global expansionary stimulus is much greater in Western Europe than in China.

Japan's situation is similar to Germany's: top performer in exports (which grew at an average annual rate of 9.3 per cent between 2001 and 2007) but lagging in terms of domestic demand (with an average annual increase of only 1.1 per cent in the same period). As in Germany, consumer demand has been sluggish due to many years of falling or stagnating real wages and slow employment growth. In this environment deflation has prevailed. Neither the zero interest rate policy of the Bank of Japan nor expansive budgetary policies or the recent export boom have been able to turn the tide. It appears that direct government intervention in the labour market and a new round of deficit spending will be necessary to eventually get the country out of its deflationary trap and help mitigate the global economic slowdown.

Given their soaring export earnings in a relatively short period of time, net exporters of primary commodities, particularly oil-exporters, may not be able to increase their imports in parallel at the same rate and thereby stimulate output growth in the rest of the world. If these countries have limited capacity to immediately absorb their higher revenues, they could play an active role in promoting financial stability by smoothly and effectively recycling the capital account equivalent of their large

> Monetary policies are diverging more than ever.

surpluses, including through sovereign wealth funds. The fact that sovereign wealth funds of developing countries have been solicited for helping some large European and United States banks in their efforts to rebuild their capital base shows how important this recycling could be.[2]

Nevertheless, some governments are wary of investments by the sovereign wealth funds of developing countries. While there is little transparency in the activities of most of these funds, there is also no evidence that their objectives are fundamentally different from those of other institutional investors. This implies that part of their portfolio may be invested in short-term, and partly speculative, assets. On the other hand, since these wealth funds are operating in the public interest of preserving part of the currently accumulated national wealth for future use, there is reason to believe that a large proportion of their financial investments will be undertaken with a long-term perspective. This implies that they also have considerable potential to support the financing of public infrastructure projects or high-yielding real investments in the manufacturing, services or agricultural sectors of other developing countries. In any case, it will be important to find ways of appropriately using the accumulating surpluses of oil-exporting countries that will satisfy the interests of both their country of origin and the international financial system. This is particularly important because the large current-account surpluses of the major oil-exporting countries are likely to remain a feature of the world economy for several years to come.

Overall, the major central banks have shown considerable coherence and coordination in their response to the sub-prime crises by providing liquidity to affected banks and financial institutions. But their monetary policies diverge more than ever. The United States Federal Reserve has been very aggressive in cutting policy rates, whereas other central banks have been much more timid, and some, including the ECB and the central banks of a number of emerging-market economies, have even raised their interest rates in an attempt to reduce the risk of an acceleration of inflation. Central banks of countries directly affected by the unwinding of carry trade positions have even sharply increased their interest rates in order to defend their exchange rates. These divergent polices may invite new speculation in foreign-exchange markets instead of calming the system.

Hence, there is a strong case for more and better coordination of macroeconomic policies and international surveillance of exchange-rate changes. The international community should not neglect the shortcomings in the existing governance of international financial and monetary relations because that may nullify any progress made in multilateral trade negotiations. Arbitrary and large swings of the exchange rate are more damaging for world trade than most tariffs. It is not enough to fight problems induced by increased uncertainty in domestic financial markets; what is also needed is an internationally coordinated approach to tackling the much larger challenges of global imbalances and instability in international financial markets (see also UNCTAD, 2007).

D. Macroeconomic policy responses to the commodity boom

1. Commodity price shocks and the risk of inflation

In the past decade, the world has seen an explosion of oil prices for the third time since the end of the Second World War. At more than $140 per barrel in mid-2008, the oil price spiked at a new peak, not only in nominal terms but also in real terms (chart 1.2). In the developed countries the fuel import bill increased from 1.6 per cent of their GDP in 2002 to 3.6 per cent in 2007. With an average oil price of $125 per barrel in 2008 it could reach the equivalent of about 6 per cent in 2008. In developing countries, the fuel import bill rose from 2.7 per cent of GDP in 2002 to about 5 per cent in 2007, and it may reach more than 8 per cent in 2008.

The oil price hike has been accompanied by a massive increase in the prices of several other primary commodities, and this combined price surge has pushed up the CPI in many developed and developing countries. In addition to their direct impact on the CPI, oil prices also affect the prices of many other goods and services for which oil is an important intermediate input. This has raised concerns about inflation amongst many of those responsible for monetary policy and has encouraged calls for rigorous action by central banks to take pre-emptive action against a further acceleration of inflation.

Even though high commodity prices are exerting an upward pressure on prices, a rise in the CPI due to a one-off increase in import costs resulting from structural changes is not the same as inflation, which implies a continuous increase in all prices. Whether higher relative prices cause a once-and-for-all increase in the CPI or trigger an inflationary process largely depends on the response of wages, which are the most important domestic price in any economy. Wages are not only the largest component of production costs in developed and developing countries, they are also the most important source of permanent income for the majority of the population. In the 1970s, higher oil prices induced an increase in nominal wage rates, and higher wage rates then resulted in a further increase in consumer prices, as higher wage costs were passed on by employers to consumers. The wage-price spiral ultimately ended in stagflation and rising unemployment, because central banks in the leading consumer countries stopped this spiral through highly restrictive interest rate policies.

Chart 1.2

CRUDE PETROLEUM PRICES, NOMINAL AND REAL, JANUARY 1970–JUNE 2008

(Dollars per barrel)

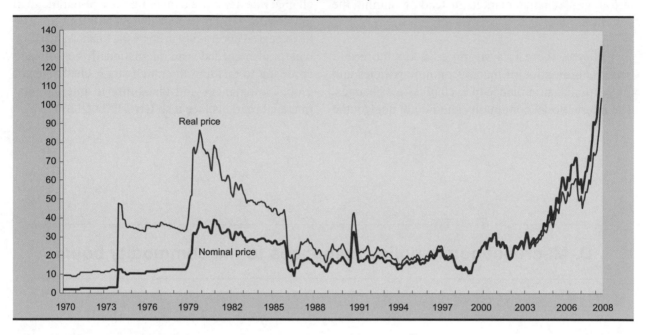

Source: UNCTAD secretariat calculations, based on UNCTAD, *Commodity Price Statistics* online; IMF, *International Financial Statistics* database; and World Bank, *Commodity Price Data* (Pink Sheet).

Note: Crude petroleum price is average of Dubai/Brent/Texas equally weighted; the real price is the nominal price deflated by United States Consumer Price Index (CPI), 2000 = 100.

The risk that the experience of a combination of galloping inflation, economic recession and increasing unemployment will be repeated today appears to be small. Trade unions in developed countries are rarely demanding exorbitant wage increases, as they have learned their lessons from the past oil crises or have lost negotiating power (Flassbeck and Spiecker, 2008; Krugman, 2008). The risk of galloping inflation also seems to be relatively low in the majority of developing countries in light of the behaviour of the key determinants of inflation in recent years. Between 2000 and 2007 nominal wages (or the compensation per employee) increased faster than the CPI in developed countries, and also in Eastern Europe, Asia and Latin America (chart 1.3). However, over this period, labour productivity also increased in most countries. As a result, unit labour costs rose, on average, at about the same rate as consumer prices. This indicates a low risk of a wage-inflation spiral. In East and South-East Asia unit labour costs fell while consumer prices rose, on average, indicating that the risk of a wage-price spiral is even lower. And

also in Latin America, which experienced considerable fluctuations in prices and unit labour costs, the latter did not push up prices in the medium-term. By contrast, in Eastern Europe, on average, unit labour costs rose faster than consumer prices.

The group averages hide considerable cross-country differences. The countries at highest risk of a wage-inflation spiral are those where unit labour costs increased at a faster rate than inflation over the period 2000–2006, and where this trend was not reversed in 2007 (the latest year for which data were available). These countries include Azerbaijan, Iceland, Kazakhstan, Latvia, Norway, Romania, the Russian Federation and Ukraine. Countries with a low or moderate, but increasing risk of an inflationary spiral include Argentina, Australia, Bulgaria, Denmark, Ecuador, Estonia, Lithuania, New Zealand, Poland, Singapore, Sweden and Switzerland. Countries with a moderate or high but decreasing risk of such a spiral include China, Hungary, Indonesia and Mexico. By contrast, in other European countries, Japan and the

Chart 1.3

UNIT LABOUR COST, LABOUR COMPENSATION, PRODUCTIVITY AND CONSUMER PRICE INDEX, SELECTED COUNTRY GROUPS, 2000–2007

(Annual changes in per cent)

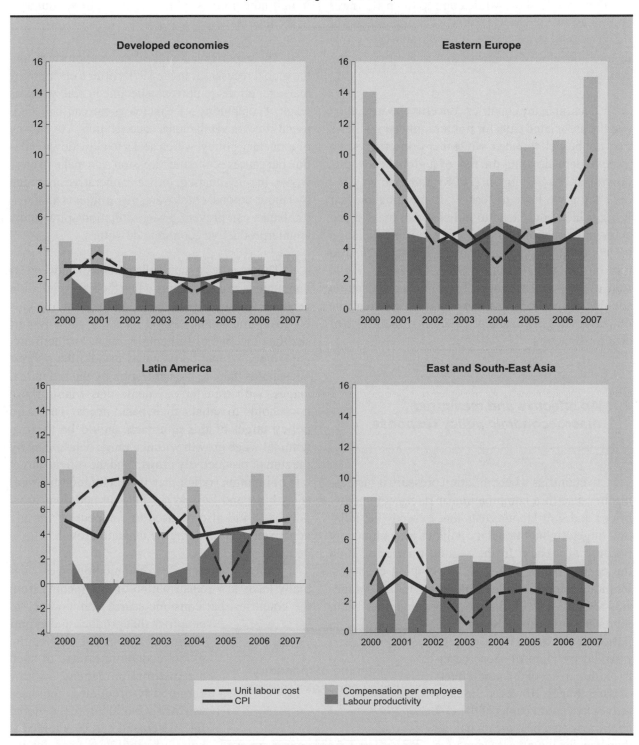

Source: UNCTAD secretariat calculations, based on OECD; European Commission, AMECO database; Economist Intelligence Unit databases; and national sources.

Note: Regional groups refer to simple average. Developed economies exclude Eastern Europe. Eastern Europe: Bulgaria, the Czech Republic, Estonia, Hungary, Latvia, Lithuania, Poland, Romania, Slovakia and Slovenia. Latin America: Argentina, Chile, Colombia, Ecuador, Mexico and Peru. Asia: China, Indonesia, the Philippines, the Republic of Korea, Singapore, Taiwan Province of China and Thailand.

United States, as well as most developing economies for which relevant data were available, namely Colombia, Egypt, the Philippines, Peru, the Republic of Korea, Taiwan Province of China, Thailand, and Turkey, unit labour costs have risen less than consumer prices. In short, while commodity prices have continued to increase in 2008, at the beginning of the year unit labour costs remained relatively stable in most developed countries and many developing countries.

Thus, in many countries concerns about inflation and the associated calls for tighter monetary policies may not be well founded, while many observers seem to be underestimating the risk of a global economic downturn. As Krugman (2008) commented, "the only thing we have to fear ... is the inflation fear itself, which could lead to policies that make a bad economic situation worse". Following strict inflation targets and tightening monetary policies could indeed turn out to be the wrong strategy, given the fragile state of the global economy. Therefore, consideration should be given to innovative ways of reconciling the objectives of growth and price stability in the face of cost push factors.

2. An effective and measured macroeconomic policy response

In countries where inflation pressure is increasing because of a combination of rising commodity prices and unit labour costs that exceeds the inflation target, tighter monetary policies may ultimately become necessary. In the second quarter of 2008 the central banks of several developing countries, including Brazil, Chile, Colombia, India, Indonesia, Mexico, the Philippines, Peru and Viet Nam, increased interest rates amid inflation fears. Such fears may be justified in some of these countries, due to second-round effects of rising wages. However, the early moves by central banks of the G-7 countries could be more damaging than beneficial for macroeconomic stability. For instance, the decision of the ECB to raise the policy interest rate in early July 2008 in order to prevent the inflation rate from rising even further above the rather low inflation

Tightening of monetary policy can make matters worse.

target of 2 per cent, can negatively affect economic growth in the euro area and beyond. Available data casts doubts as to whether the interest rate increase was necessary, given that rising prices of commodities were not accompanied by unsustainable increases in unit labour costs in the majority of the countries in the region.

The experiences with oil price explosions and the global recessions in the 1970s offer a clear policy message: efforts to prevent a decline in real wages as result of commodity price increases can cause second-round effects and inflationary acceleration. A tightening of monetary policy, which seeks to slow down inflation but causes economic recession, can make matters worse. In this situation, only a cooperative approach by labour unions, employers, governments and central banks can prevent a wage-inflation spiral and a counterproductive economic downturn.

This requires a standstill agreement between labour unions and employers when the risk of inflation is acute. At the same time it requires commitments by governments and central banks to actively pursue the objective of full employment. Furthermore, governments must be prepared to help the poorest households that are the hardest hit by the fall in real wages, with transfer payments that enable these households to satisfy their basic needs. The main policy target of this approach should be to keep nominal wage growth within a range determined by the sum of productivity growth and the official target rate of inflation (rather than the actual inflation rate) (Flassbeck and Spiecker, 2008). In addition, fiscal policies could also be used to compensate for any negative effect on domestic demand growth.

Globally, an increase in commodity prices eventually leads to a redistribution of real income from the countries that consume scarce commodities to countries that produce and export them. As discussed above, the global economic effects of such a redistribution depend on how commodity-producing countries use their windfall profits. A global fall in demand can be avoided if windfall profits are used for increased imports or are channelled smoothly through capital markets into productive investments in other countries. The stark lesson to be learned from former experiences with oil price explosions is that this process must be supported by accommodative monetary policies at the global level.

The current situation should not be viewed by governments and central banks as a dilemma. An assessment of the risks shows that, on average, the risk of economic recession associated with an orthodox policy response is great, whereas the risk of galloping inflation, associated with heterodox policy responses, is considerably overestimated. Although rising commodity prices have lifted general price levels, most developed economies and many developing and transition economies do not yet face the threat of uncontrollable inflation. ∎

Notes

1   *TDR 2007* explained carry trade with the following example: "For example, an established speculator such as a hedge fund might borrow 120 yen in Japan, buy $100 dollars in the United States, invest this amount in United States bonds and obtain an interest revenue equal to the difference between the borrowing rate in Japan, say 0.25 per cent, and the higher lending rate in the United States, say 5 per cent. Exchange rate changes between the time of borrowing and paying back the funding currency can add to the gains, or induce smaller gains or even losses. But with stable exchange rates, the *interest rate gain* amounts to 4.75 per cent. However, both gains and losses are largely magnified by high leverage ratios, since traders typically use huge amounts of borrowed funds and very little equity. For instance, owning a capital of $10 and borrowing 10 times the equivalent of that value in yen, the leverage factor of 10 leads to a net interest return on equity of 47.5 per cent."

2   International Financial Services London (IFSL, 2008) estimates that sovereign wealth funds have invested over $60 billion in United States and Swiss bank equities since the start of the sub-prime crisis. For a more detailed analysis of recent activities by sovereign wealth funds, see UNCTAD, 2008.

References

Flassbeck H and Spiecker F (2008). Fatale Fehlwahrnehmung. *Financial Times Deutschland*, 2 July.

IFSL (2008). Sovereign Wealth Funds. International Financial Services London, April.

Klein MR and Mak W (2008). Current quarter model of the United States. Forecast summary. Weekly update on the United States economy and financial markets. University of Pennsylvania, 30 June.

Krugman P (2008). A return of that 70s show? *New York Times*, 2 June.

UNCTAD (2007). Global and Regional Approaches to Trade and Finance. United Nations publication, New York and Geneva.

UNCTAD (2008). *World Investment Report*. United Nations publication, sales no. E.08.II.D.23.

UNCTAD (various issues). *Trade and Development Report*. United Nations publications, New York and Geneva.

REAL EFFECTIVE EXCHANGE RATES, 2001–2007

(Index numbers, 2000 = 100)

Region/country	2001	2002	2003	2004	2005	2006	2007
Developed countries							
Australia	97.8	103.8	116.7	126.8	130.7	129.9	138.9
Canada	96.3	95.7	106.7	113.1	119.8	125.9	131.2
Czech Republic	106.2	112.2	108.8	113.9	119.7	124.9	127.3
Denmark	101.3	103.3	108.3	108.8	107.1	106.1	107.1
Euro area	100.4	104.8	116.1	117.3	113.6	110.8	113.9
Austria	99.6	100.9	103.8	104.2	103.2	101.6	101.2
Finland	100.5	102.6	108.2	105.7	101.4	99.5	100.2
France	99.9	101.9	107.8	108.6	107.5	105.5	107.3
Germany	98.7	100.2	105.3	106.4	104.1	102.5	103.8
Greece	100.1	104.3	110.1	111.7	110.9	110.1	111.9
Ireland	102.6	107.9	119.3	122.4	121.6	123.3	126.3
Italy	100.4	103.6	110.9	112.2	109.7	108.3	109.6
Netherlands	103.7	107.0	111.7	109.2	107.2	105.7	109.0
Portugal	102.4	104.8	109.3	109.2	107.9	107.1	108.7
Spain	100.9	104.3	109.9	111.8	112.1	113.0	114.6
Hungary	107.9	103.8	104.8	125.9	126.5	118.3	130.4
Japan	89.2	83.9	85.7	87.0	81.3	73.7	68.3
New Zealand	98.9	108.4	125.3	134.7	140.8	129.9	140.2
Norway	102.7	110.8	110.5	104.0	106.7	105.7	106.7
Poland	111.9	100.0	89.0	92.9	102.5	103.2	105.4
Romania	101.6	103.4	100.4	100.5	117.6	124.3	133.3
Slovakia	100.5	94.2	107.3	127.7	128.7	135.0	147.6
Sweden	91.8	93.9	101.0	100.6	95.5	93.9	96.8
Switzerland	102.6	106.9	108.0	106.6	103.9	100.8	97.2
United Kingdom	96.9	97.3	93.6	101.5	100.0	99.8	96.0
United States of America	104.9	104.9	98.9	94.5	91.7	90.2	86.2
South-East Europe and CIS							
Albania	104.1	106.4	99.7	107.5	110.5	112.6	112.6
Armenia	95.2	90.3	82.7	87.2	93.8	97.8	109.7
Azerbaijan	98.2	89.9	75.8	74.7	82.7	85.3	92.4
Belarus	92.5	98.3	96.2	93.5	97.2	97.0	92.7
Bosnia and Herzegovina	100.5	98.8	98.8	96.8	98.1	101.6	101.9
Croatia	102.8	103.4	103.6	104.7	106.9	108.4	108.5
Georgia	102.6	98.2	94.4	104.5	101.6	109.4	111.1
Kazakhstan	101.0	98.1	95.9	99.6	104.1	112.4	112.2
Russian Federation	117.2	121.0	123.3	130.4	139.4	151.7	156.3
Serbia and Montenegro	134.5	171.9	189.6	174.8	161.7	258.6	297.4
The former Yugoslav Republic of Macedonia	101.8	103.1	103.9	101.5	97.3	95.8	94.1
Turkmenistan	80.7	67.7	58.2	52.8	47.8	41.4	39.8
Ukraine	111.0	109.0	100.6	97.2	104.9	107.9	106.7
Uzbekistan	53.1	46.8	36.6	33.9	30.8	29.1	28.1

/...

Annex table to chapter I (continued)

REAL EFFECTIVE EXCHANGE RATES, 2001–2007

(Index numbers, 2000 = 100)

Region/country	2001	2002	2003	2004	2005	2006	2007
Developing economies							
Africa							
Algeria	104.2	96.5	87.9	90.6	85.9	85.9	86.6
Angola	115.2	120.0	132.7	163.7	183.1	222.3	246.6
Benin	102.7	103.5	117.1	122.9	123.4	116.4	118.4
Burkina Faso	103.9	107.7	118.5	120.5	125.7	121.9	123.4
Cameroon	102.2	102.7	105.6	109.0	103.6	105.2	108.0
Chad	110.5	115.6	122.9	134.0	141.3	149.2	162.7
Congo	100.5	108.9	128.7	134.7	136.6	137.9	153.5
Côte d'Ivoire	100.6	101.5	108.2	110.7	114.0	111.6	113.2
Egypt	90.4	78.6	56.5	55.0	59.9	61.4	61.4
Equatorial Guinea	104.9	115.3	132.1	147.3	150.6	158.0	170.0
Gabon	98.9	101.5	117.0	122.4	118.2	119.2	127.9
Ghana	101.7	99.9	100.5	98.8	108.8	114.9	112.5
Kenya	106.3	106.9	114.2	113.4	122.1	141.4	149.0
Madagascar	111.7	119.2	114.0	80.0	85.5	84.8	98.9
Mali	107.2	111.7	120.6	122.3	125.9	118.8	121.3
Mauritius	95.5	94.5	92.9	89.5	84.7	83.2	84.2
Morocco	96.4	97.0	94.1	92.4	89.9	91.5	91.1
Mozambique	86.2	89.2	77.9	77.4	79.8	80.2	94.0
Nigeria	109.7	113.1	108.4	116.2	129.2	135.4	137.2
Senegal	101.1	103.7	106.8	109.9	107.7	107.4	108.7
South Africa	87.7	75.8	100.2	109.8	110.9	105.0	114.7
Sudan	108.5	116.8	117.9	127.7	143.0	179.2	199.3
Tunisia	99.2	101.3	96.3	91.2	88.7	89.6	86.1
Uganda	96.5	91.8	77.0	78.7	82.9	81.4	82.6
United Republic of Tanzania	98.5	87.4	76.4	65.5	66.6	61.3	63.9
Zambia	111.0	111.5	109.0	112.2	134.0	181.3	188.4
Latin America and the Caribbean							
Argentina	105.9	44.4	49.2	47.0	47.0	46.0	45.1
Barbados	102.5	100.1	97.7	92.8	94.7	98.5	98.6
Bolivia	99.6	97.0	91.4	88.7	83.7	79.4	79.0
Brazil	83.0	74.0	76.0	80.8	99.3	110.9	118.9
Chile	89.8	84.4	80.2	85.6	91.8	95.4	93.5
Colombia	94.6	92.5	82.2	92.5	104.6	102.6	115.2
Costa Rica	102.5	99.9	94.6	92.8	93.4	91.5	92.7
Cuba	92.1	96.3	84.9	78.1	78.4	81.7	76.3
Dominican Republic	102.9	97.0	72.3	77.1	107.4	101.3	103.8
Ecuador	136.7	151.0	153.7	152.1	147.6	147.2	141.9
El Salvador	100.9	100.5	100.2	100.9	100.1	99.4	98.6
Guatemala	104.3	111.3	112.5	116.8	126.2	129.1	130.8
Haiti	96.3	87.2	82.8	108.6	112.3	123.6	142.7
Honduras	102.7	101.4	100.1	99.6	101.5	103.2	106.5
Jamaica	99.5	97.4	83.1	82.8	88.0	89.8	85.1

REAL EFFECTIVE EXCHANGE RATES, 2001–2007

(Index numbers, 2000 = 100)

Region/country	2001	2002	2003	2004	2005	2006	2007
Mexico	105.2	105.4	95.6	92.9	96.1	96.2	96.2
Nicaragua	92.4	87.7	83.9	82.2	81.5	81.8	85.2
Panama	99.0	97.8	92.4	87.8	86.0	83.8	82.1
Paraguay	98.9	92.9	90.6	98.9	89.1	98.8	108.0
Peru	102.8	100.3	97.1	96.5	97.1	94.7	94.0
Trinidad and Tobago	105.4	107.0	107.4	107.4	109.9	112.6	116.9
Uruguay	99.6	75.9	62.9	62.5	70.8	69.5	70.3
Venezuela (Bolivarian Republic of)	103.9	78.0	69.6	71.0	70.3	74.8	84.3
Asia and Oceania							
Bahrain	101.5	98.7	94.1	92.0	90.2	88.6	86.6
Bangladesh	95.6	91.4	85.7	83.0	80.2	77.1	74.5
Brunei Darussalam	105.3	102.1	97.4	92.3	90.5	88.3	90.2
Cambodia	96.5	97.4	92.1	89.0	95.3	96.1	100.7
China	103.9	101.7	96.3	94.2	92.7	92.8	96.1
India	100.2	98.8	99.6	100.1	102.6	100.6	109.7
Indonesia	95.7	116.4	125.8	120.8	118.5	137.3	137.6
Iran (Islamic Republic of)	110.2	109.6	97.0	96.9	100.7	107.5	117.5
Jordan	98.3	95.2	98.4	99.2	98.6	98.8	97.1
Kuwait	107.8	107.7	103.6	100.0	100.3	100.8	101.0
Lebanon	99.7	98.0	92.6	91.0	86.5	86.3	81.6
Malaysia	104.9	104.9	99.9	95.3	95.0	97.0	99.2
Nepal	97.9	95.2	95.1	94.4	98.5	100.6	101.3
Oman	104.9	102.8	97.5	92.8	89.7	87.2	84.7
Pakistan	90.2	92.5	90.7	89.2	90.2	91.7	89.9
Papua New Guinea	95.9	88.3	95.7	95.8	98.6	99.8	96.1
Philippines	95.2	95.8	89.6	87.1	92.7	102.9	111.8
Qatar	111.1	111.9	106.6	105.4	108.9	121.5	131.4
Republic of Korea	93.1	97.2	99.9	101.5	111.8	118.0	116.1
Saudi Arabia	103.4	101.3	94.6	89.2	86.6	86.3	84.2
Singapore	99.4	97.3	95.3	94.6	93.1	95.0	95.1
Sri Lanka	98.6	98.1	96.8	90.8	98.5	104.0	97.1
Syrian Arab Republic	106.1	97.3	81.8	76.2	84.1	91.5	94.2
Thailand	94.5	96.9	96.0	96.0	97.5	104.3	110.0
Turkey	78.9	89.2	98.5	102.9	115.1	113.4	116.4
United Arab Emirates	110.3	112.4	108.4	105.8	107.1	116.0	119.0
Viet Nam	99.4	96.3	90.8	90.8	94.0	95.2	94.9
Yemen	111.1	116.8	120.3	127.6	131.8	141.7	144.0

Source: UNCTAD secretariat calculations, based on IMF, *Direction of Trade* and *International Financial Statistics* databases.
Note: Real effective exchange rate index is the index of the trade-weighted average nominal exchange rate adjusted for changes in the consumer price index. A rise in the index indicates a loss of competitiveness.

Chapter II

COMMODITY PRICE HIKES AND INSTABILITY

A. Introduction

One of the main features of the world economy since 2002 has been the price boom in international markets for primary commodities. This has been driven by the relatively strong and stable performance of the world economy, fast growth and structural change in a number of large developing economies, and increasing attention by policymakers and market participants to the challenges of climate change and shrinking oil reserves.

Higher prices for primary commodities have an immediate positive impact on the developing and transition economies that export such commodities, through improved export earnings. This increases the potential for financing new investments in infrastructure and productive capacities that are necessary to advance the process of diversification, structural change, and output and employment growth. Whether this potential is used to create new productive capacities and raise productivity depends on how commodity export earnings are distributed between domestic and foreign stakeholders, and how the part of these earnings that remains in the exporting countries is spent.

On the other hand, developing countries are not only exporters of primary commodities but also importers. For many of them, higher prices of certain commodities lead to an increase in their import bill,

and a worsening of their terms of trade, depending on their trade structure. Moreover, the recent tightening in the markets for some food crops has created serious problems for many developing countries in supplying food at affordable prices to the poorer segments of the population. The dramatic social and humanitarian consequences of this are jeopardizing progress towards attaining the Millennium Development Goals (MDGs).

Surging food and energy prices are also raising concerns in both developed and developing countries about their potential impact on inflation. In this context, what matters is not only the direct effect of higher commodity prices on the consumer price index. It is also, and perhaps even more importantly, the indirect effects that may result from subsequent attempts to increase other prices and wages in response to perceived real income losses caused by the initial price rises in energy and food. Central banks may be prompted to react to these upward pressures on the price level with monetary tightening.

The current situation, with soaring prices of key commodities and a high degree of uncertainty about short-term trends, illustrates the different facets of the commodity price issue. The stereotyping of developing countries as exporters of primary commodities and developed countries as importers is no longer valid, and for an individual country, rising prices may mean higher incomes from one type of commodity but it may also mean higher import costs for another. The response of private actors and policymakers to the changes in relative prices and to their effects on real income is extremely important for the stability of growth and for further progress in development, including achievement of the MDGs. Indeed, the macroeconomic and social implications of commodity price developments are an issue that is high on the policy agenda, not only of developing countries, but also of developed countries, as reflected in the repeated reference in G-8 communiqués to commodity prices and their volatility.[1]

Uncertainty about key prices generally has a negative impact on investment and production planning of both sellers and buyers, and renders macroeconomic, fiscal and financial management more difficult. This is why, from the perspective of developing countries whose export earnings and national income are highly dependent on commodity markets, not only the long-term trend of primary commodity prices, but also their volatility have always been a concern. Partly as a result of this volatility, commodity-dependent economies have lower long-term average growth rates than economies with diversified production structures, and greater difficulty in reducing poverty (UNCTAD, 2002a).

This chapter addresses current issues related to commodity markets. It first reviews recent price developments and the factors that have shaped them, including the link between the financial and commodity markets, especially since the latter seems to have gained in importance in recent years. Section C of the chapter discusses in greater detail the origins and implications of the food crisis that emerged in the first half of 2008, and section D revisits the issue of commodity price instability, its implications – particularly for developing countries – and possible policy measures to resolve problems resulting from instability.

B. Recent trends in commodity prices and terms of trade

1. Trends in commodity prices

Since 2002, there has been an upward trend in the nominal prices of all commodity groups (chart 2.1). In 2008, their levels were generally much higher than the previous peaks of the mid-1990s, except for tropical beverages. The surge in prices has been mainly the result of rapidly increasing demand from several fast growing developing economies, in particular China and India, owing to their highly intensive use of energy and raw materials for industrialization, urbanization and infrastructure development (*TDR 2005:* chap. II). Growing demand encountered supply constraints because during the period of relatively low prices in the 1990s, investment in new capacity had been low in the oil and mineral sectors. Although investment in exploration and new production capacity has increased since 2002, it has met with severe technological and geological constraints, so that the supply response so far has been weak.

The evolution of prices of different commodity groups has varied (chart 2.1). Until 2006, the average price increase of mining products (minerals, ores and metals) and of crude petroleum exceeded the average price increase of agricultural products (food, tropical beverages, vegetable oilseeds and oils, and agricultural raw materials). In 2007, prices surged for all commodity groups, except for a brief correction

Chart 2.1

MONTHLY COMMODITY PRICE INDICES BY COMMODITY GROUP, JANUARY 1995–MAY 2008

(Index numbers, 2000 = 100)

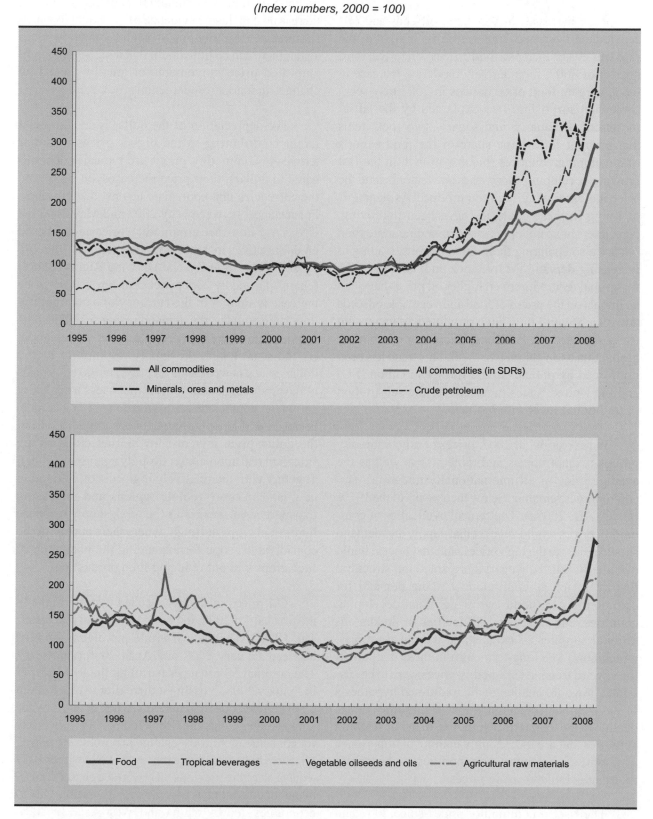

Source: UNCTAD, *Commodity Price Statistics* online.

Note: Crude petroleum price is the average of Dubai/Brent/Texas, equally weighted. Prices are in current dollars unless otherwise specified.

in mining products. However, these averages hide considerable differences within the different commodity groups (table 2.1).

Price increases of vegetable oilseeds and oils accelerated from mid-2006 onwards. In light of the rapid increase in most food prices since the third quarter of 2007, the relatively moderate increase in the aggregate food price indices in 2007 may seem somewhat surprising. It is explained by the fall in the prices of bananas and sugar – two food items that account for a large share of the food exports of developing countries. Income growth in the fast growing developing countries is one factor behind the price increases of agricultural produce. As standards of living in these countries have been improving, consumers have not only been demanding more food but are also changing their dietary habits, leading to increasing demand for livestock and, consequently, for animal feed. Moreover, higher oil prices have had an impact on the prices of food and vegetable oilseeds and oils, because they have prompted an increasing use of scarce arable land for growing crops for biofuel production as an alternative to oil. This trend has been reinforced by policies in the European Union (EU) and the United States to accelerate the substitution of traditional fuels with biofuels.

In real terms, in 2007, prices of all commodity groups (except metals and minerals) as well as the average price of all internationally traded primary commodities remained below their peaks of the 1970s (UNCTAD, 2008a). The typical cyclicality of commodity prices would suggest that supply and demand should adjust to the high prices, and that prices should eventually fall. However, there are some structural features, such as continuously rising demand for commodities in the fast growing Asian developing countries, and increasing difficulties in finding additional supplies of exhaustible natural resources, which point to a long-term shift in these markets. If the upward trend in commodity prices were to be sustained, it would challenge the traditional hypothesis in development economics that commodity prices decline in the long term. Moreover, many developing countries that are increasingly gaining in importance as importers of primary commodities are becoming more vulnerable to rising prices.

The rise in commodity prices since 2002 and the slow supply response has resulted in low inventory levels for many commodities, a situation that generally gives rise to increased speculation. Financial investors have also been investing more in commodities futures and options because of the recent turbulence in financial markets. Although there is no conclusive evidence of the extent to which speculation is contributing to rising commodity prices so far, there can be little doubt that it has significantly amplified price movements originally caused by changes in market fundamentals (box 2.1).

The depreciation of the dollar is an additional factor contributing to the higher prices in dollar terms. As commodity prices are typically denominated in dollars, their price increases are smaller in the currencies that appreciate against that currency. For instance, between May 2007 and May 2008 the UNCTAD non-fuel commodity price index based on dollar prices increased by 41.9 per cent, but only by 32.7 per cent in Special Drawing Rights (SDRs) (chart 2.1), and by 23.3 per cent in euros. If the price increase is smaller in the currency of a commodity-importing country, the demand response will also be smaller than in the absence of a dollar depreciation. By the same token, the supply response to higher dollar prices is weakened as prices in the currencies of the producing countries rise much less when those currencies appreciate against the dollar. For example, in the case of Brazil, producers benefited little from the dollar price increase for biofuel crops as the Brazilian real appreciated strongly against the dollar. Together with the relatively high cost of cultivating new land in more remote regions and increasing transport costs, it explains the weak supply response for biofuel crops in Brazil, where there appears to be considerable scope for expanding the plantation of such crops without reducing food production.

Oil prices in dollars reached historic highs in the first half of 2008, in both nominal and real terms. The UNCTAD index of crude petroleum doubled between January 2007 and April 2008 (chart 2.1). The nominal oil price per barrel hit the $100 barrier in January 2008, crossing it thereafter to reach about $140 in June 2008. In real terms, when deflated by the United States Consumer Price Index (CPI) as a proxy for consumer countries' change in purchasing power, oil prices today are above the level of November 1979 – the peak of the previous oil crisis (see chart 1.2). Demand for oil continues to grow strongly in non-OECD economies, led by China and West Asia. In 2007, non-OECD oil demand increased by 3.9 per cent, and Chinese oil consumption increased by 4.2 per cent.

Table 2.1

WORLD PRIMARY COMMODITY PRICES, 2002–2007

(Percentage change over previous year)

Commodity group	2002	2003	2004	2005	2006	2007	2002–2007[a]
All commodities[b]	**0.8**	**8.1**	**19.9**	**11.7**	**30.4**	**12.9**	**113.2**
All commodities (in SDRs)[b]	**-0.8**	**-0.2**	**13.6**	**12.0**	**30.7**	**8.5**	**80.1**
All food	**2.9**	**4.1**	**13.2**	**6.3**	**16.3**	**13.3**	**65.0**
Food and tropical beverages	**0.4**	**2.3**	**13.2**	**8.8**	**17.8**	**8.6**	**61.2**
Tropical beverages	11.7	6.2	6.4	25.5	6.7	10.4	67.0
Coffee	4.7	8.7	19.8	43.8	7.1	12.5	125.6
Cocoa	63.3	-1.3	-11.8	-0.7	3.5	22.6	9.8
Tea	-9.5	8.4	2.1	9.1	11.7	-12.3	18.2
Food	-0.5	1.9	13.9	7.2	19.0	8.5	60.5
Sugar	-20.3	2.9	1.1	37.9	49.4	-31.7	46.4
Beef	-0.3	0.4	17.8	4.1	-2.4	1.9	22.6
Maize	10.4	6.5	5.0	-12.0	24.4	38.2	69.2
Wheat	16.6	-0.7	6.8	-1.4	26.6	34.3	77.7
Rice	11.0	4.1	23.1	17.1	5.5	9.5	73.4
Bananas	-9.6	-28.7	39.9	9.9	18.5	-0.9	28.6
Vegetable oilseeds and oils	**24.9**	**17.4**	**13.2**	**-9.5**	**5.0**	**52.9**	**93.1**
Soybeans	8.6	24.1	16.1	-10.4	-2.2	43.0	80.6
Agricultural raw materials	**-2.4**	**19.8**	**13.4**	**3.9**	**15.0**	**11.2**	**80.5**
Hides and skins	-2.9	-16.8	-1.7	-2.1	5.1	4.5	-12.1
Cotton	-3.6	37.2	-3.3	-11.6	5.9	10.2	36.8
Tobacco	-8.2	-3.5	3.6	1.8	6.4	11.7	20.9
Rubber	33.1	41.7	20.3	15.2	40.4	8.6	199.4
Tropical logs	-10.5	20.1	19.2	0.3	-4.7	19.5	63.6
Minerals, ores and metals	**-2.7**	**12.4**	**40.7**	**26.2**	**60.3**	**12.8**	**260.8**
Aluminium	-6.5	6.0	19.8	10.6	35.4	2.7	95.4
Phosphate rock	-3.3	-5.9	7.8	2.5	5.3	60.5	75.7
Iron ore	-1.1	8.5	17.4	71.5	19.0	9.5	184.7
Tin	-9.4	20.6	73.8	-13.2	18.9	65.6	258.1
Copper	-1.2	14.1	61.0	28.4	82.7	5.9	356.5
Nickel	14.0	42.2	43.6	6.6	64.5	53.5	449.4
Tungsten ore	-41.8	18.0	22.9	120.7	36.2	-0.6	333.5
Lead	-4.9	13.8	72.0	10.2	32.0	100.2	469.9
Zinc	-12.1	6.3	26.5	31.9	137.0	-1.0	316.4
Gold	14.4	17.3	12.6	8.7	35.9	15.3	124.7
Crude petroleum	**2.0**	**15.8**	**30.7**	**41.3**	**20.4**	**10.7**	**185.1**
Memo item:							
Manufactures[c]	**0.6**	**9.2**	**8.3**	**2.5**	**3.4**	**7.5**	**34.8**

Source: UNCTAD secretariat calculations, based on UNCTAD, *Commodity Price Statistics* online; and United Nations Statistics Division (UNSD), *Monthly Bulletin of Statistics*, various issues.

Note: In current dollars unless otherwise specified.

   a Percentage change between 2002 and 2007.

   b Excluding crude petroleum.

   c Export unit value of manufactured goods of developed countries.

Box 2.1

COMMODITY PRICE FORMATION AND SPECULATION

Traditionally, speculators have played a useful role in primary commodity markets by providing opportunities for sellers and buyers of primary commodities to hedge against commodity price risks. However, in recent years speculation may well have become excessive, amplifying price movements to such an extent that they no longer reflect market fundamentals (Masters, 2008).

Major commodity exchanges around the world have witnessed record trading volumes helped by the wider use of electronic trading and greater interest by institutional investors. In 2007, agricultural futures and options trading grew by 32 per cent, energy by 28.6 per cent and industrial metals by 29.7 per cent (Burghardt, 2008). In addition, according to statistics of the Bank of International Settlements (BIS), outstanding amounts of over-the-counter commodity derivatives increased by close to 160 per cent between June 2005 and June 2007.[a] New actors in commodity markets, such as investment, pension and hedge funds – and, more recently, sovereign wealth funds – have become significant players in international markets for commodity futures and options. According to one estimate, investment in commodity indices has surged, from less than $13 billion at the end of 2003 to $260 billion in 2008 (Masters, 2008). In addition, media reports suggest that derivatives trading in petroleum has increased 30 to 35 times more than physical petroleum trading between 2000 and 2006.

For various reasons, it is difficult to assess the extent to which price formation is influenced by speculation. Statistics do not distinguish between commercial customers and speculators. Moreover, speculative operations are partly executed over the counter (such as directly between banks and their clients), and therefore are not recorded by commodity exchange regulators. Besides, operations on commodity exchanges are not fully transparent. Nevertheless, a report by staff of the United States Senate (2006: 2) concluded for the oil market: "Although it is difficult to quantify the effect of speculation on prices, there is substantial evidence that the large amount of speculation in the current market has significantly increased prices. Several analysts have estimated that speculative purchases of oil futures have added as much as $20–$25 per barrel to the current price of crude oil, thereby pushing up the price of oil from $50 to approximately $70 per barrel."

Movements in petroleum prices also influence the prices of other commodities because much of the derivatives trading is done on the basis of index trading (i.e. a bundle of commodities in which petroleum often has the largest share). Index speculators behave differently from traditional speculators. The latter contribute to price discovery as they both buy and sell options and futures contracts. Index speculators, on the other hand, are attracted to commodity markets because movements in commodity prices traditionally have been uncorrelated to price movements on stock and bond markets. These speculators turned their attention to commodity exchanges following the burst of the dot-com bubble on stock markets and, more recently, following the sub-prime mortgage crisis. Index speculators see buying commodity derivatives as a portfolio allocation decision. They allocate a certain proportion of their portfolio to commodity futures irrespective of the actual price on commodities markets. These speculators usually roll over one futures contract into another when the initial contract approaches maturity. They sell their positions only when they change the composition of their portfolio; thus they normally do not provide market liquidity. This insensitivity to price multiplies the impact of index speculators on commodity exchanges.

Futures prices are one criterion that guides spot prices.[b] For example, a producer of wheat will be happy to sell the entire future wheat harvest already at the time of planting if the futures price that can be locked in is high enough to guarantee the producer a satisfactory profit. The futures prices will go up if more and more people try to buy wheat for future delivery, for example because of an expected shortage of supply. Standard accounts of commodity futures markets postulate that speculative activities on such

Box 2.1 *(concluded)*

markets affect spot markets only in terms of price expectations, but with no change in the behaviour of spot traders. However, an expected shortage of supply and the associated continued increase in futures prices also encourages consumers (e.g. bakeries) to buy as much wheat flour as possible at the outset (i.e. before spot prices move up even further). Thus it may well be that a sustained rise in futures prices encourages physical traders (such as bakeries) also to engage in speculative activities. This would mean in the above example that the bakeries start hoarding flour so as to avoid, for as long as possible, the expected increase in the spot price of flour. Bakeries will do this because of very limited possibilities to substitute wheat flour in the short run. If there is substantial index speculation, and if it is combined with low price elasticity of demand, the level of spot prices will remain high. And only a sizeable supply shock will be able to reverse the speculation-driven price increase.

The cumulative process of rising futures and spot prices will continue until expectations of future supply shortages have vanished. If the price increase triggers an increase in supply, this new price level is likely to be close to the one that prevailed prior to the speculative surge. But if there is a sluggish supply response, the new price level will be established on the basis of declining demand. This would be the case for food, for example, when consumers can no longer afford as much food as they used to.

Speculation is not a driver of commodity prices but rather a factor that may accelerate and amplify price movements driven by fundamental supply and demand factors, and the impact of speculation on prices is limited in time (Burkhard, 2008; IMF, 2006: 15–18). This view is also supported by the United States Commodity Futures and Trading Commission (CFTC), which notes that prices of commodities for which no futures contracts exist, or in which there is little or no index trading, have also shown rapid increases (Harris, 2008).

Improved market supervision and regulation of derivatives trading could limit the impact of speculation on spot prices. One regulatory measure could be to limit the value of outstanding futures contracts; another could be to limit the amount of futures contracts that can be rolled over in the final days preceding maturity of a futures contract. In view of the recent developments in commodity prices, the CFTC has undertaken several initiatives directed at enhancing oversight of the energy and agricultural markets. These initiatives include increasing information and transparency, ensuring proper market controls, continuing aggressive enforcement efforts and improving coordination of oversight (Lukken, 2008). The Commission has also stressed the urgent need for more international dialogue and cooperation on this matter.

In any case, the growing presence of financial investors is most likely adding volatility to commodity markets, as it causes prices to react quickly – and often to overreact – to new information in the market (UNCTAD, 2007a). A bullish sentiment on commodities investment can suddenly change, and if speculators were to decide to take profits or to change the composition of their portfolios in response to changes in financial markets, such as an increase in interest rates or a recovery in stock markets, there could be a sharp correction in prices.

---

[a] BIS over-the-counter derivatives statistics are available at: http://www.bis.org/statistics/derstats.htm (accessed 9 April 2008). Data refer to nominal or notional amounts outstanding, defined as the gross nominal or notional value of all deals concluded and not yet settled at the reporting date.

[b] For a further discussion of the relationship between futures and spot prices, see the website of the Commodity Futures Trading Commission (CFTC) at: http://www.cftc.gov/educationcenter/economicpurpose.html.

This robust growth more than compensated for the 0.4 per cent decline in oil consumption in the OECD countries. Overall, global oil demand increased by 1.3 per cent, and the pace and pattern of this demand is expected to continue in 2008 (IEA, 2008).

Supply response to the rising oil prices has been sluggish. In 2007, global oil production increased by only 0.2 per cent.[2] Even though oil companies substantially increased their investment outlays, these had a relatively small impact on additional supply capacity. This is because new exploration and the creation of new production capacity have become much more costly due to difficulties of access to remote deposits with existing equipment and technology (IMF, 2008: box 1.5).[3] The costs associated with constructing new oil and gas facilities upstream have doubled since 2005 to reach a new record high, according to the IHS/Cambridge Energy Research Associates Upstream Capital Costs Index (CERA, 2008). Moreover, as a result of the high price levels, many extractive companies may become complacent about increasing investment in new facilities.[4]

After the Organization of the Petroleum Exporting Countries (OPEC) decided to cut oil production in late 2006 and early 2007, oil supply fell from 36.7 million barrels per day in the third quarter of 2006 to 35.5 in the second quarter of 2007. Its members then decided to raise production again in late 2007, which resulted in the production of 37.3 million barrels per day in the first quarter of 2008. In 2007, demand exceeded supply, but in March and April 2008 the oil market swung back into surplus, and it is expected to remain so for the rest of the year (IEA, 2008). Most OPEC members decided to maintain their output levels, as they believe the price increase in 2008 is due to geopolitical tensions, dollar depreciation and speculative investment rather than to supply shortages (OPEC, 2008). However, in late June 2008 Saudi Arabia agreed to increase production further, by about 500,000 barrels per day (according to media reports). Indeed, many observers believe that it is currently the only OPEC country that is in a position to increase production. In oil-producing countries that are not members of OPEC, the increase in oil production has been below expectations.

Overall, the measures taken by OPEC and the additional oil production by non-OPEC countries have been insufficient to calm the market. As a result of the tight supply and demand conditions, the lower levels of oil stocks in consuming countries and the very limited spare capacity in producing countries, the oil market has become highly sensitive to any supply disruption, which is immediately reflected in much higher prices. But even if the production of crude oil were to increase, it is unclear whether refineries have the capacity to cope with such an increase.

However, there is no clear knowledge of how much oil is left in the world, and by when exactly peak oil would be reached. According to some analysts, the oil price could reach $200 per barrel in two years.[5] In this uncertain context, energy markets react quickly to any news concerning supply, such as OPEC decisions to change or maintain production quotas, geopolitical tensions, the status of reserves in major consuming countries, or demand prospects in China. But certainly, the daily oil price changes of the magnitude seen in May and June 2008 cannot be attributed to market fundamentals alone; speculators might also be playing a significant role.

> The combination of a slowdown in global growth and sharply rising primary commodity prices has important implications for monetary policy.

In the short-term, as the elasticities of supply and demand are low, oil prices are likely to remain high. However, the slowdown of the world economy could lead to a downward adjustment in oil consumption. Also, at the current price level, governments in those developing countries where oil is subsidized may find subsidies unsustainable in budgetary terms; a reduction in subsidies would cause demand to fall. In the long term, adjustment should come from reduced oil consumption, through the implementation of more energy-saving and efficiency measures. Greater use of alternative energies, which become more profitable when oil prices are high, will also help. Additionally, higher investment in oil-producing countries should eventually bear fruit and lead to an increase in production.

Changes in oil prices influence the evolution of prices of other commodities, as some of these have become increasingly interlinked.[6] Most importantly, higher oil prices are leading to greater demand for agricultural commodities for biofuel production, which compete with food commodities. They also raise the cost of production of other commodities. For instance, global fertilizer prices tripled in 2007 (IFDC, 2008). Oil prices can also affect the prices of commodities that are used as substitutes for oil by-products, such as cotton as a substitute for synthetic fibres or natural rubber for synthetic rubber. The closer links between oil prices and other commodity prices also mean that the greater volatility of oil prices is transmitted to other commodity markets.

Higher freight rates, which are driven in part by rising oil prices, also influence the final price of commodities and commodity-related products. The Baltic Dry Index for transport costs of bulk commodities jumped from about 4,400 in early January 2007 to over 11,000 in early June 2008, due to the combination of higher oil prices and booming demand. The average Overall Liner Trade Index for container transport in the first quarter of 2008 was 96.3, compared with 88.6 in the first quarter of 2007.[7] In the past, lower transport costs was one of the major forces behind globalization. Now, the rise in oil prices to unprecedented levels, and the consequent increase in transportation costs, may lead to a greater tendency to seek supplies from domestic and regional markets (Rubin and Tal, 2008).

Moreover, the combination of a slowdown in global growth and sharply rising prices of oil and other primary commodity prices has important implications for monetary policy. With the inflation targets set by many central banks likely to be breached for yet another year, it will be difficult to ease monetary policy, even though doing so would prevent a sharper economic slowdown. A rise in commodity prices has a lasting inflationary impact only if so-called second-round effects (i.e. a vicious circle of rising nominal wages and further rising prices) cannot be avoided. There can be little doubt that such second-round effects must be minimized. However, while monetary restrictions are a suitable instrument for preventing an economy from overheating as a result of a cyclical increase in aggregate demand, they are not an appropriate instrument for curbing increases in relative prices resulting from a structural shift in the international commodity markets. International cooperation in macroeconomic policy could be helpful in avoiding an accumulation of such restrictive actions.

While it is likely that the prices of most commodities, including oil, will remain relatively high for quite some time, for the structural reasons discussed above, the short-term evolution of most commodity prices will largely depend on the performance of the world economy in the course of 2008 and 2009. A sharp slowdown, or even a recession, cannot be excluded. A recession in the United States alone, which accounts for about 16 per cent of world commodity imports, could have a significant impact on the global demand for commodities, and a downward price trend resulting from changes in real demand could be amplified by speculative sales. This would hit developing countries in particular, as commodities account for a large proportion of their exports and of their national income. The impact would also depend on the extent to which the fast growing developing countries that are major producers of manufactures and services are able to "decouple" their macroeconomic development from the United States. In view of all these uncertainties, the case for stabilization measures to mitigate the negative effects of volatility in commodity markets is as valid as ever.

2. Terms of trade

The overall impact of price changes differs considerably, depending on the trade structure of each economy and on the relative weight of commodity exports and imports in their gross national income. The recent evolution of prices of internationally traded goods also affects the distribution of income among and within different countries. Changes in income distribution within countries result from the fact that the social and economic groups that benefit from higher prices received for exported commodities are not identical to those that have to bear the burden of higher prices for imported goods.

The distribution effects across countries are largely determined by the evolution of the terms of trade, i.e. the ratio between the index of the unit price of exports and that of the unit price of imports. At a given level of export earnings or import expenditure, terms-of-trade gains indicate a relative increase in real income (because the same volume of exports enables a greater volume of imports) and terms-of-trade losses indicate a relative loss of real income (because the same volume of exports buys a smaller volume of

Chart 2.2

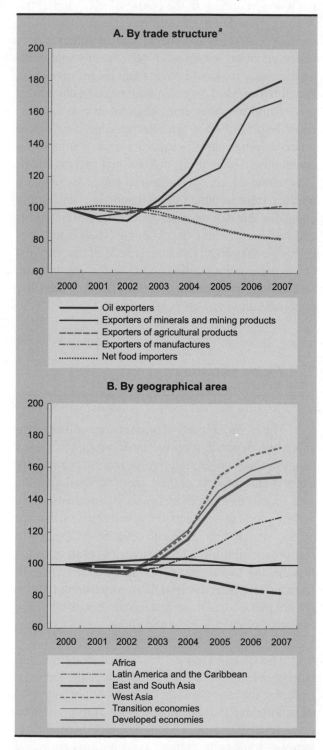

**NET BARTER TERMS OF TRADE,
SELECTED COUNTRIES, 2000–2007**

(Index numbers, 2000 = 100)

A. By trade structure[a]

— Oil exporters
— Exporters of minerals and mining products
----- Exporters of agricultural products
·—·—·— Exporters of manufactures
············· Net food importers

B. By geographical area

— Africa
·—·—·— Latin America and the Caribbean
— — East and South Asia
----- West Asia
— Transition economies
— Developed economies

Source: UNCTAD, secretariat calculations, based on *UNCTAD
Handbook of Statistics* database.
Note: Net food importers are low-income food-deficit countries, excluding exporters of fuel, minerals and mining
products.
a Developing and transition economies.

imports). There is broad agreement that during most
of the twentieth century, developing countries –
which typically exported raw materials and imported
manufactures – suffered from a long-term deterioration in their terms of trade, due to a declining trend in
the prices of primary commodities (which constituted
most of their exports to the developed countries)
vis-à-vis those of manufactures (which were mostly
imported from developed countries).

Terms-of-trade trends have changed significantly since the beginning of the new millennium,
not only because the prices of most primary products
have risen sharply, but also because prices of many
manufactures have risen more slowly – or have even
fallen – especially prices of low-skill-intensive manufactures. The change in the trend has been related to
two main structural changes: on the demand side,
the emergence of a group of developing countries as
major importers of primary products, and on the supply side, the fast expansion of manufactured exports
by developing countries with relatively low labour
costs. The latter was reinforced by currency devaluations in Asian countries following the 1997–1998
financial crisis, as the devaluations contributed to
slower increases in the average price of internationally traded manufactures. As a result of the changes
in the demand and supply patterns, stereotyping
developing countries as exporters of primary commodities and importers of manufactures, on the one
hand, and developed countries as importers of such
commodities and exporters of manufactures, on the
other, is no longer valid.

Between 2000 and 2007, on average, the greatest improvements in the terms of trade occurred
in developing and transition economies that are
exporters of fuels and mining products. In contrast,
developing countries that have emerged as important
exporters of labour-intensive manufactures and are
net oil importers saw their terms of trade deteriorate
(chart 2.2A). Data for developing and transition
economies covering the period up to 2007 indicate
that the terms of trade for the group of exporters of
agricultural products have changed very little since
2003, but, within the group, the terms of trade have
evolved quite differently for individual countries, depending on their specific export products and on their
degree of dependence on imports of food and energy.
For instance, exporters of cotton (Benin, Burkina
Faso), tobacco (Malawi) and some tropical agricultural products (Guinea Bissau) suffered significant

losses, as their export prices did not compensate for the higher food and oil bills. On the other hand, significant recovery in the prices of coffee, maize, wheat and soybeans brought terms of trade gains, or at least avoided losses, for countries such as Argentina, Ethiopia, Paraguay and Rwanda. Given that prices for food crops and oil have risen faster in the first half of 2008 than the prices for tropical beverages and agricultural raw materials, variations within this group are likely to have increased further.

The Food and Agriculture Organization of the United Nations (FAO) has identified 82 "low-income food importers" that are vulnerable to food price hikes.[8] For 48 of these countries, which do not export oil or minerals and mining products, food price increases have led to deterioration in the terms of trade by 20 per cent since 2001. In the remaining 34 countries, the terms of trade effect was offset by substantial increases in the prices of the commodities that they export.

A comparison of geographical regions further reveals the diverging trends in the terms of trade among developing and transition economies (chart 2.2B). The most dramatic improvement in terms of trade since 2003 have been observed in West Asia, which has several major petroleum exporters. This region is followed by the transition economies, on account of important hydrocarbon exporters such as the Russian Federation, Kazakhstan and Azerbaijan. The strong improvement in the terms of trade of Africa as a whole has been due not only to the rise in the prices of oil and mining products, which have benefited several countries, but also to the fact that in recent years a number of countries that traditionally have been exporters of agricultural products have begun exporting fuels and minerals. However, there are particularly large differences among the various countries of this region in terms of the evolution of the terms of trade. The situation of 20 sub-Saharan countries that do not export fuels or mining products has deteriorated since 2000, as the rate of increase in the prices of their imports (fuels, food and relatively sophisticated manufactures) has exceeded that of their exports (comprising mainly tropical agricultural products or labour-intensive manufactures).

The main challenge for countries that benefit from improved terms of trade is to use the additional revenues in a way that enhances development prospects.

Latin America and the Caribbean also show significant gains in their terms of trade, although more moderate, owing to a more diversified trade composition. Gains have been more important in South America, while most Central American and several Caribbean countries (most of which depend heavily on fuel imports and export labour-intensive manufactures) have suffered terms-of-trade losses. Finally, East, South-East and South Asian countries have experienced a significant deterioration in their terms of trade, owing to the large share of labour-intensive manufactures in their exports, and to their increasing dependence on imports of energy and industrial raw materials.

The changes in the terms of trade have led to significant gains or losses in the real income of trading countries. In fact, between 2004 and 2007, developing countries classified as exporters of manufactures suffered losses from changes in their terms of trade equivalent to almost 1 per cent of GDP per year. On the other hand, oil exporters and exporters of mining products obtained windfall gains from improving terms of trade, which were 7.5 and about 4 percentage points of GDP respectively. For many of these countries, windfall gains from terms-of-trade changes appear to have been offset in part by a rise in profit remittances by transnational corporations involved in the exploitation of natural resources. In those cases, the gross domestic *income* grew faster than the gross domestic *product* (the difference resulting from gains in the terms of trade), but the gross *national* income grew less than the gross *domestic* income (owing to higher net payments to non-residents). This was the case, in particular, for a number of mineral exporters such as Chile, Peru and Zambia between 2004 and 2007, where 60 per cent or more of the gains from price increases of minerals and mining products went into profit remittances (table 2.2). Similarly, in several sub-Saharan African countries and transition economies that are oil exporters, foreign companies appear to have captured a substantial share of the windfall revenues. On the other hand, in other oil- and gas-exporting countries, such as Algeria, Angola, Bolivia, the Bolivarian Republic of Venezuela, Ecuador, the Islamic Republic of Iran, Kuwait, the Russian Federation and Saudi Arabia, the rise in prices and related improvements in

Table 2.2

IMPACT OF CHANGES IN TERMS OF TRADE AND NET INCOME PAYMENTS ON NATIONAL DISPOSABLE INCOME IN SELECTED DEVELOPING-COUNTRY GROUPS, AVERAGE OF 2004–2006

(Per cent of GDP)

	Effects from changes in		
	Terms of trade	Net income payments	Net impact
Oil and gas exporters	**7.5**	**-2.0**	**5.5**
of which:			
Algeria	4.6	0.0	4.6
Angola	16.4	-3.9	12.5
Azerbaijan	9.3	-7.1	2.2
Bolivia	2.6	0.2	2.9
Equatorial Guinea	18.7	-11.6	7.1
Iran, Islamic Republic of	3.9	0.6	4.5
Kazakhstan	8.6	-4.9	3.6
Kuwait	10.2	2.4	12.6
Nigeria	5.5	-3.3	2.2
Russian Federation	4.3	-0.5	3.8
Saudi Arabia	9.5	0.6	10.0
Venezuela, Bolivarian Republic of	7.1	1.0	8.1
Exporters of minerals and mining products	**3.9**	**-2.1**	**1.8**
of which:			
Botswana	-0.8	-0.3	-1.1
Chile	6.3	-3.7	2.5
Jamaica	2.3	-1.1	1.2
Papua New Guinea	6.6	-1.5	5.0
Peru	2.7	-2.1	0.6
Zambia	6.5	-4.0	2.5
Exporters of agricultural products	**-0.2**	**-0.1**	**-0.4**
Exporters of manufactures	**-0.6**	**-0.1**	**-0.7**

Source: UNCTAD secretariat calculations, based on UN data; IMF, *Balance of Payments Statistics* database; ECLAC, *Balance of Payments Statistics* database; Economist Intelligence Unit, *Country Reports*; national sources; and UNCTAD estimates of unit value and volume of exports and imports.

Note: For an explanation of net income payments, see text.

the terms of trade were not accompanied by a higher share of net factor payments abroad in gross domestic income. This suggests that the producer countries themselves appropriated most or all of the gains. These are countries where State-owned companies dominate the extraction and export of oil and gas, or countries that have recently renegotiated contracts with foreign companies to appropriate a larger share of the income from oil and gas exploitation.

The main challenge for countries that benefit from improved terms of trade is to use the additional revenues in a way that enhances long-term development prospects. It is therefore important that the windfall income be captured by the producing countries to the largest extent possible, either through local ownership of producing firms or through a well-designed taxation and royalty system that ensures a fair distribution of the rent between domestic actors and foreign investors. The present high prices for oil and mining products may offer an opportunity for re-negotiating the conditions of rent distribution where it remains unfavourable for the producing countries. In addition, these resources need to be used for financing investment in infrastructure development and in social and productive sectors in a sustainable way.

C. The global food crisis

1. Soaring food prices in 2007 and 2008

World food prices roughly doubled between January 2006 and May 2008, and they have increased by over 80 per cent since April 2007 (chart 2.1). The increases apply to a wide range of food commodities. The current price surge, which started in June 2007, has been led by wheat, the price of which more than doubled by March 2008, although it declined slightly thereafter. The price of maize has risen by 66 per cent since July 2007, while that of rice has tripled since September 2007 and surged by about 160 per cent in the short period between January 2008 and May 2008 (chart 2.3). Vegetable oilseeds and oils have also registered spectacular increases, with prices multiplying by about 2.5 times since early 2006 (chart 2.1).

There are a number of reasons for the dramatic increase in food prices in 2007 and 2008, including a slowdown in the expansion of global production due to a lower rate of growth of crop yields and cultivated land[9] on the one hand, and strongly increasing demand by fast growing developing countries on the other (*TDR 2005,* chap. II). However, an analysis of world consumption and production data for the last two decades for wheat, maize and rice (chart 2.3) shows that previous price increases in comparable deficit situations were much smaller than the present one. Thus recent price hikes cannot be explained solely by underlying consumption and production trends. As mentioned above, they are also related to higher fuel prices and transport costs and, to some extent, to dollar depreciation (IMF, 2008). Furthermore, today, many food stocks have fallen to historic lows,[10] suggesting that positive demand shocks and negative supply shocks can only be accommodated through sharp price movements (Merryll Lynch, 2008).

Under these conditions, the effect of speculation is also magnified. It is more than a mere coincidence that the recent price surge started at the same time as the financial turmoil resulting from sub-prime mortgage lending in the United States. Speculators, looking for high returns in the short run, may well have sensed strains arising in world food markets and readjusted their portfolios to contain a greater share of commodity futures contracts (see box 2.1). On the other hand, if food stocks had been high, any supply or demand shock could easily have been absorbed through a reduction in stocks, thus reducing the incentives for speculation. Thus, as the general evolution of global food prices since mid-2007 has been driven by a series of shocks that occurred in the context of increasing sensitivity of global food markets to events in other markets, these shocks had a much stronger impact on global food prices than in normal circumstances.

The shocks that triggered the price explosion have differed by commodity. For wheat, adverse weather conditions were the main factor, which considerably reduced crops in Australia and Europe. The higher price of maize was largely the result of a policy-driven push for biofuel production of ethanol

> Recent price hikes cannot be explained solely by underlying consumption and production trends.

Chart 2.3

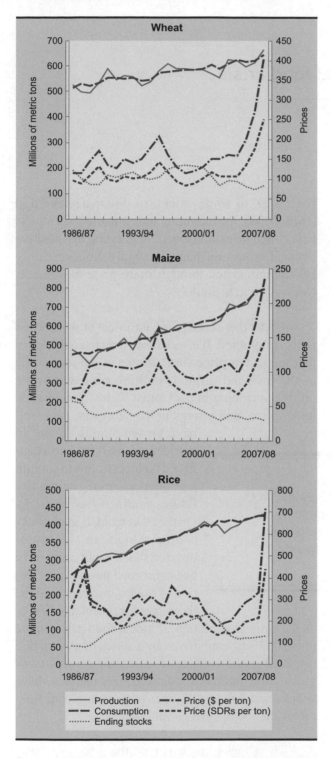

WORLD CEREAL CONSUMPTION, PRODUCTION, STOCKS AND PRICES

Source: UNCTAD secretariat calculations, based on United States Department of Agriculture, *Production, Supply and Distribution Online* database; UNCTAD, *Commodity Price Statistics* online; and IMF, *International Financial Statistics* database.

Note: Data on prices for 2008 are only an indication as they are the average of January to May.

in the United States, which led to a doubling of the maize output used for biofuel production between 2006 and 2008, partly at the expense of maize produced for food consumption (WAOB, 2008). Demand for biofuels is also behind the strong increases in the prices of vegetable oils. According to OECD-FAO (2008), biofuels accounted for more than half of the increase in demand for grains and vegetable oils between 2005 and 2007. The United States accounts for a large proportion of the increase in the use of grains, mainly maize, for biofuel production. The FAO reports that, of the nearly 40 million ton increase in global maize consumption in 2007, 30 million tonnes were absorbed by ethanol plants alone, mostly in the United States, which is the world's largest producer and exporter of maize (FAO, 2008a). Indeed, the United States Department of Agriculture recognizes that the increase in that country's ethanol production over the past five years and the related changes in the structure of the domestic corn market have had a more pronounced impact on the world's supply and demand balance for total coarse grains recently than in the 1980s and 1990s (USDA, 2008a: 18). Although there is strong evidence that the demand for biofuels has driven up the price of food, the relationship between both in the long term will depend on future trends in petroleum prices as well as on the "second generation" of biofuels.

The substitution effects of crops have also been important. As the price of maize increased, consumers shifted to alternative grains (such as rice and wheat), while producers shifted from rice, wheat and soybean production to maize. The combined effect of this was higher prices of rice, wheat and soybeans. With regard to soybeans, their higher price in 2007 was mainly the result of a sharp drop in production due to a reduction in the area under cultivation. This situation seems to be reversing in 2008, with prospects for higher production of these food commodities and lower production of maize. For instance, wheat prices started falling after March 2008 following expectations of higher yields. By contrast, recently the price of maize has been rising due to unfavourable weather conditions. As for rice, its price has surged, mostly as a result of policy measures adopted by major rice-exporting countries to restrict exports and by importing countries to build up their strategic stocks of grains. These measures were taken to protect domestic consumers in response to concerns about food scarcity. They were also a reaction to domestic food price inflation due to higher production costs, mainly of fuels and fertilizers. But these measures also reduced the already relatively low supply in international markets and increased food prices even further.

However, the recent developments in food markets also have deep historical reasons. One important reason for today's food shortages – as characterized by low supply and declining stocks – is neglect of the agricultural sector over the past two decades. Since the 1980s, in many developing countries this sector has suffered from underinvestment, as now also recognized by the World Bank (2008). In the context of structural adjustment programmes, many developing countries, especially in Africa, had been encouraged to dismantle agricultural support institutions and abandon other instruments of agricultural policy, such as input subsidies, output price stabilization and territorial pricing, which encouraged agricultural use of even remote land areas (*TDR 1998*: Part Two). One objective of the reforms was to raise prices of agricultural goods in order to trigger higher production in the agricultural sector. But this did not happen. Furthermore, while developing countries were encouraged to liberalize their external trade in agricultural products, developed countries continued to provide substantial support to their agricultural sector.

Farmers in the least developed countries (LDCs) were particularly hard hit by these developments. They were unable to weather the competition from imports of cheaper, subsidized agricultural products from developed countries. As a result, food imports surged and farmers suffered income losses (FAO, 2003a).[11] They also had insufficient access to finance for investment aimed at increasing productivity (UNCTAD, 2007b). To make matters worse, ODA in support of agriculture has been falling from an annual average of about $7.5 billion in the 1980s to about half this amount in 1995–2005 (World Bank, 2008: 41).

While prospects for some food crops are better in 2008, it will take some time before stocks are replenished to normal levels. There may be some easing of prices from current levels, but they will continue to be high and volatile (FAO, 2008b; OECD-FAO, 2008; and USDA, 2008b). Markets are likely

> With better prospects for some food crops in 2008, there may be some easing of prices, but they will remain high and volatile.

to remain extremely sensitive to new supply shocks and shifts in investor sentiment, depending on further developments in international financial markets and regulatory measures that have a bearing on the profitability of biofuel production.

2. Impact of the rise in global food prices

The impact of higher food prices varies across countries and population groups. At the country level, this impact depends to a large extent on the trade structure. Net food exporters can benefit from improved terms of trade, although some of them are currently foregoing this opportunity by regulating exports in order to assure food security for domestic consumers. By contrast, several net food-importing countries have been finding it difficult to meet domestic food demand.

Data show that developments in 2006–2007 in international markets for food (including vegetable oilseeds and oils) had only a minor impact on the food trade balance of the developed countries (table 2.3). The strongest impact was felt in Australia and New Zealand, where the food export surplus fell more than 1 percentage point of GDP since 2000, mainly due to lower export volumes. The food trade deficit in Japan increased slightly, to 1 per cent of GDP, while the developed countries of North America and Europe maintained a fairly even balance between food exports and imports.

The impact of changes in international food markets was felt much more in developing countries. Net imports increased in Central America (including Mexico) and in the Caribbean, whereas a growing surplus was registered in South America, mainly on account of Argentina. The South-East Asian economies maintained a food trade surplus in the order of 1.9 per cent of their GDP, while the deficit in the food trade of the transition economies fell from 1.3 per cent of GDP in 2000 to 0.7 per cent in 2007. At the same time, net food imports of sub-Saharan Africa (excluding South Africa) increased from 1.3 per cent of GDP in 2000 to 1.9 per cent in 2007.

Table 2.3

FOOD TRADE AS A SHARE OF GDP, BY MAIN COUNTRY GROUPS, 2000–2007

(Per cent)

	Net imports			Gross imports			Gross exports		
	2000	*2006*	*2007*	*2000*	*2006*	*2007*	*2000*	*2006*	*2007*
World	**0.1**	**0.0**	**0.1**	**1.1**	**1.3**	**1.3**	**1.1**	**1.2**	**1.3**
Developed economies	**0.1**	**0.1**	**0.1**	**1.0**	**1.2**	**1.2**	**0.9**	**1.1**	**1.1**
America	-0.2	-0.1	-0.2	0.4	0.5	0.5	0.6	0.6	0.7
Asia	0.9	0.9	1.0	0.9	1.0	1.1	0.1	0.1	0.1
Europe	0.1	0.2	0.2	1.7	1.9	1.9	1.6	1.7	1.7
Oceania	-3.1	-2.2	-1.7	0.7	0.7	0.7	3.8	3.0	2.4
Developing economies	**0.0**	**-0.2**	**-0.1**	**1.6**	**1.5**	**1.5**	**1.6**	**1.7**	**1.6**
Africa	1.4	1.3	1.6	2.8	2.7	2.9	1.4	1.3	1.2
Northern Africa	2.4	1.9	2.3	3.4	3.1	3.4	1.1	1.2	1.1
Southern Africa	-0.5	-0.2	0.1	1.2	1.3	1.4	1.7	1.5	1.4
Eastern Africa	0.3	1.1	1.8	3.0	4.1	4.5	2.8	3.0	2.7
Western Africa	1.4	1.9	2.0	2.7	3.1	3.2	1.3	1.2	1.2
Middle Africa	3.5	2.1	2.1	4.0	2.3	2.3	0.5	0.2	0.1
America	-0.9	-1.6	-1.4	1.2	1.2	1.3	2.1	2.8	2.6
South America	-1.7	-2.8	-2.5	0.8	0.7	0.7	2.5	3.5	3.2
Central America, incl. Mexico	0.2	0.3	0.6	1.7	1.9	2.1	1.5	1.6	1.5
Caribbean	2.2	3.2	3.7	3.7	4.1	4.5	1.5	0.9	0.8
Asia	0.2	0.1	0.2	1.6	1.4	1.5	1.4	1.3	1.3
South Asia	0.2	-0.1	0.1	1.2	1.0	1.0	1.0	1.1	0.9
East Asia	0.4	0.4	0.5	1.2	1.2	1.2	0.9	0.8	0.7
West Asia	1.7	1.0	1.1	2.5	2.0	2.1	0.8	1.0	1.0
South-East Asia	-1.7	-1.9	-1.9	2.5	2.4	2.4	4.2	4.3	4.3
Oceania	1.9	1.6	1.5	5.4	5.7	6.0	3.6	4.2	4.5
Transition economies	**1.3**	**0.9**	**0.7**	**2.4**	**1.9**	**1.6**	**1.1**	**1.0**	**1.0**
Asia	0.9	0.8	0.7	2.8	2.2	2.0	1.9	1.4	1.3
Europe	1.4	0.9	0.6	2.4	1.9	1.6	1.0	0.9	0.9
Memo items:									
Sub-Saharan Africa, excl. South Africa	1.3	1.7	1.9	3.2	3.2	3.3	1.9	1.5	1.4
Least developed countries	2.1	2.0	2.2	3.7	3.6	3.7	1.6	1.6	1.5
Landlocked countries	0.4	0.6	0.6	3.1	2.9	2.8	2.6	2.3	2.2
Small island developing States	2.1	1.9	2.4	5.7	5.7	6.0	3.6	3.8	3.6
Heavily indebted poor countries	1.1	2.1	2.4	4.0	4.5	4.8	2.9	2.4	2.3
G-7	0.2	0.3	0.2	0.8	1.0	1.0	0.6	0.7	0.8

Source: UNCTAD secretariat calculations, based on *UNCTAD Handbook of Statistics* database; UNCTAD, *Commodity Price Statistics* online; and national sources.

Note: Food includes vegetables oilseeds and oils. Data for 2007 are estimates.

On average, the poorest developing countries were more adversely affected by the recent increase in food prices than the more advanced developing countries. According to FAO estimates, the food import bill for the LDCs and low-income food-deficit countries (LIFDCs) could grow by another 37 to 40 per cent in 2008, after rising 30 and 37 per cent, respectively, in 2007 (FAO, 2008b).[12] This implies that by the end of 2008, the food basket in these countries could cost about four times as much as it did in 2000. Most of the heavily indebted poor countries (HIPC) and small island developing States have also witnessed a substantial rise in their food import bill since 2006.

At the household level, those with the lowest purchasing power were particularly hard hit by the surging and volatile food prices. In developing countries, and particularly in the LDCs, households spend a much higher share of their income on food than those in developed countries. According to FAO estimates, this share amounts to 60–80 per cent in developing countries, compared to 10–20 per cent in developed countries (FAO, 2008c). And for the poorest segments of the population, the share of staples in total food consumption is much higher than for the average household.

The degree to which higher international prices get passed on to domestic prices differs from country to country, depending on the exchange rate, transport costs and domestic policies to control prices, as well as on trade policies and food distribution structures. As the share of processed products in the food basket is usually small in developing countries, increases in international commodity prices are likely to be more directly transmitted to retail prices. For many developing countries, the recent inflation in food prices has considerably exceeded overall inflation, and it has been much higher than in developed countries. In the latter, the direct contribution of higher food prices to overall inflation is modest compared to developing countries (OECD-FAO, 2008: box 2.1). The United Nations (2008) reports that the increase in global food prices contributed from about a third to over a half of headline inflation in developing countries in 2007, and that the impact was particularly strong in Asia, including West Asia. Upward pressures on prices have been intensifying in the course of 2008 in all developing regions, especially in oil- and food-importing countries.

A simulation by USDA (2008a) shows the different impact of food price hikes in developing and developed countries. A 50 per cent increase in staple food prices causes retail food expenditures to rise by 6 per cent for a consumer in a high-income country, but by 21 per cent for a consumer in an LIFDC. This implies that the percentage of income spent on food increases only from 10 to 10.6 per cent for the high-income consumer, but it jumps from 50 to more than 60 per cent for the low-income consumer. The likely result is that poor households that are typically net purchasers of food, including smallholder farmers, landless labourers and the disadvantaged segments of the urban population, will be forced to reduce their consumption of food and other basic necessities. By contrast, better-off farmers and agro-businesses may directly benefit from higher food prices, as they tend to be better equipped to respond to changing price incentives and market opportunities. While the impact of the recent rise in food prices will differ among developing countries, depending on the patterns of poverty, income and expenditure, they could substantially increase overall poverty in low-income countries (Polaski, 2008; Ivanic and Martin, 2008).

3. Policy implications of the food crisis

The recently soaring global food prices may well be more than just another short-lived phenomenon, the last of which occurred in 1995–1996; it could represent a structural change in the world food economy. Hence, while emergency measures, such as greater food aid, can address the most urgent needs, in the medium to long term the food crisis must be tackled through investment, innovation and productivity growth.

> Emergency measures can address urgent needs, but for the longer term the food crisis must be tackled through investment and productivity growth.

There is undoubtedly need for emergency measures to ensure that the poorest households have access to sufficient food. This aid should be provided in a manner that does not affect market incentives or undermine local production. Governments in developing countries will also need to provide safety nets for the poor to enable them to buy food. Indeed, a key challenge is how to maintain the real income of poorer households in developing countries to enable them to buy enough food without triggering a wage-price spiral. Income support for the most needy households through targeted transfer payments would also help to contain the inflationary impact of higher food prices. Such payments must be based on a broad social consensus on how the higher costs of food are to be distributed. Yet, in many of the concerned countries it will be very difficult for the public budget to accommodate such additional social expenditure without reducing public spending for other purposes, including urgent infrastructure investments. This dilemma suggests that additional foreign assistance to solve this distribution problem in poor countries is justified. It also demonstrates the importance, from both the macroeconomic and social perspective, of new measures to achieve greater commodity price stability and of quick-response instruments to mitigate their impact.

Equally important, and even more important for solving the problem of food supply in the medium and long term, will be measures to encourage smallholder farmers to boost production, for example by providing financial support to improve their access to vital production inputs such as seeds and fertilizers. Such measures must be undertaken in the context of broader programmes to reform the financial system in developing countries in support of investment in the productive sectors (see also chapter IV). In this context it might be worth considering the possible contribution of environmentally sustainable agricultural production methods.[13] Such methods generally require less imported energy and have lower carbon intensity, thereby reducing the vulnerability of farmers to external shocks. They rely more on local resources and local traditional knowledge. This form of agriculture is also particularly well suited to small farmers.

> International action may be needed to tackle the problem of excessive speculation in global commodity markets.

At the international level, a concerted and coordinated global response to food shortages must take into account the link between markets for food crops, biofuels and petroleum, in addition to considering the broader need for mitigating climate change through reduced consumption of fossil fuels. In this context, it might be worth taking a fresh look at producer-consumer cooperation schemes, including in the oil sector, where an orderly, long-term management of the remaining reserves is in the interest of both producers and consumers. Moreover, in light of recent experiences, developed-country policymakers may wish to consider changing the relative weight of reduction of total emissions and substitution of fossil fuels by biofuels or substitution by other renewable forms of energy in their policy objectives. This might imply reviewing policies for the provision of subsidies for domestic biofuel producers, erection of protectionist barriers against ethanol and biodiesel, and mandating an increased use of biofuels in total fuel combustion. In any case, it is imperative that biofuel production does not reduce the availability of food supplies.

In addition, international action may be needed to tackle the problem of excessive speculation in global commodity markets, which is also closely related to movements on financial markets. This should include measures to allow concerted intervention of governments in food markets if there is a strong indication that speculation is driving prices. By contrast, measures such as country-specific export bans, bilateral food trade accords, or national targets for the use of a certain percentage of biofuels in total energy consumption should be discouraged, as they tend to contribute to instability in global markets and they may undermine the incentives created by rising prices to boost production.

Poor developing countries that experience deterioration in their trade balance because of higher commodity prices depend heavily on external financial assistance. Such assistance, in the form of ODA grants, is particularly important for those poor countries that are net importers of both oil and food. In this context the calculations for the amount of ODA required to achieve the Millennium Development Goals (see chapter V of this *Report*) may need to be revised on a country-by-country basis.[14]

In the medium to long term, agricultural output needs to be increased, including through sustained improvement in agricultural productivity. This will require substantial investment in the agricultural sector, including in infrastructure, water supply, improved seeds and fertilizers, education and agricultural research and development.[15]

D. The persistent problem of instability in commodity markets

1. Background

Traditionally, the "commodity problem" of developing countries has been understood to have three dimensions: first, the long-term deterioration in prices of commodities, primarily those exported by developing countries, vis-à-vis the prices of manufactures, exported mainly by developed countries; second, the high volatility of prices in commodity markets; and third, the small share of the final price of commodities that accrues to the commodity producers in developing countries.[16] With trade among developing countries increasing, the geographical pattern of trade in primary commodities and manufactures has changed considerably. Although many developing countries still depend on exports of a few primary commodities and on imports of manufactures, particularly capital goods, others have become important exporters of manufactures and importers of primary commodities from other developing countries.[17]

Many developing countries continue to depend on earnings from exports of primary commodities to finance their imports of capital and intermediate goods that cannot be produced at home but are indispensable for advancing structural change. Movements in commodity prices thus have an immediate impact on the potential for capital formation and growth in the exporting countries. Many other economies, including an increasing number of developing countries rely on imports of primary commodities as industrial raw materials or for current consumption. For these countries, price movements change both the cost of production and consumer prices.

But in an increasingly integrated world economy, the level and stability of commodity prices is not only an issue at the national level; it also has a global dimension. Similar to wages in a national economy, which determine incomes and the purchasing power of workers as well as the costs of production for firms, commodity prices have a significant effect on the incomes of producers and the costs for users. This gives them an important role in macroeconomic stability and growth in the world economy. The global macroeconomic impact of commodity price movements depends on the reaction of demand in the exporting countries. If, with unchanged export volumes, the additional income from higher commodity prices is spent entirely on additional imports by the commodity exporting countries, the price increases tend to have a global expansionary impact. This is because most demand for commodities is relatively inelastic so that the higher import bill tends to translate into lower savings. On the other hand, if rising commodity prices do not result in higher imports by the commodity-exporting countries, they tend to have a global contractionary effect. Such an effect is also likely to arise from a fall in commodity

> Movements in commodity prices have an immediate impact on the potential for capital formation and growth in the exporting countries.

prices, unless the level of imports of the commodity-exporting countries can be maintained by means of external financing that compensates for the shortfall in export earnings.

Another international aspect is that price hikes for essential primary commodities may generate inflationary pressures prompting central banks to adopt a tighter monetary policy, even when the cyclical situation would call for an expansionary monetary policy stance instead. Thus, short-term price stability and carefully managed price movements of internationally traded primary commodities could contribute substantially to stabilizing demand and supply conditions, and thus, to an investment-friendly macroeconomic environment, not only in the exporting countries but also in importing countries.

Notwithstanding the recent improvement in the growth potential of exporters of primary commodities, many developing countries will remain highly vulnerable to changes in supply and demand in international commodity markets, as long as progress towards diversification and industrialization is slow. Indeed, they may even experience a severe slowdown if a recession occurs in the global economy. The next subsection reviews commodity dependence in developing and transition economies and its implications for investment and growth.

2. Commodity dependence and price volatility

The share of primary commodities (including fuels) in total developing-country exports plunged to 33 per cent in 2003–2006, from around 73 per cent in 1980–1983. The shift in the structure of exports towards a greater share of manufactures occurred in all developing regions. However, diversification into manufactures has been highly concentrated in a small number of countries, mainly in the newly industrializing economies (NIEs) of East and South-Asia. Excluding this region, primary commodities still accounted for about 51 per cent of developing-country exports in 2003–2006, and fuel exports alone for 34 per cent. The number of countries that rely heavily on the export of primary commodities has not changed significantly since 1995 (table 2.4). This dependence is particularly high in Africa, where

primary commodity exports represented 79 per cent of total exports in 2003–2006.[18] Although oil exports from Africa account for a large share of the region's total commodity exports, only a small number of African countries are involved; the majority of African countries depend on exports of non-oil primary commodities. Dependence on primary commodity exports is closely related to poverty and high external indebtedness, as indicated by the particularly high share of primary commodities in exports (83 per cent) of the heavily indebted poor countries (HIPCs).[19]

Commodity-dependent economies are exposed to considerable external shocks stemming from price booms and busts in international commodity markets (Cashin and McDermott, 2002; Cashin, McDermott and Scott, 1999). These relatively strong price swings are also reflected in relatively high volatility in the barter terms of trade of many developing countries, and movements in the terms of trade have a strong effect on the current-account position and growth of developing countries (as discussed in chapter III, section D of this *Report*).

While the trend since 2002 is of increasing commodity prices, volatility continues to be very high and has even increased over the past 30 years. A comparison of overall non-fuel commodity price volatility as measured by the deviation of prices from their exponential trend level over the past four decades reveals that commodity price instability in 1998–2007 was lower than in 1968–1977, but higher than in 1978–1987 and 1988–1997.[20]

The higher volatility of commodity prices compared to manufactures can be illustrated by showing the evolution of the commodity price index for all commodities (excluding fuels), the export unit value index of manufactured goods of developed countries and the price index of crude petroleum, around their corresponding trends (chart 2.4A). Chart 2.4B shows the quarterly changes in these indices in nominal terms. The UNCTAD non-fuel commodity price instability index showed a slight increase in volatility between 1996–2001 and 2002–2007.[21] This was mainly due to higher price volatility of vegetables and oilseeds and of the minerals, ores and metals group.

The particular reasons for commodity price volatility differ by country and commodity. But in general, sharp price fluctuations are the result of

Table 2.4

COMMODITY DEPENDENCE BY GEOGRAPHICAL REGION, 1995–1998 AND 2003–2006

(Number of countries for which exports of commodities account for more than 50 per cent of total exports)

	Total primary commodities[a]		Three or less commodities		One commodity	
	1995–1998	2003–2006	1995–1998	2003–2006	1995–1998	2003–2006
Developing and transition economies	**118**	**113**	**82**	**84**	**47**	**50**
Developing economies	**108**	**103**	**78**	**78**	**45**	**46**
Africa	46	45	37	34	21	23
Latin America	30	27	15	17	6	7
East and South Asia	7	8	4	6	1	2
West Asia	9	9	9	9	8	6
Oceania	16	14	13	12	9	8
Transition economies	**10**	**10**	**4**	**6**	**2**	**4**
Memo items:						
Least developed countries	38	38	31	31	19	20
Heavily indebted poor countries	38	36	30	28	15	15

Source: UNCTAD secretariat calculations, based on *UNCTAD Handbook of Statistics* database.
a Primary commodities: SITC Rev. 2: 1 to 4 plus 68, 667 and 971.

low elasticities of demand and supply in the short-term. Price changes therefore tend to overshoot any supply or demand shock. For metals and minerals, industrial raw materials and energy, price movements are strongly determined by demand, and are closely linked to global industrial and economic activity. Prices of agricultural commodities are highly influenced by the supply side and by external factors such as weather. In addition, as explained above, low inventory levels lead to greater price volatility of the concerned commodity. In the particular case of oil, other factors also influence price volatility, such as geopolitical tensions.[22] Furthermore, as commodity prices are denominated in dollars, part of their variability is due to changes in exchange rates. As discussed in box 2.1, speculation also plays an increasingly important role.

Volatility has negative effects at both macroeconomic and microeconomic levels. In developing countries, particularly the poorest, the problems created by commodity price volatility are aggravated because of the lower resilience of their economies to external shocks.[23]

At the macroeconomic level, large short-term movements of commodity prices and export earnings have a direct impact on the trade balance, but they can also have an indirect impact through their influence on the real exchange rate of the exporting country. For example, a sharp price increase can lead to a currency appreciation and a worsening of the international competitiveness of other export goods. This is because sudden increases in export earnings do not always translate immediately into higher import demand. In the case of emerging-market economies, if such pressure for an appreciation of the currency cannot be addressed through monetary or exchange-rate policies, this may increase the incentives for carry trade speculators to purchase assets in the local currency, which in turn will reinforce the appreciation. On the other hand, if there is a sharp fall in prices, it may be difficult for an exporting country to maintain the level of its imports of essential goods,

Chart 2.4

PRICE VOLATILITY OF NON-FUEL COMMODITIES AND CRUDE PETROLEUM VIS-À-VIS MANUFACTURES

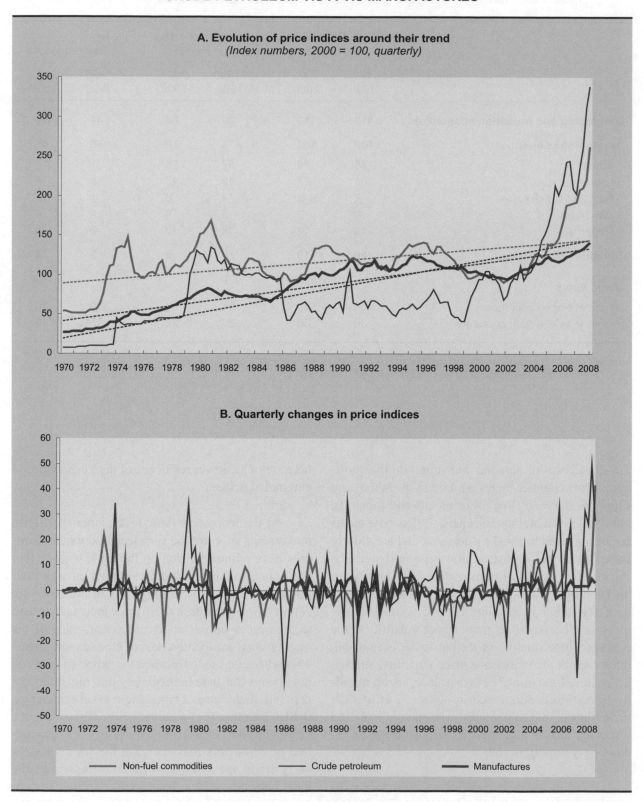

A. Evolution of price indices around their trend
(Index numbers, 2000 = 100, quarterly)

B. Quarterly changes in price indices

Non-fuel commodities   Crude petroleum   Manufactures

Source: UNCTAD secretariat calculations, based on UNCTAD, *Commodity Price Statistics* online; and UNSD, *Monthly Bulletin of Statistics*, various issues.

Note: The dotted lines represent the trend of the relevant price indices.

and uncertainty about price developments translates into perceptions of a higher country risk by potential trading partners and international lenders.

Moreover, government budgets in many of these countries depend heavily on taxation and other revenues from the commodity sector. Increases in government expenditures and public investment after a price upswing are often unsustainable when prices fall and increased public borrowing is to be avoided. Price fluctuations can therefore adversely affect a country's ability to consistently maintain and upgrade its infrastructure, which is essential for sustaining the process of diversification as a complement to private investment in productive capacities. They may also pose a constraint on the public sector's ability to maintain the level of education and health services and other social spending aimed at poverty reduction. Furthermore, price increases on imports of basic food and energy commodities may require governments to provide different forms of subsidies in order to avoid socially unacceptable increases in consumer prices that may jeopardize poverty reduction efforts and the achievement of other human development objectives. Commodity price volatility adds to the difficulties in maintaining a sustainable domestic and external public debt (discussed at greater length in chapter VI of this *Report*), and it has been identified as a major factor behind the debt crises of the poorest countries (Cohen et al., 2008).

At the level of the individual commodity producer, instability and unpredictability of earnings increases uncertainty about the viability of investment, which is a major obstacle to rational investment decisions. The uncertain income situation of potential investors also creates reluctance on the part of banks and other financial institutions to provide financing for such investments and increases the cost of finance.

3. Measures to deal with commodity price instability

Although the causes of the recent price hikes may differ from those of previous ones, and their economic and social implications may also differ from past experiences, they highlight the need for greater attention to be given to the problem of commodity price volatility more generally. Indeed, both have been referred to in numerous political declarations in recent years. But large movements in the prices of primary commodities are not a new phenomenon. Indeed, the international debate on commodity price stabilization and the measures needed to address problems arising from instability in commodity markets has a long history.[24] Some measures employed to overcome the problem of commodity price instability aim at: (a) reducing price fluctuations through market intervention; (b) reducing the impact of price fluctuations on the income of producers; and (c) enabling producers to maintain their levels of expenditure at times of falling prices and incomes.

(a) Price stabilization mechanisms

In the 1970s and 1980s international commodity agreements (ICAs) between producers and consumers aimed at price stabilization through direct intervention in the markets, mainly in the form of buffer stocks and/or export quotas. Internationally financed buffer stocks, which bought the commodity and stored it when the prices fell below their long-term trend and sold it when prices increased, sought to reduce price volatility by artificially balancing supply and demand over time. Export quotas functioned more as a price support measure. The agreements on natural rubber and cocoa worked with buffer stocks, whereas the coffee and sugar agreements worked with export controls, and the tin agreement combined both.

The ICAs suffered from a number of technical, operational and political problems. Technical problems related to the determination of the long-term price level around which prices should be stabilized, and the need to be flexible on this. Maintaining buffer stocks was costly, particularly when it had to be done over a long period of low prices, and ICAs did not dispose of sufficient financial resources. Operational problems were also related to the inability of the agreements to effectively cope with problems of cheating, rent-seeking and free-riding. Furthermore, they suffered from broader collective action problems, such as securing agreement among a relatively large number of countries that did not always share the same interests. A major problem, for example, was that the objective of price stabilization as pursued by some members of the agreement was not always compatible with the objective of price level support as pursued by others.

Political support for ICAs dwindled in the course of the 1980s because, in addition to the operational and financial difficulties with the existing ICAs, an increasingly influential strand of thinking, propagated in particular by the international financial institutions, viewed intervention in markets as leading to inefficient allocation of factors of production. Those supporting this view advocated market liberalization "to get prices right". As a result of these different factors, all ICAs but one lapsed, or collapsed, by the end of the 1980s.[25] The record of ICAs in the 1970s and 1980s was mixed, but some of them were relatively successful in stabilizing prices in those years and, had they been equipped with larger financial resources, they might have operated longer. Although producer cartels pursue objectives different from short-term price stabilization, they have at times also been successful in stabilizing prices, such as OPEC for oil or the Central Selling Organization of De Beers for diamonds (Gilbert, 1996).

> Greater price stability on international commodity markets has characteristics of a global public good ...

Greater stability of prices on international commodity markets has characteristics of a global public good that could facilitate macroeconomic management and contribute to greater stability in the global economy. It would also serve the objective of income stabilization in the exporting countries.

(b) Income stabilization policies

The objective of stabilizing producers' incomes can be pursued not only by minimizing price fluctuations, but also through measures aimed at reducing the impact of such fluctuations on incomes. At the national level, developing-country governments frequently intervened in commodity markets until the 1990s through national marketing boards and *caisses de stabilisation*. They had no direct impact on international market prices but provided a buffer between these and the prices received by domestic agricultural producers. In addition, they provided various extension services to commodity producers, including credit at affordable rates. However, these institutions were often found to lack efficiency and to suffer from serious governance problems.

Along with the general trend towards reducing market intervention, often in connection with structural adjustment programmes, these institutions were also dismantled in most developing countries. Yet most developed countries have continued to maintain complex and costly schemes of income support and stabilization for their farming sectors. Reduced intervention in developing countries did not lead to the desired results in terms of greater efficiency, faster growth and structural change in the exporting countries (see, for example, UNCTAD, 2003b). Instead, it left commodity producers exposed and vulnerable to considerable instability in world commodity markets (Akiyama et al., 2001). Exposure to previously unknown price risks has combined with growing difficulties in financing investment and shortfalls in earnings. Such investment is indispensable for increasing productivity and enabling producers to react to any price signal from international markets. In the example of cocoa, Ul Haque (2003) notes that market liberalization led to higher volatility of producer prices in countries that had dismantled their marketing boards (e.g. Cameroon and Côte d'Ivoire) than in Ghana, which kept its marketing board.

(c) Compensatory financing schemes

Independent of these national stabilization schemes that aim to mitigate the impact of commodity price fluctuations on incomes in the commodity producers, the IMF and the EU provided compensatory financing to governments. Such financing has sought to make up for losses in export income resulting from commodity-related external shocks in order to prevent downward adjustment of these countries' imports. The main international compensatory financing schemes that have been implemented so far include the Compensatory Financing Facility (CFF)[26] of the IMF, and the STABEX, SYSMIN and FLEX systems[27] agreed between the EU and the African, Caribbean and Pacific (ACP) group of countries under the Lomé and Cotonou agreements. However, these have not been able to solve the problems arising for developing countries in a manner that would satisfy the interests of the different stakeholders (UNCTAD, 2007c).[28]

One of the main shortcomings was that there was generally a time lag in delivery of compensation so that it would end up having a procyclical effect, rather than a countercyclical one as intended. Both CFF and STABEX worked well until the mid-1990s, but access for countries in need became more complicated over time, with increasingly tight conditionalities attached, when the mechanisms were repeatedly revised. The CFF has hardly ever been used since 2000. It lost its attractiveness, particularly for low-income countries, not only because it was non-concessional, but also because it "became a complex facility that was difficult to use and administer" (IMF, 2004: 5). So far, there has been no resort to the recently introduced Exogenous Shock Facility, under which concessional loans can be provided to meet the needs of the poorest countries that are eligible for lending under the Poverty Reduction and Growth Facility. While the EU schemes did not cover all developing-country commodity exporters, compensatory financing had a concessional element. Indeed, STABEX support was provided in the form of grants, but since these were considered as part of ODA, there was a tendency for ODA for these compensatory funds to be diverted from other forms of ODA.

In general, the scope of the facilities and the resources to face external shocks were too small in proportion to the magnitude of the shocks (Griffith-Jones and Ocampo, 2008), and compensatory financing became unsustainable with the persistent decline in commodity prices until the late 1990s. The schemes have also been criticized because they do not guarantee pass-through of the assistance from the governments who receive the funds to the producers who suffer a loss of income.

(d) *Market-based commodity-linked financial instruments*

Since the 1990s, considerations of how to mitigate the impacts of instability have focused on the use of market-based commodity price risk management

> ... that could facilitate macroeconomic management and contribute to greater stability in the global economy.

instruments.[29] By transferring their risk to other market operators, producers can better predict their earnings in the short run, and obtain better access to credit because their risk of default is reduced. Hedging is also a useful measure for reducing the impact of risk relating to imports.

Commodity price risk management instruments are traded in organized futures and options exchanges. Futures contracts are agreements to buy or sell a quantity of a commodity at a predetermined price. An option is a contract that gives the right, but not the obligation, to buy or sell a futures contract at a specified price, at or before a future date. It provides protection against unfavourable price movements, while retaining the possibility to profit from higher prices, unlike futures. In addition, tailored products, such as swaps, are traded in the over-the-counter market. Swaps lock in commodity prices over the medium to long term.[30]

Although increasing, the use of commodity risk management tools is not widespread in developing countries, particularly in Africa. The reasons for this include lack of knowledge and understanding on the part of producers and governments of these usually complex instruments, the high costs and liquidity needed to carry out such transactions and a limited time horizon, particularly with regard to agricultural commodities. Moreover, there are very few local intermediaries, if any, that participate in these markets, and access to and connectivity with international markets providing these instruments are limited.

Some of these shortcomings can be overcome with the development of commodity exchanges. Since 2003 the volume of trading in commodity exchanges in developing countries has grown twice as fast as that of their more established counterparts in developed countries (UNCTAD, 2007d). This has led to an increasing share of developing countries in overall commodity futures and options trading, approaching one third in 2006. This expansion has been largely facilitated by advances in information and communication technologies. Commodity exchanges in developing countries can offer hedging opportunities which are better adapted to the needs of domestic producers and traders and bring them closer to the producer. They help reduce transaction costs, provide a price discovery mechanism and price transparency, reduce counterparty risk, offer enforcement rules, and facilitate the provision of finance. To some extent, these exchanges can help fill the institutional gap that arose from government withdrawal from the commodity sector.

4. Commodity price instability and policy coherence

Although industrialization is progressing in developing countries, and the share of manufactures and services in total output has risen considerably over the past two decades, primary commodity prices remain a key variable in development strategies for the majority of developing countries. Stable growth of earnings from the production of primary commodities not only influences the propensity to invest, but also facilitates the financing of new productive capacities, be it in the primary sector itself or in manufacturing and service activities. Relatively stable commodity prices would be in the interest not only of exporters but also of importing countries, and thus the world economy as a whole. Stable income growth in the primary sector helps sustain international demand for other goods and services, and improves predictability of the costs of production in industries where primary commodities are used as inputs.

Diversification and industrialization are the best means in the long run for countries to reduce their dependence on a few primary commodities, and thus their vulnerability to the adverse effects of commodity price volatility and unfavourable price trends. But diversification is a complex process achieved over a long period of time, as it requires capital formation and skill acquisition, and depends heavily on stable earnings from primary commodity exports.

Market liberalization and privatization in the commodity sector have not resulted in greater stability of international commodity prices. There is widespread dissatisfaction with the outcomes of unregulated financial and commodity markets, which fail to transmit reliable price signals for commodity producers. In recent years the global economic policy environment seems to have become more favourable to fresh thinking about the need for multilateral actions against the negative impacts of large commodity price fluctuations on development and macroeconomic stability in the world economy. One reason is that developing countries have become larger importers of primary commodities, and many of them have the potential to provide additional financing for price or income stabilization measures. Another reason for the changing policy environment is the increasing attention of the major industrialized countries to the problem of commodity price volatility. However, international price stabilization mechanisms agreed multilaterally between producers and consumers are unlikely to become a political option in the near future; therefore other measures, which deal with either the causes or the effects of commodity price volatility, are urgently needed.

> Adequate countercyclical official liquidity to deal with external shocks should be a key aim of a development supportive international financial architecture.

While the causes of instability in commodity markets cannot be entirely eliminated, regulatory measures that prevent excessive speculation on commodity markets could be an important step to reduce the extent of price fluctuations. Greater exchange-rate stability would also help. Regarding international measures to address the effects of instability, a realistic option would be the improvement and scaling up of compensatory financing mechanisms in light of past experiences. Adequate countercyclical official liquidity to deal with external shocks should be one of the key aims of a development supportive international financial architecture (Griffith-Jones and Ocampo, 2008). In order to contribute to sustained development and global macroeconomic stability, such compensatory financing schemes would need to be equipped with much more financial resources than were available for this purpose in the past. They should not only cover shortfalls in export earnings resulting from sharp dips in prices of export commodities but also, similar to the concept of the CFF, sharp increases in the import bill resulting from higher prices for essential commodity imports, particularly food and energy.

Different external shocks may require different forms of compensatory payments. In the case of a decline in prices that is likely to be reversed, compensatory payments might take the form of concessional loans for balance-of-payments support from international financial institutions. These can be repaid eventually, once prices rise and exceed a certain threshold. By contrast, when compensatory financing is provided for income support, either to producers of certain agricultural commodities or to consumers suffering from soaring prices for imported basic energy and food items, compensatory payments in the form of grants would appear to be more appropriate, because these payments aim at helping parts of the population to maintain a certain level of consumption. However, such grants should not be at the expense of current ODA provided in support of economic infrastructure and productive sectors (see also chapter V of this *Report*).

A compensatory financing scheme that is more effective and administratively less cumbersome than previous schemes would certainly need to avoid pro-cyclicality. One way of achieving this would be to envisage automatic payouts made at predetermined trigger prices. In terms of eligibility, in principle it should be sufficient that a country has no control over the cause of the shock that led to its need for compensatory financing. Conditionality, if any, should be linked directly to the way in which the financial resources provided under the scheme are used. If they are provided as grants, it would be justified to require their pass-through to producers in the form of income support, while pass-through to consumers should be the aim of conditionality attached to compensatory financing for food or energy import stress.

On the other hand, when compensatory financing is provided in the form of loans, decisions by creditors and beneficiary governments about the actual use of those loans should take into account the need to produce a return from which the future debt service can be paid, rather than relying on an uncertain future price

> The international economic system would gain coherence if new efforts were made at the multilateral level to contain international commodity price fluctuations …

> … while allowing for smooth price adjustments that reflect market fundamentals and structural change.

reversal to enable such repayment. In this case, it would seem more appropriate to channel the financial resources into investment in support of productive capacity in other sectors so as to reduce commodity dependence.

At the national level, institutional arrangements that serve as a buffer between prices on international commodity markets and incomes received by domestic producers may be useful. Their aim would be not only to influence domestic income distribution and reduce existing or avoid future poverty, but also to enable producers to carry out necessary investments to maintain steady productivity growth. Experience with systems of income support, for example in many developed countries, could provide useful lessons, but the costs of these systems normally exceed the budgetary possibilities of developing countries. However, in situations of high primary commodity prices, an institutional arrangement whereby developing countries retain part of the windfall gains from high commodity prices in national funds for release when international market conditions are unfavourable would be helpful. Such an arrangement would assure a smooth income stream for their producers without unduly straining budgetary resources. In some cases, especially when windfall gains arise from price increases for oil and mining products, which are exhaustible natural resources, similar funds could be instrumental in supporting investments in other sectors in order to accelerate diversification and structural change, which ultimately will reduce commodity dependence.

Obviously, different measures, both national and international, should be complementary. In addition, greater use of new tools for commodity price risk management and finance can make an important contribution to development and poverty reduction efforts in developing countries. The use of such tools will not eliminate or even reduce price volatility as such, but it could help to reduce the vulnerability of producers to price fluctuations. If undertaken in coordination with broader efforts to strengthen the role of domestic banking for investment financing, measures that promote the provision and intermediation of such instruments by local banks, together with appropriate regulatory measures to prevent excessive speculation, could help mitigate the impact of commodity price volatility on producers. They could thereby improve the context in which investment in new production capacities or higher productivity takes place. If such measures succeed in making the national economic environment more stable, it might be justified to consider subsidizing the costs that the use of hedging instruments implies for certain producers.

Notwithstanding the merits of such national mechanisms to deal with the effects of commodity price instability, the international economic system would gain coherence if new efforts were made at the multilateral level to contain price fluctuations on international commodity markets while allowing for smooth price adjustments that reflect market fundamentals and structural changes, for example in connection with climate change. Institutional and financial strengthening of support mechanisms is needed to reduce or avoid the negative impact that sharp commodity price fluctuations can have, not only on commodity exporters, especially when prices are headed downwards, but also on commodity importers in developing countries when prices are headed upwards.   ■

Notes

1   See, for example, the communiqué of the meeting of G-8 Finance Ministers in Osaka, Japan, 14 June 2008 (available at G8 Information Centre: http://www.g7.utoronto.ca/finance/fm080614-statement.pdf), wherein the Ministers expressed their concern not only about high commodity prices, especially oil and food, but also their volatility.

2   See IEA (2008). According to data from BP (2008), oil production even fell by 0.2 per cent in 2007.

3   According to some observers, renegotiated contracts on the extraction of natural resources in order to modify the distribution of rents between producing countries and transnational companies, constitute an additional investment cost (IMF, 2008: box 1.5).

4   See, for example, the *Financial Times*, 9 May 2008.

5   Goldman Sachs, as reported by the *Financial Times*, 6 May 2008.

6   Baffes (2007) examines the effect of crude oil prices on the prices of other commodities, and concludes that if crude oil prices remain high for some time, the recent commodity boom is likely to last much longer than earlier booms, at least for food commodities, fertilizers and precious metals.

7   Data for Baltic Dry Index are from Capital Link Shipping at: http://shipping.capitallink.com/baltic_ exchange/stock_chart.html and for Overall Liner Trade Index from ISL, 2008.

8   FAO classification of low-income food-deficit countries (LIFDC), at: http://www.fao.org/country-profiles/lifdc.asp?lang=en (accessed 8 July 2008).

9   Global aggregate yield growth averaged 2 per cent annually between 1970 and 1990, but declined to 1.1 per cent between 1990 and 2007. The area under cultivation has grown at an average rate of only about 0.15 per cent during the past 38 years. The slow growth in yields is probably related to climate change, reduced research and development in the agricultural sector and difficulties in obtaining additional water for agriculture (USDA, 2008a).

10   Cereal stocks are at their lowest level in three decades. According to the Food and Agriculture Organization of the United Nations (FAO, 2008a): "A number of changes in the policy environment since the Uruguay Round Agreements have been instrumental in reducing stock levels in major exporting countries, namely: the size of reserves held by public institutions; the high cost of storing perishable products; the development of other less costly instruments of risk management; increases in the number of countries able to export; and improvements in

information and transportation technologies". The United States Department of Agriculture (USDA, 2008a) provides some additional reasons for the low levels of stocks, apart from greater liberalization of trade, which lowered trade barriers and facilitated trade, and reduced the need for countries to hold stocks. The reasons include: a reduction of grain stocks in China, the lower importance attached by governments to maintaining buffer stocks following about two decades of low and stable food prices. In addition, the private sector reduced its stockholdings due to years of readily available global supplies, the cost of holding stocks and use of "just-in-time" inventory management.

11 For a more comprehensive discussion of this issue, see Herrmann, 2007.

12 The global food import bill is expected to grow by 26 per cent in 2008. And, looking at different products, the import bill is expected to increase by as much as 77 per cent for rice and about 60 per cent for wheat and vegetable oils.

13 This is among the recommendations contained in the report of the International Assessment of Agricultural Knowledge, Science and Technology for Development (IAASTD), an intergovernmental process supported by over 400 experts and cosponsored by the FAO, the Global Environment Facility (GEF), the United Nations Development Programme (UNDP), the United Nations Environment Programme (UNEP), the United Nations Educational, Scientific and Cultural Organization (UNESCO), the World Bank and the World Health Organization (WHO).

14 Quite independent of the terms-of-trade and balance-of-payments effects, from the point of view of food security it will be necessary to provide food-importing countries with additional short-term trade financing in line with higher import values. The Marrakesh Ministerial Decision on Measures Concerning the Possible Negative Effects of the Reform Programme on Least-Developed and Net Food-Importing Developing Countries sought to address the possible difficulties low-income countries might face in financing food imports as a result of liberalization and reform of trade in agriculture in the context of multilateral trade agreements. However, the principle underlying this decision is equally relevant in the context of the recent food price hikes caused by other factors, since it aims at avoiding a shortage of basic foodstuffs stemming from insufficient trade financing possibilities. To ease the liquidity constraints of least developed and net food-importing developing countries and to facilitate the emergency import of food, which may arise quite independently of the net impact on the trade balance, UNCTAD and FAO jointly formulated a proposal in 2003 for the creation of an international Food Import Financing Facility (FAO, 2003b). Given the current global food crisis,

this proposal could be reviewed and given serious consideration.

15 For a more detailed account of possible policy options to address the food crisis, see UNCTAD, 2008b.

16 The fact that only a small share of the final price of primary commodities accrues to commodity producers in developing countries has been attributed to the weak negotiating power of exporters vis-à-vis importers, especially transnational corporations (TNCs), and also to the increasing power of retail chains for food commodities.

17 Even though rapidly growing emerging-market developing economies, such as China and India, have accounted for much of the incremental demand for commodities in recent years, thus supporting the increase in South-South trade, developed countries still represented over 65 per cent of total world imports of commodities in 2006.

18 For instance, fuels account for 95 per cent of Angolan exports, cocoa for 90 per cent of the exports of Sao Tome and Principe, iron ore for 64 per cent of Mauritania's exports, and cotton for 64 per cent of Benin's exports.

19 Data on the share of commodity exports are UNCTAD calculations based on *UNCTAD Handbook of Statistics* and UN COMTRADE databases.

20 This analysis is based on the UNCTAD non-fuel commodity price instability index. It should be noted that in historical comparisons of commodity price volatility, the period considered is important. However, an increase in volatility can also be identified when periods other than those referred to in the main text are chosen for the analysis. For example, overall non-fuel commodity price volatility was higher in 1986–2007 than in 1973–1985, periods that were suggested for the measurement of changes in volatility over time by Dehn, Gilbert and Varangis, 2004.

21 This index is calculated on a monthly basis, while the data used for chart 2.4 are calculated on a quarterly basis because monthly data for the export unit value of manufactured goods of developed countries are not available.

22 For a more detailed analysis of commodity price volatility, see Dehn, Gilbert and Varangis, 2004, and for oil price volatility, see UNCTAD, 2005.

23 For detailed discussions on the negative effects of commodity price instability, see World Bank, 2000; Dehn, Gilbert and Varangis, 2004; and Parimal, 2006. For a more focused analysis on the effects on government revenues, see Asfaha, 2007.

24 For detailed accounts on the evolution of international commodity policy, see UNCTAD, 2002b; 2003a; 2004; and 2008c.

25 At present, ICAs serve more as a forum for debate and market transparency, and none of them include economic clauses to stabilize prices. For more details on the functioning of the different ICAs and their

problems, see Gilbert,1996; and South Centre, 2004. For a broader assessment of supply management policies, see Lines, 2007.

26   The CFF was established in 1963 to assist countries facing balance-of-payments difficulties due to temporary shortfalls in export earnings resulting from external shocks that were beyond the control of the local authorities. It was expanded in 1979 to cover shortfalls in receipts from tourism revenues and workers' remittances, and in 1981 to include excess cereal import costs. In 1988, it was renamed the Contingency and Compensatory Finance Facility (CCFF), until the contingency element was dropped.

27   Until 2000, the EU provided compensatory financing to its ACP partners, through the STABEX system for agricultural products and the SYSMIN for mining products. The two mechanisms had been introduced under the Lomé Convention in 1975, and were revised in subsequent renewals of that convention. With its successor, the Cotonou Agreement of 2000, the STABEX and SYSMIN systems were replaced by the FLEX (for financing of short-term fluctuations in exports earnings), which provided additional short-term budget support to ACP countries that lost 2 per cent or more of their export earnings. The aim was to safeguard macroeconomic and sectoral reforms and policies that were at risk as a result of a fall in export revenue (European Commission, 2004). Financial support from this source does not depend on price movements of a specific commodity, but on losses of export earnings and an increasing public sector deficit. FLEX seems to suffer from similar shortcomings as other mechanisms, notably slowness of disbursements and apparent resource constraints. In the context of the negotiations of European partnership agreements following the expiration of the Cotonou Agreement, a reformed FLEX system is likely to be introduced.

28   For a review, see Hewitt, 2007.

29   UNCTAD has played a critical role in promoting the use of commodity risk management instruments since the early 1990s (see, for instance, UNCTAD, 1998). In 1999, the World Bank, with the participation of UNCTAD, among other institutions, established the International Task Force on Commodity Risk Management for enhancing access to these instruments by developing-country players. The work of this task force was inspired by an influential paper of the World Bank (1999). However, it seems that so far only a small number of pilot projects have been successfully implemented under this task force.

30   For detailed reviews of commodity risk management instruments, their advantages and problems, see UNCTAD, 1998; UNCTAD, 2005; and Rutten and Youssef, 2007. The latter authors present a case study on the application of these instruments to the coffee market, which is the second most important commodity in international trade, after oil.

References

Akiyama T et al. (2001). Commodity market reforms: Lessons of two decades. World Bank Regional and Sectoral Studies. Washington, DC, March.

Asfaha S (2007). National revenue funds: their efficacy for fiscal stability and intergenerational equity. Winnipeg, International Institute for Sustainable Development.

Baffes J (2007). Oil spills on other commodities. Policy Research Working Paper WPS4333. Washington, DC, World Bank.

BP (2008). *Statistical Review of World Energy*. British Petroleum, June.

Burghardt G (2008). Volume surges again. *Futures Industry Magazine*. March/April.

Burkhard J (2008). The price of oil: A reflection of the world. Testimony before the Committee on Energy and Natural Resources, United States Senate, Cambridge Energy Research Associates, Washington, DC, 3 April.

Cashin P and McDermott CJ (2002). The long-run behavior of commodity prices: Small trends and big variability. IMF Staff Papers, 49(2). Washington, DC, International Monetary Fund.

Cashin P, McDermott C J and Scott A (1999). Booms and slumps in world commodity prices. IMF Working Paper 99/155. Washington, DC, International Monetary Fund.

CERA (2008). IHS/CERA Upstream Capital Costs Index: Cost of constructing new oil and gas facilities reaches new high. Cambridge Energy Research Associates. 14 May. Press release. Available at: http://www.cera.com/aspx/cda/public1/news/pressReleases/pressReleaseDetails.aspx?CID=9487.

Cohen D et al. (2008). Lending to the poorest countries: A new counter-cyclical debt instrument. OECD Development Centre Working Paper 269. Paris, OECD.

Dehn J, Gilbert C and Varangis P (2004). Commodity price volatility. In: Aizenman J and Pinto B, eds. *Managing Volatility and Crises*: *A Practitioner's Guide*. Washington, DC, World Bank.

European Commission (2004). Agricultural commodity chains, dependence and poverty: A proposal for an EU action plan, COM(2004)89 final. Brussels.

FAO (2003a). Some trade policy issues relating to trends in agricultural imports in the context of food security. Report of the 64th Session of the Committee on Commodity Problems. Rome, 18–21 March.

FAO (2003b). Financing normal levels of commercial imports of basic foodstuffs in the context of the Marrakesh Decision on least-developed and net food-importing developing countries. Rome.

FAO (2008a). Soaring food prices: Facts, perspectives, impacts and actions required, HLC/08/INF/1. Rome.

FAO (2008b). Food outlook. Rome, June.

FAO (2008c). Crop prospects and food situation. Rome, April.

Financial Times (2008). Analyst warns of oil at $200 a barrel, 6 May.

Financial Times (2008). The Lex Column. Commodities: mining, and Commodities: oil, 9 May.

Gilbert C (1996). International commodity agreements: an obituary notice. *World Development*, 24(1).

Griffith-Jones S and Ocampo JA (2008). Compensatory financing for shocks: What changes are needed? Initiative for Policy Dialogue Working Paper. New York.

Harris J (2008). Written testimony before the Senate Committee on Homeland Security and Governmental Affairs, Commodity Futures Trading Commission, United States Senate. Washington, DC. 20 May. Available at: http://hsgac.senate.gov/public/_files/052008Harris.pdf.

Herrmann M (2007). Agricultural support measures of advanced countries and food insecurity in developing countries: Economic linkages and policy responses. In: Guha-Khasnobis B, Acharya SS and Davis B, eds. *Food Security: Indicators, Measurement, and the Impact of Trade Openness*. Oxford, Oxford University Press.

Hewitt A (2007). Compensatory finance: Options for tackling the commodity price problem. Winnipeg,

International Institute for Sustainable Development.

IEA (2008). Oil market report. Paris, International Energy Agency, May.

IFDC (2008). World fertilizer prices soar as food and fuel economies merge. International Center for Soil Fertility and Agricultural Development. Press release, 19 February. Available at: http://www.ifdc.org/i-wfp021908.pdf.

IMF (2004). Review of the compensatory financing facility. Washington, DC.

IMF (2006). *World Economic Outlook*. Washington, DC, September.

IMF (2008). *World Economic Outlook*. Washington, DC, April.

ISL (2008). *Shipping Statistics and Market Review*, 529(4). Bremen, Institute of Shipping Economics and Logistics.

Ivanic M and Martin W (2008). Implications of higher global food prices for poverty in low-income countries. Policy Research Working Paper, WPS 4594. Washington, DC, World Bank.

Lines T (2007). Supply management: Options for commodity income stabilization. Winnipeg, International Institute for Sustainable Development.

Lukken W (2008). Written testimony before the Senate Appropriations Subcommittee on Financial Services and General Government and the Senate Committee on Agriculture, Nutrition and Forestry, United States Senate. 17 June. Available at: http://www.cftc.gov/stellent/groups/public/@newsroom/documents/speechandtestimony/opalukken-41.pdf.

Masters MW (2008). Testimony before the Committee on Homeland Security and Governmental Affairs, United States Senate. Masters Capital Management LLC. Washington, DC, 20 May. Available at: http://hsgac.senate.gov/public/_files/052008Masters.pdf.

Merryll Lynch (2008). Commodity volatility: a primer. Global Commodity Paper No. 7. New York.

OECD-FAO (2008). Agricultural Outlook 2008–2017. Organisation for Economic Co-operation and Development and Food and Agriculture Organization. Paris and Rome.

OPEC (2008). OPEC Monthly Oil Market Report. Vienna, May.

Parimal J (2006). Rethinking policy options for export earnings. South Centre Research Papers, No. 5. Geneva.

Polaski S (2008). Rising food prices, poverty, and the Doha round. *Policy Outlook*, No. 41. Washington, DC, Carnegie Endowment for International Peace.

Rubin J and Tal B (2008). Will soaring transport costs reverse globalization? *CIBC World Markets StategEcon*, 27 May.

Rutten L and Youssef F (2007). Market-based price risk management: An exploration of commodity income stabilization options for coffee farmers. Winnipeg,

International Institute for Sustainable Development.

South Centre (2004). Commodity market stabilization and commodity risk management: Could the demise of the former justify the latter? South Centre analytical note, SC/TADP/AN/COM/, Geneva.

Ul Haque (2003). Commodities under neoliberalism: The case of cocoa. G-24 Discussion Paper No. 25. New York and Geneva, UNCTAD, January.

UNCTAD (1998). A survey of commodity risk management instruments. UNCTAD/COM/15/Re.2, Geneva.

UNCTAD (2002a). *The Least Developed Countries Report 2002: Escaping the Poverty Trap.* United Nations publication, sales no. E.02.II.D.13, New York and Geneva.

UNCTAD (2002b). The effects of financial instability and commodity price volatility on trade, finance and development. Note prepared by the UNCTAD Secretariat for the WTO Working Group on Trade, Debt and Finance. Geneva, 10 July.

UNCTAD (2003a). Economic development in Africa: Trade performance and commodity dependence. United Nations publication, New York and Geneva.

UNCTAD (2003b). Report of the Meeting of Eminent Persons on Commodity Issues. TD/B/50/11, Geneva.

UNCTAD (2004). *Beyond Conventional Wisdom in Development Policy: An Intellectual History of UNCTAD*, 1964-2004. New York and Geneva.

UNCTAD (2005). The exposure of African Governments to the volatility of international oil prices, and what to do about it. Paper prepared for the African Union Extraordinary Conference of Ministers of Trade on African Commodities. UNCTAD/DITC/COM/2005/11, Geneva, 6 December.

UNCTAD (2007a). The development role of commodity exchanges. TD/B/COM.1/EM.33/2, Geneva.

UNCTAD (2007b). *The Least Developed Countries Report 2007: Knowledge, Technological Learning and Innovation for Development.* United Nations publication, sales no. E.07.II.D.8, New York and Geneva.

UNCTAD (2007c). Commodities and development. TD/B/COM.1/82, Geneva.

UNCTAD (2007d). The development role of commodity exchanges. TD/B/COM.1/EM.33/2, Geneva.

UNCTAD (2008a). *Development and Globalization: Facts and Figures 2008.* United Nations publication, New York and Geneva.

UNCTAD (2008b). Addressing the global food crisis: Key trade, investment and commodity policies in ensuring sustainable food security and alleviating poverty. A note by the UNCTAD secretariat for the High-level Conference on World Food Security: The Challenges of Climate Change and Bioenergy, Rome, 3–5 June.

UNCTAD (2008c). The changing face of commodities in the twenty-first century. TD/428, Geneva.

UNCTAD (various issues). *Trade and Development Report.* United Nations publication, New York and Geneva.

United Nations (2008). *World Economic Situation and Prospects 2008: Update as of mid-2008.* New York.

United States Senate (2006). The role of market speculation in rising oil and gas prices: A need to put the cop back on the beat. Staff report prepared by the Permanent Subcommittee on Investigations of the Committee on Homeland Security and Governmental Affairs. Washington, DC.

USDA (2008a). Global agricultural supply and demand: Factors contributing to the recent increase in food prices. United States Department of Agriculture. Washington, DC, May.

USDA (2008b). Grains: World markets and trade. United States Department of Agriculture. Washington, DC, May.

WAOB (2008). World Agricultural Supply and Demand Estimates No. 460. World Agricultural Outlook Board, United States Department of Agriculture. Washington, DC.

World Bank (1999). Dealing with commodity price volatility in developing countries: A proposal for a market-based approach. Washington, DC, International Task Force on Commodity Risk Management, World Bank. Washington, DC.

World Bank (2000). *Global Economic Prospects 2000.* Washington, DC.

World Bank (2008). World Development Report 2008: Agriculture for Development. Washington, DC.

Chapter III

INTERNATIONAL CAPITAL FLOWS, CURRENT-ACCOUNT BALANCES AND DEVELOPMENT FINANCE

A. Introduction

Heads of State and Government gathered in Monterrey, Mexico, in March 2002 committed themselves through the Monterrey Consensus, *inter alia*, to attract and enhance inflows of productive capital (para. 21) and to make debt sustainable (para. 47). The beginning of the millennium also saw the shift of developing countries as a group from net capital importers to net capital exporters. Indeed, since the Asian financial crisis in 1997–1998 capital has increasingly been flowing "uphill" – from poor to rich countries. The magnitude of this new phenomenon has caused some observers to conclude that some developing countries have been creating a global "savings glut" (Bernanke, 2005).[1]

The emergence of developing countries as net capital exporters contrasts with expectations derived from standard growth theories. These theories postulate that with open capital markets, capital will flow from rich to poor countries in order to exploit the higher expected rates of return on capital and bridge the "savings gap" in capital-scarce countries. The theories also predict that capital inflows will spur economic growth.

However, these predictions are not supported by developments over the past few years. Not only is capital flowing "uphill", but net capital-exporting developing countries also tend to grow faster and invest more than those developing countries that receive net capital inflows. These developments also call into question another hypothesis of standard economic theory, namely that there is a close and positive relationship between capital account liberalization and economic growth.

The divergence between these expectations and empirical findings has been described as a "puzzle". However, this divergence is puzzling only if viewed from the perspective of the basic tenets of neoclassical economic theory, particularly the idea that the evolution of the current account is driven by the behaviour of a representative agent that has perfect foresight and maximizes an intertemporal utility function. It is not puzzling once it is recognized that these assumptions do not reflect what actually happens in the real world.

This chapter addresses the main issues associated with capital flowing "uphill" – a phenomenon also called the "capital flows paradox" – with a view to providing a unified framework to enhance an understanding of the mechanisms that determine current-account balances and their interaction with the determinants of investment and growth. The chapter examines those factors that have played a key role in improving the external balances of many developing countries, in particular swings from current-account deficit to surplus and the associated net capital outflows.

The main finding is that in countries which are heavily dependent on primary commodities, swings in the current account are driven to a large extent by changes in commodity prices, and that in countries with more diversified export and production structures, the real exchange rate plays the key role in determining changes in the current-account balance. Particularly the latter finding is in line with recent research that has shown not only that an overvalued exchange rate has detrimental effects on the external balance, but also that a competitive real exchange rate is a key factor for achieving growth of aggregate demand in the short run and of employment in the long run (Frenkel and Taylor, 2006; Eichengreen, 2007; and Rodrik, 2007).

Section B of this chapter briefly traces the recent evolution of the current account in different groups of developing countries. Section C analyzes episodes of current-account reversals in developing economies over the past three decades and highlights the conditions that are generally conducive to a strengthening of both the external balance and output growth. Section D takes up the fundamental building blocks of the traditional theoretical frameworks to examine the relationship between financial openness, net capital flows, investment and growth. It highlights the divergence between predictions of the standard "savings gap" model and the standard neoclassical growth model on the one hand, and the empirical observations that net capital inflows are not always necessary for growth and that faster growth in developing economies can even be associated with net capital exports on the other. Section E draws conclusions, outlining implications for economic policies at the national and international levels.

B. Recent evolution of the current account in developing countries

In the late 1990s, the current account of developed countries as a group moved from a surplus to a deficit and developing economies as a group moved from a deficit to a large surplus (chart 3.1). The evolution of the aggregate current-account balance (chart 3.1A) is strongly influenced by the behaviour of the two largest economies in each group, the United States and China respectively. While China can build on an enormous labour force it is also an outstanding example of a developing country that has succeeded in creating a sizeable amount of capital and in combining a significant current-account surplus with fast domestic capital accumulation.

There is considerable heterogeneity within the developed and developing country groups, as can be seen by comparing charts 3.1A and 3.1B. The latter

shows the evolution of the non-weighted, simple average of current-account balances. While the average for developing countries still showed a deficit after the turn of the millennium, the difference in current-account performance between developing and developed countries has narrowed substantially since then. But at the same time, the dispersion within the two groups of countries has increased, as indicated by the curves showing the evolution of the country at the 25th and 75th percentile of the distribution of the current-account balances. The inter-quartile range rose from 6 per cent of GDP in 1997 to 11.5 per cent of GDP in 2007.

The reversal of the current-account balances of developing countries started around 1998, probably largely in response to the wave of financial crises

Chart 3.1

CURRENT-ACCOUNT BALANCE IN DEVELOPING AND DEVELOPED COUNTRIES, AND EMERGING ECONOMIES IN EUROPE, 1980–2007

(Per cent of GDP)

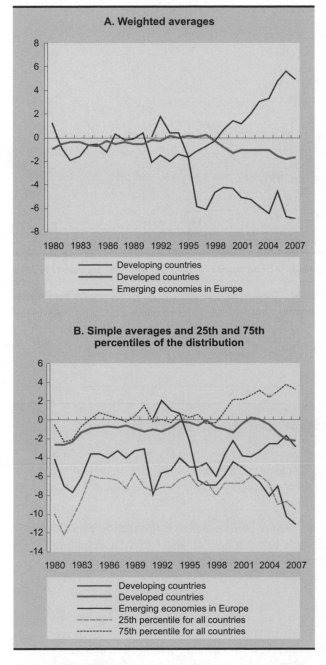

Source: UNCTAD secretariat calculations, based on United Nations Statistics Division, Department of Economic and Social Affairs (UNSD/DESA) National Accounts data; *UNCTAD Handbook of Statistics* database; and IMF, *Balance of Payments* database.

Note: Emerging economies in Europe comprise the Czech Republic, Estonia, Latvia, Lithuania, Slovakia and Slovenia. A 75th (25th) percentile is the value below which 75 (25) per cent of observations are found.

that hit the developing world in the second half of the 1990s. The reversal was driven mainly by emerging-market economies (chart 3.2). By 2007, the emerging-market economies among the developing countries had eliminated, or almost eliminated, their current-account deficits (chart 3.2A), while other developing countries continued to maintain a substantial deficit (chart 3.2B). The transition economies of South-East Europe and the Commonwealth of Independent States (CIS) did not follow the same trend: whereas the emerging-market economies in this group registered, on average, a dramatic increase in their current-account deficit, other transition economies managed to reduce their deficits substantially.

The observation that the overall improvement in the current-account balances is mainly attributable to emerging-market economies can be explained by the fact that the other countries had only limited access to international capital markets and were only marginally affected by the financial crises of the last 10 years. This observation is even more perplexing from the perspective of mainstream economic theory, because it is the emerging-markets economies that, due to their greater openness to the international financial markets, would be expected to benefit the most from net capital inflows (or inflows of "foreign savings"), and thus have greater current-account deficits (box 3.1). Yet it was in the Asian emerging-market economies in particular that greater gross inflows were more than offset by gross outflows (chart 3.3).[2]

Chart 3.3 also illustrates the three waves of capital flows to and from developing countries and how these affected different regions. The first wave began in the mid-1970s and ended with the debt crisis in the early 1980s. The second started after the Brady swaps of the early 1990s and ended with the sudden halt in flows that followed the Asian and Russian crises. The third wave started in the early 2000s and has not yet ended. The first wave brought a large net inflow of capital, as gross outflows from developing countries were very small. During the second wave, rising gross capital inflows were accompanied by rising gross outflows. And during the third wave, gross outflows, largely associated with the accumulation of foreign-exchange reserves, particularly from Asia, outpaced gross inflows, leading to net capital outflows from developing countries.

For a number of countries whose trade performance is determined primarily by world demand for

Chart 3.2

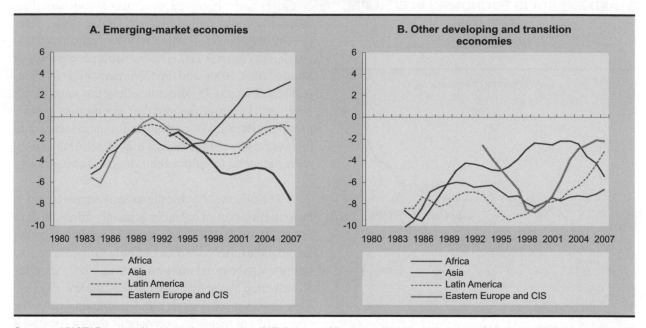

CURRENT-ACCOUNT BALANCE IN DEVELOPING AND TRANSITION ECONOMIES BY REGION, 1980–2007

(Average as per cent of GDP)

Source: UNCTAD secretariat calculations, based on IMF, *Balance of Payments* and *World Economic Outlook* databases; and *UNCTAD Handbook of Statistics* database.

Note: Cross-country simple averages and five-year-moving averages. Eastern Europe and CIS does not include the Russian Federation.

Box 3.1

CURRENT ACCOUNT AND NET CAPITAL FLOWS: SOME DEFINITIONS

In standard terminology, capital inflows represent the acquisition of domestic assets by non-residents (plus grants), whereas sales of domestic assets by non-residents are defined as a negative capital inflow. Similarly, capital outflows measure the acquisition of foreign assets by residents, while sales of foreign assets by residents are defined as a negative capital outflow.

In the system of national accounts, the current-account balance corresponds to both the difference between national savings and investment and the difference between national income and expenditure. This implies that when domestic expenditure exceeds national income the resulting current-account deficit measures the transfer of resources from abroad that finances excess expenditure; this transfer is sometimes called "foreign savings".

The current-account balance is equal to the sum of the balance of imports and exports of goods and services plus the balance of factor payments between residents and non-residents, as well as current transfers. It is in the logic of the balance of payments as an accounting identity that the current-account balance equals the sum of all capital flows, changes in international reserves, and errors and omissions. Although in balance of payments accounting the latter three items are recorded separately, the terms *"net capital inflow"* and *"net capital outflow"* as used in this *Report* comprise the balance of the capital account, changes in reserves and net errors and omissions, unless otherwise mentioned, and are, thus, identical to the current-account balance (with opposite sign). This means that a current account surplus is identical with a net capital outflow and a current-account deficit is identical with a net capital inflow. This differs from the definition used in the *TDR 1999* (Part two, chap. V).

Chart 3.3

CAPITAL FLOWS, CURRENT-ACCOUNT BALANCE AND CHANGE IN RESERVES IN DEVELOPING AND TRANSITION ECONOMIES, BY REGION, 1981–2007

(GDP weighted averages as per cent of GDP)

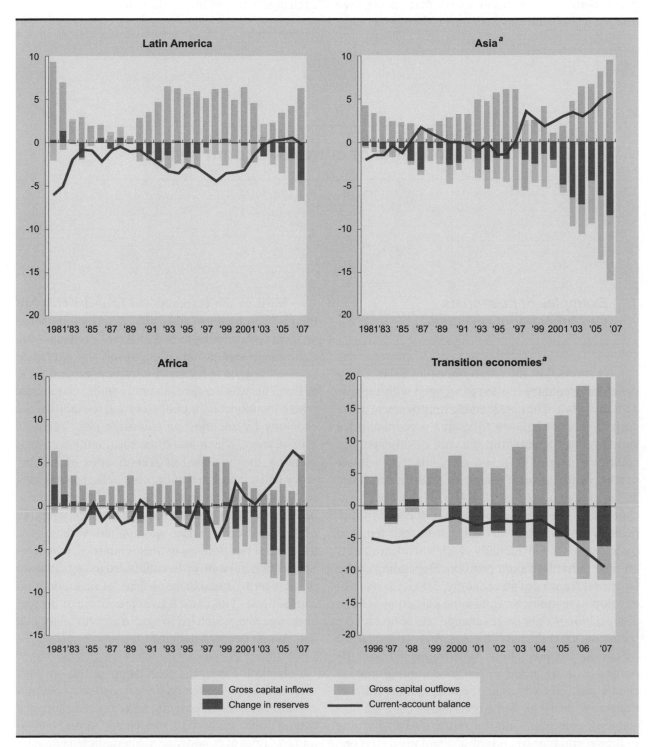

Source: UNCTAD secretariat calculations, based on IMF, *Balance of Payments, International Financial Statistics* and *World Economic Outlook* databases; and national sources.

Note: For change in reserves, a negative value indicates an increase in reserves. Gross capital inflows are the sum of direct investment in the economy, portfolio investment liabilities and other investment liabilities. Gross capital outflows are the sum of direct investment abroad, portfolio investment assets and other investment assets.

a Excluding major oil exporters. Transition economies include Bulgaria and Romania.

primary commodities the improvement in their current account occurred with the rise in prices of primary commodities. Oil exporters, in particular, experienced a large turnaround of their current accounts when oil prices started to increase, whereas net importers of commodities recorded a negative effect on their current accounts. Many emerging-market economies in Asia fall in the latter group. But these countries compensated for an increase in their commodity-related import bill through a proportionately larger increase in revenues from manufactured exports, as their policymakers decided to keep real exchange rates slightly undervalued.

C. Determinants of current-account swings

1. Examples of post-crisis current-account reversals

A reversal in the current-account balance of a developing country is often associated with a terms-of-trade shock. The considerable improvement of the current account balance following a positive price shock is most apparent in the case of oil-exporting countries (chart 3.4A), and also, albeit to a lesser extent, in the case of countries with mineral, ore and metal exports (chart 3.4B). However, in recent years developing-country producers of other primary commodities have also seen their terms of trade improve considerably, with attendant effects on their current-account position. Depending on the structural features of an economy, deficit reversals in developing countries can also be caused by a large depreciation in their real exchange rate or by a severe recession. Over the past 20 years, reversals triggered by currency depreciations have frequently been the outcome of financial crises in emerging-market economies. The Republic of Korea and the Russian Federation in 1998, and Argentina in 2002 are outstanding examples. China also provides an example of the second type of current-account reversal if one considers the adjustments made after its currency crisis in 1992, when the yuan depreciated markedly before it was fixed for a long time to the dollar (see chart 3.5).

Most of the currency and financial crises of the past can be reasonably well described by some stylized facts relating to two different exchange-rate regimes. In one group of countries, the exchange rate was pegged to a reserve currency, generally the dollar. This was the case in many smaller economies where the monetary authorities tried to stabilize the economy by adopting an exchange-rate "anchor". This strategy, which was often successful in cutting inflation, mostly ended in overvaluation of the currency and a large current-account deficit, as imports from the anchor economy became cheaper (Flassbeck, 2001). In another group of countries, a regime of flexible exchange rates was applied. Variations in the interest rate policies of these countries, which reflected their inflation differentials, led to large inflows of short-term capital in the absence of restrictions on capital flows. This caused an appreciation of the real exchange rate, which led to a rapid growth of imports and current-account deficits.

In both cases, the worsening of the current-account balance increased the perception of international investors of a growing currency risk, and, at a certain point, triggered a sudden and strong capital outflow. Loss of confidence in international financial markets usually provokes defensive actions by governments and central banks, including an increase in interest rates, intervention in the currency market, and an attempt to reduce fiscal deficits despite the

Chart 3.4

CURRENT-ACCOUNT BALANCE AND COMMODITY PRICES FOR COUNTRIES EXPORTING OIL, AND MINERAL AND MINING PRODUCTS, 1980–2007

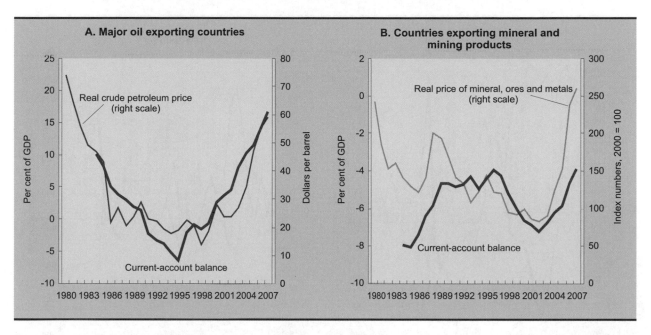

Source: UNCTAD secretariat calculations, based on IMF, *Balance of Payments* and *World Economic Outlook* databases; UNCTAD, *Commodity Price Statistics* online; and *UNCTAD Handbook of Statistics* database.

Note: Current-account balance data are cross-country simple averages and five-year-moving averages. Exporters of mineral and mining products comprise Chile, Ghana, Guinea, Mozambique, Niger, Papua New Guinea, Peru, Suriname and Zambia. Real crude petroleum price: average of Dubai/Brent/Texas, equally weighted (dollars per barrel), deflated by United States consumer price index (2000 = 100). Real price of mineral, ores and metals: price index of mineral, ores and metals deflated by United States consumer price index (2000 = 100).

worsening domestic economic situation. This happened in the Republic of Korea in 1998, when its economy, despite relatively sound fundamentals, was subject to the contagion effects of the financial crisis that hit some other East Asian countries which were pursuing the anchor approach. The problem was that the exchange rate of the Korean currency had been de facto fixed after the opening up of its capital account, without considering the risk of speculative net capital inflows as a result of the relatively low dollar interest rates. The sharp current-account reversal in this country was driven by output and import contraction. Subsequently, a real currency depreciation helped sustain a moderate surplus for quite some time (chart 3.5A).

The current-account reversal in Argentina in 2002 followed a similar pattern (chart 3.5B): the currency board arrangement with the dollar led to an unsustainable overvaluation of the real exchange rate, which was exacerbated by the fact that, while

the United States accounted for only a small fraction of the country's exports, Argentina's main trading partner, Brazil, had devalued its currency in 1999. When the currency board was abandoned in 2002, this regime change caused a sharp currency depreciation. Combined with extremely severe economic contraction, this led to a swing in the current-account balance of 10 per cent of GDP in 2002, and subsequently to a fast acceleration of growth that was initially driven by import substitution and an increase in exports.

In China, a surge in the current-account surplus, accompanied by moderate inflation, began in 2001. It took place in an environment of fast growth of the world economy and with an exchange rate that was still at the low level of 1993 when the Chinese authorities had allowed a sharp depreciation of the nominal exchange rate and pegged the yuan unilaterally to the dollar. This depreciation led to a reversal of the current account, which turned positive, but the

Chart 3.5

**CURRENT-ACCOUNT REVERSALS, GDP GROWTH AND REAL
EFFECTIVE EXCHANGE RATE FOR SELECTED COUNTRIES**

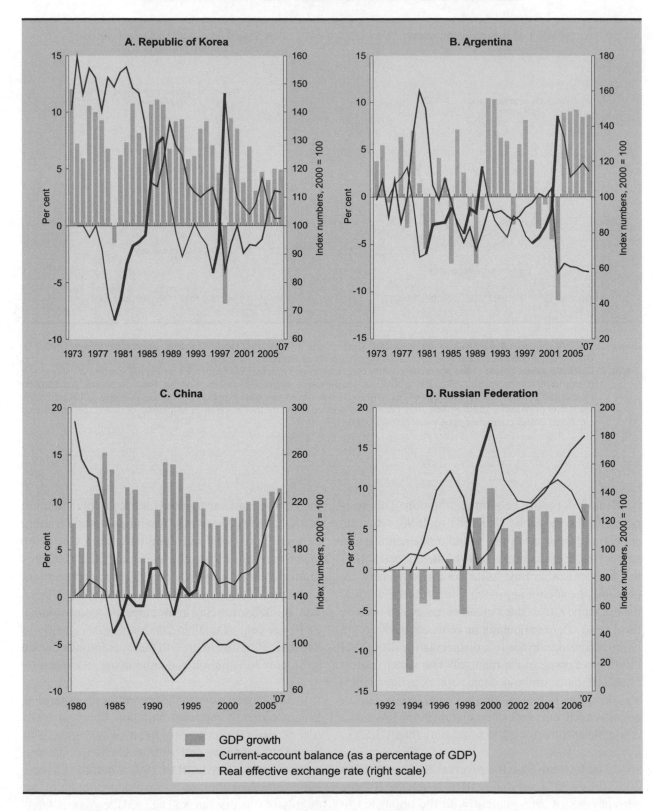

Source: UNCTAD secretariat calculations, based on IMF, *Balance of Payments* and *International Financial Statistics* databases;
          JPMorgan; and *UNCTAD Handbook of Statistics* database.
Note: A thick segment of the line depicting the current-account balance denotes a deficit reversal.

surplus diminished somewhat in the aftermath of the Asian financial crisis (chart 3.5C). This was because the currencies of other Asian economies – whose producers competed with Chinese exporters on world markets – depreciated sharply, and Chinese exports stagnated as a result of recession in these countries.

The improvement in the current account of the Russian Federation after its 1998 financial crisis was primarily due to favourable terms-of-trade developments and growing exports of energy-related commodities (chart 3.5D). Although the interest rate differential vis-à-vis the dollar narrowed after 1998, the potential for speculative gains returned with rising inflation and higher nominal interest rates. The ensuing appreciation of the rouble nullified the competitive gains for the Russian economy accruing from the currency depreciation associated with the 1998 crisis. This may compromise Russian efforts to diversify the economy sufficiently to be able to deal with future dips in oil prices or a depletion of reserves.

The four cases discussed above show that large improvements in the current account are usually accompanied by either a positive terms-of-trade shock or by a depreciation of the real exchange rate. The results of an econometric exercise, aimed at estimating the cross-country determinants of positive current-account reversals and the conditions under which such reversals are associated with an increase in GDP growth, suggest that this pattern is also valid for a larger sample of countries. The main results of this exercise are discussed below, while the methodology used to define the reversal episodes and detailed results of the econometric analysis are described in the annex to this chapter.

2. Factors influencing current-account reversals

For the quantitative analysis, 268 reversal episodes were identified. Their main characteristics are summarized in table 3.1. More than three quarters of the episodes took place in developing economies, about 10 per cent in transition economies, and the remaining 15 per cent in developed economies.[3] The average episode started with a current-account deficit of approximately 10 per cent of GDP. It lasted for about four years and brought about a cumulative

current-account reversal of approximately 12 per cent of GDP. In developed economies the initial deficit and the size of the reversal were about half those of the developing and transition economies. GDP growth during the period in which the reversal took place was generally lower than GDP growth in the period before the reversal, but at 0.5 percentage points, the difference was not very large. On average, economic activity tended to pick up after the reversal was completed, and in the period following the reversal GDP growth was about one percentage point higher than in the period in which the reversal took place.

The reversals were usually associated with large depreciations of the real exchange rate and they were followed by a limited appreciation of the real exchange rate. Thus, after the reversal was completed, the real exchange rate was about 20 per cent lower than in the period before the episode. Domestic producers were thus internationally more competitive after the reversal than before. An exception to this pattern is the transition economies, where the period in which the reversal took place was characterized by an appreciation of the real exchange rate.

The evolution of several variables during the reversal episode is illustrated in chart 3.6, which distinguishes between developed and developing economies. GDP growth reached a trough in the year after the beginning of the episode and then started to recover in both the developed and developing economies. In both groups of countries reversals tended to occur when there was a large negative output gap (i.e. when the actual output was higher than trend output).[4] In developing countries, the real exchange rate peaked one period before the reversal and kept depreciating for several periods after the beginning of the reversal. By contrast, in developed economies, the real exchange rate began to depreciate several periods before the episode and then flattened at the time of the episode. Reversals in developing countries, unlike those in developed countries, were often preceded by positive terms-of-trade shocks. Real interest rates rose sharply in both groups before the reversal took place, probably as a result of unsuccessful attempts by the monetary authorities to defend a nominal exchange rate. In developed and developing countries alike, the real interest rate started falling immediately after the reversal.

To sum up, evidence shows that current-account reversals are typically preceded by positive

Table 3.1

ANALYSIS OF CURRENT-ACCOUNT REVERSALS:
SUMMARY OF CHANGES IN GDP GROWTH AND THE REAL EFFECTIVE EXCHANGE RATE (REER)

	Current-account balance at the beginning of the episode	Current-account reversal	Duration	Change in						No. of episodes
				GDP growth			REER			
				(t - t-1)	(t+1 - t)	(t+1 - t-1)	(t - t-1)	(t+1 - t)	(t+1 - t-1)	
	(Per cent of GDP)		(Years)	(Percentage points)						
All economies	-10.0	12.3	4.2	-0.5	1.3	0.6	-21.5	4.7	-19.4	268
Developed economies	-5.4	6.4	4.0	-0.6	1.4	0.6	-9.0	6.4	-3.3	40
Transition economies	-12.3	14.5	4.6	7.3	4.3	10.7	-24.4	28.8	-14.0	22
Developing economies	-10.7	13.2	4.2	-1.1	1.0	-0.3	-23.6	2.7	-22.6	206
Africa	-13.2	14.6	4.3	-1.4	0.7	-0.9	-26.6	1.1	-26.1	97
Latin America and the Caribbean	-7.7	10.6	4.1	-1.8	2.4	0.3	-18.0	8.9	-12.7	52
Asia and the Pacific, excl. West Asia	-6.8	9.9	4.0	-1.2	1.4	0.3	-24.1	-3.0	-26.6	37
West Asia	-13.0	19.6	4.9	2.3	-2.2	0.3	-25.7	4.5	-27.0	20

Source: UNCTAD secretariat calculations, based on *UNCTAD Handbook of Statistics* database; World Bank, *World Development Indicators*; IMF, *Balance of Payments and International Financial Statistics* databases; JPMorgan; and national sources.

Note: Values in period "t" are the averages of the values over the reversal episodes, while values in periods "t-1" and "t+1" are the averages values of the three years before the beginning and three years after the end of the episode, respectively.

Chart 3.6

MAIN ECONOMIC VARIABLES AROUND A CURRENT-ACCOUNT REVERSAL

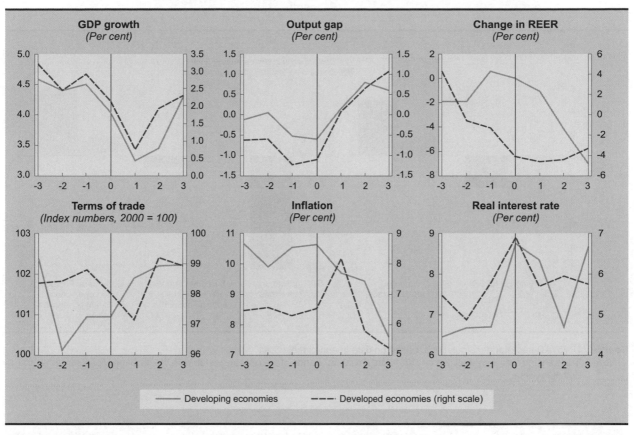

Source: See table 3.1.
Note: The horizontal axis marks years before and after the reversal episode.

terms-of-trade shocks and real depreciations, and that the subsequent improvement in the current-account balance enables implementation of a more investment- and growth-friendly monetary policy stance. But changes in the current account are influenced by a variety of factors in addition to the real exchange rate and the terms of trade. An econometric investigation provides some indications of the relative importance of changes in some other variables that contribute to possible current-account reversals in developed or developing economies.[5]

The main results of this analysis are summarized in chart 3.7 (for details see table 3.A1 in the annex to this chapter). The chart shows the effect of a "one standard deviation" change in each variable on the probability of occurrence of a current-account reversal.[6] The "one standard deviation" represents a normalization of changes in different variables, which is useful because, under standard assumptions,

the probability that a variable will change by more than one standard deviation in either direction is not very high.[7]

Current-account reversals are correlated with real depreciations in all economies – developed, developing and transition – but further analysis also shows that the effect of exchange-rate shocks is stronger in the developed economies. If a depreciation of the real effective exchange rate in developed economies increases the probability of a current-account reversal by 4.2 per cent, the corresponding effect in developing and transition economies is 2.8 per cent.[8] The probability of a current-account reversal occurring due to changes in the terms of trade is almost three times higher for developing and transition economies than for developed economies. In the former, an improvement in the terms of trade is associated with a 5 per cent increase in the probability of a current-account reversal, while the

Chart 3.7

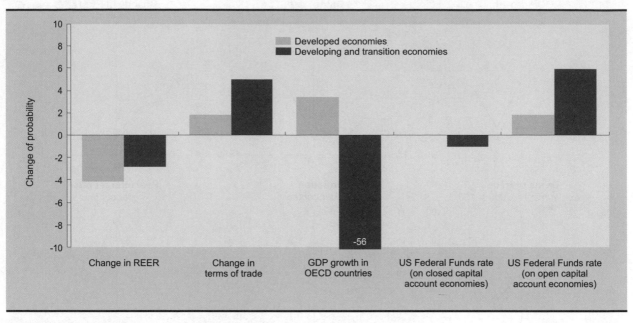

DETERMINANTS OF THE PROBABILITY OF A CURRENT-ACCOUNT REVERSAL

(Per cent)

Source: UNCTAD secretariat calculations, based on data in annex table 3.A1.
Note: The bars indicate the effect of a one standard deviation change of the relevant variable on the probability of a current-account-deficit reversal.

corresponding value for the latter is 1.8 per cent. This finding indicates that external shocks have a significant effect on the current account of developing countries.

Along similar lines, the econometric analysis also confirms that current-account reversals in developing and transition economies are negatively correlated with GDP growth in developed economies (i.e. that faster growth in the latter increases the probability of a reversal in the former). A decrease in GDP growth in the OECD countries increases the probability of a current-account reversal in developing countries by more than 50 per cent (the bar in chart 3.7 is truncated at -10 per cent). The opposite relationship holds in the developed economies, but in this case the effect is smaller and the coefficient is not statistically significant.[9] The chart also shows that external financial shocks (as measured by changes in the United States interest rate policy), have practically no effect on the probability of a current-account reversal of developing countries with a closed capital account. But for those with an open capital account, it can have a large positive effect: an increase in the

Federal Funds Rate increases the probability of a current-account reversal by approximately 6 per cent.

Taken together, these results suggest that, rather than being driven by autonomous saving and investment decisions of domestic agents, current-account reversals in developing countries tend to be driven by external shocks emerging from goods as well as financial markets.

In order to examine the conditions under which a country can move from a current-account deficit to a current-account surplus without suffering a large and protracted economic crisis, the reversal episodes shown in table 3.1 have been divided into three groups: expansionary, contractionary and unclassified. Episodes that were followed by an increase in GDP growth of at least one percentage point are classified as expansionary, those followed by a one percentage point decrease in GDP growth are classified as contractionary, and all remaining episodes are defined as unclassified. Based on this methodology, out of 193 episodes, 57 were expansionary, 77 were contractionary and 59 could not be classified.[10]

Table 3.2

CHANGES IN EXCHANGE RATES AND TERMS OF TRADE DURING CURRENT-ACCOUNT REVERSALS, BY TYPE OF EPISODE

	Type of episode							
	Expansionary		Contractionary		Not classified		Total	
Episodes with:	*No. of episodes*	*Terms-of-trade change (per cent)*	*No. of episodes*	*Terms-of-trade change (per cent)*	*No. of episodes*	*Terms-of-trade change (per cent)*	*No. of episodes*	*Terms-of-trade change (per cent)*
Depreciation of real exchange rate	42	26	58	20	50	18	150	21
Appreciation of real exchange rate	15	120	19	10	9	33	43	53
Total	57	51	77	17	59	20	193	28

Source: See table 3.1.

Within each of these groups, a further distinction can be made between episodes that were accompanied by a currency depreciation and a currency appreciation. Table 3.2 shows that more than 75 per cent of the episodes were accompanied by a real depreciation of the exchange rate. The few episodes accompanied by a real appreciation of the exchange rate were characterized by positive terms-of-trade shocks which were more than twice as large as those associated with the episodes accompanied by a depreciation. Moreover, expansionary episodes that were accompanied by a currency appreciation also experienced large positive changes in their terms of trade.[11] This provides *prima facie* evidence that unless a country receives a large positive terms-of-trade shock, a real exchange rate depreciation is a necessary, but not sufficient, condition for an expansionary current-account deficit reversal. If developed economies were to be excluded from this analysis, it would lead to even stronger results in the same direction.

The finding that expansionary reversals need either a large positive terms-of-trade shock or a real depreciation is strengthened by a formal test that controls for a host of other factors that may affect the probability of such a reversal (chart 3.8).[12] A real depreciation increases the probability of an expansionary reversal by approximately 3.5 per cent, and an improvement in the terms of trade increases

Chart 3.8

DETERMINANTS OF THE PROBABILITY OF AN EXPANSIONARY CURRENT-ACCOUNT REVERSAL, DEVELOPING AND TRANSITION ECONOMIES

(Per cent)

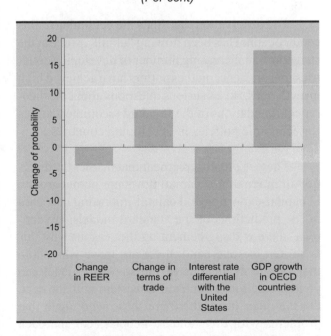

Source: UNCTAD secretariat calculations, based on data in annex table 3.A2.

Note: The bars indicate the effect of a one standard deviation change of the relevant variable on the probability of an expansionary current-account-deficit reversal.

the probability of such a reversal by approximately 7 per cent. Moreover, an increase in the difference between the domestic and the United States nominal interest rate reduces the probability of an expansionary reversal by 13 per cent. This suggests that high nominal interest rates have a large negative effect on the probability of an expansionary reversal. Another important factor is the global macroeconomic environment: an increase in the GDP growth of the OECD countries is associated with an 18 per cent increase in the probability of an expansionary reversal occurring in developing and transition economies.

An attempt at explaining the determinants of contractionary reversals did not produce satisfactory results: the statistical model showed that the only robust predictors are the output gap and the nominal interest rate (the higher the nominal interest rate the more likely it is that the reversal will be contractionary). Some of the regressions described in the annex found that greater trade openness is associated with a higher probability of a contractionary episode occurring, and that greater capital-account openness is associated with a lower probability of a contractionary episode occurring. These results can lead to the conclusion that successful reversals tend to have many features in common: a depreciated real exchange rate, positive terms-of-trade shocks and an accommodating monetary policy. However, each contractionary reversal has its own explanation.

D. Foreign capital and growth

The observation that since the beginning of this century capital has been flowing "uphill", while at the same time an increasing number of developing countries that are net capital exporters have achieved high growth rates, raises serious questions about the theoretical foundations of the standard recommendations for economic policies in developing countries.

There is broad agreement that neither the direction of international capital flows nor output growth in capital-exporting and capital-importing countries fit the predictions of the standard models. By contrast, there is disagreement on the reasons why this is so. On the one hand, there are those who claim that simple extensions of the standard model can yield predictions which are consistent with the data. On the other hand, there are those who argue that problems with the standard neoclassical approach go deeper, and that a completely different economic model needs to be applied. This section suggests several reasons why the latter interpretation may be sounder than the former.

1. Standard economic models of savings and development

(a) The savings gap model

Typically, theories of economic growth and explanations for large income differences between countries focus on countries' endowments in terms of factors of production and/or natural resources. Economies with more capital equipment and/or better educated workers are expected to generate higher per capita income than countries with low-skilled labour and meagre capital equipment. Thus, in order to be able to catch up, poor countries need more capital. However, if the creation of capital is a function of the level of income, developing countries face the dilemma of not having enough capital precisely *because* they are poor. In other words, their savings are insufficient to free up a part of the domestic production potential for the production of capital goods or for the production of exports that could finance imports of such goods. In this theoretical framework, economies are not expected to grow fast enough to initiate a catching-up process before reaching critical benchmarks of savings and investment (see, for example, Sachs et al., 2004). The attempt to fill this "savings gap" by capital inflows from countries with higher income and savings has guided traditional development thinking.

According to this thinking, the strategy to reduce global poverty and to allow the catching up of poorer countries is built on two blocks. Firstly, the endowments of less developed countries can be enriched by giving them access to those factors of production that they lack – through the provision of private foreign capital or official development assistance. Secondly, as developed countries open up their markets to the products of developing countries that possess natural resources or abundant labour but little capital, the developing countries are able to raise their export earnings and, consequently, to import more sophisticated equipment.

The savings gap theory refers to the standard growth model of the 1940s and 1950s: the Harrod-Domar model (Harrod, 1939; and Domar, 1957). This capital-labour model identifies certain necessary components of growth, but it does not explain the functional relationships that determine the interaction of these components. Most approaches based on this growth theory see the rate of capital accumulation determined by the difference between capital deepening (the capital-labour ratio) and capital widening (the amount of saving per capita needed to hold the capital-labour ratio constant as the population grows and the existing capital stock depreciates). If total factor productivity is constant "the economy grows in per capita terms as long as saving per capita exceeds capital widening" (Sachs et al., 2004: 124).

Accordingly, countries with relatively low growth rates are encouraged to increase their savings enough to keep up with the requirements of capital widening. This conclusion is plausible, as productive investment is found to be decisive for growth. However, if domestic saving is essentially equated with productive domestic investment, the result is trivial. It amounts to saying that economies with briskly growing investment grow more rapidly than economies with less dynamic investment. Thus the Harrod-Domar model predicts what it assumes: savings are needed to grow and a high ratio of savings is better than a low ratio.[13]

Because of its tautological nature, this approach does not enable far-reaching policy conclusions. The argument that total savings must be increased by an inflow of external savings in order to raise productive investment is based on the assumption that households are the only source of domestic savings and that savings are invariably used for productive investment in fixed capital. If either of these two assumptions is relaxed, the inflow of foreign savings becomes less important for the promotion of productive investment. In that case, other sources of domestic savings, including company profits, and the kinds of activities in which these savings are invested are of crucial importance for economic growth, as discussed in chapter IV. The Latin American experience during the last quarter of the past century has shown that higher capital inflows (i.e. the availability of foreign savings) cannot be equated with higher investments. Despite sizeable net capital inflows investment ratios remained low and output growth subdued.

(b) The neoclassical model

The more recent textbook descriptions of the behaviour of the economy in the long run are rooted in the purely neoclassical growth model originally developed by Solow (1956) and Swan (1956). According to this model, savings determine capital accumulation (as in the Harrod-Domar model), but savings and investment are not always related to economic growth (in contrast to the Harrod-Domar model). Savings (and investment) drive growth only when the economy is out of equilibrium, but they do not influence growth when the economy is in equilibrium. In the long run, growth is determined solely by technology, which in turn is determined exogenously by non-economic variables.

Successive work based on this model, such as the Cass-Koopmans model (Cass, 1965; and Koopmans, 1965) "endogenized" the saving rate. It did so by modelling the behaviour of a representative individual who seeks to optimize lifetime utility. This strand of the literature assumes perfect foresight and risk-aversion: it hypothesizes that consumers prefer a stable consumption path and that any transitory shock to income is, under normal circumstances, compensated for by a change in savings in the same direction (i.e. a temporary drop in income leads to lower savings and a temporary increase in income leads to higher savings). A permanent shock to income has the opposite effect. If GDP growth increases permanently, individuals will immediately jump to a higher consumption path and the increase in growth will lead to lower savings.

By contrast, if a shock has its origin in the savings rate, for example if a change in preferences leads to higher savings, then both investment and growth increase (as in the Harrod-Domar model), at least in the transition to a "new steady state". Thus, the model predicts different relationships between savings and growth, depending on the nature of the shock and on whether the shock is permanent or temporary. In response to a temporary shock to GDP growth, income and savings change in the same direction, while in response to a permanent shock to GDP growth, income and savings change in opposite directions. In response to a shock to the savings rate (for example resulting from a change in preferences), income and savings change in the same direction. In this case, however, causality goes from savings to income.

These assumptions are based on a closed economy model, in which ex-post national savings are always equal to ex-post investment. Things are different in open economy models that allow free capital flows. Since savers can invest in other countries, the open economy neoclassical model predicts that there should be no correlation between domestic savings and investment decisions.

As first pointed out by Lucas (1990), under the model's assumption that profits per unit of output are the same in all countries, the marginal product of capital should be higher in countries with a relatively small capital stock (i.e. in poor countries) so that poor countries should record net capital inflows. Accordingly, the observed relatively small capital flows from developed to developing countries have been labelled the "Lucas Paradox". This paradox triggered a vast body of literature that sought to explain the factors that limit the incentives to invest in developing economies. The recent literature seeks to explain the Lucas Paradox by switching the emphasis from factor accumulation to total factor productivity (TFP), which (in the Solow-Swan model) is the part of the overall productivity increase that cannot be attributed to either labour or capital. It argues that if TFP correctly reflects the return on investment, countries with faster productivity growth will invest more. It also argues that countries with faster productivity

growth will have lower savings rates because agents anticipate the potential for future consumption, which increases with rising productivity growth.

Given that the current account equals, by definition, the difference between national savings and investment, the neoclassical model predicts that countries with relatively fast productivity growth have current-account deficits (Gourinchas and Jeanne, 2007). If there are no capital controls, there should be no direct link between domestic investment and savings decisions. This means that the neoclassical open economy model predicts that an exogenous increase in national savings will be associated with an improvement in the current account, but that it will have no effect on domestic investment and growth.

To summarize, similar to the savings-gap model, the neoclassical model predicts a positive correlation between savings (equal to investment) and growth for a closed economy. But while the savings-gap model predicts that open economies with current-account deficits grow faster than countries with surpluses, in the neoclassical model the growth impact of capital inflows depends on whether savings or productivity were subject to the initial shock.

(c) Evidence

The neoclassical model is based on three central assumptions: (i) the economy can be described by studying the behaviour of a representative agent; (ii) the representative agent is fully rational and maximizes intertemporal utility under perfect foresight; (iii) the economy is in a long-run equilibrium characterized by full employment (see also box 3.2). If one of these assumptions is violated, the model is not applicable and its policy recommendations are unfounded. While the assumptions have been called into question, proponents of the model have argued that the strength of the model is to be judged not only by its assumptions, but also by its predictive power. Yet, the model's predictive power is challenged by empirical evidence.

Empirical evidence points to a highly significant positive correlation between savings and growth over the past 20 years (chart 3.9). This observation is not consistent with the prediction of the standard neoclassic model, according to which there is no

Box 3.2

THE FAILURE OF THE NEOCLASSICAL MODEL

While most economists would agree that the assumptions of the neoclassical model are far from reality, the model continues to serve as a basis for economic policy prescriptions. One problem is that it approaches macroeconomic issues with microeconomic reasoning that can lead to erroneous policy recommendations. Kaldor (1983: 83) commented on this problem as follows:

> Primitive religions are anthropomorphic. They believe in gods which resemble human beings in physical shape and character … [Anthropomorphic economics applies] to the national economy the same principles and rules of conduct as have been found appropriate to a single individual or a family - paying your way, trimming your expenditure to fit your earnings, avoiding living beyond your means and avoiding getting into debt. These are well-worn principles of prudent conduct for an individual, but when applied as policy prescriptions to a national economy they lead to absurdities.

> If an individual cuts his expenditure he will not thereby reduce his income. However, if a Government cut their public expenditure programme in relation to tax rates and charges, they will reduce the total spending in the economy and hence the level of production and income … It is a policy that is appropriate only in times of excess demand and over-full employment.

For many reasons it is wrong to assume that a complex economy, with millions of agents with diverging interests, functions in a way that would be found in a Robinson Crusoe world. For example, prices only clear markets if supply and demand are determined independently. This is not the case for one of the most important prices, that of labour. Wages are a cost factor, and thus influence the supply of goods and services, but they also determine the income of the largest segment of the population and thereby influence the demand for goods and services. In the same vein, an individual agent may reduce its consumption in order to invest more, but in a complex economy, where investment and savings decisions are made independently by different actors, higher savings (equivalent to lower demand for consumer goods) do not automatically lead to an increase in investment; rather, the opposite may be true. Keynes (1936) argued that the decision "not to have dinner today" depresses the business of preparing dinner today without immediately stimulating any other business. Unless companies have "accurate information about the future", they will react to lower demand and falling profits by reducing investment, thereby reducing income.

In neoclassical models, the assumption of full employment prevents a fall in aggregate demand brought about by an increase in the savings rate. In the closed economy version of the model, this leads to an immediate reduction in the interest rate, and, since firms supposedly have perfect foresight and anticipate higher growth in the future, they react by increasing investment. This implies that firms increase investment even as involuntary inventories rise and their capacities are not fully utilized. It is hard to think of a real world entrepreneur who would behave in this way. Nor is there any country where the interest rate is determined by the supply of financial savings (let alone real savings). Short-term rates are either the result of central bank policy – when monetary policy operates without external constraints – or are influenced by short-term financial speculation.

In the open economy version of the neoclassical model, foreign savings (equivalent to the current-account deficit) close any gap between the demand and supply of national savings that may exist at the prevailing real interest rate, or in other words, they provide additional financial resources for investment. However, since the global current-account balance is zero by definition (although, due to statistical errors, actual records may show a different balance), the question arises as to how the "decision" of a specific country to have a current-account deficit is made consistent with the decisions in the rest of the world to have a surplus. This is a question for which the model does not provide an answer but which is essential for the conduct of successful growth-oriented macroeconomic policies.

While most economists would agree that the assumptions mentioned above are questionable, the standard answer of neoclassical economists is that one should not focus too much on the assumptions. Models should be judged based on the accuracy of their predictions and not on the validity of their assumptions. The evidence discussed in this chapter suggests that the neoclassical model fails on both the validity of its assumptions and its ability to predict.

Chart 3.9

RELATIONSHIP BETWEEN DOMESTIC SAVINGS AND PER CAPITA GDP GROWTH, AVERAGE FOR 1985–2005

(Per cent)

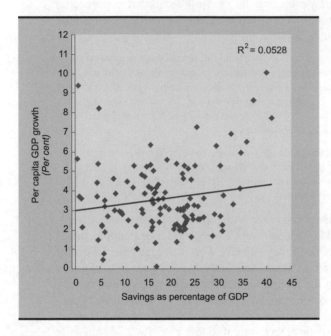

Source: UNCTAD secretariat calculations, based on *UNCTAD Handbook of Statistics* database; and World Bank, *World Development Indicators*.

Note: The sample comprises 130 developed, developing and transition economies.

correlation between domestic savings and invest-ment in open economies.[14] The empirical relationship between the current-account balance and growth is much less clear. The long-term relationship between growth and the current-account balance is negative and statistically significant for developed economies, as predicted by the model (chart 3.10A), but it is positive and statistically significant, albeit less so, for developing and transition economies and thus contradicts the model's prediction (chart 3.10B).[15]

The empirical findings of Gourinchas and Jeanne (2007) indicate a positive correlation between the current-account balance and TFP growth and a negative correlation between net capital inflows and convergence towards the world technological fron-tier. Both these findings refute the predictions of the neoclassical model; most importantly in the present context, the findings contradict the neoclassical

prediction that developing countries with a relatively rapid rate of convergence towards the world tech-nology frontier will import more capital (i.e. run a relatively large current-account deficit). Their focus on TFP growth also allows Gourinchas and Jeanne (2007) to explain the Lucas Paradox (given that most developing countries have lower TFP growth than the advanced economies). However, they uncover another puzzle as they find that capital seem to flow to developing countries that are growing slowly rather than to those that are growing rapidly. They call this finding the "allocation puzzle".

Some authors claim that marginal changes to the neoclassical model suffice to reconcile these diver-gences between the model's predictions and empirical evidence. Prasad, Rajan and Subramanian (2007), for instance, interpret the absence of a positive growth impact of capital inflows in developing countries as being caused by the inefficiency of financial inter-mediation in the financial systems of these countries. According to these authors, institutional deficiencies (such as weak protection of property rights) limit the ability of financial intermediaries to effectively use foreign capital to finance arm's length transactions, especially investment projects that have a long gesta-tion period and low initial profitability.

But Prasad, Rajan and Subramanian (2007) also show that the strong link between net capital inflows and the behaviour of the real exchange rate has a large negative effect on export industries. Indeed, export-oriented industries are very often the most dynamic component of the domestic economy and the negative relationship between capital inflows and GDP growth could well be explained by the fact that capital inflows tends to lead to an appreciation of the real exchange rate or even an overvaluation.

Rodrik and Subramanian (2008) propose a fur-ther explanation for the absence of a positive growth impact of capital inflows by distinguishing between savings-constrained and investment-constrained economies. They postulate the existence of a savings constraint if several potentially profitable investment projects cannot be realized because of the high costs of capital. Capital inflows would relax the savings constraint and, by lowering interest rates, stimulate investment and growth. In investment-constrained economies, by contrast, capital inflows have no effect on investment and growth, but they raise con-sumption. In economies of this type, capital inflows

Chart 3.10

RELATIONSHIP BETWEEN CURRENT-ACCOUNT BALANCE
AND PER CAPITA GDP GROWTH, 1985–2005

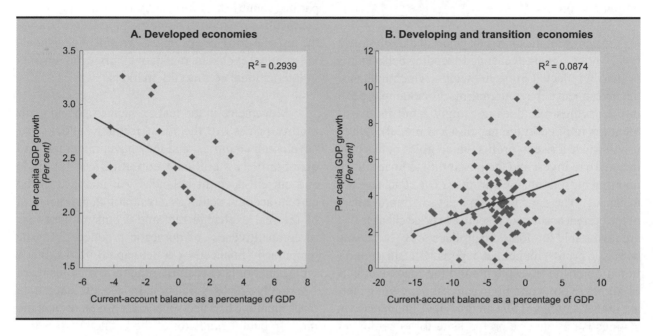

Source: UNCTAD secretariat calculations, based on *UNCTAD Handbook of Statistics* database; and World Bank, *World Development Indicators*.

Note: The sample in chart A comprises 19 developed economies and the sample in chart B comprises 111 developing and transition economies.

impact negatively on growth because they lead to an appreciation of the real exchange rate and thus hurt the tradeables sector. However, Rodrik and Subramanian (2008) stop short of explaining the underlying reasons that make an economy subject to the savings or the investment constraint.

To summarize, a significant number of empirical findings call into question the predictions of neoclassical growth models. While both the structure of these models and the econometric techniques designed to test the validity of their predictions have been developed further with a view to reconciling the differences between these empirical findings with the model's predictions, the remaining difference is often interpreted in a somewhat *ad hoc* fashion as pointing to structural problems of developing countries – such as imperfections of their financial markets – or policy failures. However, it may be at least as plausible to try and explain the empirical findings by means of an alternative model. The following subsection outlines such a model.

2. An alternative approach to savings and investment

Explanations of the relationship between savings and investment based on the work of Schumpeter and Keynes focus on the role of profits in the adjustment of savings and investment. These explanations share the perspective that economies do not develop along a known and somehow predetermined path, but that they are subject to external quantity and price shocks, as well as to policy shocks. Given that this approach does not assume perfect information and foresight, it does not postulate the existence of a mechanism that would automatically preserve or restore full employment. It therefore presents a more realistic image of developing economies, which are often characterized by weak economic structures and slack capacity. In such a set-up, profits are the residual element of income, unlike wages or rents, which are normally the outcome of contracts that are agreed at a certain periodic interval. One implication of this approach is that, if an economy has not yet reached its full-employment level and/or if its potential to grow is not fully exploited, any increase in aggregate demand (either domestic or foreign) will increase output and profits.

Another implication is that most of the adjustment to new price signals or changed spending behaviour is primarily reflected in profit swings, which influence the investment behaviour of firms. For example, a fall in the savings rate does not imply a fall in investment (as implied in the neoclassical model); rather, it will cause a rise in profits which gives both a new incentive to invest and the possibility to finance such investment from retained profits (*TDR 2006*, annex 2 to chap. I). The same logic applies to an improvement of the current account in response to price changes that are favourable for domestic producers. By increasing domestic profits, higher net exports will trigger additional domestic investment, and the income effects of higher exports and higher investment will generate higher savings. Thus, in this view, an increase in savings is no longer a prerequisite for either higher investment or a current-account improvement.

On the other hand, a current-account deficit that emerges in the wake of negative shocks from a rise in import prices, a fall in export prices or a real currency appreciation can have large negative effects on domestic output, and can thus lead to lower savings and lower planned investment. The emerging current-account deficit is equivalent to a net capital inflow, but this inflow is the symptom of a negative shock, and it will certainly not induce higher planned investment in plant and equipment. On the contrary, it is likely that planned investment will fall as a result of lower profits or sales volumes.[16]

Viewing developing countries as having a persistent "savings gap" implies a confusion between the low savings of households in developing countries and the behaviour of the current-account of the economy as a whole. A country does not take decisions over savings, consumption, investment and the current-account balance. The behaviour of the current-account balance is normally driven by shocks that are often induced by differences in the stance of domestic macroeconomic policy among trading partner countries, as well as by large changes in the competitive position of domestic producers vis-à-vis the rest of world (for example as a result of overshooting nominal exchange rates), or by price movements in international commodity markets.

Movements in the real exchange rate and commodity prices are the most frequent shocks for developing countries, and they have immediate and quantitatively significant consequences for trade and current-account balances. An increase in the current-account deficit as a result of an appreciation of the real exchange rate and a concomitant loss of competitiveness of domestic producers may be temporarily financed by a net capital inflow, but it will sooner or later require some form of adjustment – normally a real depreciation. Indeed, exchange-rate overvaluation has been the most frequent and the most "reliable" predictor of the financial crises that have characterized the developing world over the past 15 years.[17]

If current-account imbalances are understood as the outcome of export performance and import demand, rather than an international savings transfer, it is also possible to understand why current-account surpluses and net foreign asset accumulation can favour longer term growth. The fact that a number of developing countries are rapidly accumulating foreign exchange reserves, instead of using these funds to further increase their imports, is due to their attempts to defend their favourable competitive position arising from an undervalued exchange rate – mostly reached after a severe financial crisis. It is also due to their strategy to avoid dependence on the international capital markets and their volatility. It is only under such circumstances that open developing economies are able to set their monetary conditions in a way that favours domestic investment and the building of productive capacity.

E. Implications for economic policy

---

1. Macroeconomic policies

One of the outstanding features of the economic process is its proneness to shocks and cyclicality. Uncertainty, falling profits and shrinking demand may depress the activity of investors and bring a successfully ignited process of capital formation and growth to a sudden halt. Therefore, it is of the utmost importance for sustained growth and catching up that macroeconomic policies effectively absorb shocks, allow a quick resolution of cyclical disturbances and provide enterprises with a stable environment conducive to investment in productive capacity. One crucial element is the availability of adequate, reliable and cost-effective financing of investment.

Monetary instability, periods of hyperinflation and frequent financial crises have often forced many developing countries to adopt economic policies that generate the exact opposite of what would be favourable investment conditions. "Sound macroeconomic policies" as prescribed by the Washington Consensus, combined with financial liberalization, seldom led to the desired result of higher investment and faster growth, whereas the alternative policy approaches helped the newly industrializing economies of East and South-East Asia to accelerate their catch-up process.

In Asia, accommodative and stimulating monetary policies, with low policy interest rates and government intervention in the financial markets, have been accompanied by undervalued exchange rates since the financial crisis in 1997–1998. Fiscal policy has been used pragmatically to stimulate demand whenever that was required to respond to cyclical developments. Chart 3.11 reveals the degree

of monetary stimulation: in South, East and South-East Asia, the policy interest rate (in real and nominal terms) has been, on average, consistently lower than the growth rate (in real and nominal terms) over the past 20 years, except during the Asian financial crisis (see also chapter IV, box 4.1). By contrast, policy interest rates have been considerably higher in Latin America, where monetary policy has focused entirely on avoiding inflation, with the result that investment ratios and growth rates remained low. It is only since 2003 that more accommodative monetary policies and an overall good growth performance have prevailed in the majority of the countries in that region.

This evidence suggests that sustained income growth needs proactive economic management so that there is a permanent tendency for planned investment to exceed planned savings. Such an environment enables vigorous economic expansion, even if the propensity of private households to save remains unchanged. The additional savings that correspond to the increased investment are eventually generated by higher profits and a higher total income, while the initial increase in investment is financed by credit creation in the banking system (see also chapter IV).

By the same token, if growth and fixed investment are constrained by monetary conditions, including the exchange rate, many efforts aimed at good governance or strengthening of market forces may not generate the expected results, and overly restrictive monetary conditions may become prohibitive for development. In pursuing the agenda of the Washington Consensus, which aimed at "getting the prices right", many countries got two of the most important prices – the exchange rate and the interest rate – wrong. This may explain why the Washington

Chart 3.11

REAL SHORT-TERM INTEREST RATE AND GDP GROWTH IN ASIA AND LATIN AMERICA, 1986–2007

(Per cent)

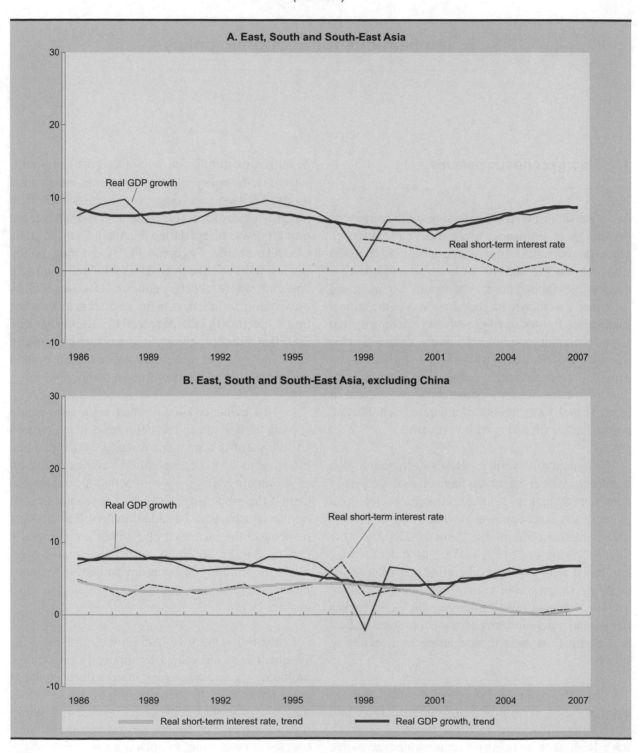

Chart 3.11 (concluded)

REAL SHORT-TERM INTEREST RATE AND GDP GROWTH
IN ASIA AND LATIN AMERICA, 1986–2007

(Per cent)

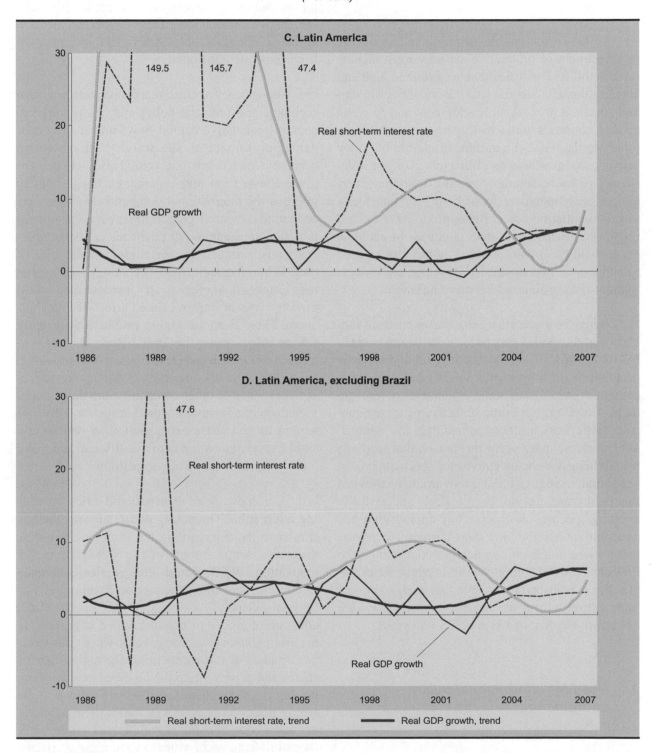

Source: UNCTAD secretariat calculations, based on OECD, *International Development Statistics* (IDS) online; IMF, *International Financial Statistics* database; *UNCTAD Handbook of Statistics* database; and Thomson Datastream.

Note: Real short-term interest rates are GDP weighted. East, South and South-East Asia: Bangladesh, India, Indonesia, Malaysia, the Philippines, the Republic of Korea, Singapore, Taiwan Province of China and Thailand. Latin America: Argentina, Brazil, Chile, Colombia, Costa Rica, Mexico, Peru, Uruguay and Venezuela (Bolivarian Republic of).

Consensus was not applied in Washington: the United States, after flirting briefly with monetarist orthodoxy at the beginning of the 1980s, returned to fine-tuning the interest rate and to an extraordinarily accommodative monetary policy stance over the past two decades.

To be sure, a stable environment conducive to investment in productive capacity must include price stability. Countries that are prone to high and accelerating inflation may find it more difficult to start and sustain a process of development and catching up than countries with a history of price stability. In other words, without a sufficient number of policy instruments available to effectively dampen inflationary pressure, attempts to spur development by expansionary macroeconomic policy are more likely to fail as inflation soars. But appropriate wage and incomes policies could help countries to maintain price stability so that monetary policy can be used to support an investment-led development process without risking an acceleration of inflation.

It may be argued that the Asian experience suggests that this policy mix needs to be complemented by some form of capital-account regulation. It is true that controls on capital inflows have helped to contain crises, and to some extent even to prevent them. However, the prime objective of these countries' policy mix has been to maintain low nominal interest rates, and it is for this reason that arbitrage possibilities and the incentives for speculation have been small to begin with. It is only in situations when this policy mix has not been entirely successful in averting speculation on currency appreciation and concomitant destabilizing short-term capital inflows that a more hands-on approach to controlling such flows has proved helpful, as in Malaysia, for example. But it is important to note that such additional interventionist measures have been episodic and are not a core element of Asian policy strategies.

2. Need for international policy coordination

It is mainly international speculation searching for interest arbitrage and gains from exchange-rate appreciation that makes it difficult to prevent currency overvaluation and financial crises (see also *TDRs 2004* and *2007*). Revaluation of currencies as a result of speculative capital flows undermines the normal functioning of the exchange-rate mechanism that would prevent the emergence of large and persistent current-account deficits. Moreover, the adjustment to currency overvaluation driven by speculative capital flows can be extremely costly, as the Asian and the Latin American financial crises have amply demonstrated.

Strengthened international cooperation in macroeconomic and financial policy may be required to contain speculative capital flows and reduce their damaging impact on the stability of the world economy. Such cooperation could also help prevent governments from manipulating exchange rates to improve the international competitiveness of their economies. Overall competitiveness of countries is a zero sum game. All countries can simultaneously raise productivity and wages and the level of trade to improve their overall economic welfare, but they cannot all simultaneously increase their world market shares or improve their current-account balances. There is an adding up problem, as recently acknowledged also in the Growth Report of the Commission on Growth and Development (2008: 94–96). Whereas efforts of companies to gain market shares at the expense of other companies, are an essential ingredient of a functioning market system, efforts of nations to gain at the expense of other nations at a similar level of development is a different and much more problematic type of competition.[18]

A framework of international rules governing international monetary and financial relations similar to those governing the use of trade policy measures in agreements of the World Trade Organization (WTO) could lend greater coherence to the system of global economic governance. The Secretary-General of UNCTAD has suggested the adoption of a code of conduct aimed at preventing the manipulation of exchange rates, wage rates, taxes or subsidies in the competition for higher market shares and at preventing the financial markets from driving the competitive positions of nations in the wrong direction (UNCTAD, 2008). The adoption of such a code of conduct would mark a new spirit of multilateralism in global economic governance and would allow balancing the potential advantages resulting from real exchange rate adjustment for one country against the potential disadvantages of other countries that would be affected by that adjustment.

For example, major changes in the nominal exchange rate should be subject to multilateral oversight and negotiations. Only if such rules were to apply could all trading parties avoid unjustified overall loss or gains of competitiveness, and developing countries could systematically avoid the trap of overvaluation that has been one of the greatest impediments to prosperity in the past. ∎

Notes

---

1   For an earlier discussion, see TDR 2006, chapter I, section D.

2   It has also been observed that fast growing developing economies tend to have smaller deficits than slowly growing developing economies (Prasad, Rajan and Subramanian, 2007).

3   The sample includes 22 developed countries, 20 transition economies and 91 developing countries, and the relative frequencies were 0.55, 0.90 and 0.44, respectively.

4   The relationship in transition economies is a different one: growth picked up before the reversal episodes and reversals tended to occur when output was above trend.

5   This statistical analysis allows isolating the effect of a single variable by assuming that all other variables included in the experiment are held constant.

6   Thus, for example, the observation in the following discussion that "a real depreciation increases the probability of a current-account reversal by 4.2 per cent" signifies that "a real depreciation equal to a one standard deviation change in the movement of the real exchange rate increases the probability of a current-account reversal by 4.2 per cent."

7   If the relevant variable has a normal (Gaussian) distribution, this probability is about 30 per cent.

8   Moreover, the annex shows that the real exchange rate is statistically significant in the regressions that focus on developed countries but only marginally significant in the regressions that focus on developing and transition economies.

9   Moreover, by including OECD growth in the developed countries, the regression may lead to an endogeneity bias.

10   For 75 of the episodes listed in table 3.1 there were not enough data to calculate GDP growth both before and after the episode.

11   Similarly, among the reversals that could not be classified, the change in the terms of trade is almost twice as large for episodes that are accompanied by a real appreciation than it is for episodes that are accompanied by a real depreciation.

12   As above, the following discussion assumes a one standard deviation change of the relevant variable.

13   Traditionally, overall investment is defined as being equal to national savings plus foreign savings. This is a highly questionable terminology because foreign savings is just the counterpart of the current-account deficit. However, the purchasing power which is transferred by the net capital inflow can also be used for consumption; there is no mechanism that would guarantee the use of capital inflows for investment.

14   This was first highlighted by Feldstein and Horioka (1983) who interpreted their result as indicating low – or restricted – capital mobility, even among the industrialized countries. Otherwise, capital would "seek out the most productive investment opportunities worldwide" (Obstfeld and Rogoff, 1996: 162).

15   The figure for the advanced economies does not include Ireland and Luxembourg, which are two large outliers. If these countries are included, the relationship remains positive but not statistically significant (it is positive and statistically significant if only Luxembourg is excluded). While chart 3.10A presents a simple correlation, which does not control for other factors that may also affect GDP growth and the current-account balance, Prasad, Rajan and Subramanian (2007) show that these results are robust when controlling for standard determinants of GDP growth, including investment.

16   The same reasoning holds for a scenario where a current-account surplus is the result of a positive shock to exports, leading to higher profits in the

tradable sector and to positive second-round effects on aggregate output and investment.

17 This reasoning is also relevant in the context of policies related to external debt and its repayment. A net repayment of external debt always requires a shift in the current account. This shift can originate from either a growth differential between the debtor and the creditor countries (with a relative fall in real income of the debtor country) or an improvement of the competitiveness of producers in the debtor country that leads to the switching of expenditure from foreign to domestic goods. But this implies a loss of competitiveness and market shares of producers in the creditor countries. If governments of the creditor countries do not accept this loss of competitiveness of their producers and therefore influence the exchange rate, a default by the debtor is unavoidable. In other words, a creditor economy cannot retain its export position and expect the repayment of debt. Standard analyses of net capital flows between countries and of foreign debt of countries do not normally take this paradox into account.

18 This kind of fallacy of composition does not refer to efforts by developing countries to catch up and gain globally vis-à-vis developed economies. Rather, it describes the competition of nations at a similar level of development, and a permanent loss of market shares which would normally not result from catching up by developing countries.

References

Bernanke B (2005). The global saving glut and the United States current account deficit. Remarks at the Sandrige Lecture, Virginia Association of Economics. Richmond, Virginia, 14 April. Available at: www. federalreserve.gov/boarddocs/speeches/2005/200503102/default.htm.

Cass D (1965). Optimum growth in an aggregate model of capital accumulation. *Review of Economic Studies*, 32: 233–240, July.

Chinn M and Ito H (2007). A new measure of financial openness. Mimeo. Madison, University of Wisconsin.

Commission on Growth and Development (2008). The growth report: Strategies for sustained growth and inclusive development. Washington, DC, World Bank.

Domar ED (1957). Essays in the theory of economic growth. New York, Oxford University Press.

Eichengreen B (2007). The real exchange rate and economic growth. Berkeley, University of California. Mimeo. July.

Feldstein M and Horioka CY (1983). Domestic saving and international capital flows. *Economic Journal*, 90: 314–329.

Flassbeck H (2001). The exchange rate: Economic policy tool or market price? UNCTAD Discussion Paper No. 157. Geneva, UNCTAD.

Frenkel R and Taylor L (2006). Real exchange rate, monetary policy and employment. New York, United Nations Department of Economic and Social Affairs. Working Paper No. 19, February.

Gourinchas PO and Jeanne O (2007). Capital flows to developing countries: The allocation puzzle. NBER Working Paper No. 13602, November.

Harrod RF (1939). An essay in dynamic theory. *Economic Journal*, 49: 14–33.

IMF (2007). Exchange rates and adjustment of external imbalances. *World Economic Outlook*, April.

Kaldor N (1983). The economic consequences of Mrs. Thatcher. London, Gerald Duckworth & Co. Ltd.

Kaufmann D, Kraay A and Mastruzzi M (2007). Governance matters VI: Aggregate and individual governance indicators, 1996–2006. World Bank, Policy Research Working Paper Series 4280.

Keynes JM (1936). General theory of employment, interest and money. London, Macmillan, Cambridge University Press, for Royal Economic Society.

Koopmans TC (1965). On the concept of optimal economic growth. In: *The Economic Approach to Development Planning*. Amsterdam, North-Holland.

Levy Yeyati E and Sturzenegger F (2005). Classifying exchange rate regimes: Deeds vs. words. *European Economic Review*, 49: 1603–1635, August.

López de Silanes F et al. (2004). The regulation of labor. *Quarterly Journal of Economics*, 119(4): 1339–1382. Available at: http://works.bepress.com/florencio_lopez_de_silanes/3.

Lucas RE Jr. (1990). Why doesn't capital flow from rich to poor countries? *American Economic Review*, 80(2): 92–96. Papers and proceedings of the hundred and second annual meeting of the American Economic Association, May.

Obstfeld M and Rogoff K (1996). *Foundations of international macroeconomics*. Cambridge, MA, MIT Press.

Prasad E, Rajan R and Subramanian A (2007). Foreign capital and economic growth. NBER Working Paper 13619.

Rodrik D (2007). The real exchange rate and economic growth: Theory and evidence. Mimeo. Kennedy School of Government. Harvard University, Cambridge, MA, August.

Rodrik D and Subramanian A (2008). Why did financial globalization disappoint? Mimeo. March.

Sachs JD et al. (2004). Ending Africa's Poverty Trap. *Brookings Papers on Economic Activity*, Issue 1.

Solow R (1956). A Contribution to the theory of economic growth. *Quarterly Journal of Economics*, 70(1): 65–94.

Swan T (1956). Economic growth and capital accumulation. *Economic Record*, 32(2): 334–61.

UNCTAD (2008). Report of the Secretary-General of UNCTAD to UNCTAD XII: Globalization for development: Opportunities and challenges, document TD/413. United Nations publication, New York and Geneva.

UNCTAD (various issues). *Trade and Development Report*. United Nations publications, New York and Geneva.

ECONOMETRIC ANALYSES OF DETERMINANTS OF EXPANSIONARY AND CONTRACTIONARY CURRENT-ACCOUNT REVERSALS

With a view to getting a better understanding of the relative importance of different factors, in particular changes in real exchange rates and terms-of-trade shocks, in bringing about positive current-account reversals, the UNCTAD secretariat has undertaken a cross-country analysis of the determinants of such reversals and the conditions under which the reversals are associated with an increase in GDP growth. This annex describes the methodology used to define the reversal episodes and provides detailed results of the econometric analyses.

1. Identifying reversal episodes

Current account reversals are defined by using an approach similar to that discussed by IMF (2007). An episode was considered to begin (time 0) when the current account improved by at least 0.5 percentage points of GDP over the next three years, and it was considered to end (time T) when at least 50 per cent of the original reversal was overturned and the current account remained below its level at time T for at least three years. In order to be considered for this exercise, episodes also needed to be large and persistent. Therefore, all episodes in which the cumulative adjustment of the current-account balance was less than 2.5 per cent of GDP and all episodes in which the current-account balance deteriorated below the level at time 0 within five years from the beginning of the episode were excluded from the sample. Episodes that lasted more than 8 years were truncated and terminated by choosing the largest current-account surplus (or smallest deficit) realized between years 5 and 8. The episodes were taken from the experiences of 133 countries (22 developed countries, 91 developing countries and 20 transition economies) for the period 1975–2006.

2. Econometric analyses of the determinants of current-account reversals

The estimates of a Probit model aimed at evaluating the multivariate relationship between the probability of a reversal episode and the behaviour of several macroeconomic variables are reported in table 3.A1. The dependent variable takes a value of 1 in the first and second year of the reversal episode and 0 in tranquil periods. All turbulent periods which did not occur during the first or second year of the episode were dropped from the sample.[1]

Explanatory variables comprise the following:

- the current-account balance as a share of GDP (CAB),

- the change in the real effective exchange rate (DREER),

- GDP growth (GDPGR),

- the output gap (OUTPUTGAP),

- the change in terms of trade (DTOT),

- credit growth (CRGR),

- log inflation (ln(INF)),

- trade openness (OPEN),

- the log of GDP per capita (ln(GDP_PC)),

- average GDP growth in the OECD economies (OECDGR),

- the United States Federal Funds rate (US FF RATE),

- a dummy variable that takes a value of 1 for countries with an open capital account (KA OPEN),

- the interaction between KA OPEN and US FF RATE (KA OPEN*US FF RATE),

- a dummy variable that takes a value of 1 for countries with a fixed exchange rate (FIX XRATE), and

- a dummy variable that takes a value of 1 for countries with an intermediated exchange rate (INTER XRATE).[2]

Since the US FF RATE only varies over time and not across countries, standard errors were clustered at the year level. The point estimates cannot be interpreted as showing a causal relationship going from the explanatory variables to the probability of a reversal episode. However, the result can shed light on the correlates of reversal episodes.

Table 3.A1 shows that, as expected, a reversal tends to occur when an economy has a current-account deficit and that it is accompanied by a depreciation of the real exchange rate.[3] A corollary of this finding is that countries with a floating exchange rate are less likely than countries with a fixed exchange rate to be able to improve their current account. Indeed, the statistical analysis shows that the FIX XRATE dummy variable is negative and statistically significant. The regression model also confirms the findings of the analysis in chart 3.6, and suggests that a reversal tends to occur in periods of low GDP growth and when output is below capacity, while inflation does not play an important role. Trade openness has a positive coefficient (though not always statistically significant) in the developed countries and a negative effect in developing and transition economies. The positive sign of GDP per capita indicates that reversals are more prevalent in middle-income developing countries than in low-income developing countries. With

Table 3.A1

DETERMINANTS OF CURRENT-ACCOUNT REVERSALS

	(1)	(2)	(3)	(4)	(5)	(6)
CAB	-1.198	-1.260	-0.745	-0.611	-1.388	-1.474
	(7.94)***	(8.12)***	(3.39)***	(3.23)***	(7.72)***	(7.79)***
DREER	-0.093	-0.086	-0.197	-0.126	-0.090	-0.086
	(1.96)*	(1.57)	(2.56)**	(2.20)**	(1.56)	(1.32)
GDPGR	-0.510	-0.692	-1.063	-1.033	-0.559	-0.731
	(2.19)**	(3.24)***	(3.85)***	(3.53)***	(2.10)**	(3.10)***
OUTPUTGAP	-0.835	-0.970	-0.402	-0.370	-0.799	-0.960
	(4.19)***	(4.73)***	(1.16)	(1.24)	(3.65)***	(3.88)***
DTOT	0.097	0.110	0.063	0.052	0.126	0.142
	(1.98)**	(2.29)**	(0.86)	(0.91)	(2.08)**	(2.37)**
CRGR	0.055	0.043	-0.060	-0.052	0.054	0.044
	(1.69)*	(1.17)	(2.65)***	(2.96)***	(1.55)	(1.10)
ln(INF)	0.009	0.008	0.002	-0.001	0.001	0.001
	(1.16)	(0.97)	(0.22)	(0.15)	(0.08)	(0.11)
OPEN	-0.008	0.011	0.029	0.053	-0.054	-0.037
	(0.35)	(0.44)	(1.12)	(3.18)***	(1.90)*	(1.14)
ln(GDP_PC)	0.021	0.018	0.014	0.014	0.053	0.046
	(3.01)***	(2.58)***	(0.55)	(0.80)	(4.80)***	(4.11)***
OECDGR	-0.591	-0.530	0.019	0.040	-0.684	-0.658
	(2.59)***	(2.65)***	(0.22)	(0.56)	(2.34)**	(2.55)**
US FF RATE	-0.005	-0.003	-0.001	-0.001	-0.004	-0.003
	(1.67)*	(1.08)	(0.22)	(0.45)	(1.14)	(0.82)
KA OPEN*US FF RATE	0.015	0.014	0.006	0.006	0.020	0.020
	(3.04)***	(3.55)***	(1.93)*	(2.58)***	(2.49)**	(2.57)**
KA OPEN	-0.127	-0.115	-0.125	-0.196	-0.123	-0.113
	(4.35)***	(4.38)***	(1.77)*	(2.25)**	(3.21)***	(3.20)***
FIX XRATE		-0.056		-0.041		-0.053*
		(2.42)**		(2.68)***		(1.74)
INTER XRATE		-0.026		-0.019		-0.027
		(1.43)		(1.40)		(1.10)
No. of observations	1 382	1 285	365	342	1 017	943
Group	All countries		Developed		Developing and transition	

Note: For definitions of variables and sources, see explanatory note at the end of this annex.

Probit estimates with standard errors clustered at the year level. The dependent variable is a dummy that takes a value of 1 in the first two years of the episode and a value of 0 in tranquil periods. Turbulent periods which do not occur in the first two years of the episode are not included in the sample. The explanatory variables are averages over the three years preceding the episode. Robust z statistics in parentheses.

  * Significant at 10 per cent.
  ** Significant at 5 per cent.
  *** Significant at 1 per cent.

regard to external factors, there is strong evidence that the probability of a current-account reversal in developing countries is negatively associated with GDP growth in the developed world. The behaviour of the United States interest rate is very important in countries with an open capital account, but has no effect on the probability of a reversal in developing countries with a closed capital account.

3. Distinction between expansionary and contractionary reversals

The next econometric exercise focuses on the conditions under which an economy can move from a current-account deficit to a current-account surplus without suffering a large and protracted economic crisis. This question was approached by classifying the reversal episodes analysed in the first exercise into expansionary and contractionary ones. Expansionary reversals are all the episodes that are followed by an increase of GDP growth of at least one percentage point. Similarly, contractionary reversals are followed by a one percentage point decrease in GDP growth. All remaining episodes are defined as "neutral".

The hypothesis that expansionary reversals need either a large, positive terms-of-trade shock or a real depreciation, is confirmed by a formal test that controls for possible other factors that may affect the probability of such a reversal. Table 3.A2 presents the results of a multivariate analysis of the determinants of expansionary reversals. In this case, each observation is one episode and the dependent variable takes a value of 1 if the episode is expansionary and a value of 0 if the episode is neutral or contractionary. Like table 3.A1 the regressions control for:

- the current-account balance as a share of GDP (CAB),

- the change in the real effective exchange rate (DREER),

- the output gap (OUTPUTGAP),

- the change in terms of trade (DTOT),

- log inflation (ln(INF)),

- trade openness (OPEN),

- the log of GDP per capita (ln(GDP_PC)),

- average GDP growth in the OECD economies (OECDGR), and

- capital account openness (KA OPEN).

In addition this exercise controls for:

- the difference between the domestic and the United States interest rate (DIR-FFR), as a measure of how accommodating monetary policy is compared to that of the United States;

- the quality of institutions (INSTQUAL, computed as an average of the six indices assembled by Kaufmann, Kraay and Mastruzzi, 2007);[4] and

- an index of labour market rigidity (LMR).

As expected, the regressions show that the output gap variable is positive and highly significant, indicating that countries that are in a deep crisis are more likely to rebound and sustain higher growth in the post-reversal period. Moreover, the data show that the presence of a competitive exchange rate and positive terms-of-trade shocks are strong predictors of an expansionary reversal, and that the same is true for an accommodating monetary policy, which has a direct and an indirect effect, mediated by the competitive real exchange rate. The data show that countries where a policy of high interest rates is applied are less likely to observe an expansionary reversal. Inflation, the size of the current-account deficit at the beginning

Table 3.A2

DETERMINANTS OF EXPANSIONARY CURRENT-ACCOUNT REVERSALS

	(1)	*(2)*	*(3)*	*(4)*	*(5)*	*(6)*
DREER	-0.449	-0.583	-0.534	-0.557	-0.704	-0.651
	(2.08)**	(2.41)**	(2.40)**	(2.60)***	(3.08)***	(2.86)***
DTOT	0.131	0.116	0.135	0.103	0.081	0.111
	(2.15)**	(1.83)*	(2.34)**	(1.59)	(1.09)	(1.70)*
OUTPUTGAP	6.228	5.533	6.050	6.125	4.915	5.847
	(4.58)***	(4.28)***	(4.46)***	(4.44)***	(4.13)***	(4.39)***
DIR-FFR	-0.032	-0.042	-0.047	-0.043	-0.053	-0.057
	(1.81)*	(1.83)*	(2.01)**	(2.27)**	(2.51)**	(2.53)**
ln(INF)	-0.041	-0.186	-0.062	-0.180	-0.422	-0.222
	(0.16)	(0.66)	(0.24)	(0.76)	(1.70)*	(0.92)
CAB	0.011	0.012	0.012	0.013	0.011	0.012
	(1.59)	(1.69)*	(1.64)	(1.75)*	(1.59)	(1.60)
KA OPEN	0.112	0.193	0.248	0.309	0.412	0.418
	(0.86)	(1.30)	(1.62)	(1.98)**	(2.33)**	(2.36)**
OECDGR	5.530	5.756	5.462	6.042	6.275	5.932
	(3.83)***	(3.42)***	(3.22)***	(4.55)***	(4.35)***	(3.92)***
ln(GDP_PC)				0.081	0.081	0.097
				(1.55)	(1.53)	(1.77)*
OPEN				-0.033	-0.166	-0.105
				(0.42)	(1.62)	(1.07)
INSTQUAL				-0.208	-0.246	-0.232
				(2.30)**	(2.26)**	(2.08)**
LMR				0.003	0.002	0.002
				(1.44)	(0.68)	(0.99)
No. of observations	155	129	135	152	126	132
Group	All	Developing	Developing and transition	All	Developing	Developing and transition

Note: For definitions of variables and sources, see explanatory note at the end of this annex.

Probit estimates with robust standard errors. The dependent variable is a dummy that takes a value of 1 for reversal episodes characterized by a subsequent sustained increase in GDP growth and a value of 0 for other reversal episodes. DREER and DTOT are the changes in the real effective exchange rate and the terms of trade, respectively, between the episode and three years before; the other variables are averages for the duration of the episode.

   * Significant at 10 per cent.
  ** Significant at 5 per cent.
 *** Significant at 1 per cent.

of the reversal, the presence of capital controls, trade openness, GDP per capita, and the index of labour market rigidities are not significantly correlated with the probability of observing an expansionary reversal. A further result is that economies with "good institutions" as defined by Kaufmann, Kraay and Mastruzzi (2007) are significantly less likely to observe an expansionary current-account reversal.

By contrast, the analysis shows again that external factors (proxied by GDP growth in OECD countries) are a key determinant of the probability of observing an expansionary reversal.

Table 3.A3 contains the results of the same analysis focusing on contractionary reversals. In this case, the model is unable to explain why countries do

Table 3.A3

DETERMINANTS OF CONTRACTIONARY CURRENT-ACCOUNT REVERSALS

	(1)	*(2)*	*(3)*	*(4)*	*(5)*	*(6)*
DREER	0.048	0.073	0.082	0.058	0.118	0.120
	(0.23)	(0.31)	(0.38)	(0.28)	(0.48)	(0.53)
DTOT	-0.099	-0.076	-0.085	-0.090	-0.068	-0.079
	(1.04)	(0.80)	(0.94)	(1.01)	(0.73)	(0.94)
OUTPUTGAP	-7.326	-7.331	-7.390	-7.390	-7.558	-7.565
	(4.86)***	(4.68)***	(4.75)***	(5.02)***	(4.89)***	(4.93)***
DIR-FFR	0.032	0.034	0.034	0.055	0.063	0.061
	(1.70)*	(1.40)	(1.44)	(2.50)**	(2.24)**	(2.26)**
ln(INF)	0.033	0.046	0.008	0.130	0.200	0.128
	(0.14)	(0.19)	(0.03)	(0.54)	(0.83)	(0.54)
CAB	-0.003	-0.006	-0.006	-0.008	-0.007	-0.009
	(0.40)	(0.87)	(0.89)	(1.02)	(0.83)	(1.03)
KA OPEN	-0.107	-0.228	-0.272	-0.362	-0.588	-0.597
	(0.75)	(1.29)	(1.64)	(2.09)**	(2.67)***	(3.00)***
OECDGR	-1.795	-2.644	-2.489	-2.353	-3.210	-2.983
	(1.33)	(1.61)	(1.54)	(1.61)	(1.77)*	(1.71)*
ln(GDP_PC)				0.018	-0.008	-0.005
				(0.31)	(0.13)	(0.09)
OPEN				0.116	0.389	0.298
				(1.09)	(2.25)**	(2.10)**
INSTQUAL				0.084	0.081	0.111
				(0.83)	(0.64)	(0.93)
LMR				-0.003	-0.001	-0.001
				(1.13)	(0.36)	(0.32)
No. of observations	155	129	135	152	126	132
Group	All	Developing	Developing and transition	All	Developing	Developing and transition

Note: For definitions of variables and sources, see explanatory note at the end of this annex.
    Probit estimates with robust standard errors. The dependent variable is a dummy that takes a value of 1 for reversal episodes characterized by a subsequent contraction in GDP growth and a value of 0 for other reversal episodes. DREER and DTOT are the changes in the real effective exchange rate and the terms of trade, respectively, between the episode and three years before; the other variables are averages for the duration of the episode.
    * Significant at 10 per cent.
    ** Significant at 5 per cent.
    *** Significant at 1 per cent.

not grow after the episode. The only robust predictors are the output gap and the nominal interest rate: the higher the nominal interest rate the more likely it is that the reversal will be contractionary. In some regressions, greater trade openness is associated with a higher probability of occurrence of a contractionary episode, and greater capital account openness is associated with a lower probability of observing a contractionary episode. However, these results do not appear to be particularly robust.

DEFINITIONS OF VARIABLES AND SOURCES

Variable	Definition	Source
CAB	Current-account balance divided by GDP	World Bank, *World Development Indicators*
DREER	Change in the real effective exchange rate: deviation of the real effective exchange rate from its average level in tranquil periods. Tranquil periods begin three years after the end of the episode and ends three years before beginning of it.	IMF, *International Financial Statistics*; and national sources
GDPGR	GDP growth	*UNCTAD Handbook of Statistics* database
ln(GDP_PC)	Logarithm of per capita GDP (PPP at constant 2000 international dollars)	IMF, *World Economic Outlook*; and national sources
OUTPUTGAP	Output gap: Per cent deviation of GDP trend from its current value	IMF, *World Economic Outlook*; and national sources
DTOT	Change in the terms of trade	UNCTAD calculations, based on IMF, *World Economic Outlook*; and national sources
CRGR	Growth of total credit to residents	World Bank, *World Development Indicators*
Ln(INF)	Logarithm of inflation	IMF, *International Financial Statistics*; and national sources
OPEN	Trade openness: sum of imports and exports divided by GDP	IMF, *World Economic Outlook*; and national sources
OECDGR	Average GDP growth in OECD economies	*UNCTAD Handbook of Statistics* database
US FF RATE	United States federal funds rate	National sources
KA OPEN	Dummy variable that takes value one for countries with open capital account	Chinn and Ito (2007)
KA OPEN*US FF RATE	Interaction between KA OPEN and US FF RATE	Chinn and Ito (2007)
FIX XRATE	Dummy variable that takes value one for countries with a fixed exchange rate regime	Levy Yeyati and Sturzenegger (2005)
INTER XRATE	Dummy variable that takes value one for countries with an intermediate exchange rate regime	Levy Yeyati and Sturzenegger (2005)
DIR-FFR	Difference between domestic and United States interest rate	National sources
INSTQUAL	Quality of institutions index	Kaufmann, Kraay and Mastruzzi (2007)
LMR	Labour market rigidity index	López de Silanes et al. (2004)

Notes

1 Assuming that a country has a reversal episode that starts in 1998 and lasts until 2002, the dependent variable takes value of 0 in 1975–1997 and 2003–2006 and a value of 1 in 1998 and 1999. The observations for the 2000–2002 period are dropped from the sample.

2 Floating exchange rate is the excluded dummy.

3 However, the real depreciation significantly anticipates the reversal only in the sub-sample of developed countries.

4 See also the discussion of governance indicators in chapter VI, section D of this *TDR*.

Chapter IV

DOMESTIC SOURCES OF FINANCE AND INVESTMENT IN PRODUCTIVE CAPACITY

A. Introduction

There is general agreement that a sustainable rise in living standards can only be achieved through expanded production and continuous productivity growth. This presupposes high rates of investment in physical infrastructure and plant and equipment, as well as in more intangible elements, such as education and research and development. But opinions differ as to the most appropriate modes of financing these different types of investment. For private investment to take place, entrepreneurs not only need an incentive in terms of expectations of future profits, they should also be able to finance the purchase of the required capital goods.

An influential strand of economic thought views investment as being financed from a savings pool created mainly by household savings. According to this view, entrepreneurial investment will be maximized by increasing national savings and the efficiency of financial intermediation. Policy recommendations stemming from this view include lowering fiscal expenditure to improve government fiscal accounts, and increasing household savings rates and capital imports ("foreign savings") through higher interest rates. Greater efficiency of banks and non-bank financial intermediaries and securities markets is expected to increase financial resources for investment

in enterprises, along with better monitoring of the investment and spreading of risk.

An alternative approach to the financing of investment – associated with Keynes and in particular Schumpeter – suggests that capital accumulation in industry is financed primarily by savings from corporate profits, while the contribution of voluntary household savings to productive investment is considered relatively less important. In examining the successful economic catch-up of the East Asian economies in the post-Second World War period, UNCTAD emphasized the importance of the link between corporate profits and savings and a dynamic profit-investment nexus (see in particular *TDRs* 1994, 1996, 1997 and 2003). It attributed high national savings rates to high corporate savings, rather than to high household savings. Strong enterprise profits simultaneously increased the incentive of firms to invest and their capacity to finance new investment, which in turn further boosted profits by enhancing both the rates of capacity utilization and productivity growth.

These alternative views relate to the broader controversy regarding the causal relationship between savings, investment and credit discussed in chapter III. One of the hypotheses discussed in this chapter is that the quality of a country's monetary and financial institutions, and particularly the role of banks, has important implications for the relationship between savings, investment and credit: if investment can be financed by banks, which have the power to create money *ex nihilo* during the credit operation, then the prior existence of savings is not a necessary condition for investment; higher savings would be generated as a result of expanding income. In other words, the structure and operation of domestic financial systems are not neutral in the process of "mobilizing resources" and financing investment. The way an economy functions and its response to monetary policy may differ depending on whether capital markets ("capital market economies") or bank intermediation ("overdraft economies") are more predominant in the financial system. Moreover, financial institutions, particularly commercial and development banks, are not passive intermediaries that only facilitate transactions between non-financial

agents. Rather, they are dynamic actors that distribute resources among different economic agents and sectors for specific purposes (e.g. consumption or investment) in accordance with their own objectives or policy orientations. Hence financial institutions actively shape a country's economic structure and activities. Indeed, their activities are often part of strategic development plans of private conglomerates or governments.

Section B of this chapter discusses the principal sources of financing investment in developing and transition economies. Section C examines the recent transformation of financial systems as a result of financial globalization and domestic reforms. Section D analyses the main results of these changes and the present characteristics of financial systems in developing and transition economies. The final section summarizes the most important findings of these experiences and discusses the policy recommendations that can be derived from them.

B. Main sources of investment finance

From a microeconomic perspective, financing may come from internal sources, such as self-financing or retained earnings, or from external sources such as loans, bonds or equity. From a macroeconomic perspective (i.e. for the economy as a whole), financing may come from domestic or foreign sources, but it is only the foreign sources that create a liability for the economy. A complementary distinction refers to foreign and national savings, the latter of which can be further decomposed into household, business and government savings. From an accounting point of view, the savings generated in the whole economy during a certain period of time must equal total investment.

1. The role of corporate profits

One important condition for economic development is for firms to have access to reliable, adequate and cost-effective sources for financing their investments. This condition is best met when profits themselves are the main source of investment financing. Indeed, government policy that helps create an investment-profit nexus will support both a firm's incentive to invest and its capacity to finance new investments.[1]

The decision by firms as to what proportion of profits they should retain is related to their decisions

Table 4.1

SAVINGS AND INVESTMENT BY HOUSEHOLDS AND NON-FINANCIAL FIRMS, SELECTED ECONOMIES AND PERIODS

(Per cent of GDP)

		Households		Non-financial firms		*Memo item:* Share of profits in manufacturing value added
	Period	*Savings*	*Fixed investment*	*Savings*	*Fixed investment*	
Brazil	1995–2003	7.0	5.5	12.3	11.4	..
Chile	1996–2003	8.4	6.0	9.8	14.9	81.7[a]
China	1995–2003	17.3	4.8	12.8	25.5	..
China, Taiwan Province of	1995–2003	12.4	1.0	10.6	14.8	..
Colombia	1995–2002	5.5	3.0	8.1	9.6	..
Côte d'Ivoire	1995–2000	2.8	1.6	4.1	7.4	..
Egypt	1996–2003	10.6	4.7	8.1	6.8	..
Iran (Islamic Republic of)	1996–2003	18.4	10.3	6.6	11.7	75.0
Mexico	1995–2002	7.5	4.8	10.2	13.0	82.0[a]
Niger	1995–2003	8.9	3.1	1.8	5.3	54.1[b]
Rep. of Korea	1995–2003	..	..	11.0	20.1	78.0[b]
Tunisia	1995–2002	7.8	6.5	8.8	12.4	..
Memo items:						
China, Taiwan Province of	1983–1990	17.0	4.3	9.6	12.4	58.9
Japan	1960–1970	13.3	8.0	15.0	22.7	67.2[c]
Republic of Korea	1980–1984	10.3	5.3	8.3	20.0	72.8

Source: UNCTAD secretariat calculations, based on *UN National Account Statistics*; *TDR 1997*, table 44; Taiwan Province of China National Statistics MacroEconomics Database; and UNIDO, *Industrial Statistics* database.
Note: Profits are manufacturing value added less total gross earnings of employees.
a 1995–2000.
b 1995–2002.
c 1963–1970.

on investment. To the extent that a high rate of profit retention is associated with a high rate of corporate investment, over the long term a strong propensity to retain profits is an indication of a strong accumulation drive and corporate dynamism. This dynamism and the division of profits between reinvestment and distribution to stakeholders vary considerably from one country to another, and play a crucial role in the overall pace of accumulation and industrialization.

Evidence on the respective role of corporate and household savings in inter-country differences in savings and investment performance is scarce due to the absence of comprehensive data. Table 4.1 presents, for those developing countries for which

data are available, the distribution of savings and investment between the household and non-financial corporate sectors over the period 1995–2003, which is the period for which cross-country coverage is the most comprehensive.

Although it is difficult to draw general conclusions from the relatively small sample in the table, the evidence suggests that high corporate fixed investment rates are in most cases associated with high corporate savings, while the association of corporate investment and household savings rates is much weaker. High corporate fixed investment in China, the Republic of Korea and Taiwan Province of China during the period 1995–2003 – as well as during the

Chart 4.1

CHINA: SHARES OF SAVINGS BY SECTOR IN TOTAL SAVINGS, 1992–2004

(Per cent)

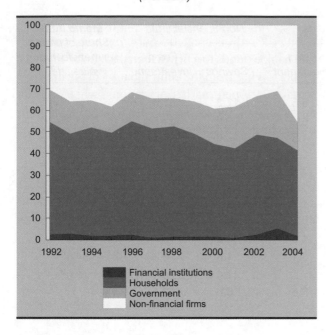

Source: UNCTAD secretariat calculations, based on *China Statistical Yearbook*, various issues.

rapid catch-up periods of Japan in the 1960s and of the Republic of Korea and Taiwan Province of China in the 1980s – was associated with considerably higher corporate savings rates than those found in most of the other countries. While household savings rates were also higher, the differences with the other countries are less striking than with corporate savings, in particular if China is excluded. By contrast, the relatively high household savings rates in Egypt and the Islamic Republic of Iran were not accompanied by high corporate savings rates, nor were they associated with high corporate investment rates. It is also noteworthy that relatively high corporate savings rates in some of the Latin American countries have not translated into similarly high rates of corporate fixed investment. This may indicate a tendency in these countries to spend capital income on consumption or portfolio investment rather than on fixed investment.

Table 4.1 also shows that variations in the importance of corporate savings do not fully reflect variations in the share of profits in value added.

Hence, factors other than the propensity to save from profits must play an important role in determining the extent to which corporate profits are retained for investment. Such factors include the burden of corporate taxation and depreciation allowances.

China's sectoral savings and investment pattern stands out for at least two reasons. First, its corporate investment ratio significantly exceeds that of other countries. Moreover, while China's corporate savings rate is also very high, its household savings rate is even higher. This may give the impression that the country's high corporate investment depends on high household savings, which in turn result from high precautionary savings by urban households owing to China's imperfect social security system, the substantial rise in educational expenditure and uncertainty about future income developments (see, for example, Chamon and Prasad, 2007).[2] However, the contribution of households to national savings has declined, from over 50 per cent during most of the 1990s to slightly under 40 per cent in 2004 (chart 4.1). On the other hand, the savings contributions of non-financial corporations and the Government have increased since the mid-1990s, and the business sector became the most important source of national savings in 2004. Estimates for the period since 2004 (not reflected in chart 4.1) suggest that the contribution of non-financial corporations to China's total national savings has continued to exceed that of the household sector (Barnett and Brooks, 2006; Yu, 2008). This increase has been due to a combination of greater profitability of Chinese enterprises, particularly State-owned enterprises, and the tightening of monetary policy, which reduced the availability of bank loans (Barnett and Brooks, 2006; He and Cao, 2007).

2. External financing of corporate investments

External financing of corporate investment is usually provided by financial intermediaries, notably banks. Financial intermediaries may facilitate transactions of financial instruments without modifying their terms of maturity and remuneration, and without buying or issuing financial assets themselves. In this sense, they constitute "capital markets" and their operations are called "direct finance". On the other hand, financial institutions – and particularly banks

– can de-link the terms of the financial assets bought by borrowers from those of the liabilities incurred by lenders. Banks typically incur short- and medium-term liabilities and distribute longer term loans. These classical bank operations, where contractual relations are between the bank and the depositors, on the one hand, and the bank and the borrowers on the other, are called "indirect finance".

The predominance of "direct" or "indirect" finance may have macroeconomic consequences and shape some aspects of the economic process. The lack of term transformation in direct finance leaves bond and equity holders with long-term financial assets, meaning that they must sell them in capital markets if they need liquidity. This can lead to price instability in these markets, which are exposed to boom-and-bust episodes. On the other hand, indirect finance exposes the commercial banks to liquidity risks (i.e. they may lose deposits without being able to recover long-term loans), which may pose a dilemma for the central bank: it could finance ailing banks, which requires the creation of money and might encourage moral hazard, or risk a contagion of financial distress, which might change a confined liquidity problem into a systemic solvency crisis. Another important aspect is that bank financing tends to create durable relations between banks and firms, leading to long-term partnerships that can influence corporate strategies and governance.[5]

The role of banks – both public and private – in sourcing productive investment goes beyond their advantage of being large-scale, which makes them more efficient than private households in maturity transformation and savings intermediation, and their informational advantage, which makes them more efficient than stock markets in addressing information asymmetries between insiders and outsiders. Credit creation by banks through lending to firms in support of productive economic activity plays an important role, particularly in countries with a bank-based financial system that is characterized by relationship or house banking. According to Minsky (1982), it is impossible for a firm to coordinate cash inflows and outflows in a way which ensures that outflows never exceed inflows. From that perspective, credit

creation is fundamental because it allows firms to invest without previous savings.

Credit creation by the banking system is particularly important for enterprises, especially new enterprises, that are heavily dependent on borrowing to meet their need for fixed investment and working capital.[4] Credit is created *ex nihilo* when a commercial bank extends to a firm a loan that can be financed by borrowing from the central bank via the discount window or open market operations, which implies an increase in the money supply. The nominal value of the firm's expansion of productive capacity and production of additional goods and services, for which the additional credit was used, increases aggregate income and creates the real economy counterpart to an increase in the money supply. The firm's larger cash inflow allows the loan to be paid back. The increase in corporate profits and household savings resulting from these additional activities on the real side of the economy lead to an *ex post* balancing of aggregate investments and savings.

> In addition to retained profits, credit creation in the banking system plays an important role in financing productive investment.

This process of credit creation can be inflationary if it runs up against resource constraints; for example if the rate of credit expansion exceeds the economy's rate of potential output growth. But the risk of this happening will be limited when credit creation increases real output by putting previously underutilized or unutilized production factors to productive use, or by increasing the productivity of production inputs.

Several factors can impede this process of credit creation through controlled monetary expansion. First, a firm may not have the kind of collateral that a commercial bank requires to grant a loan: for instance, the bank may not be willing to accept the collateral the firm is able to offer, or property rights may not be guaranteed, which could make a potential collateral an actual one. Second, the amount of credit (and of money issued) cannot exceed specific limits, which are determined by the ability of the bank to receive deposits, its access to other banks' financing (including that of the central bank) and financial regulations. Moreover, the ability of banks to create credit does not preclude the need for generating savings in the future, since the borrower must reimburse the credit. But in this case the causal relationship between savings, investment and credit is the opposite of that assumed by conventional theory: bank credit finances investment, which, if successful, generates savings (profits), which in turn are used to reimburse the loan.

Third, the central bank will not be able to pursue an independent monetary policy and increase the supply of base money if the economy is officially "dollarized" (i.e. uses a foreign currency as sole legal tender). Furthermore, it will be greatly limited if it has a currency board, which allows its central bank to expand the supply of domestic base money only to the extent that it is backed by foreign exchange reserves. Fourth, the central bank will also not be able to fully accommodate demand for credit to finance investment if it pursues a fixed nominal exchange-rate target and uses money supply or interest-rate policies to attain this objective.

Contrary to private commercial banks, public and development banks have a development objective: their loan analysis takes account of the economic and social development impact of an investment project in addition to its financial return. Public and development banks provide finance for investment projects that would typically be judged too risky by a private bank, either because full recovery of the cost of investment is a long-term process, such as from infrastructure investment, or because investment is carried out by small and/or innovative enterprises that aim to produce new products or apply new production processes. The developmental role of public banks implies that their activities tend to be concentrated in areas characterized by information asymmetries and intangible assets. Hence, public banks should not be expected to have the same degree of profitability as private commercial banks. Indeed, disproportionate pressure for profitability would cause managers of public banks to deviate from their developmental mandate (Levy Yeyati, Micco and Panizza, 2007).[5] Some of the projects that finance innovative investment will necessarily be a commercial failure for the very reason that it is only by undertaking such projects that their profitability – or lack of it – will

be discovered.[6] Hence, in order to act as a source of public risk capital, an optimal strategy of a development bank would be to minimize the costs of mistakes when they occur, rather than minimizing the risks of making such mistakes.

Another aspect of the development objective of State-owned and development banks has to do with coordination of investment projects. Investment can fail to be profitable unless there is simultaneous investment in upstream and downstream activities, particularly if such activities are not tradable or require geographic proximity. Physical infrastructure is a prime example. But a similar argument applies to the availability of appropriate production inputs (i.e. appropriately skilled labour as well as physical inputs that match a country's level of technology) or to the presence of a buyer of a firm's production.

In this sense, a major problem for entrepreneurs, who act as independent agents and only in their self-interest, is how to coordinate investment in a way that enables them to mutually benefit from upstream and downstream linkages. Where such mutual benefits occur, the economy-wide impact of an investment project exceeds its private profitability. Hence it is likely that a bank acting in the interest of national economic development as a whole (i.e. a public or development bank) will have an advantage in financing investments, the profitability of which depends strongly on complementary investment. This was the role played by development banks in Japan, the Republic of Korea and Taiwan Province of China (see, for example, Khan, 2004).

> Public banks that play a developmental role should not be expected to have the same profitability as private commercial banks.

National development banks often suffer from underfunding, particularly when they lack access to resources through client and government deposits. This is one of the reasons why their loan disbursements are often made in association with private banks. For example, over the past few years, Brazil's development bank, Banco do Desenvolvimento de Todos os Brasileiros (BNDES), has made about half of its loans in association with private commercial banks.[7] This kind of syndicated loan allows the development bank to invest in more projects and diversify its project-related risk. At the same time, involving another bank offers the benefit of a second opinion on the viability of the investment opportunity thereby reducing the risk of funding bad projects.

The experience of China's State-owned banks has been less successful, lending support to the argument that in the absence of a complementary institutional set-up, State-owned banks may not allocate credit optimally. Lending decisions based on political and other non-economic reasons caused non-performing loans of the four largest State-owned banks to become a serious problem for China's banking system during the 1990s. In recent years, the Chinese Government has taken various measures to resolve this problem.[8] According to official statistics, non-performing loans have fallen both in value and as a percentage of total loans[9] despite the emergence of new non-performing loans (Allen, Qian and Qian 2008).

In most developing and transition economies, financial intermediation remains concentrated in banks. However, it is increasingly recognized that well-functioning local bond markets can make a significant contribution to financial intermediation.[10] The public sector has had a particular interest in developing local bond markets, because government bond markets help to fund budget deficits in a non-inflationary way and also sterilize large capital inflows. Moreover, local bond markets provide private borrowers with access to long-term finance, in particular for investment in construction and infrastructure development. To the extent that domestic banks offer mostly short-term loans, the absence of a functioning domestic bond market will force enterprises to finance long-term investments out of short-term debt. This can result in their accumulating maturity mismatches in their balance sheets, or it can lead them to source more of their investment funding from international markets, with the risk of accumulating currency mismatches. Both these factors cause greater financial fragility. Indeed, their combination was at the root of the financial crisis in East Asia.

Equity markets have come to play a significant role in some more advanced developing and transition economies, particularly those that have undertaken extensive privatization. The importance of equity markets in a financial system is often gauged by the value of stock market capitalization. However, such capitalization might reveal the market value of one type of financial asset, but it tells very little about the financial flows obtained through equity issues during a given period. For instance, stock capitalization will increase with rising equity market prices without generating any new financing. It is true that the existence of large stock markets and relatively high share prices provide a favourable framework for issuing new shares, but this does not necessarily happen: firms' owners may be reluctant to open their capital to new investors, as this may weaken their control over the company. In other words, stock capitalization tells more about the structure of financial portfolios than about investment financing. What is relevant for investment financing is the amount of new equity issues in stock markets, as discussed below.

3. Investment finance and information asymmetries

In making their decisions on how to finance investment, entrepreneurs have a well-grounded microeconomic rationale not to consider different sources of investment financing as perfect substitutes.[11] The so-called "pecking order theory" of capital structure postulates the relevance of specific forms of investment finance for investment and production decisions. It suggests that the choice of capital structure depends on financial factors (e.g. the availability of internal finance, access to new debt or equity finance, and the functioning of particular credit markets) and a firm's characteristics (e.g. the firm's investment opportunities, its profitability and its size). On this view, firms generally follow a hierarchy in financing real investment, with a preference for internal over external finance, and for debt over equity. Highly profitable firms might be able to finance their growth by using retained earnings and by maintaining a constant debt ratio. By contrast, firms that are less, or not yet, profitable are forced to resort to external financing. Accordingly, changes in a firm's debt ratio are driven by its need for external funds, which in turn is determined by the extent to which investment opportunities exceed internally generated funds (Myers and Majluf, 1984; Fazzari, Hubbard and Petersen, 1988).[12]

According to the pecking order theory, a firm prefers internal sources (i.e. internal cash flow stemming from depreciation and retained earnings) because they allow it to safeguard the manager's insider information on the value of the firm's existing assets and the quality of its investment opportunities. Asymmetric information makes it very costly, or even impossible, for providers of external finance to fully assess the quality of a firm's assets and its investment opportunities.[13] Moreover, internal finance avoids agency costs (i.e. costs associated with mitigating a potential conflict of interest between the firm's management and providers of external finance).

Information asymmetry is also the reason why debt financing is preferable to issuing equity, according to the pecking order theory of capital structure. The degree of information asymmetry, and hence the agency cost, is relatively lower for debt than for equity finance. This is because debt financing, such as through bank loans, allows screening and monitoring of investment projects and their execution directly at the level of the firm. Banks can demand collateral, and, in events of financial distress, debt generally has the prior claim on assets and earnings, while equity has the residual claim. Seniority of claims of various kinds in general is an important factor in external financing decisions by financiers.

Moreover, capital markets may assume that an enterprise issues equity only when it considers its existing assets to be overvalued. They also tend to view the firm's resort to equity financing as an indication that it is unable to obtain other financing because its investment opportunities are extremely risky, or as an indication that the enterprise's debt ratio is already at a level that raises serious concern about upcoming financial distress (i.e. difficulties in meeting debt service obligations).[14] As a result, for a firm that is seeking financing for investment, the conditions attached to issuing equity will tend to be worse than those associated with debt financing.

A further reason for preferring debt to equity is that equity financing exposes a firm to the risk of a takeover, especially when financial markets undervalue the firm's assets.[15] The pricing process on stock markets may work well in terms of information arbitrage efficiency, or financial arbitrage, which ensures that all stock market participants have immediate access to all new information concerning a

firm's shares so that no participant can make a profit on such public information. However, this pricing process may not work so well in terms of fundamental valuation efficiency, which would ensure that share prices accurately reflect a firm's fundamentals (i.e. its long-term expected profitability) (Kregel and Burlamaqui, 2006).

Firms in developing countries often face different problems from those in developed countries in sourcing finance for their investment projects. Financing needs may frequently exceed the availability of internal finance, particularly when technological upgrading and new product development require a fast turnover of capital equipment investment. According to Singh (1997), this was the case for many firms in East Asia, which had to use both internal and external resources to finance their investments and expand their world market shares.

> The financing needs of firms in developing countries frequently exceed the availability of internal finance ...

Industrialization and economic catch-up generally require the application of novel techniques (i.e. novel for the respective economy) for producing new products or using new processes. Traditionally, large firms and business conglomerates were considered to have an advantage in driving industrialization in sectors that required large-scale, heavy capital investment, prior manufacturing experience and the coordination of investment activities across a number of industries (Amsden, 2001). However, over the past few years increasing importance has been given to the use of information and communication technologies (ICTs) as an important condition for achieving productivity growth. This has resulted in a growing emphasis on the role of new and often small firms in the application of novel techniques.

New firms, as well as particularly innovative firms whose projects may be deemed excessively risky by outsiders, are not likely to have the possibility to resort to internal finance or to be able to rapidly generate sufficient cash flows. In these cases, information asymmetries are particularly pronounced because there is no track record of either the entrepreneurial skills of the manager or the profitability of the innovative enterprise; moreover, information about the firm's previous engagement in non-innovative activities may not be of much help. Innovative firms are likely to encounter enormous difficulties in procuring bank credit because the only collateral they may be able to provide will be in the form of intangible assets, which are partly embedded in human capital and generally very specific to the particular firms in which they reside (Hall, 2002). Therefore potential sources of outside finance cannot easily distinguish between high- and low-value opportunities. While the innovator could convey all the information about the innovative investment project to potential outside sources, this would involve disclosure of insider information, which would expose the firm to imitation and severely diminish the firm's ability to appropriate the returns on its investment. On the other hand, banks will be reluctant to finance an initial investment that could make productive investment and productivity gains possible if they are unable to appropriate a share of the productivity gains commensurate with the banks' earlier risk-taking.[16] This may create a situation where every bank waits for others to move first so that they can reap the benefits of other banks' revelation of information about the capability of the entrepreneur to undertake profitable investment (Emran and Stiglitz, 2007).[17]

In such a situation, informal financing from the entrepreneur's family or friends can be an important source of risk capital in the early stages of an innovative project when the need for financial resources is limited.[18] But when this need strongly increases, informal financing will no longer suffice and the project may try to access venture capital.[19] Venture capital is equity or equity-linked investment finance in young, privately held companies, where the investor is a financial intermediary that collects financing from a group of investors (e.g. banks, pension funds, insurance companies and foundations).[20] Venture capitalists may be considered specialists in the accumulation of information on balance sheet positions and on investment projects of firms with a high growth potential. Since venture capitalists often also possess technical knowledge, they suffer less from information asymmetry than a provider of traditional bank loans or equity capital. Venture

... particularly when technological upgrading and new product development require a frequent renewal of capital equipment.

capitalists often lend their expertise to the firms in exchange for part of the value that the firms generate. Their technical knowledge and experience also enable them to perform non-financial advisory or managerial functions, which permit a better assessment of the industrial and commercial viability of an investment project. These non-financial functions may actually prove to be more important than their mere financial contribution, because it helps manage the downside risks and maximize the return from a given investment (Lerner, 1995). Since the venture capitalist usually disinvests after some time, venture capital may be best considered a hybrid form of debt and equity finance (Hall, 2002). This means that an innovative enterprise is likely to follow a slightly different hierarchy in the pecking order of capital structure and, as far as external finance is concerned, resort to bank financing only after obtaining resources from venture capitalists.[21]

However, the venture capital solution to financing investment has its limitations, particularly in developing countries, because there must be an active stock market to provide an exit strategy for venture capitalists typically through an initial public offering in which the enterprise issues shares to the public. This would also allow them to move on to financing other enterprises (Hall, 2002).[22] Moreover, in order to limit the number of partners in a firm, venture capitalists need to invest a certain minimum amount. This amount may exceed the means at the disposal of most potential venture capitalists in developing countries. Developing countries have traditionally used public sector banks, including national development banks, to cover gaps in access to investment finance.[23] Amsden (2001), for example, provides a detailed account of the role played by national development banks in many late industrializing economies.[24] As a result of a large share of non-performing loans in their liabilities, several public and national development banks were dismantled in many countries as part of financial reforms in the 1990s. However, more recently, there has been renewed interest in their usefulness as an instrument in development strategies.

C. Financial reforms in developing and transition economies

Until the 1980s, government intervention in the financial sector was widespread in developed and developing countries alike. The main objective was to support industrialization, post-war reconstruction and development. In many developing countries these objectives were pursued through the provision of low-cost finance to selected sectors and activities by means of controlling interest rates and patterns of lending. Regulation of banking activities, government support for cooperative banking networks, the establishment of specialized financial intermediaries, and direct State ownership of commercial and development banks were key elements of financial policies. Moreover, the degree of openness to international financial transactions and the entry of foreign banks were restricted.

> Development policy advice emphasized the problems associated with interventionism and the merits of laissez-faire.

These policies came under increasing criticism in the 1970s, and, in the aftermath of the debt crisis of the early 1980s, mainstream thinking and advice on development policy emphasized the problems connected with interventionism and the merits of laissez-faire, including in the financial sphere.[25] According to the theory of "financial repression" (Shaw, 1973; McKinnon, 1973) savings were depressed by low or negative real rates of return on financial assets. These low rates of return were believed to result in a highly inefficient use and allocation of the savings, encourage the holding of foreign-exchange-denominated assets and capital flight, and induce savers to hold unproductive physical assets instead of lending funds to entrepreneurs for productive investment.

Low interest rates and credit allocation directed by the State were also believed to reduce the quality of investment and increase its capital intensity, thereby distorting the pattern of production and trade. Lack of competition among banks was deemed responsible for inefficiencies in financial intermediation. Public intervention in the domestic financial system was also considered costly on account of the relatively large proportion of non-performing loans in the public banks (see, for example, World Bank, 1989: 2, 60).

It was expected that removing ceilings on interest rates by encouraging savings and attracting resources to the banking system would lead to higher investment and growth. By leaving credit allocation to market forces, only the projects that showed greater profitability than the market interest rate would be financed. Market segmentation between a formal market with abnormally low costs for a group of privileged borrowers and an informal, expensive one for the rest was expected to end. The external component of financial deregulation consisted of opening up national financial markets to foreign banks with a view to increasing competition in the banking sector, and allowing free movement of capital to attract foreign savings.

The most radical financial reforms took place in Latin America. Notwithstanding the experience of the Southern Cone countries,[26] where early reforms in the late 1970 and early 1980s had ended in currency and banking crises, unregulated credit allocation and free interest rates became the rule in the region. The capital account was opened up in most countries, with the partial exceptions of Chile and Colombia, and in the 1990s, foreign banks were increasingly allowed to expand their activities. In Mexico, commercial banks were re-privatized in 1991–1992, 10 years after their nationalization in the midst of the debt crisis, and the number of private banks rose from 18 to 37 within a short period of time.

Several Latin American countries and countries with economies in transition also tried to accelerate development of their securities markets, which were seen as a possible source of long-term financing largely free from government intervention. In many countries, securities and exchange commissions were created, the regulatory and supervisory framework for securities trading was improved, and clearance and settlement systems enhanced (Quispe-Agnoli and Vilán, 2008: 16). These reforms took place in an environment that was conducive to the development of capital markets. Stock prices rose fast in several countries as a result of increasing foreign portfolio investments, and external government debt in the form of bank loans was exchanged for securities under the Brady Plan.

Another key element in capital market development was the reform of the pension scheme, in which the public pay-as-you-go system was complemented or substituted by a privately managed funding system. In the new system, contributions were accumulated in personal funds that would be administrated by specialized institutions. These long-term forced savings could be invested in different financial assets, including bank deposits, equities and bonds. While the primary objective of pension reforms was to strengthen the pension system, it was also supposed to "increase long-term saving, capital market deepening and growth" (World Bank, 1994: 23 and 254).[27]

> Removing ceilings on interest rates was expected to attract resources to the banking system and increase investment.

> Many African countries undertook financial reforms in an attempt to overcome crises related to historically low commodity prices.

Financial reforms similar to those in Latin America were also undertaken in other regions. Many African countries undertook such reforms in an attempt to overcome a crisis related to a substantial worsening of their terms of trade and historically low prices for primary commodities. This situation was exacerbated by the lack of diversification and structural change, and most of the countries in the region were cut off from private capital flows. As a consequence of their need for assistance from the international financial institutions for financing their external deficits, many African countries undertook far-reaching trade and financial liberalization as part of structural adjustment programmes (Brownbridge and Harvey, 1998).

Distinct from Latin America, financial liberalization in East and South-East Asia was not a response to financial and macroeconomic crises; on the contrary, it followed many years of sustained growth and industrialization, driven by high rates of capital formation. Strategic State intervention in the financial system, including directed credit and interest subsidization, played an important role in the successful catch-up process of several countries. In the Republic of Korea, banks were gradually privatized from 1981 onwards, while the State retained ownership of development banks and specialized banks. Control over interest rates and credit allocation was gradually relaxed (Amsden and Euh, 1990). Financial liberalization accelerated from 1993 onwards, including a departure from the post-war practice of control over private external borrowing.[28]

The second-tier newly industrializing economies (NIEs) carried financial liberalization even further. In Indonesia, the central bank gave up direct control over credit allocation and interest rates in the early 1980s. Liberalization of market entry in 1988 led to a rise in the number of private and foreign banks and to a sharp increase in their lending (Batunanggar, 2002). In Thailand, financial liberalization advanced rapidly in the early 1990s as interest rate ceilings were lifted and foreign exchange transactions liberalized. Openness to capital transactions was further extended with the creation in 1993 of the Bangkok International Banking Facility (BIBF), as part of a bid to promote Thailand as a regional financial centre, and access of domestic firms to external loans was to be facilitated (Khan, 2004: 10–13). The development of bond and equity markets in the NIEs was pursued through measures to strengthen the institutional framework, such as the creation of supervisory entities, clearing and settlement processes, and information mechanisms. More recently, several countries have sought to harmonize such institutions and regulations within the region in order to create an integrated regional bond market (Eichengreen, Borensztein and Panizza, 2006; *TDR 2007,* chapter V).

> Financial liberalization in East and South-East Asia followed many years of sustained growth and industrialization ...

In China financial reforms advanced more slowly. Until the early 1980s, the People's Bank of China acted both as a central bank and a commercial bank. The first step in financial reforms was the transfer of its commercial bank functions to four banks, which remained under State ownership but each specialized in lending to specific non-financial sectors, namely construction, agriculture, industry and commerce. In addition, a number of regional banks, rural credit cooperatives, urban credit cooperatives and trust and investment corporations were created (Allen, Qian and Qian, 2008). A bond market started operating in 1981, but to date it has not yet assumed a major role in the financing of the private corporate sector. The stock exchanges created at the beginning of the 1990s have been quite volatile and segmented, and remain less important for business and investment financing than company profits and bank loans.

> ... that had been supported in several countries by strategic State intervention in the financial system.

With the exception of Turkey, financial reforms in West Asian countries were pursued more cautiously and gradually, and several countries only partially opened up their banking systems to private and foreign banks.[29] In parallel, since the late 1970s several West Asian and other Islamic countries

developed Islamic banking.[30] This aims to apply *sharia* principles in the financial sphere, which forbid the payment of interest from borrowers to lenders; depositors receive a share of the banks' profits, while borrowers pay a share of the estimated future profits from the activities being financed, instead of making an interest payment.[31] In addition, borrowers can be charged different transaction fees.

As in China, financial reform in the transition economies was part of a broader change in the economic system from central planning to market-determined resource allocation. As a first step, most transition economies created a two-tier banking system comprising a central bank and newly established commercial banks. In the Russian Federation, in the 1990s hundreds of new private domestic banks started to operate, and by 1997 domestically owned private banks accounted for more than 50 per cent of total bank assets. Some of the largest banks were part of large industrial groups, and most of their business was conducted within these groups (Aslund, 1996; Bonin and Wachtel, 2004). In the Central Asian transition economies, the financial system continued to be dominated by State-owned banks which assumed the functions of the former Soviet financial institutions, from which they mostly also inherited a portfolio of badly performing loans. Banking regulation was almost non-existent, and a large number of banks remained small and undercapitalized (Bonin and Wachtel, 2002). Financial reforms included liberalization of interest rates and opening up of the capital account. In most of the transition economies, State-owned financial institutions lost importance with progressive privatization in the course of the 1990s, while the activities of foreign banks and some domestic private banks grew rapidly.

D. Reform outcomes and financial market patterns

1. Financial crises and restructuring of the banking sector

In all but a few cases, financial reform in emerging markets was followed by a crash, while the objective of improving the conditions for investment financing was rarely attained. This was partly because it was often undertaken when financial markets had been weakened as result of economic stagnation and instability. It was also because deregulation of interest rates and financial activity was often not accompanied by sufficiently strengthened prudential regulation and supervision, leaving scope for increasing speculation and excessive risk-taking and irregularities.

The typical sequence of the effects of financial reform was that, during an initial phase in which financial activities expanded rapidly, the system became increasingly vulnerable to shocks from international capital markets, and domestic borrowers became over-indebted. When this ended in banking and currency crises, substantial government intervention was needed to mitigate the impact of the crisis on the real economy and to rescue and restructure the financial system. The ways in which these crises were handled shaped the financial systems of the countries concerned as much as the initial reform, especially in the emerging-market economies. Moreover, in many countries the experience also led to a rethinking of macroeconomic strategies from the late 1990s onwards, and a shift away from a reliance on external financing as a means to accelerate growth.

> Credit allocation changed considerably, but it rarely favoured productive investment.

The immediate effect of financial liberalization in emerging-market economies was a rise in interest rates and an increase in the number of banks and other financial institutions. Domestic credit expanded rapidly, but often without an adequate evaluation of risks. In countries where deregulation of the domestic financial market was coupled with liberalization of the capital account, as was frequently the case, this process was fuelled by a rapid increase in capital inflows that were attracted by the possibility of short-term gains from higher interest rates. In this process, the risks arising from the exposure of borrowers to exchange-rate devaluation were often underestimated.

During this phase, credit allocation changed considerably, depending on the particularities of each country, but it rarely favoured higher productive investment. In most Latin American countries, credit for consumption purposes increased much faster than investment credit, as rising interest rates discouraged productive investment. At the same time, an appreciation of the real exchange rate caused a widening of the current-account deficit in a period of low growth of domestic output. In East and South-East Asia, banks often extended their credits to the conglomerates or business groups of which they were a part. This contributed to overinvestment in industry, as in Malaysia and the Republic of Korea, or fuelled a construction boom, as in Thailand and Indonesia (Pangestu, 2003: 4–5; Khan 2004: 37–40).

High financing costs also increased the debt service burden of domestic debtors, so that many of them became over-indebted and evolved into "Ponzi" financing schemes (i.e. borrowing in order to pay interest on the outstanding debt). This led to a significant rise in non-performing loans, and currency mismatches in the balance sheets of financial institutions became more frequent. Once the financial weaknesses became evident and deposits were withdrawn, banks faced increasing liquidity problems and had to cut lending – even to creditworthy borrowers – thereby adding to the financial distress in the non-financial sector and exacerbating the economic downturn. In the process, the space for growth-oriented monetary policy shrank, as central banks frequently had to raise interest rates to avoid currency devaluation with a view to restoring confidence among international investors.

Although financial crises were triggered by different factors in individual countries, they were almost always the outcome of changes in key variables in international capital markets, combined with increasing current-account deficits. These deficits were brought about by a sharp loss of competitiveness of domestic producers, which in turn was largely the result of an appreciation in the real exchange rate. According to standard financing gap models, the ensuing increase in the external deficit could have been interpreted as evidence of the growing availability of foreign savings to boost investment. However, international investors sooner or later realized that it was a sign of weakness, and this perception led to a sudden halt in capital inflows and sharp currency devaluations that caused an immediate surge in debt service obligations. While high interest rates, restrictive fiscal policies – frequently backed by IMF stabilization programmes – and sharply reduced domestic demand led to recession, devaluation of the exchange rate laid the ground for a reversal of the current-account balance and subsequent recovery (see also chapter III, section D).

In most emerging-market economies that underwent such a cycle, governments and central banks had little choice but to intervene to rescue financial institutions and to restructure the financial system, generally at considerable fiscal cost. In Mexico, for example, the central bank sought to rescue the banking system through liquidity financing and the purchase of low-quality loans, intervening in 15 banks between 1994 and 2000. In Argentina, in connection with the banking crisis in 1995, the central bank resumed its role as lender of last resort[32] and established two trust funds to support the recapitalization or the transfer of ailing private banks and to finance the privatization of banks owned by provincial governments (Calcagno, 1997: 78–79).

Similarly, in Brazil in 1995, the Government began to take over the bad loans of private banks and financed their acquisition by other banks. Moreover, publicly owned banks, many of which where unable to recover loans provided to the State, were restructured and 12 of them were privatized between 1997 and 2005 (Freitas, 2007). Large central government expenditures for rescuing and restructuring banks, estimated at around 11 per cent of 1998 GDP, were a major factor contributing to the growth of the domestic public debt. However, this early intervention to address the solvency problems in the banking sector probably helped prevent a more dramatic banking crisis when a currency crisis occurred in 1999. This crisis was the result of an abrupt halt in capital inflows due to contagion from the East Asian financial crisis of the late 1990s and to a widening current-account deficit (Sáinz and Calcagno, 1999: 28).

In the Republic of Korea, the cost of government intervention in the form of purchases of non-performing loans, repayments on bank deposits and recapitalization of domestic financial institutions amounted to one quarter of the average annual GDP in the period 1997–2007 (Bank of Korea, 2007).[33] Many private banks closed down and others merged, which increased the market share of foreign and publicly owned banks: in 2006 the latters' share amounted to more than 40 per cent of total bank assets. Similarly, in Thailand, the public sector acquired bad loans, injected funds into the banking system and took control of ailing banks, some of which were subsequently privatized while others remained under State ownership. The share of public sector financial institutions in the financial market rose to 35 per cent

> Governments had to rescue financial institutions at considerable fiscal cost.

Table 4.2

MARKET SHARES OF BANKS BY OWNERSHIP, SELECTED ECONOMIES, 1994–2007

(Per cent in total bank assets)

	Public banks[a]			Private domestic banks			Foreign banks		
	1994–1995	2000–2001	2006–2007	1994–1995	2000–2001	2006–2007	1994–1995	2000–2001	2006–2007
Argentina	37.8	29.3	40.1	42.9	19.8	32.3	19.3	51.0	27.6
Azerbaijan	79.1	59.4	51.0[b]	..	36.1	42.9[b]	..	4.5	6.1[b]
Brazil	51.9	34.6	29.5	40.0	36.5	48.4	8.1	28.9	22.2
Georgia	58.4	0.0	0.0[b]	38.6	84.1	13.1[b]	3.0	15.9	86.9[b]
India[c]	83.8	76.9	69.2	8.9	15.7	23.4	7.3	7.4	7.4
Indonesia	..	52.8	45.3	..	38.8	45.3	..	8.4	9.4
Mexico	28.5[d]	25.2	14.2	60.3[d]	25.9	16.6	11.2[d]	49.0	69.3
Pakistan	92.0[e]	53.2	41.2	0.0[e]	30.3	47.1	8.0[e]	16.5	11.6
Republic of Korea[f]	31.1[d]	42.9	41.8	60.0[d]	43.0	26.6	8.9[d]	14.1	31.6
Serbia	94.4	79.5	14.9[b]	5.4	13.7	6.4[b]	0.2	6.9	78.7[b]
Thailand	12.8[g]	35.5	35.0	78.0[g]	49.3	50.5	9.2[g]	15.2	14.6
Turkey	..	44.7	31.9	..	49.6	55.7	..	5.7	12.4
Ukraine	13.5[d]	11.9	8.9[b]	78.3[d]	76.6	56.1[b]	8.2[d]	11.6	35.0[b]

Source: UNCTAD secretariat calculations, based on national sources; and European Bank for Reconstruction and Development, *Structural Change Indicators*.

a Public banks include: for Brazil, Caixa Econômica Federal; for India, State Bank of India and its associates and nationalized banks; for the Republic of Korea, specialized cooperative banks; for Thailand, specialized financial institutions; and for Mexico, they are development banks.
b 2006.
c Private domestic banks include regional rural banks.
d 1997.
e 1990.
f Foreign banks include the Shinhang Group, partly owned by domestic private capital.
g 1996.

by 2006. Meanwhile, financial restructuring also led to a drastic reduction in the activities of non-bank financial institutions and to a greater share of foreign banks in the financial system (table 4.2).[34]

In Indonesia, where by the end of 1997 almost half of total bank loans had become non-performing (Batunanggar 2002: 9), public resources provided to the banking sector for recapitalization and liquidity support amounted to around 50 per cent of one year's GDP by December of 2000.[35] Although the number of banks was drastically reduced, State intervention helped a number of big private and public banks to survive, so that the ownership structure in the banking system changed much less than in other countries (table 4.2).

Similarly in Turkey, where the number of banks had also increased rapidly after liberalization and deregulation of the financial system, the Government had to come to the rescue of the banking system when it was threatened by a financial crisis. In response to financial distress in both public and private banks resulting from a combination of capital outflows, interest rate increases and, eventually, currency devaluation, the Treasury provided State-owned banks with securities to cover their losses. It also supported the recapitalization of private banks, which, following their insolvency, were managed by the Saving Deposit Insurance Fund. Thus, overall, an amount equivalent to almost 25 per cent of GDP was injected into the banking system in early 2001 (BDDK, 2001).

China had experienced a currency crisis in the early 1990s, leading to a sharp devaluation of the real exchange rate, but it was not affected by the Asian financial crisis. Although the country did not suffer from an open banking crisis, its banking system accumulated a significant amount of non-performing loans as a result of imprudent lending by State-owned banks to State-owned enterprises. By the mid-1990s, non-performing loans represented, on conservative estimates, 25 per cent of all bank loans (Yu, 2008), requiring the Government to address solvency problems in the banking sector and to actively intervene in its restructuring. In this context, the central bank recapitalized the "big four" State-owned banks and created four asset-management companies, which were to acquire non-performing loans from the banks, restructure the over-indebted enterprises and then sell their shares in the stock market.[36] Smaller commercial banks and rural credit cooperatives could also exchange bad loans for securities issued by public entities, including the central bank. Once the solvability and profitability of the principal banks had been restored, they opened their capital to foreign investors, that were allowed to acquire minority stakes of up to 20 per cent. The aim was to bring governance and the performance of the local banks closer to international standards. Although financial reforms and restructuring have dramatically changed the financial structure in China, and created new agents and markets, its banking system remains dominated by State-owned banks, and the central bank continues to set benchmark interest rates for deposits and loans.

As in East Asia, the financial crisis in the Russian Federation was a combination of banking and currency crises, linked to excessive currency exposure and domestic lending that was funded by foreign borrowing and capital inflows. However, macroeconomic imbalances and structural

> Despite financial reforms, the banking system in China remains dominated by State-owned banks ...

> ... and the central bank continues to set benchmark interest rates for deposits and loans.

and institutional weaknesses played a much greater role in this country. Russian banks had financed their purchase of large amounts of treasury securities by borrowing in dollars, thus generating considerable arbitrage profits from the wide differential between Russian and foreign interest rates. When the Federal Government defaulted on its domestic debt obligations as a result of an erosion of its revenues, this, combined with a rise in domestic interest rates to defend the rouble in the wake of the Asian crisis, led to insolvency of many domestic banks. Here too, the banking sector underwent major restructuring following the crisis. The smaller banks were supported by the central bank with stabilization credits, and the Government encouraged mergers and acquisitions of insolvent banks by larger ones in order to secure the stability of the system (Bonin and Wachtel, 2002).

As a result of the rescue operations and restructuring, the banking sector in most developing and transition economies became more concentrated and the shares of foreign banks increased, particularly in Latin America (table 4.2). In Mexico, for example, foreign banks accounted for less than 0.5 per cent of all banking assets in 1993, but this share rose to 70 per cent by December 2007 (Banco de México, 2007). In Brazil, foreign banks increased their share in total assets from 7.5 per cent in 1994 to 30 per cent in 2001, but their participation has declined in recent years, following the acquisition of some foreign banks by domestic private banks. In Argentina, the influence and market share of foreign banks grew dramatically after the 1995 crisis, favoured by the currency board regime. By mid-1997, only one of the 10 largest private banks was still Argentine-owned. On the other hand, the number of public banks fell from 33 in 1994 to 12 in 2007, while cooperative banks almost completely disappeared. However, following the breakdown of the currency board system in 2001, foreign banks were no longer perceived to be safe havens, and their market share, which had exceeded 50 per cent in 2000, halved by 2007. In Brazil, the share of public banks also declined, but banks controlled by the Federal Government still retain a significant share in total banking activities (table 4.2). In the Russian Federation the number of banks fell from 2,029 in 1996 to 1,089 in 2006. Similar reforms that had led to a considerable reduction in the number of banks were also undertaken in other transition economies.[37] In the process, the role of foreign banks was greatly strengthened: by 2006, they controlled 12 per cent of total bank assets in the Russian Federation and 35 per cent in Ukraine, and significantly more in other transition economies.[38]

A number of African countries, too, were affected by severe banking crises in the 1980s and 1990s.[39] In the absence of adequate banking supervision and regulation, the crises in Africa were mostly triggered by strongly negative terms-of-trade shocks in the period 1985–1992, which led to recession and problems in servicing the external debt (Daumont, Le Gall and Leroux, 2004).[40] In the member States of the CFA franc zone (Communauté financière africaine), the negative impact of the adverse terms of trade were exacerbated by an appreciation of the CFA franc (Hoffmaister, Roldós and Wickham, 1997). These crises also resulted in high fiscal costs associated with rescue operations: they generally exceeded 10 per cent of GDP, and even reached 25 per cent in Côte d'Ivoire in the late 1980s. In Africa the response to these crises was typically not a reversal of previous liberal reforms but their continuation, and even acceleration, under structural adjustment programmes. In the process, the banking sector in most African countries underwent significant changes, especially with regard to ownership. Honohan and Beck (2007) estimate that today only 7 per cent of African banks are government-owned, compared with 12 per cent in other developing countries, and that about 45 per cent of the African banks are foreign-owned, compared with 30 per cent in other developing countries. Measured by their share in total assets, the weight of foreign banks is even stronger. Concentration in the African banking sector is also considerably higher than elsewhere. According to Honohan and Beck (2007: 41), the market share of the top three banks in the 22 countries for which data were available has averaged 73 per cent in recent years, compared with 60 per cent in the rest of the world. Thus financial sector liberalization in African countries has led to increasing concentration in their banking sector, associated with a declining number and weight of domestic private and public banks on the one hand, and an increasing dominance of foreign-owned banks on the other.

In general, despite heavy government involvement in the restructuring of the banking system and the greater role of foreign banks in most countries that liberalized and deregulated their financial sector, financing conditions have remained unfavourable for corporate and investment finance. Access to credit continues to be segmented and financing costs high, even though financial reforms were expected to introduce more competition and reduce the cost of credit.

2. Evolution of bank credit

Bank credit to the private sector as a share of GDP has increased since the early 1990s in all regions except Africa (table 4.3). It has been the highest in East and South-East Asia, although it fell in that region after the financial crisis in the late 1990s. In China, Malaysia, the Republic of Korea and Singapore loans to the private sector have exceeded 90 per cent of GDP (chart 4.2). They have been below 25 per cent of GDP only in a few low-income countries in

Table 4.3

BANK CLAIMS ON THE PRIVATE SECTOR IN DEVELOPING AND TRANSITION ECONOMIES, BY REGION, 1990–2007

(Median in per cent of GDP)

	1990–1992	1996–1998	2004–2007
South America	17.9	26.6	21.2
Central America	12.9	18.2	30.2
South Asia	14.0	21.8	28.4
East and South-East Asia	45.3	54.6	50.5
West Asia	27.3	33.5	35.4
Africa	12.8	9.8	12.3
Transition economies	..	5.6	22.9

Source: UNCTAD secretariat calculations, based on IMF, *International Financial Statistics* database.
Note: South America includes Mexico; Central America includes Dominican Republic and Haiti.

Chart 4.2

BANK CLAIMS ON THE PRIVATE AND PUBLIC SECTORS, SELECTED COUNTRIES, 1990–2007

(Per cent of GDP)

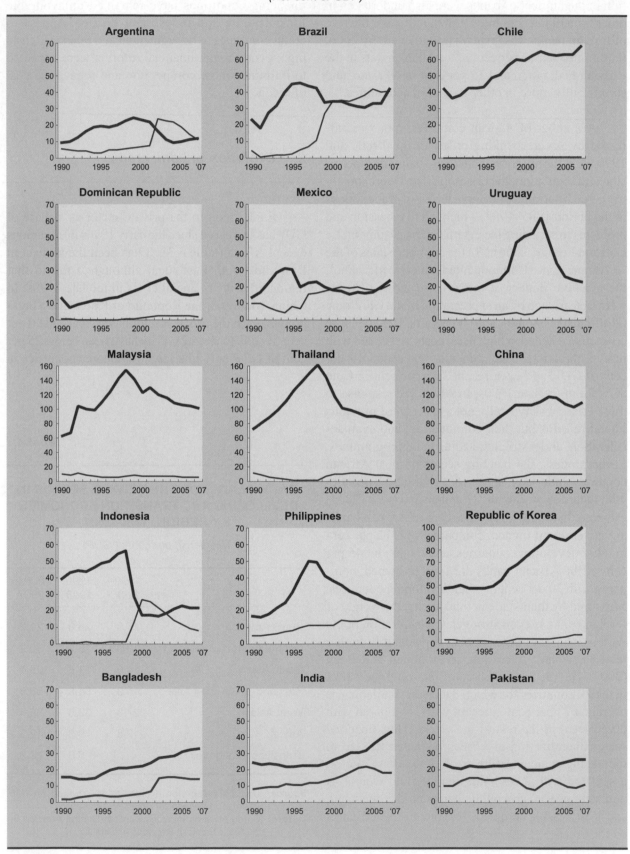

Chart 4.2 (concluded)

BANK CLAIMS ON THE PRIVATE AND PUBLIC SECTORS, SELECTED COUNTRIES, 1990–2007

(Per cent of GDP)

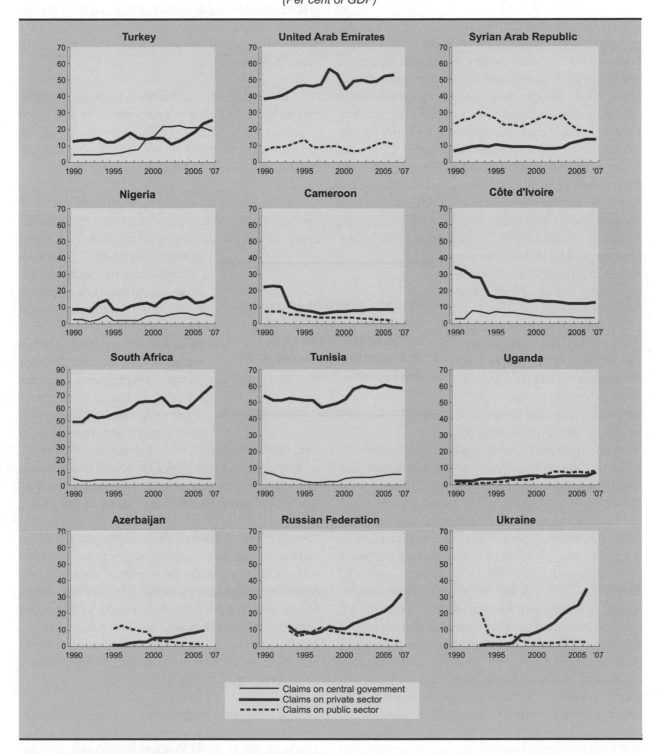

Source: UNCTAD secretariat calculations, based on IMF, *International Financial Statistics database*; and national sources.
Note: For China claims on private sector include claims on State-owned firms and the regional governments.

the region where the banking sector is very small, as well as in Indonesia and the Philippines, where bank credit has not recovered from the 1998 financial crisis.

In South and Central America, credit to the private sector was at low levels in the early 1990s.[41] It rose in the course of the last decade but, due to the banking crises (discussed in the previous subsection), credit growth could not be sustained. Many emerging-market economies in Latin America and East and South-East Asia followed a similar pattern during the 1990s, with bank financing of the private sector characterized by boom-and-bust cycles, the most notable exceptions being Chile, China and the Republic of Korea (chart 4.2). Banking crises in Mexico (1995), Indonesia, Malaysia, the Philippines, Thailand, Brazil (1999), Turkey, Argentina (2001), Uruguay (2002) and the Dominican Republic (2003) resulted in significant reductions in credit to the private sector. The same is true for Cameroon, Côte d'Ivoire and Benin (Daumont, Le Gall and Leroux, 2004). With the exception of Turkey, lending to the private sector has not fully recovered from the contraction in any of these countries. By contrast, in the South Asian and transition economies, bank lending to the private sector has followed a steady upward trend since the early 1990s.

> In many emerging-market economies, bank financing of the private sector was characterized by boom-and-bust cycles.

In African countries, the main challenges to the financial sector are perceived to be insufficient scale, a high degree of informality and weak governance (Honohan and Beck, 2007). The more advanced economies in North and Southern Africa (Algeria, Egypt, Morocco and Tunisia, as well as South Africa and Namibia), and the larger economies of East and West Africa (Kenya and Nigeria) have more developed and diversified financial sectors, including banks, insurance companies, pension funds and capital markets. The majority of countries in sub-Saharan Africa have no, or extremely thin, capital markets and few non-bank financial institutions, so that bank lending constitutes almost the only external source of investment finance for firms (see, for example, Senbet, 2008). The IMF estimates that out of a sample of 25 African countries for which data were available, in 10 countries banks have accounted for 90 per cent or more of the total assets of the financial system, and in 15 countries they have accounted for 70 per cent or more in recent years (Quintyn, 2008). Yet in Africa as a whole, bank credit to the private sector remains very limited, and in many countries it does not even reach 10 per cent of GDP. It is considerably higher than average in Namibia, Morocco, South Africa and Tunisia, as well as in some small island States.

In the transition economies, bank credit to the private sector has grown faster than in the developed countries since the mid-1990s, in parallel with the growing size of the private sector in these countries, but it is still relatively low.

In several countries, the decline in credit to the private sector as a percentage of GDP was accompanied by an expansion of credit to the central government (chart 4.2). Indeed, in most emerging-market economies the proportion of public securities in bank assets has been much higher than in economies with more mature financial markets. This is partly related to how governments have responded to the crisis: some of them took over bad loans from banks' assets and replaced them with public securities, as in Indonesia and Mexico, or they compensated banks for losses that resulted from the crises themselves, as in Argentina and Turkey.[42] The increasing share of claims on the public sector in the total assets of the banking system also stemmed from a credit crunch in the private sector and the simultaneous issuance of new public debt that was needed to cover the fiscal costs of the crisis, part of which was bought by banks. The fact that claims on the central government remained an important component of bank assets several years after the crises seems to reflect a more conservative lending behaviour on the part of the banks, with a tendency to prefer low-risk credit.

In many emerging-market economies there has been a strong tendency since the beginning of the 1990s for the share of loans to households for consumption and housing credits to rise at the expense of lending to the productive sectors, including manufacturing (table 4.4). This rapid expansion in loans to households is partly related to financial liberalization, which removed restrictions on consumer credit

Table 4.4

COMPOSITION OF BANK CLAIMS ON THE PRIVATE SECTOR IN SELECTED ECONOMIES, 1990, 2000 AND 2007

(Per cent of total)

	Primary sector			Manufacturing industry			Wholesale and retail trade			Households			Other private		
	1990[a]	2000	2007	1990[a]	2000	2007	1990[a]	2000	2007	1990[a]	2000	2007	1990[a]	2000	2007
Argentina	10.1	10.4	13.1	31.9	15.3	18.9	8.1	9.0	6.9	20.8	29.7	32.5	29.1	35.6	28.6
Brazil	11.3	8.8	9.9	26.8	27.9	23.1	10.7	10.3	10.6	35.8	38.0	39.8	15.4	15.0	16.6
Chile	14.8	6.6	5.3	17.1	11.1	6.1	19.8	12.0	11.1	18.9	29.9	36.6	29.4	40.4	40.9
Egypt	8.8	2.4	1.8	31.7	34.1	35.9	27.4	22.8	17.7	2.8	12.8	16.4	29.3	27.9	28.2
Gabon	21.1	13.6	..	8.7	1.1	..	15.3	17.6	..	15.4	33.8	..	39.5	33.9	..
India	12.1	11.0	12.5	45.0	42.3	27.6	13.9	15.6	9.9	9.3	11.2	23.3	19.7	19.9	26.7
Indonesia	8.3	10.0	8.2	29.7	40.8	20.5	21.9	16.9	21.7	9.8	15.3	28.3	30.3	17.0	21.3
Kuwait	0.4	1.7	0.4	4.9	6.1	5.3	19.0	15.0	9.4	26.4	36.1	35.2	49.3	41.1	49.7
Namibia[b]	..	9.7	6.7	..	5.4	1.8	..	4.8	4.1	..	44.1	54.9	..	36.0	32.5
Russian Federation	..	1.7	6.9	..	33.0	13.7	..	18.1	18.2	..	6.4	27.4	..	40.8	33.8
Thailand	7.2	3.1	1.9	25.1	28.7	25.2	28.3	20.1	16.3	10.6	11.1	30.4	28.8	37.0	26.2

Source: UNCTAD secretariat calculations, based on national Central Banks; and IMF, *Financial System Stability Assessments Country Report*, various years.
Note: Other private: construction, electricity, gas and water, and other services.
 a 1995 for Brazil, 1991 for Egypt, 1997 for Gabon and India, and 1996 for Indonesia.
 b Data correspond to 2001 and 2005.

Chart 4.3

AGRICULTURE: SHARE OF BANK LOANS, VALUE ADDED AND LABOUR FORCE IN TOTAL, SELECTED AFRICAN COUNTRIES

(Per cent)

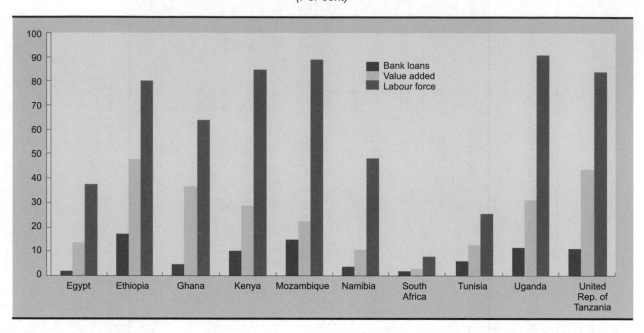

Source: UNCTAD secretariat calculations, based on national central banks; IMF, *Financial System Assessment Reports*, various; and *UNCTAD Handbook of Statistics* database.

Note: Data correspond to latest available year: 2002 for Kenya, Mozambique, Uganda and the United Republic of Tanzania; 2005 for Namibia, South Africa and Tunisia; 2006 for Egypt and Ethiopia; and 2007 for Ghana.

and reduced credit that had formerly been directed towards manufacturing and agriculture. Also, greater openness to foreign banks permitted the entry of lenders with well-developed expertise in consumer lending (IMF, 2006: 48, 60). Moreover, by increasing household loans, banks could expect to obtain higher revenues with lower risks. This paradox is related to the fact that consumers tend to be willing to pay high interest rates because they do not compare the credit cost to an expected rate of return of a project financed with the loan; at the same time, household loans are subject to lower default rates, and when losses occur, they tend to be smaller and more predictable than those arising from larger corporate loans (IMF, 2006: 47).

This development runs counter to the two main objectives of financial reforms: raising household savings and improving the allocation of credit to the most productive purposes. The IMF's *Global Financial Stability Report 2006* warned that the rapid expansion of household credit "can compound the

problems of excessive consumption, current account imbalances, and property boom-bust cycles. If credit is predominantly financed by external capital flows, it can heighten the vulnerability to sudden stops and financial crises" (IMF, 2006: 69).

The relative reduction of bank lending for the productive sectors makes it more difficult for these sectors to undertake the investments required to enhance their productivity and compete successfully in an increasingly open economic environment. In particular, bank financing of agriculture is very low in countries where it is probably needed the most: in a sample of African countries the share of the credit allowed for agriculture is systematically and significantly lower than the sector's contribution to GDP and employment (chart 4.3). On average, loans to agriculture constitute about 8 per cent of total bank credits in the sample of African economies, yet that sector generates one quarter of the total value added and 60 per cent of employment – and even up to 80 per cent in several sub-Saharan countries.

Table 4.5

SELECTED INDICATORS OF BANK FINANCING IN SELECTED REGIONS, 1995–2007

(Per cent)

	Real deposit rate (1)			Real lending rate (2)			Real interest rate spread (2) - (1)		
	1995–1997	1998–2002	2003–2007	1995–1997	1998–2002	2003–2007	1995–1997	1998–2002	2003–2007
Developed economies	0.5	1.4	0.4	6.2	5.7	4.0	5.7	4.3	3.5
Transition economies	-1.2	1.4	0.0	22.1	14.1	10.3	23.4	12.6	10.3
Developing economies *of which:*	0.8	2.4	-0.3	10.3	11.5	8.2	9.2	9.1	8.4
Africa *of which:*	-0.4	2.6	0.7	9.7	13.3	10.2	9.3	10.6	9.4
Sub-Saharan Africa, excl. South Africa	-1.0	2.3	0.6	10.3	13.9	10.7	10.1	11.6	10.0
Latin America *of which:*	0.9	3.3	-0.7	12.8	13.9	9.0	11.9	10.6	9.7
Caribbean	1.2	2.2	-0.2	8.8	9.6	6.7	7.6	7.4	7.0
Central America	-2.6	2.6	-2.9	7.8	13.2	9.3	10.4	10.6	12.2
South America	2.8	5.2	0.0	21.5	20.1	11.9	18.7	14.9	11.9
Asia *of which:*	1.8	1.2	-0.7	7.9	7.1	5.3	6.1	5.8	5.9
East and South-East Asia	3.2	0.8	-0.2	9.8	6.2	5.6	6.5	5.3	5.8
Memo item:									
Emerging economies in Asia	3.1	3.3	0.1	6.2	6.9	4.1	3.0	3.6	4.0
Other economies in Asia	1.1	0.1	-1.1	8.8	7.1	5.9	7.7	7.0	7.0

Source: UNCTAD secretariat calculations, based on IMF, *International Financial Statistics* database.

Present trends in credit allocation across sectors are consistent with some basic indicators of the banking system. Real lending rates in developing and transition economies are substantially higher than in developed countries, despite a declining trend in the past five years (box 4.1). High real lending rates discourage demand for credit in productive activities, which must compare the cost of financing with the expected profit of the activity to be financed. Households and the State generally do not rely on such a comparison.

Real lending rates are particularly high in South America, sub-Saharan Africa and in transition economies; they averaged about 10 per cent between 2003 and 2007. In Asia, these rates are, on average, half that level. The emerging-market economies in Asia tend to have lending rates below the regional average, whereas the low-income economies have lending rates above this average. High real lending rates are related to large spreads between lending and deposit rates, rather than to high real deposit rates, which, in developing and transition economies are slightly lower than the levels in developed countries (i.e. close to zero or slightly negative) (table 4.5). To some extent, larger spreads in Africa, Latin America and the transition economies may be related to the fact that unit costs of banking tend to be higher in countries with a lower ratio of loans to GDP. Spreads are lower in Asia and the Caribbean, where this ratio is higher. In Africa, in particular, large interest rate spreads are typically attributed to higher risk. However, high spreads are also related to high returns on assets in Africa, Latin America and the transition economies, meaning that the higher costs of banking do not absorb the entire spread. Moreover, the strong and increasing profitability of banks suggests that it is often the lack of effective competition – and not

Box 4.1

PATTERNS OF INTEREST RATES, INFLATION AND GROWTH

In the banking system of developed countries there is a stable relationship between different interest rates. The lowest rate is the one charged to banks by the central bank. This rate is normally 1–2.5 per cent higher than the rate of inflation, depending on the monetary policy stance. Deposit rates paid by banks can be slightly higher or lower than the central bank rate, depending on the overall liquidity situation as determined by the central bank and credit demand. The interest rate charged by the commercial banks for loans is higher by a relatively stable margin, which amounted to 2.3–3 per cent between 2000 and 2007 (see chart).

In real terms, all these rates remain close to the real growth rate of the economy. One of the most important conditions for successful development is that income growth of the different sectors, including the financial sector, cannot deviate permanently from the growth of value added of the economy as a whole.

In developing countries, on average the central bank rate is considerably higher than in developed countries, partly due to higher inflation rates of the former. Moreover, the margin between the central bank rate and commercial bank lending rates is also much greater and less stable. For the period 2000–2007, the average spread between the money market rate, taken as a proxy for the central bank rate, and the commercial bank lending rate in developing countries was 7.9 per cent, fluctuating between 6.3 and 9.4 per cent. In the transition economies the average spread was even higher but more stable.

Among the developing countries, both the average money-market rate and the spread vis-à-vis the commercial bank lending rates were the lowest in East, South-East and South Asia, at 4.7 and 3.8 per cent respectively. In real terms, lending rates in these subregions were, on average, higher than in the developed countries by only about one percentage point (5.4 compared to 4.3 per cent) despite much higher real growth rates than in the latter. This means that the domestic monetary conditions for growth, investment and jobs have been extremely favourable.

In the other developing and transition economies for which data are available the relationships between the different interest rates and the rates of inflation are dramatically distorted. Commercial bank lending rates have remained extremely high in Latin America and in the transition economies of South-East Europe and the Commonwealth of Independent States, although they have fallen since 2002. The average for the period 2005–2007 was more than 15 per cent in both regions in nominal terms, and in real terms it was 7.5 per cent for the transition economies and 9.3 per cent for Latin America. In Africa, the real lending rate was, on average, 8.2 per cent during this period. With real GDP growth in Africa and Latin America at around 6 and 5 per cent, respectively, and at about 7 per cent in the transition economies, such conditions are certainly prohibitive for many potential investors in fixed capital, in particular for small businesses and smallholder farmers. Under such conditions it is not surprising that the banks and other financial institutions are unwilling to provide sufficient affordable credit for risky fixed investment in machinery and equipment, and instead prefer to lend to the government and for less risky real estate activities.

High lending rates and the huge spreads between central bank rates and deposit rates, on the one hand, and commercial bank lending rates on the other are often explained by the high risk of bankruptcy and other problems with credit contracts. However, in an economy that is growing at 5 per cent in real terms the average firm can pay a real interest rate in the order of 10 per cent or more only with an increased risk of bankruptcy. If, as is the case in many countries, non-competitive banking systems charge such rates, frequent default should not come as a surprise.

Such a vicious circle of excessively high interest rates and a high risk of default call for more proactive financial policies. Governments can directly restrict the size of bank spreads through the kind of legislation that is used to stop usury in many developed countries. Moreover, public banks offering reasonable rates for private savers as well as for smaller private companies could directly compete with a non-competitive private banking system on a broad scale.

Box 4.1 (concluded)

LENDING RATES, MONEY MARKET RATES AND GDP GROWTH, 2000–2007

(Simple average, per cent)

Developed economies

Developing economies

East, South and South-East Asia

Latin America

Africa

Transition economies

Real GDP growth
Lending interest rate
Money market interest rate
Inflation

Source: UNCTAD secretariat calculations, based on *Thomson Datastream*; IMF, *International Financial Statistics* database; *UNCTAD Handbook of Statistics* database; and national sources.

Note: Data for periods with inflation rates larger than 100 per cent were excluded. Calculations are based on data for 71 countries: 23 developed economies, 38 developing economies and 10 transition economies in South-East Europe and the CIS. Developed economies exclude Eastern Europe and Baltic countries.

Table 4.6

NON-PERFORMING LOANS AND RETURN ON ASSETS, SELECTED REGIONS, 2000–2007

(Per cent)

	Share of non-performing loans in total loans		Return on assets	
	2000–2002	2003–2007	2000–2002	2003–2007
Developed economies	2.9	1.9	0.7	0.8
Transition economies	14.3	8.7	-0.3	2.3
Developing economies	14.2	8.6	1.0	2.0
of which:				
Africa	17.9	13.5	2.3	2.6
of which:				
Sub-Saharan Africa, excl. South Africa	19.5	13.3	2.8	3.1
Latin America	9.5	5.1	0.1	1.9
of which:				
Central America	6.2	5.4	1.5	1.9
South America	11.4	5.1	-0.8	1.8
Asia	17.4	9.9	0.9	1.4
of which:				
East and Southeast Asia	16.4	9.6	0.8	1.3
Memo item:				
Emerging economies in Asia	16.4	10.0	0.8	1.0
Other economies in Asia	19.4	10.4	1.0	1.6

Source: UNCTAD secretariat calculations, based on IMF, *Global Stability Report*, various issues.
   Note: Due to lack of data, the sample covers only 41 developing economies: 13 in Africa, 17 in Latin America and 11 in Asia.

merely higher risk and operating costs – that allows banks to charge relatively high real interest rates. [43]

As shown by recent experiences of crises, the search for high profitability through large spreads and lending rates presents risks for the banking system. It may have led to adverse selection of entrepreneurs (since only speculators or firms already in trouble borrow at very high interest rates) and an accumulation of bad loans in the banks' assets. Yet the banks needed to be highly profitable to reduce the remaining heavy burden of non-performing loans with which they had started the new millennium (table 4.6). Relatively fast income growth over the past few years, owing to a particularly favourable external environment, and the increased shares of claims on governments and households, have allowed banks to improve their solvency. But with high interest rates, there is a greater risk that a deterioration of the external environment, due to the slowdown of global growth or a recession, could lead to a worsening of banks' loan portfolios once more. It would therefore be in their own interest to reduce their interest spreads and lending rates in line with lower policy rates.

3. Capital markets

Expanding the role of capital markets in the financial system has been part of the reform programmes of several emerging-market economies. As a potential source for long-term financing, these markets could meet the need for financing investment in business that is frequently neglected by banks. They are seen as a complement to the banking system rather than a substitute for it, in particular because

Chart 4.4

STOCK MARKET CAPITALIZATION IN DEVELOPING AND TRANSITION ECONOMIES, BY REGION, 1995–2006

(Per cent of GDP)

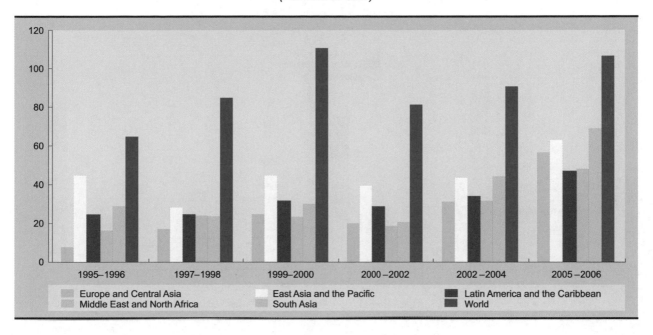

Source: World Bank, *World Development Indicators* database.
Note: Country groups as defined in the source.

banks underwrite bond issues, provide bridging loans and distribution channels for bonds and equities, form part of the primary dealer network and may also be conducive to secondary market liquidity (Eichengreen, Borensztein and Panizza, 2006: 10).

Capital markets in developing and transition economies have expanded since the early 1990s, but they remain insignificant in most low-income countries, especially in sub-Saharan Africa. Capitalization of stock markets showed an impressive (although unstable) increase in all developing regions, but most notably in Asian emerging economies and the Russian Federation (chart 4.4). Bond markets in emerging-market economies also expanded dramatically: the stock of outstanding domestic bonds of 26 of these economies grew from $700 billion in 1993 to $6,400 billion in 2007. This represented 17 per cent of GDP in 1993 and more than 100 per cent of GDP in 2007 (chart 4.5). Asian economies led, with a stock of outstanding bonds equivalent to 122 per cent of their GDP, followed by Latin American (90 per cent of GDP) and European emerging-market economies (47 per cent).

Growth in securities markets has been stimulated by factors on both the demand and supply side. On the demand side, some institutional investors that generally prefer long-term assets gained importance in several developing and transition economies. In Latin America, social security reforms led to the creation of pension funds, which, by December 2007, had accumulated assets amounting to $275 billion in 10 countries.[44] These assets represented 16 per cent of their aggregate GDP (AIOS, 2007). In Malaysia, the Republic of Korea and Singapore, and also in South Africa, insurance companies gained in importance. Another category of institutional investors typically holding a relatively high share of long-term assets in their portfolio is mutual funds. In recent years, such funds have been managing financial assets exceeding 10 per cent of GDP in Brazil, Chile, Malaysia, the Republic of Korea and South Africa (IMF, 2005). International factors have also encouraged the demand for domestic financial assets, and the opening up of the capital account to foreign investors was a deliberate policy aimed at developing capital markets and gaining economies of scale. Moreover, since 2003, rising export income has expanded domestic liquidity

Chart 4.5

OUTSTANDING DOMESTIC BONDS IN EMERGING MARKETS BY TYPE OF ISSUER: SELECTED REGIONS, 1993, 2000 AND 2007

(Per cent of GDP)

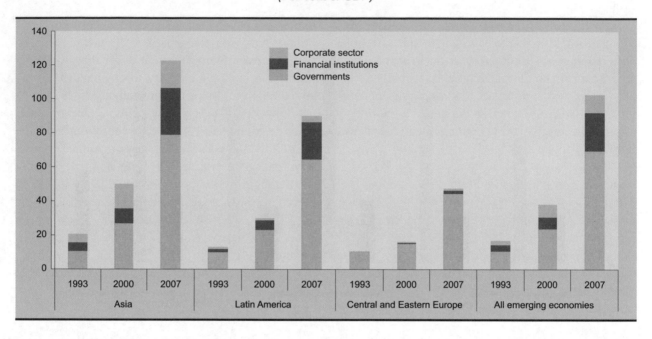

Source: UNCTAD secretariat calculations, based on Bank of International Settlements (BIS) statistics database, available at: www. bis.org/statistics/secstats.htm.

Note: Asia comprises China, Hong Kong (China), India, Indonesia, Lebanon, Malaysia, Pakistan, the Philippines, the Republic of Korea, Singapore, Taiwan Province of China, Thailand and Turkey. Latin America comprises Argentina, Brazil, Chile, Colombia, Mexico, Peru and Venezuela (Bolivarian Republic of). Europe comprises: Croatia, Czech Republic, Hungary, Poland, Russian Federation and Slovakia.

in several countries – especially in oil exporting countries. In West Asian countries, where much of the household saving has traditionally been held in the form of short-term deposits and real estate, increased liquidity has encouraged diversification to other assets and led to a spectacular stock market boom: notwithstanding a significant correction of share prices in 2006, market capitalization increased 6.5-fold in the countries of the Gulf Cooperation Council (GCC) between 2002 and 2007, and largely exceeded 100 per cent of their GDP (Corm, 2008).

> Larger capital markets do not necessarily equate with better access to investment finance.

On the supply side, in the context of external public debt restructuring through the mechanisms of the Brady Plan, outstanding bank loans were replaced by government bonds that could be traded in foreign or domestic capital markets. In several countries this represented a turning point in the way governments covered their financing needs: it reduced the demand for monetary and bank financing and increased the issuance of government securities. The partial or total privatization of public firms also provided new financial assets that attracted domestic and/or foreign investors. This structural transformation was particularly important in the transition economies. Other firms increasingly resorted to capital market financing for various reasons. Some of them that were adversely affected by bank credit restrictions in the aftermath of financial crises turned to capital markets as an alternative source of financing, as seems to have been the case, for example, in Malaysia, the Republic of Korea and the Russian Federation (IMF, 2005: 114–115). Others may have seen in thriving stock markets the opportunity for cheap funding with few constraints, as happened to some extent in China (Yu, 2008; EURASFI, 2006: 139–140). In some countries, big companies also appear to have benefited from regulations requiring institutional investors to channel their investments in bonds and equities to a small number of eligible firms. In Chile, for example, pension funds provided abundant financing to a handful of firms in the energy and telecommunications sectors (ECLAC, 1994).

However, larger capital markets do not equate with a proportionate increase in investment finance. In particular, the relatively high stock market capitalization in developing and transition economies has not always improved access to finance for a large number of firms. Stock market capitalization increases without generating any new financing if the market value of outstanding equity rises. Indeed, the amount of new equity issues has been quite limited in most developing and transition countries, with the exception of a few countries, mainly offshore centres (table 4.7). This source of financing has been negligible in Latin America and in the transition economies.

Bond markets in developing countries mainly serve to finance the public sector (chart 4.5). In 2007, government securities represented 64 per cent of total outstanding bonds in Asia, whereas the non-financial corporate sector accounted for only 13 per cent. In other regions, the share of government debt in total domestic bond financing was even higher, reaching 71 per cent in Latin America and 94 per cent in European emerging-market economies. Financing of the non-financial corporate sector through bond issues has been comparatively small: in 2007, the stock of corporate bonds amounted to 3.8 per cent of GDP in Latin America and 0.8 per cent of GDP in the emerging-market economies of Europe; in the emerging-market economies of Asia this ratio was much greater, although it exceeded 5 per cent of GDP only in a few economies (Malaysia, the Republic of Korea, Taiwan Province of China and Thailand). Moreover, only a small group of relatively large private firms can issue debt in capital markets. This is mainly because bond issues are associated with high fixed costs, which make large issues much more economical than small ones, and also because most

institutional investors restrict their bond purchases to issues by large firms (IMF, 2005: 104, 119).

In a number of countries, the increase in domestic government bond debt as a percentage of GDP has been the result of a debt management strategy aimed at replacing external public debt by domestic public debt (see also chapter VI). Moreover, the cost of government intervention in the restructuring of the banking industry after financial crises, as well as reforms of pension schemes, resulted in new financing needs for the public sector. In many countries, the financing needs arising from a change from a pay-as-you-go system to a funded system were partly covered by government securities that were bought by the pension funds themselves.[45] In December 2007, government debt represented 37 per cent of total assets of the pension funds in 10 Latin American countries that had reformed their pension systems.[46]

4. Foreign financing

From a firm's perspective, it may seem advantageous to rely on foreign borrowing if such borrowing is available at a lower cost than domestic borrowing, or when financing from domestic sources is simply not available. Foreign borrowing may also be the preferred choice for firms that obtain a substantial proportion of their cash inflows in foreign currency, and for which diversifying the liability side of the balance sheet can be a more efficient approach to coping with exchange-rate risk than purchasing derivatives (World Bank, 2007).

In recent years, leading private and public enterprises from developing and transition economies have sharply increased their borrowing from overseas, particularly after 2004 (chart 4.6). Relatively fast and sustained growth in most of these economies has improved their risk ratings, while low international interest rates and ample global liquidity have increased the pressure on international portfolio investors to enhance returns through increased lending to non-traditional markets and borrowers. Private sector companies accounted for more than 60 per cent of the increase in borrowing from banks and for 75 per cent of new bond issuance during the period 2002–2006 (World Bank, 2007: 79).

Table 4.7

STOCK EXCHANGE INDICATORS IN SELECTED DEVELOPING
AND TRANSITION ECONOMIES, BY REGION, 2006

Stock exchange	Number of listed companies	Market capitalization	New capital raised by shares
		(Per cent of GDP)	
Latin America			
Buenos Aires (Argentina)	106	23.7	0.2
Colombia	94	42.9	0.1
Costa Rica	17	8.8	0.0
Lima (Peru)	221	44.4	0.4
Mexican Exchange	335	42.0	0.1
Panama	35	41.8	0.5
Santiago (Chile)	246	119.6	0.4
São Paulo (Brazil)	350	66.5	1.5
East, South and South-East Asia			
Bombay (India)	4 796	90.7	0.8
Bursa Malaysia	1 025	158.2	0.7
Colombo (Sri Lanka)	237	28.4	0.1
Hong Kong Exchanges	1 173	904.8	35.6
Jakarta (Indonesia)	344	38.1	0.5
Karachi (Pakistan)	628	12.3	0.1
Korea Exchange (Republic of Korea)	1 689	95.6	0.6
National Stock Exchange India	1 156	85.7	1.6
Philippine Stock Exchange	240	58.0	1.0
Shanghai (China)	842	34.4	0.6
Shenzhen (China)	579	8.5	0.2
Singapore Exchange	708	290.8	4.3
Taiwan (Province of China)	693	167.2	0.6
Tehran (Islamic Republic of Iran)	320	15.0	0.6
Thailand	518	68.0	1.9
Western Asia			
Abu Dhabi (United Arab Emirates)	60	44.3	0.4
Amman (Jordan)	227	207.4	23.7
Bahrain	50	131.4	6.6
Beirut (Lebanon)	11	36.9	0.1
Kuwait	181	105.9	4.0
Istanbul (Turkey)	316	41.4	0.4
Muscat Securities Market (United Arab Emirates)	235	44.9	2.6
Palestine	33	64.3	0.0
Saudi Stock Market	86	89.9	1.0
Africa			
BRVM (West Africa)	40	8.3	3.7
Cairo & Alessandria (Egypt)	595	84.9	2.9
Casablanca (Morocco)	63	75.5	0.1
Ghana	32	14.5	1.0
Johannesburg (South Africa)	389	287.0	5.2
Lusaka (Zambia)	15	26.9	0.1
Mauritius	63	77.3	0.0
Nairobi (Keynia)	52	47.9	0.9
Namibia	28	2 499.7	0.3
Nigeria (2005)	215	16.8	3.0
Swaziland	6	7.3	0.0
Transition economies			
Banja Luka (Bosnia and Herzegovina)	793	44.5	0.1
Kazakhstan	68	73.4	2.3
MICEX (Moscow)	190	90.0	0.0
Russian Trading System	346	98.3	0.0
Zagreb (Croatia)	182	68.7	0.1

Source: World Federation of Exchanges, at www.world-exchanges.org; and *UNCTAD Handbook of Statistics* database.

Chart 4.6

FOREIGN BORROWING BY FIRMS IN DEVELOPING AND TRANSITION ECONOMIES, BY TYPE, 1998–2006

(Billions of dollars)

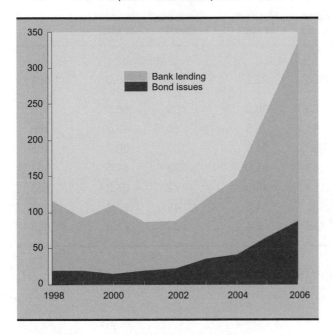

Source: World Bank, 2007, based on Dealogic.

According to Ratha, Sutle and Mohapatra (2003: 458) the foreign debt of the corporate sector in developing countries of the East Asia and Pacific region grew at a compound annual rate of 27 per cent between 1990 and the beginning of the Asian financial crisis in 1997.[47] While corporate foreign-currency-denominated debt fell sharply in East Asia following the Asian crisis, the exposure of Latin American corporations remained high until 2001. Since then, corporations from the transition economies of Eastern Europe and Central Asia have led the expansion of corporate foreign-currency-denominated borrowing and now account for about 40 per cent of total external borrowing by corporations in developing and transition economies (chart 4.7).

Six countries (Brazil, China, India, Mexico, the Russian Federation and Turkey) account for more than half of the outstanding international debt owed by firms from developing and transition economies (table 4.8). In all developing and transition economies taken together, as well as in the six above-mentioned

economies, syndicated bank loans provide most – on average about two thirds – of overseas financing. Foreign borrowing through corporate bond issues is the second largest source in most countries. Equity issues have been much more important for Indian and, in particular, Chinese corporations than for corporations of other developing and transition economies.

Most of the firms that have been able to borrow from international capital markets are large, have strong growth potential, and are in the banking, infrastructure or extractive industry sectors. The correlation between access to financial markets and firm size is not surprising, given that large firms mostly operate internationally, are less vulnerable than small firms to adverse shocks and are considered more creditworthy by investors. Moreover, large firms can negotiate more favourable terms, and they may be judged "too big to fail" and more easily able to attract

Chart 4.7

FOREIGN BORROWING BY FIRMS IN DEVELOPING AND TRANSITION ECONOMIES, BY REGION, 1999–2006

(Billions of dollars)

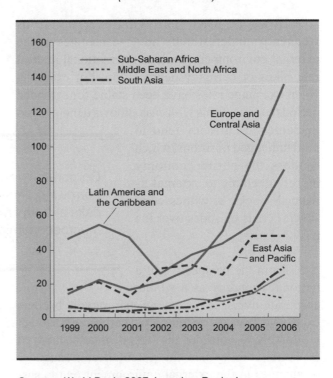

Source: World Bank, 2007, based on Dealogic.
Note: Country groups as defined in the source.

Table 4.8

FOREIGN FINANCING OF FIRMS IN SELECTED DEVELOPING AND TRANSITION ECONOMIES, BY TYPE, AVERAGE OF 1998–2006

(Billions of dollars)

	Equity issues	Per cent of total	Bond issues	Per cent of total	Syndicated bank	Per cent of total	Total
Developing and transition economies	133	9.1	325	22.2	1 004	68.6	1 461
Russian Federation	14	8.0	63	36.0	99	56.0	176
China	72	43.2	14	8.5	80	48.2	166
Brazil	9	5.3	56	34.0	100	60.7	165
Mexico	6	3.7	48	31.7	98	64.6	151
Turkey	2	1.9	9	10.9	72	87.2	83
India	13	18.9	8	11.5	49	69.7	71
Others	17	2.7	126	19.4	505	77.9	648

Source: World Bank, 2007, based on Dealogic.

government support when they are in a financially fragile situation (World Bank, 2007).

However, when borrowing overseas, firms frequently underestimate adverse changes in the external environment, such as international interest rate hikes or currency depreciation. For example, when exchange rates have been stable for extended periods of time, firms with cash inflows denominated in domestic currency tend to hold unhedged positions, which renders the entire economy more vulnerable to external financial shocks, as witnessed in several crisis episodes over the past 20 years.

From the perspective of a national economy as a whole, corporate overseas borrowing may rapidly become excessive, because an individual corporate borrower is unlikely to consider the overall indebtedness of its home country and the potential consequences of changes in the external environment on the sustainability of the country's balance-of-payments

> Corporate overseas borrowing entails substantial risks at both firm and macroeconomic levels.

position. A major task of financial policy is therefore to find ways to monitor corporate overseas exposure effectively and intervene before minor problems of corporate indebtedness turn into major macroeconomic ones. In this context, it is important for policymakers to understand the determinants of corporate overseas borrowing. Restrictions on corporate overseas investment finance could help avoid currency mismatches in the balance sheets of firms whose cash inflows are denominated entirely in domestic currency, but it would also risk stifling investment if firms are unable to find the required long-term financing at home, or only at costs that far exceed those of foreign loans. Tight standards on corporate transparency and clear and consistent rules for access to overseas borrowing could provide an early warning system for impending currency mismatches in the foreign-currency segments of a firm's balance sheet. An important objective of such standards and rules would be to indicate instances of speculative currency positions in firms' balance sheets.

5. Investment financing from the perspective of the firm

Given the difficulties for potential investors to gain access to financing from the banking system and capital markets, it is not surprising that retained earnings are the main source of investment finance in all the regions (table 4.9).[48] This finding is derived from empirical evidence based on cross-country averages for more than 32,000 firms from 100 developed, developing and transition economies for the period 2002–2006. Firms worldwide finance about two thirds of their investments from retained earnings and another 16 to 23 per cent, depending on the size of the firm, from bank loans. Equity financing is of relatively little importance, accounting for only about 3 per cent of investment financing – a share that is even smaller than financial support from family and friends.

The pattern of financing in the corporate sector varies substantially both among different sized firms and regional groups of countries. Bank financing is generally more prevalent among larger firms (particularly in Africa), whereas small firms rely more on retained earnings, and family and friends. The sample in table 4.9 shows a below average reliance on retained earnings by firms in developed countries, emerging economies (excluding the transition economies), Latin America and the Caribbean, and in developing Asia, but alternative sources of investment finance that compensate for this difference vary across the four country groups. Equity financing is of greater importance in Asia and in the emerging-market economies of Eastern and Central Europe, while for firms in Latin America and the Caribbean trade credit accounts for a relatively larger proportion of their total financing. Leasing, which is included in the category labelled "other", is relatively more important for firms in developed countries and in the emerging-market economies of Eastern and Central Europe than elsewhere. The last row in the table shows that young firms source their fixed investment from banks to a much lesser extent than do older firms; they rely much more on family and friends, as well as on equity finance.

Constraints due to limited access to bank credit are particularly severe in Africa, where more than 80 per cent of small enterprises (and about 80 per cent of the adult population) are excluded from formal banking services (table 4.9; see also Honohan and Beck, 2007). The result is a dual financial structure, in which the less advantaged firms are forced to rely on family and friends and informal financial intermediation, including various types of microfinance institutions. These financial intermediaries fill an important gap left by the formal financial system, but their financing is of limited utility for real productive investment. This is because it is characterized by relatively small volumes with very short maturities and high costs, and can therefore be used only to provide temporary working capital or to finance the purchase of simple equipment for the provision of services (Kota, 2007).

Country-specific evidence further underlines the varying importance of different sources for the financing of fixed investment (table 4.10). Perhaps most importantly, the capital structure of Chinese firms in 2003 significantly differed from that of firms in other countries in that they appear to have sourced a very low share of investment finance from retained earnings, while the category "other" played a significant role. This category includes funds raised by enterprises from various sources and, for State-owned enterprises, financing by local governments, as well as external sources of funds raised through various channels, including capital markets.[49] Given that the category "other" cannot be disaggregated further, it may also largely include misclassified retained earnings. Indeed, according to the results from a 1999 survey (reported in the third panel for China in the table), Chinese firms financed about 60 per cent of their fixed investments from retained earnings at that time (i.e. roughly as much as firms in other countries). Informal financing channels – including informal associations, private money houses and underground lending organizations that function like banks but charge very high interest rates – have played a significant role in the Chinese economy, particularly for those private entrepreneurs who have no access to the formal banking system (Allen, Qian and Qian (2005). Chinese firms also make relatively extensive use of equity finance. This reflects, in large part, the partial or total privatization of State-owned enterprises, while the number of domestic enterprises

> Constraints resulting from limited access to bank credit are particularly severe in Africa.

Table 4.9

SOURCES OF INVESTMENT FINANCE, SELECTED COUNTRY GROUPS, 2002–2006

	Number of countries	Number of firms	Internal funds and retained earnings	Local and foreign-owned commercial banks	Investment and State funds[a]	Trade credit	Equity	Family and friends	Other
					(Per cent)				
All countries									
All firms	100	32 809	65.5	16.1	1.3	3.2	3.0	3.8	7.1
Small firms	100	12 388	69.0	12.4	1.1	3.0	3.4	4.7	6.4
Medium firms	100	11 235	63.1	17.9	1.5	3.4	3.4	3.1	7.7
Large firms	100	9 036	59.7	22.9	2.5	3.4	2.9	1.5	7.1
Developed countries									
All firms	5	2 592	59.3	20.0	0.6	3.0	3.8	1.2	12.0
Small firms	5	1 618	63.2	18.1	0.3	2.7	3.2	1.7	10.9
Medium firms	5	575	53.4	22.8	0.8	3.0	5.0	0.4	14.5
Large firms	5	399	50.0	25.5	1.5	3.4	5.0	0.5	14.2
Emerging-market economies in Europe									
All firms	8	2 334	59.6	13.9	1.1	2.4	7.4	2.5	13.1
Small firms	8	1 290	62.8	10.1	0.2	2.8	7.5	4.2	12.3
Medium firms	8	621	55.3	18.3	1.4	2.4	8.2	0.4	14.0
Large firms	8	423	57.8	18.0	3.0	1.4	6.5	0.1	13.2
Latin America and the Caribbean									
All firms	20	7 845	60.6	20.2	1.5	6.8	1.2	2.7	7.0
Small firms	20	2 622	62.2	18.6	1.1	6.4	0.8	3.2	7.8
Medium firms	20	3 265	58.9	21.2	1.1	7.6	1.6	2.8	6.9
Large firms	20	1 938	58.8	24.4	2.8	6.3	1.1	1.3	5.3
Africa									
All firms	31	6 100	73.8	12.7	1.3	2.1	0.8	3.7	5.6
Small firms	31	2 642	77.8	8.9	1.1	2.4	0.8	4.3	4.8
Medium firms	31	2 059	69.9	16.1	2.0	1.9	1.0	2.5	6.6
Large firms	31	1 372	63.4	24.3	2.0	2.3	1.1	0.8	6.1
East, West, South and South-East Asia									
All firms	17	9 309	49.3	21.0	1.6	2.8	8.9	7.2	9.3
Small firms	17	2 055	53.4	14.4	2.1	2.5	11.4	8.3	7.8
Medium firms	17	3 223	50.2	19.2	1.4	2.8	9.3	7.4	9.7
Large firms	17	3 928	46.4	25.9	2.8	3.1	8.0	5.0	8.8
Transition economies in Europe									
All firms	12	3 008	72.5	14.5	1.0	2.3	1.9	3.2	4.6
Small firms	12	1 448	77.0	10.4	0.4	1.7	2.0	5.0	3.5
Medium firms	12	915	69.8	16.5	1.0	2.5	2.3	2.5	5.4
Large firms	12	645	65.7	20.6	2.3	4.1	1.2	0.3	5.8
Transition economies in Central Asia									
All firms	7	1 621	81.4	10.1	1.9	1.3	0.2	2.9	2.2
Small firms	7	713	84.6	7.7	1.0	0.4	0.0	4.5	1.8
Medium firms	7	577	79.6	11.1	2.0	2.3	0.4	2.5	2.0
Large firms	7	331	77.8	14.0	3.1	1.2	0.1	1.0	2.8
Memo items: **firm-based averages**									
All firms		32 809	58.9	19.5	1.3	3.7	4.7	3.6	8.2
Small firms		12 388	67.7	12.5	0.7	3.5	4.2	4.9	6.4
Medium firms		11 235	56.8	20.6	1.4	4.3	4.8	3.4	8.7
Large firms		9 036	49.6	27.5	2.1	3.3	5.4	2.1	10.0
New firms		1 070	63.9	13.8	1.7	2.7	6.0	6.1	5.8

Source: UNCTAD secretariat calculations, based on World Bank, *Enterprise Survey* database.

Note: New firms = firms aged 2 years or less. Small firms = less than 20 employees; medium firms = 20–99 employees; large firms = more than 99 employees. The numbers for small, medium and large firms may not add up to the total number given for all firms because some firms gave no indication of their size. Emerging-market economies in Europe: Czech Republic, Estonia, Hungary, Latvia, Lithuania, Poland, Slovakia and Slovenia.

a Aggregate funding by investment funds, development banks and other State services.

Table 4.10

SOURCES OF INVESTMENT FINANCE, SELECTED COUNTRIES, 1999–2006

	Number of firms	Internal funds and retained earnings	Local and foreign-owned commercial banks	Investment and State funds[a]	Trade credit	Equity	Family and friends	Other
		(Per cent)						
Brazil (2003)								
All firms	1 351	56.3	14.3	8.5	8.7	4.3	1.2	6.7
Small firms	226	58.0	10.8	5.7	13.0	3.5	2.2	6.7
Medium firms	736	58.6	14.8	6.4	8.2	3.8	1.4	6.9
Large firms	384	51.2	15.0	14.1	7.4	5.7	0.3	6.2
China (2003)								
All firms	1 342	15.2	20.4	0.5	1.0	12.4	5.9	44.5
Small firms	169	13.7	8.6	0.9	0.0	16.7	11.0	49.0
Medium firms	478	14.6	15.2	0.6	1.1	12.4	8.6	47.5
Large firms	686	16.2	26.8	0.4	1.2	11.4	2.7	41.1
China (1999)								
All firms	94	59.6	9.7	6.4	2.9	2.8	6.2	12.5
Small firms	42	64.9	6.8	5.0	1.0	0.3	9.0	13.0
Medium firms	27	61.6	8.0	10.1	3.9	3.9	3.9	8.6
Large firms	25	48.4	16.3	4.6	5.0	5.6	4.1	15.9
China (2003)								
State-owned firms	263	11.5	25.3	1.0	0.0	4.7	1.2	56.3
Private domestic firms	831	15.9	18.4	0.3	1.1	14.1	8.7	41.6
Egypt (2004)								
All firms	716	86.1	6.9	0.2	0.8	3.8	0.9	1.3
Small firms	287	90.1	3.9	0.0	1.2	2.2	1.4	1.2
Medium firms	275	87.0	6.6	0.4	0.8	3.3	0.7	1.3
Large firms	154	77.4	13.1	0.3	0.0	7.6	0.3	1.2
India (2005)								
All firms	1 476	52.0	32.2	0.0	4.5	1.1	6.9	3.3
Small firms	612	51.2	25.9	0.0	6.4	1.1	10.9	4.6
Medium firms	497	54.5	33.2	0.0	4.1	0.8	4.6	2.7
Large firms	284	51.4	41.6	0.0	2.0	1.8	2.1	1.2
Russian Federation (2005)								
All firms	431	85.0	6.5	1.2	2.4	0.2	1.1	3.6
Small firms	183	90.9	3.5	0.0	1.5	0.0	1.5	2.6
Medium firms	132	82.2	7.3	1.5	3.6	0.0	1.6	3.9
Large firms	116	78.8	10.3	2.8	2.6	0.7	0.1	4.7

Source: UNCTAD secretariat calculations, based on World Bank, *Enterprise Survey* database; and World Bank, World Business Environment Survey database.

Note: Small firms = less than 20 employees; medium firms = 20–99 employees; large firms = more than 99 employees. For China (1999): Small firms = less than 50 employees; medium firms = 50–500 employees; large firms = more than 500 employees. The numbers for small, medium and large firms may not add up to the total number given for all firms because some firms gave no indication of their size.

a See note a to table 4.9.

enlarging their capital base through new equity issues is still relatively small. On the other hand, Chen (2004: 1346) suggests that equity financing may be particularly important for Chinese firms because of country-specific factors, such as insufficient enforcement of enterprise law and individual shareholders who lack adequate investment protection, with the result that equity "has become somewhat [of] a 'free' source of finance".

A major source of investment finance in Egypt and the Russian Federation is retained earnings, while in India it is the banks. In Brazil, special development finance – which falls under the investment funds category – plays a relatively important role. The Brazilian national development bank, BNDES, is an example of a financially sound institution that survived the wave of reduced State presence in banking activities in the 1990s.[50] It focuses on investment projects in infrastructure and industry, which account for about half and one third of its disbursements, respectively, and more than four fifths of its operations are in support of small enterprises.[51]

To sum up, the pattern of how firms finance their productive investments displays a number of characteristics that apply to all countries, such as the relatively greater importance of internal finance relative to external finance and the relatively lower importance of equity finance. But within this general pattern there are substantial differences both across regional country groups and firms. In particular, bank financing is generally more prevalent among larger firms, whereas small and new firms rely to a greater extent on retained earnings and finance from family and friends.

This variation in the relative importance of different sources of investment finance can be traced to information asymmetries between firm managers and potential providers of external finance with respect to the value of a firm's existing assets and the quality of its investment opportunities. The use of retained earnings allows a firm's manager to protect insider information, the disclosure of which would expose the firm to imitation and severely restrict its ability to appropriate the returns on its investment. However, small and medium-sized firms or new firms encounter serious obstacles to accessing suitable external financing for their investments. Therefore they resort to internal or informal sources of finance, not out of choice but generally for lack of an alternative.

E. Lessons and policy recommendations

The question of financing investment for strengthening productive capacities in developing countries raises empirical and theoretical issues, with important policy implications. From a macroeconomic perspective, domestic sources of finance are more appropriate and quantitatively more important than foreign ones. However, the latter can play a key role in advancing investment and growth in a number of small countries and low-income and least developed countries, because of specific structural weaknesses in these countries. From the perspective of firms, self-financing from retained earnings is the most important and most reliable source for financing investment, with bank loans playing an important complementary role. Policies aimed at mobilizing resources for investment must not undermine these empirically and strategically most important sources of financing investment. This may occur when interest rates are too high as a result of monetary and financial policies based on the assumption that prior increases in household savings and capital flows from abroad are a prerequisite for higher investment and growth. Experience has shown that such policies are counterproductive: they eventually reduce business profits through lower aggregate demand and higher domestic financing costs,

> When interest rates are too high, they reduce business profits and depress domestic investment and income.

and by doing so, lead to lower domestic investment, output growth and household income.

The financial reforms undertaken by most developing and transition economies in the 1980s and 1990s generally failed to solve the problems of inefficiency and lack of transparency in the allocation of credit, market segmentation and the high proportion of non-performing loans in bank portfolios. They rarely led to a sustained increase in bank lending to private firms, especially to small and medium-sized ones. Countries that undertook more radical financial liberalization entered into a boom-and-bust dynamic that, after a rapid and poorly supervised credit boom, caused a prolonged stagnation of bank lending to the private sector. It also generated considerable fiscal costs as governments came to the rescue of the banking system. As a result of the public bailouts and, in several cases, pension system reforms, the share of the public sector in total credit provided by the financial system increased. This outcome was precisely the opposite of the initial objective of the financial reforms.

The expectation that financial liberalization and opening up of the domestic financial sectors to foreign banks would introduce more competition, which would eventually reduce interest spreads and the cost of credit, did not materialize either; spreads and lending rates have remained generally high, to the detriment of corporate and investment financing. With high spreads between deposit rates and central bank refinancing rates on the one hand and lending rates on the other, commercial banks have found it generally more profitable to extend consumption and housing credits, or to purchase government securities, than to provide longer term loans for investment projects or new business activities. This is because risk assessment for the latter tends to be more difficult, and lending rates cannot exceed the average return of the projects financed with the loan. Financial reforms and the development of the securities market have not brought about a significant reduction in financial market segmentation. Access to bank credit

has depended largely on the size of the firm, so that new, often innovative, enterprises, in particular, have encountered severe financing constraints. Financing from securities markets is concentrated in big private corporations or in public entities.

Even though these disappointing outcomes may be explained in part by poor implementation of reforms and negative external shocks, the observation that different countries experienced similar problems and at different points in time suggests that there are more fundamental problems with the way in which financial markets function. The pro-cyclical behaviour of these markets, their protracted segmentation and their failure to allocate credit for the most productive uses point to the existence of intrinsic "market failures" which the financial reforms did not successfully address (Stiglitz, 1994). It would be unrealistic to expect problems such as adverse selection, moral hazard, pro-cyclicality and segmentation to disappear as a result of liberalization, and the real world to adapt to the assumptions of a theoretical model. However, it is possible to design policies to cope with market failures. In particular, it is unrealistic, and undesirable, to eliminate all kinds of discrimination in the process of credit allocation. A financial system must discriminate between good and bad projects, and reliable and non-reliable borrowers. The absence of discrimination is characteristic of deep financial and monetary crises – either hyper-inflationary (practically everybody obtains credit) or deflationary (credit is refused to almost everyone) (Aglietta and Orlean, 1982). But governments can influence the outcome of discrimination by means of direct provision of credit through public financial institutions, including sectorally specialized banks and development banks, or by intervening in the financial markets with the provision of interest subsidies or the refinancing of commercial loans or guarantees in support of strategically selected activities. Similarly, it is more realistic to manage market segmentation than to design financial policies as if segmentation did not exist (Ocampo and Vos, 2008).

> Governments can influence financial discrimination through direct provision of credit by public institutions ...

> ... or by intervening in the financial markets in support of strategically selected activities.

In addition to positive demand and expectations of profit, secure property rights are an important condition for entrepreneurs to envisage undertaking productive investment and for potential lenders to finance such investment. But what matters from a financial policy perspective is to give firms access to reliable, adequate and cost-effective sources for financing productive investment. To the extent that the availability of funds, and in particular the amount of profits retained by firms, determines investment, measures that increase the liquidity of firms are likely to spur investment. Possible measures include a range of fiscal incentives, such as preferential tax treatment for re-invested or retained profits and special depreciation allowances aimed at accelerating capital accumulation and enhancing productive capacities.

The impact of such measures on productive investment can be amplified if banks are encouraged to make loans more easily available for investment. The cost of finance could be reduced by an investment-friendly monetary policy stance, supported by additional instruments such as an incomes policy aimed at ensuring price stability. In a process of controlled, but growth-oriented, monetary expansion, the banking system can be provided with the necessary liquidity to create new investment credit when pre-existing savings are lacking.

Ensuring access of firms to adequate sources for financing productive investment may also require intervention by the government and public sector banks in the process of credit allocation. Restrictions on lending for consumption or for speculative purposes could induce banks to extend longer term loans for investment purposes. To the extent that high lending rates reflect perceived risks, government guarantees for loans to finance promising investment projects of firms that otherwise may have very limited access to longer term bank credit (or may be able to obtain such credit only at extremely high cost that would make their investment unviable) may be envisaged. While this may entail fiscal costs when a project financed this way fails, these costs have to be weighed against the total increase in investments that can be made only because of such guarantees, and the dynamic income effects (including higher tax revenues) these

> Restrictions on lending for consumption or for speculative purposes could induce banks to extend longer term loans for investment purposes.

additional investments may generate. It should also be weighed against the fiscal costs of large rescue operations for the banking system, as became necessary following the uncontrolled increase in credit for consumption and speculative purposes that took place in many countries after financial liberalization.

It is important to bear in mind that, from the perspective of financing development, it is not only the microeconomic profitability of an investment project that matters, but also the external benefits the project generates for the economy as a whole. This consideration is generally accepted for infrastructure projects and their public financing from budget receipts or with the support of development banks. But it is equally rational if development banks and public financial institutions with expertise in specific sectors contribute to the financing of private productive activities in agriculture, industry and services when those activities generate important external benefits and social returns but are unable to obtain the necessary financing from commercial sources of finance.

One way to bring both considerations to bear on credit allocation could be through joint financing of certain investment projects by private and public banks. Whereas the commercial bank would contribute its expertise in assessing the viability of a project from a private sector perspective, the public financial institutions would make a judgement from the point of view of the project's overall developmental merits, and through its participation in the financing it could reduce the risk of the commercial bank. This kind of arrangement has several precedents in some developed countries in the post-war period, in some successful late industrializers in East Asia, and also in the activities of BNDES in Brazil. It might also serve to leverage public financing with private financing, and reduce the risk of patronage on the part of both the private and public financial institutions involved.

The debate on the role of public banks and development banks has often centred on the argument that State ownership and the existence of national development banks may increase the opportunities for corruption and patronage, rather than on the economic merits of such institutions. It is clear that public and development banks can fulfil their developmental role only if they are subject to strict rules of accountability. On the other hand, the experience with liberalization and privatization in the financial sector shows that private ownership alone does not guarantee better corporate governance. Private banks are not immune to corruption and patronage, especially when they are linked to conglomerates that receive much of their financing.

Adequate regulation and supervision of the financial sector, particularly the effective monitoring of foreign-currency-denominated debt, is essential for maintaining sound balance sheets of financial institutions. Strict standards of corporate transparency and clear and consistent rules for access to overseas borrowing would help prevent speculative currency positions also in balance sheets in the non-financial sector.

> Without public intervention, it is unlikely that the undesired consequences of financial market failures can be overcome.

Governance structures of public financial institutions should be designed in such a way that the direct and indirect benefits arising from their activities accrue to the economy as a whole (and over a longer time horizon than the one usually considered by the private sector for profit maximization). In addition, the benefits should outweigh the inefficiencies that may be generated by their political nature. Without proactive public intervention, it is highly unlikely that the undesired consequences of market failures and segmentation of the financial system can be overcome. A proactive policy, rather than ignoring the persistent financial market imperfections and segmentation, could develop new channels for financing economically and socially important activities (such as manufacturing, agriculture and infrastructure) and actors (such as small and innovative firms) which tend otherwise to be marginalized. ∎

Notes

1   Corporate profits are influenced also by exchange rate policy (UNCTAD, 2007). Greater international competitiveness resulting from an appropriate real exchange rate can help earn extra profits through increased export market shares and/or higher profit margins, which in turn develop additional capacity for internal financing of new investment.
2   Chamon and Prasad (2007) rely on data from household surveys, rather than on national accounts data as in figure 4.1.
3   Some authors have highlighted these differences by proposing to distinguish between economies where money-creating banks play a central role (called "overdraft economies") and those where capital markets are more important ("capital-market economies") (Hicks, 1974). More recently, the evolution of bank activity has tended to blur the boundaries between direct and indirect finance (IMF, 2006). Besides their traditional role as traders of bonds and securities, many banks have "securitized" part of their assets (i.e. the issuance of securities backed by bank loans) with the aim of disseminating loan risks to other agents. However, this should not lead to the hasty conclusion that basic differences between financial mechanisms have been removed, especially as the crisis resulting from sub-prime lending in the United States showed that securitization does not eliminate credit risks for banks, and that one of their fundamental tasks must continue to be the managing of such risks.

4   The following account of credit creation *ex nihilo* is partly based on Dullien, 2008.

5   Much of the literature on the role of State-owned banks (e.g. La Porta, Lopez-de-Silanes and Shleifer, 2002) focuses on their role in growth and financial development. Levy Yeyati, Micco and Panizza (2007) demonstrate that findings showing an adverse effect of State ownership on financial development and growth are far less robust than often thought, and that evidence to support a causal adverse impact of State ownership of banks and growth relies on the unrealistic assumption that there is no correlation between the presence of public banks and the level of financial development. Moreover, they show that public banks in developing countries reduce pro-cyclicality in credit allocation.

6   In this respect, the financial performance of development banks may be similar to that of venture capital funds. Gompers and Lerner (2001), for example, cite the wide variation in the financial success of the investments made by the first true venture capital firm, American Research and Development (ARD), established in 1946. Almost half of its profits during its 26-year existence as an independent entity came from just one investment. These authors also note that the average annual return to investors in venture capital funds in the United States fluctuated sharply between the mid-1970s and the late 1990s, and was close to nil in the second half of the 1980s.

7   See the BNDES website at: http://www.bndes.gov.br.

8   In 1996, the Government adopted a central bank law, which reorganized the administrative structure of the central bank and its provincial branches with a view to weakening the influence of provincial governments on decision-making by the provincial branches of the central bank, and consequently on local commercial banks. At the same time, the four big State-owned banks centralized their decisions on loans in Beijing, and adopted a computerized monitoring system to prevent provincial and municipal governments from exerting undue influence on lending decisions. In addition, the Chinese Government formed State-owned asset management companies to assume and liquidate the non-performing loans, and injected foreign-currency reserves into two of the four big State-owned banks to improve their balance sheets (Yu, 2008).

9   According to Mohanty and Turner (2008: 45), non-performing loans as a share of total loans fell from 22.4 per cent in 2000 to 10.5 per cent in 2005.

10   For example, the G-8 meeting in Potsdam in 2007 issued an action plan for developing local bond markets in emerging market economies and developing countries (for a policy-oriented overview of bond market issues in developing countries, see Turner, 2003).

11   Perfect substitutability between different sources of investment finance had been suggested by the Modigliani-Miller Theorem (1958). According to this theorem, financial structure and financial policy are irrelevant for real investment because they have no material effects on the value of a firm or on the cost or availability of capital. For the theorem to hold, the capital market must be perfect (i.e. competitive, frictionless and complete), "so that the risk characteristic of every security issued by a firm can be matched by purchase of another existing security or portfolio, or by a dynamic trading strategy" (Myers, 2001: 84). However, subsequent research, surveyed by Myers (2001), has shown that the structure of investment finance matters for firms with different financial characteristics and specifically identified costs (such as taxes), and when there is imperfect, asymmetrical information between managers-entrepreneurs (insiders) and investors-financiers of various types (outsiders).

12   The pecking order theory contrasts with the Static Trade-Off Model (STO). The STO assumes that firms try to adhere to a target capital structure, which is determined by equalizing the marginal benefit from tax savings associated with additional debt and the cost of financial distress when the firm finds it has borrowed too much (Kim, Jarrell and Bradley, 1984). While it has proved difficult to distinguish between these hypotheses empirically, Shyam-Sunder and Myers (1999) show that the STO model cannot account for the usually observed correlation between high profits and low debt ratios (for a discussion of the empirical evidence, see also Hogan and Hutson, 2005).

13   This problem of asymmetric information between an enterprise manager and any source of external finance regarding the value of the enterprise's assets and the likely profitability of the envisaged investment project is similar to the 'lemons' problem discussed by Akerlof (1970).

14   Rajan and Zingales (1998) show that debt ratios also vary across industries with, for example, oil and chemical corporations relying more on debt for external financing than pharmaceutical companies.

15   Moreover, the threat of a takeover may lead to short-termism, and could result in economic rewards for financial engineering, rather than for entrepreneurial efforts to improve products and productivity.

16   Moreover, the short-termism of banks in project choice (aimed at maximizing the expected return on their loan portfolios by favouring short-term projects with front-loaded returns) is likely to retard entrepreneurial learning.

17   A policy of entry restraint (i.e. a limited duration monopoly for a bank investing in entrepreneurial discovery) works like a patent right for the bank in an indirect way over the object of discovery (i.e.

entrepreneurial capability). But in the presence of moral hazard, the bank may choose an interest rate that is too high. A deposit rate control can address this, but it does not address short-termism. A more feasible solution, which has the additional advantage of being relatively easy to implement, would be for the government to grant guarantees for bank loans to new and innovative firms.

18 Informal lenders are also often seen as having a monitoring and enforcement advantage over formal lenders (Ayyagari, Demirgüç-Kunt and Maksimovic, 2008).

19 A domestic market for corporate bonds denominated in domestic currency would also facilitate the provision of external finance for investment. However, such markets are absent in most developing countries.

20 The role of venture capital expanded considerably during the 1970s and early 1980s. This evolution was linked to the ICT revolution and the fact that this revolution was largely propulsed by small private enterprises (Gompers and Lerner, 2001).

21 Hogan and Hutson (2005) provide evidence for this hypothesis from Ireland, and cite similar findings from other developed countries, including Finland, the United Kingdom and the United States. They argue that venture capitalists seem to be better able than banks to overcome information asymmetry problems, but that the key reason for innovative entrepreneurs to favour venture capital over debt is their willingness to forfeit independence and control in order to obtain the finance needed to proceed with their projects.

22 Mani and Bartzokas (2004) discuss the role and potential of venture capital in developing countries in Asia.

23 National development banks are only one layer among the wide institutional diversity of development banks in general. Some development banks operate at the global level, such as the Islamic Development Bank, while there are many that operate at the regional level (for example, the Asian Development, the African Development Bank or the Inter-American Development Bank). Among national development banks, only some operate at the national level, while the operations of others focus on specific provinces or economic sectors.

24 There has been an impressive growth in microcredit schemes over the past two decades, but they are not likely to play an important role in financing real investment. Microcredit usually involves very small loans with very short maturities, and therefore is mostly used to provide working capital or a fairly simple capital good for service sector activities (Kota, 2007).

25 For a survey, see *TDR 1991*, Part Two, chap. III, and Williamson and Mahar, 1998.

26 Argentina, Chile and Uruguay.

27 In Latin America, the most radical reforms of the pension scheme took place in Chile (1981), Bolivia (1997), Mexico (1997), El Salvador (1998), and the Dominican Republic (2003). Other Latin American countries, including Argentina, Colombia, Costa Rica, Ecuador, Nicaragua, Peru and Uruguay, also introduced private capitalization, but without totally eliminating the public element.

28 For a more detailed account of financial reforms in the broader context of industrial policy, see Chang, 2006.

29 For instance, in Saudi Arabia, the authorities have encouraged shareholdings by residents in the existing large foreign banks, and have allowed new foreign banks to acquire stakes in local banks. In the Syrian Arab Republic, the banking system was opened in 2002 to new banking ventures with a foreign participation of up to 49 per cent. In Bahrain, the large number of banks is due to the success of the offshore banking centre created in the1970s, but this does not imply that the Bahraini banking market is open to competition: banks operating in the offshore zone are not allowed to conduct business in the domestic Bahraini market, where only six banks have been allowed to operate (Corm, 2008).

30 Sharia-compliant assets account for more than 25 per cent of total financial assets in the Islamic Republic of Iran, Kuwait, Lebanon, Malaysia, Pakistan, Saudi Arabia and Sudan.

31 The most common types of agreements are Ijara, Murabaha, Mudarabah, Musharaka. Under the Ijara (leasing), the lender buys equipment and rents it to the borrower; Murabaha (cost plus) involves the purchase of a good by the lender and its sale (with a profit) to the borrower; Mudarabah is a profit-sharing agreement between the bank and the entrepreneur at a predetermined ratio; and Musharaka is a sort of joint venture between the lender and the borrower, whereby both profits and losses are shared.

32 This contravened the spirit of the convertibility regime and the charter of the central bank; but after the run on deposits the Government reformed the Act with a simple decree.

33 The Government supported the banking system through two mechanisms: the Korea Asset Management Corporation, which purchased non-performing loans, and the Korea Deposit Insurance Corporation (KDIC), which repaid deposits and recapitalized domestic institutions.

34 In December 1996, 91 financial and security companies managed 21 per cent of the financial assets in the system; four years later, there were only 21 such companies controlling 3 per cent of total assets.

35 In January 1998, the Indonesian Bank Restructuring Agency (IBRA) was established with the mandate of restructuring the banking system through closures, takeovers, mergers and recapitalizations. The

number of banks fell from 238 in October 1997 to 151 in December 2000 (Bank of Indonesia, 2000). Two new State-owned banks were created during this period: Bank Mandiri, which resulted from the merger of four insolvent banks, and Bank Ekspor Indonesia. Several remaining banks needed to be recapitalized. In principle, part of the additional capital had to be provided by shareholders; however, "the burden of recapitalisation of banks was borne fully by the Government since, given the situation, one could not hope for private investors to inject capital" (Pangestu, 2003: 16).

36 The "big four" received 270 billion yuan in 1998 and $60 billion in 2004–2005. In addition, they could transfer to the asset management companies 1,400 billion yuan ($170 billion) of non-performing loans in 1999, and an additional 780 billion yuan ($95 billion) in 2004–2005.

37 In Ukraine and Kazakhstan, for example, the number of banks fell from 229 to 170 and from 101 to 33, respectively, between 1996 and 2006.

38 The share of foreign banks in total bank assets in 2006 amounted to 46 per cent in Armenia, 53 per cent in the former Yugoslav Republic of Macedonia, 72 per cent in Kyrgyzstan, 79 per cent in Serbia, 87 per cent in Georgia, 91 per cent in Croatia, 92 per cent in Montenegro and 94 per cent in Bosnia and Herzegovina (EBRD, 2007).

39 Benin (1988–1990), Cameroon (1987–1993), Côte d'Ivoire (1988–1991), Ghana (1982–1989), Guinea (1985 and 1993–1994), Kenya (1985–1989 and 1993–1995), Nigeria (1991–1995), Senegal (1988–1991), United Republic of Tanzania (1987–1990) and Uganda (1990s).

40 According to Daumont, Le Gall and Leroux (2004: 42), "the most important factors behind the banking crises in sub-Saharan Africa appear to have been government interference, poor banking supervision and regulation, and shortcomings in management"; in other words, that there was not too much but too little liberalization and deregulation.

41 In the countries of the Caribbean region, bank credit to the private sector has, on average, been considerably higher than in Central and South America, reaching more than 50 per cent of GDP in 2004–2007. This may be explained by the relatively high degree of openness to international trade in goods and services, especially tourism, and the relatively advanced development of banking services in those countries of the region that are offshore financial centres.

42 In Argentina in 2002, as the peso was devalued after 10 years of a fixed exchange rate, both assets and liabilities of banks were converted into pesos, but at different exchange rates (i.e. 1 peso per dollar for loans, 1.4 peso per dollar for deposits). Banks were compensated for the difference with public bonds.

43 Honohan and Beck (2007) found that during the period 2000–2004 foreign banks in Africa had higher returns than their branches outside Africa, but also that these foreign banks had higher returns than domestic banks.

44 Argentina, Bolivia, Chile, Colombia, Costa Rica, the Dominican Republic, El Salvador, Mexico, Peru and Uruguay.

45 The transition from a pay-as-you-go system to a funded system implies that social security contributions are henceforth paid into new pension funds, while the government continues to pay current pensions and those that will still be due for many years under the previous regime.

46 If Chile is excluded from the group, this percentage rises to 57 per cent. As pension reform in Chile is the oldest (1980), Chilean private pension funds have accumulated the largest amount of financial assets in Latin America: $111 billion, or 64 per cent of GDP. They also have the lowest share of government bonds in total assets (8 per cent). However, this share was much higher in the years immediately following the reform (more than 40 per cent), when transitional fiscal costs were the highest.

47 This strong corporate foreign-currency-denominated leverage was a major factor contributing to the financial troubles of many East Asian economies in 1997–1998 (see *TDR 1998*, chap. III, and *TDR 2004*, chap. IV).

48 The data are from the *World Bank Enterprise Survey* (WBES) series. Regarding sources of investment finance, the survey asks enterprise managers to respond to the following question: "Please identify the contribution of each of the following sources of financing for your establishment's new investments (i.e. new land, buildings, machinery and equipment)". Information on the various sources relates to proportions of total financing rather than to assets and debt. The table considers only the most recent results where country-specific surveys were available for various years during the period 2002–2006. The 2006 surveys do not enable an identification of sourcing from foreign-owned banks, leasing and credit cards; however, judging from evidence for the other years, these sources are generally of little importance for developing and transition economies. Results from 2007 surveys were not included because they are not part of the WBES standardized database.

49 See *China Statistical Yearbook*, table 6.4, at: http://www.stats.gov.cn/tjsj/ndsj/2007/indexeh.htm. As mentioned, in the table the category "other" also includes leasing, foreign-owned banks and credit cards but, as in other developing countries, these sources are of very little importance in China.

50 Given that BNDES had a sound balance sheet, it was not affected by the Programme of Incentives for the Reduction of States' Participation in Banking

Activities (PROES) launched by the Brazilian Government in 1995 (Levy Yeyati, Micco and Panizza, 2007: 217–218).

51 BNDES finances the bulk of its activities from returns on previous investments, with the FAT (Fundo de Amparo ao Trabalhador) Worker Assistance Fund constituting another important source of funding. The data presented here are from the BNDES website: http://www.bndes.gov.br.

References

Aglietta M and Orlean A (1982). *La violence de la Monnaie*. Paris, Presses Universitaires de France.

AIOS (Asociación Internacional de Organismos de Supervisión de Fondos de Pensiones) (2007). *Boletín Estadístico* No. 18, December. Available at: www.aiosfp.org.

Akerlof GA (1970). The market for "lemons": Quality uncertainty and the market mechanism. *Quarterly Journal of Economics*. 84(3): 488–500, August.

Allen F, Qian J and Qian M (2005). Law, finance, and economic growth in China. *Journal of Financial Economics,* 77(1): 57–116.

Allen F, Qian J and Qian M (2008). China's financial system: Past, present and future. In: Rawski T and Brandt L, eds. *China's Great Economic Transformation*. Cambridge, Cambridge University Press.

Amsden AH (2001). *The Rise of the Rest: Challenges to the West from Late-Industrializing Economies*. Oxford and New York, Oxford University Press.

Amsden A and Euh Y-D (1990). Republic of Korea's financial reform: What are the Lessons? UNCTAD Discussion Paper No. 30. Geneva, UNCTAD, April.

Aslund A (1996). Russian banking: Crisis or rent-seeking? *Post-Soviet Geography and Economics*, 37(8): 495–502.

Ayyagari M, Demirgüç-Kunt A and Maksimovic V (2008). Formal versus informal finance: Evidence from China. Working Paper No. 4465, Washington, DC, World Bank, January.

Banco de México (2007). Historia sintética de la banca en México, October. Available at: www.banxico.gob.mx/sistemafinanciero/index.html.

Bank of Indonesia (2000). *Quarterly Banking Report*, Quarter IV. Jakarta.

Bank of Korea (2007). Financial system in Korea, December. Available at: www.bok.or.kr/contents_admin/info_admin/eng/home/public/public06/info/330.pdf.

Barnett S and Brooks R (2006). What's driving investment in China? Working Paper No. 06/265, International Monetary Fund, Washington, DC, November.

Batunanggar S (2002). Indonesia's banking crisis resolution: Lessons and the way forward. Paper presented at the Banking Crisis Resolution Conference (CCBS), London, 9 December.

BDDK (Banking Regulation and Supervision Agency of Turkey) (2001). Towards a sound Turkish banking sector. Ankara, 15 May.

Bonin J and Wachtel P (2002). Financial sector development in transition economies: Lessons from the first decade. BOFIT Discussion Paper No. 9, Bank of Finland, Institute for Economies in Transition, Helsinki.

Bonin J and Wachtel P (2004). Dealing with financial fragility in transition economies. BOFIT Discussion Paper No. 22, Bank of Finland, Institute for Economies in Transition, Helsinki.

Brownbridge M and Harvey C (1998). *Banking in Africa: The Impact of Financial Sector Reform Since Independence*. Oxford, James Currey Ltd.

Calcagno A (1997). Convertibility and the banking system in Argentina, *CEPAL Review* 61, April 1997.

Chamon M and Prasad E (2007). Why are saving rates of urban households in China rising? Discussion Paper No. 3191, Institute for the Study of Labor (IZA), Bonn.

Chang H-J (2006). *The East Asian Development Experience. The Miracle, the Crisis and the Future*. London, New York and Penang, Zed Books and Third World Network.

Chen JJ (2004). Determinants of capital structure of Chinese listed companies. *Journal of Business Research*, 57(12): 1341–1351.

Corm G (2008). *Financial systems in the MENA region*. Background paper prepared for the *Trade and Development Report 2008*. Geneva, UNCTAD.

Daumont R, Le Gall F and Leroux F (2004). Banking in Sub-Saharan Africa: What Went Wrong? IMF Working Paper WP/04/55, Washington DC, International Monetary Fund.

Dullien S (2008). Central banking, financial institutions and credit creation in developing countries. Background paper prepared for the *Trade and Development Report, 2008*. Geneva, UNCTAD.

EBRD (2007). *Transition Report*. London, European Bank for Reconstruction and Development.

EBRD (various years). Structural change indicators. Available at: www.ebrd.com/country/sector/econo/stats/sci.xls.

ECLAC (Economic Commission for Latin America and the Caribbean) (1994). El Crecimiento Económico y su Difusión Social: el Caso de Chile de 1987 a 1992. LC/R.1483, Santiago, Chile, December.

Eichengreen B, Borensztein E and Panizza U (2006). A tale of two markets: Bond development in East Asia and Latin America. HKIMR Occasional Paper No. 3, Hong Kong Institute for Monetary Research, Hong Kong, October.

Emran MS and Stiglitz JE (2007). Financial liberalization, financial restraint and entrepreneurial development. Available at: http://www.cid.harvard.edu/neudc07/docs/neudc07_s5_p02_emran.pdf.

EURASFI (Europe-Asie Finance) (2006). *La Chine: Un Colosse Financier? Le Système Financier Chinois à l'Aube du XXIE Siècle*. Paris, Vuibert.

Fazzari S, Hubbard G and Petersen BC (1988). Financing constraints and corporate investment. *Brookings Papers on Economic Activity* (1): 141–205.

Freitas MCP (2007). Transformações institucionais do sistema bancario brasileiro. Relatório do Projeto de Pesquisa: O Brasil na era da globalisação: condicionantes domésticos e internacionais ao desenvolvimento. Campinas: Cecon/IE/Unicamp e Rio de Janeiro: BNDES. Mimeo.

Gompers P and J Lerner (2001). The venture capital revolution. *Journal of Economic Perspectives*, 15(2): 145–168.

Hall BH (2002). The financing of research and development. NBER Working Paper No. 8773. Cambridge, MA, National Bureau of Economic Research.

He X and Cao Y (2007). Understanding high saving rate in China. *China and World Economy*, 15(1): 1–13.

Hicks J (1974). *The Crisis in Keynesian Economics*. Oxford, Basil Blackwell.

Hoffmaister AW, Roldós JE and Wickham P (1997). Macroeconomic Fluctuations in sub-Saharan Africa. IMF Working Paper WP/97/82, Washington DC, International Monetary Fund.

Hogan T and Hutson E (2005). Capital structure in new technology-based firms: Evidence from the Irish software sector. *Global Finance Journal*, 15(3): 369–387.

Honohan P and Beck T (2007). Making finance work in Africa. Washington, DC, World Bank.

IMF (various years). *Financial System Stability Assessment* (various country reports).

IMF (2005). *Global Financial Stability Report*. Washington, DC, IMF, September.

IMF (2006). *Global Financial Stability Report*. Washington, DC, IMF, September.

Khan H (2004). *Global Markets and Financial Crises in Asia: Towards a Theory for the 21st Century*. New York, Palgrave Macmillan.

Kim EH, Jarrell GA and Bradley M (1984). On the existence of an optimal capital structure: Theory and evidence. *Journal of Finance*, 39(3): 857–878.

Kota I (2007). Microfinance: banking for the poor. *Finance and Development*, 44(2): 44–45.

Kregel J and Burlamaqui L (2006). Finance, competition, instability and development. Working Papers in Technology Governance and Economic Dynamics No. 4. Tallinn, Tallinn University of Technology.

La Porta R, Lopez-de-Silanes F and Shleifer A (2002). Government ownership of banks. *Journal of Finance*, 57(1): 265–301.

Lerner J (1995). Venture capitalists and the oversight of private firms. *Journal of Finance*, 50(1): 301–318.

Levy Yeyati E, Micco A and Panizza U (2007). A reappraisal of state-owned banks. *Economia*, 7(2): 209–247.

Mani S and Bartzokas A (2004). Institutional support for investment in new technologies: the role of venture capital institutions in developing countries. In: Bartzokas A, ed. *Financial System, Corporate Investment in Innovation, and Venture Capital*. Cheltenham, Edward Elgar.

McKinnon R (1973). *Money and Capital in Economic Development*. Washington, DC, Brookings Institution.

Minsky HP (1982). The financial-instability hypothesis: capitalist processes and the behavior of the economy. In: Kindelberger CP and Laffargue JP, eds. *Financial Crises*. Cambridge and New York, Cambridge University Press: 13–39.

Modigliani F and Miller M (1958). The cost of capital, corporation finance and investment. *American Economic Review*, 48(3): 261–297.

Mohanty MS and Turner P (2008). Monetary policy transmission in emerging market economies: What is new? *BIS Papers* No 35. Basle, Bank for International Settlements.

Myers SC (2001). Capital structure. *Journal of Economic Perspectives*, 15(2): 81–102.

Myers SC and Majluf N (1984). Corporate financing and investment decisions when firms have information that investors do not have. *Journal of Financial Economics*, 13(2): 187–221.

Ocampo JA and Vos R (2008). Policy space and the changing paradigm in conducting macroeconomic policies in developing countries. In: New financing trends in Latin America: a bumpy road towards stability, *BIS Papers* No 36, Bank for International Settlements, Basel, February.

Pangestu M (2003). The Indonesian bank crisis and restructuring: Lessons and implications for other developing countries. G-24 Discussion Paper No 23. New York and Geneva, UNCTAD, November.

Quintyn M (2008). Building supervisory structures for Africa: An analytical framework to guide the process. Paper prepared for the joint IMF/Africa Institute High-Level Seminar on African Finance in the 21st Century, held in Tunis, Tunisia, 4–5 March.

Quispe-Agnoli M and Vilán D (2008). Financing trends in Latin America. In: New financing trends in Latin America: a bumpy road towards stability, *BIS Papers* No. 36, Bank for International Settlements, Basel, February.

Rajan R and Zingales L (1998). Financial dependence and growth. *American Economic Review*, 88(3): 559–586.

Ratha D, Sutle P and Mohapatra S (2003). Corporate financing patterns and performance in emerging markets. In: Litan R, Pomerleano M and Sundararajan V, eds. *The Future of Domestic Capital Markets in Developing Countries*. Washington, DC, Brookings Institution.

Sáinz P and Calcagno A (1999). La economía brasileña ante el Plan Real y la crisis. Serie temas de coyuntura 4, ECLAC, Santiago, Chile, July.

Senbet L (2008). African stock markets. Paper prepared for the joint IMF/Africa Institute High-Level Seminar on African Finance in the 21st Century, held in Tunis, Tunisia, 4–5 March 2008.

Shaw E (1973). *Financial Deepening in Economic Development*. New York, Oxford University Press.

Shyam-Sunder L and Myers SC (1999). Testing static tradeoff against pecking order models of capital structure. *Journal of Financial Economics*, 51(2): 219–244.

Singh A (1997) Savings, investment and the corporation in the East Asian miracle. *Journal of Development Studies*, 34(6): 112–137.

Stiglitz J (1994). The role of the state in financial markets. In: *Proceedings of the World Bank, Annual Conference on Development Economics*. Washington, DC, World Bank, March.

Turner P (2003). Bond markets in emerging economies: an overview of policy issues. In: Litan RE, Pomerleano M and Sundararajan V, eds. *The Future of Domestic Capital Markets in Developing Countries*. Washington, DC, Brookings Institution Press.

UNCTAD (various issues). *Trade and Development Report*. United Nations publications, New York and Geneva.

UNCTAD (2007). Global and regional approaches to trade and finance. Document UNCTAD/GDS/2007/1. New York and Geneva, United Nations.

Williamson J and Mahar M (1998). A survey of financial liberalisation. *Essays in International Finance* (211). Princeton, NJ, Princeton University, Department of Economics.

World Bank (1989). *World Development Report* 1989. Washington, DC, Oxford University Press.

World Bank (1994). *Averting the Old Age Crisis*. New York, Oxford University Press.

World Bank (2007). *Global Development Finance: The Globalization of Corporate Finance in Developing Countries*. Washington, DC, World Bank.

Yu Y (2008). China's development finance. Background paper prepared for the *Trade and Development Report 2008*. Geneva, UNCTAD.

OFFICIAL DEVELOPMENT ASSISTANCE FOR THE MDGs AND ECONOMIC GROWTH

A. Introduction

Official development assistance (ODA) has acquired a pivotal position in economic relations between developed and developing countries in the context of Goal 8 of the Millennium Development Goals (MDGs), which calls for a global partnership for development. To help developing countries achieve the MDGs, all States subscribing to the Monterrey Consensus (United Nations, 2002) recognized the need for concrete efforts to reach the quantitative targets for ODA that have long been on the international cooperation agenda. Furthermore, in 2005 most DAC donors set ambitious targets for increasing their ODA. However, despite a substantial rise in ODA disbursements, as of 2007 most donors were not on track to meet these targets (OECD, 2008).[1]

> Despite a substantial rise in ODA disbursements, in 2007 most donors were not on track to meet their ODA targets.

Since the 1980s, bilateral and multilateral donors have incorporated increasingly demanding policy conditions into aid agreements with the objective of making the use of aid more effective. Questions surrounding the type, sources, purpose and channels of aid are critically important in the larger debate on aid effectiveness. The policy framework that has guided ODA flows over the past decade or so has rested on the belief that, in the long run, better institutions lead to faster growth. Thus aid effectiveness is also increasingly associated with better institutions and policies. And, despite weak evidence of such a correlation, aid is often made conditional on good governance.

The yardstick against which aid effectiveness is measured is not always clear. Certainly, the sectoral destination of ODA (and its link to the productive economy) makes a difference in terms of the impact of a particular aid package on growth. From most donors' perspectives, the political considerations driving aid are as imperative as measures to ensure its transparent and effective use by beneficiaries. From the perspective of a poor developing country, on the other hand, harmonization, simplification and predictability of aid flows are as vital as the extent to which aid enables and empowers governments to assume their role in development. In terms of the MDGs, aid effectiveness is viewed in terms of the level and quality of aid that should enable recipient countries to achieve those goals by 2015.

The Monterrey Consensus also recognized a possible role for innovative sources of development finance, and highlighted the need to maintain adequate funding of international financial institutions. This chapter reviews the trends that have shaped ODA since the beginning of the new millennium and assesses their measurable or possible effects on key development indicators, especially the MDGs. It shows that, although donor countries have made considerable efforts to increase their ODA in line with old and new commitments, there is still a considerable gap between actual ODA flows and the aid estimated to be necessary to undertake measures in pursuit of the MDGs. Moreover, there is a risk that the design of ODA in the coming years may be too narrowly oriented towards realizing an improvement in the indicators against which achievement of the MDGs is measured. At the same time, ODA aimed at enhancing productive capacity, creating employment, increasing domestic value added and contributing to structural change risks being neglected. Yet, without such investments, poverty reduction and the improvement of other social and human development indicators are unlikely to be sustainable.

B. The rationale for ODA

The economic case for extending aid to poorer countries still largely rests on the growth and gap models of the 1950s and 1960s.[2] These suggest that aid can provide an initial boost to domestic capital formation, which will eventually augment fiscal revenues, export earnings and per capita incomes. Over time, growth and development should become self-sustaining and the need for aid should disappear (UNCTAD, 2000 and 2006).

Traditionally, the underlying premise for the transfer of financial resources from capital-rich industrialized countries to capital-scarce developing countries is rooted in the notion that additional resources are necessary for creating and upgrading productive capacity in the process of growth and structural change. One way to express this formally is through the use of an economic growth model that allows for foreign financing to fill the chronic gap between domestic savings and the total investment needed to reach a targeted higher growth rate without creating an unsustainable debt (Rosenstein-Rodan, 1961).

From another perspective, growth and structural change in a typical low-income country are understood to be constrained by the fact that the imports deemed essential for accelerating growth and structural change are greater than the country's export potential. This results in a foreign-exchange gap, which is identical to the savings gap inasmuch as it corresponds to the current-account deficit. However, the foreign-exchange-gap theory also has a structural aspect in that a current-account deficit results from the need for capital and intermediate goods that cannot be produced domestically but are necessary for strengthening the productive sectors and

> Aid can provide an initial boost to domestic capital formation.

diversifying the economies of low-income countries, which typically have no, or very limited, access to private external capital.

The fact that developing countries as a group have registered net capital outflows since the turn of the century may give the impression that some of these countries no longer require external development finance since they can ensure stable economic and social development through export led-growth and macroeconomic management aimed at avoiding current-account deficits without sacrificing growth (see chapter III above). However, it should be pointed out that the current account performance of developing countries as a group has been strongly influenced by some of the largest developing economies, while many other developing countries continue to be structurally in deficit due to a very narrow export base and their need for considerable imports of the capital and intermediate goods necessary for broadening this base. Indeed, a number of these countries saw a deterioration in their current account, which in some cases was associated with a swing from surplus to deficit between 1992–1996 and 2002–2006 (table 5.1). During this period, overall, out of 113 developing countries and economies in transition for which reliable data are available, 60 countries saw an improvement in their current-account balance, while 53 experienced a deterioration. Among the 10 transition economies in the sample, half experienced an improvement, and among the 72 developing countries in the sample that are not classified as least developed countries (LDCs) the current-account balance improved in 44 (i.e. more than 60 per cent), whereas among the 31 LDCs this was the case for only 11 (i.e. 35 per cent). Almost two thirds of the LDCs saw their current account deteriorate despite a generally development-friendly external environment. During the period 2002–2006, 39 developing countries and 3 transition economies were net exporters of capital, including 6 LDCs.

In view of what has been discussed in chapter III on the role of real exchange rates for countries' current-account positions, it may be useful to compare the current-account performance of these countries with changes in their average real exchange rates from 1992–1996 to 2002–2006.[3] In some of the developing countries that experienced a deterioration in the current account, this was associated with a sizeable appreciation of their real exchange rate, but in a majority of these countries the current account

Table 5.1

CURRENT-ACCOUNT BALANCES: CHANGES BETWEEN 1992–1996 AND 2002–2006

(Number of countries)

	Developed economies	Developing countries		Transition economies
		of which:		
		All	LDCs	
Improvement in the current-account balance				
Total	12	55	11	5
Higher surplus	7	14	2	1
Lower deficit	0	16	4	3
Swing from deficit to surplus	5	25	5	1
Deterioration of the current-account balance				
Total	23	48	20	5
Higher deficit	18	41	18	5
Lower surplus	0	1	0	0
Swing from surplus to deficit	5	6	2	0

Source: UNCTAD secretariat calculations, based on *UNCTAD Handbook of Statistics* database.

worsened despite a depreciation of the real exchange rate of more than 10 percentage points. This suggests that while the real exchange rate matters, the current account of many developing countries is also strongly influenced by terms-of-trade shocks and various structural factors that make their economies less responsive to such policies than those of the more advanced countries.

Apart from these macroeconomic considerations, there is another case for ODA, which concerns public finance. In most low-income countries the scope for the government to provide public goods in support of growth and development is constrained by their small income base and institutional difficulties in tax collection. The resulting fiscal gap remains an important reason for ODA in the form of budget support to the least developed and other low-income countries. In 23 out of 81 developing countries and economies in transition for which reliable data are

Table 5.2

SHARE OF AID IN CENTRAL GOVERNMENT EXPENDITURE, 2002–2006

(Number of countries)

	Developing countries		Transition economies
	All	of which: LDCs	
More than 25 per cent	18	13	5
More than 50 per cent	13	11	3
More than 75 per cent	10	9	1

Source: UNCTAD secretariat calculations, based on World Bank, *World Development Indicators* database.

Note: The sample comprises 69 developing countries (of which 17 LDCs) and 12 transition economies.

available, ODA by members of the OECD Development Assistance Committee accounted for more than 25 per cent of central government expenditure during the period 2002–2006, and in 16 countries this share even exceeded 50 per cent (table 5.2). As for LDCs, a particularly large proportion relied heavily on ODA for budgetary support: 76 per cent of the LDCs depended on ODA for more than one quarter of their central government expenditure, and 65 per cent for more than one half of such expenditure.

With the commitment of the international community to make achievement of the MDGs a common project, the general rationale for ODA has shifted from a focus on economic growth as a precondition for realization of the social objectives, to attainment of the social, human and environmental objectives themselves.[4]

C. Recent trends in ODA

1. Aggregate ODA flows

The main source of data on ODA is the OECD Development Assistance Committee (DAC).[5] It defines ODA as financial flows originating from official agencies, including State and local governments of DAC member States, which are "administered with the promotion of the economic development and welfare of developing countries as its main objective".[6] ODA can be provided fully as grants, or as concessional loans with a grant element of at least 25 per cent.[7] It can take the form of financial flows, debt relief or goods and services in kind. The valuation of aid other than a financial flow complicates the measurement of ODA. Moreover, certain reporting modalities can distort the perception of actually disbursed aid flows, particularly when debt stock cancellation is included, which is not connected with the flow of new financial resources to the beneficiary countries.

Aggregate ODA, as reported by OECD-DAC, has risen considerably compared to the average in the 1990s, and in particular since 2002 (chart 5.1 and table 5.3). However, given that ODA fell quite dramatically between 1993 and 1999, average ODA per capita, in real terms, since the beginning of the new millennium has not been much higher than it was in the 1960s and 1980s (chart 5.1), despite the recovery from 2000 onward.

Between 2000 – the year of the adoption of the MDGs – and 2006, total ODA grew in real terms at an average annual rate of almost 9 per cent. Bilateral ODA drove that trend with an average annual growth rate of over 11 per cent. This demonstrates a positive response by donors to the commitments made at the beginning of the new millennium. However, the question remains as to whether increases in ODA have kept pace with the increases in initial donor commitments and with the requirements for addressing the core challenges of the MDGs, not to mention

Chart 5.1

LONG-TERM TRENDS IN ODA, 1960–2006

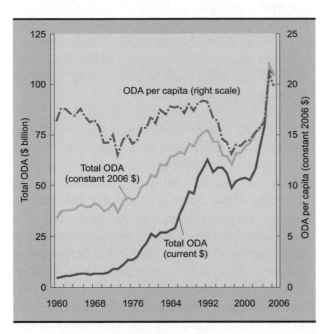

Source: UNCTAD secretariat calculations, based on OECD *International Development Statistics* online databases on aid (OECD-IDS).

Note: The data, as reported by donors, are net disbursements. Data in real terms are obtained using the OECD/DAC deflator.

the added requirements for addressing emerging new global concerns such as climate change and food and water security (discussed in section E below).

2. Sources, categories and distribution of ODA

Since the bulk of global ODA comes from OECD-DAC donors, the analysis in the remainder of this chapter is based on ODA from these sources, unless otherwise specified. However, it should be pointed out that contributions from non-DAC bilateral donors have risen, and can be an important source of funding for individual recipients. In the period 2004–2006, ODA provided by non-DAC countries doubled compared to 2000–2002, but it continued to account for less than 3 per cent of DAC ODA (table 5.3). In the 1990s, West Asian donors provided the largest share of non-DAC ODA, and

their disbursements were also the most stable. Subsequently, as a by-product of fast GNI growth in East Asia, ODA flows from that region rose rapidly and outpaced those from West Asia in 2005.[8] Non-DAC aid programmes are often attractive for developing countries, because they typically imply fewer constraints, bureaucratic procedures and conditionalities. On the other hand, non-DAC official lending is criticized on the grounds that it is non-concessional and that uncoordinated lending may heighten the risk of new debt problems and undermine progress

Table 5.3

ODA BY MAIN TYPES, AVERAGES OF 2000–2002 AND 2004–2006

	2000–2002	2004–2006	Percentage change between periods
	$ million		
Total DAC ODA	54 823	96 984	77
Multilateral	17 512	25 747	47
Bilateral	37 311	71 237	91
Non-grants	1 855	-2 146	- 216
Grants	35 456	73 383	107
Project and programme aid	7 864	16 953	116
Technical cooperation	13 940	20 559	47
Humanitarian aid (incl. food aid)	3 403	7 355	116
Debt relief	3 400	17 542	416
Other	6 848	10 974	60
	Share in total DAC ODA *(per cent)*		
Multilateral	32	27	- 16
Bilateral	68	73	7
Non-grants	3	- 2	- 168
Grants	65	75	17
Project and programme aid	14	18	22
Technical cooperation	25	21	- 16
Humanitarian aid (incl. food aid)	6	8	23
Debt relief	6	17	184
Other	13	11	- 8
Memo item:			
Total non-DAC ODA *($ million)*	1 411	2 820	100

Source: UNCTAD secretariat calculations, based on OECD-IDS.

Note: The data as reported by donors are in current dollars and represent net disbursements.

Chart 5.2

**ODA BY SELECTED TYPES OF AID,
1990–2006**

(Billions of current dollars)

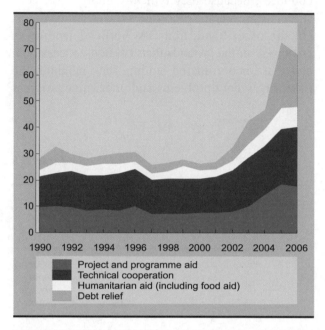

Project and programme aid
Technical cooperation
Humanitarian aid (including food aid)
Debt relief

Source: UNCTAD secretariat calculations, based on OECD-IDS.
Note: The data, as reported by donors, are net disbursements
of bilateral aid.

towards maintaining sustainable debt levels achieved in part as a result of bilateral and multilateral debt relief initiatives.

In the total ODA provided by DAC countries, the share of grants has risen continuously over the past 20 years, to reach more than 75 per cent of total net ODA flows from DAC countries in 2006. Net flows in the form of loans have been negative since 2003, indicating a net repayment of concessional loans. To a large extent, the increase in the proportion of grants in total ODA is attributable to the inclusion of debt relief in ODA statistics. Indeed, debt relief dominated the increase in average ODA between 2000–2002 and 2004–2006. It accounted for almost two thirds of the surge of ODA in 2005, when total aggregate ODA reached a historic peak, and for around 30 per cent of all grants provided in 2005–2006 (chart 5.2). Compared to 2000–2002, debt relief more than quadrupled in 2004–2006, according to OECD statistics. In the coming years, this increase in total ODA may be reversed, at least in part, as unusually large debt relief exercises in the Paris

Club for some non-HIPCs have been completed and debt write-offs under the HIPC Initiative are set to decline. Meanwhile, other categories of ODA have increased much less: in nominal terms, ODA in the form of technical cooperation increased by 47 per cent between 2000–2002 and 2004–2006, and project and programme aid, the category of ODA that provides the most fiscal space to the recipient countries, by 116 per cent (table 5.3).

Another factor, in addition to debt relief, that has driven the recent increase in aggregate ODA is the assistance provided to a few countries in special circumstances, notably Afghanistan and Iraq (chart 5.3). There can be no doubt that assistance to countries emerging from war, political conflict or other exceptional crises is an indispensable element in an effective global partnership for development. However, adding it up with regular ODA flows to other developing countries can distort the overall picture. If the temporary increase in debt relief and the additional aid flows to these two war-torn

Chart 5.3

**ODA LESS DEBT RELIEF AND AID TO
AFGHANISTAN AND IRAQ, 2000–2006**

(Index numbers, 2002 = 100)

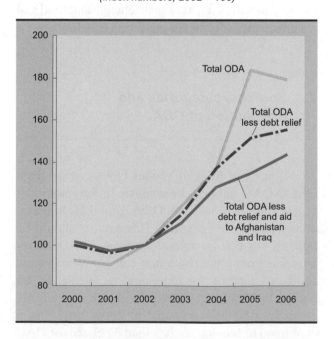

Total ODA

Total ODA
less debt relief

Total ODA less
debt relief and aid
to Afghanistan
and Iraq

Source: UNCTAD secretariat calculations, based on OECD-IDS.
Note: The data, as reported by donors, are in current dollars
and represent net disbursements of bilateral aid.

economies are excluded, the increase in ODA, while still considerable, is more modest.

Apart from the assistance to countries emerging from major crises, ODA would be expected to flow primarily to those countries that are the most in need, as indicated by low GDP per capita. However, empirically there is no significant correlation (chart 5.4). Similarly, as discussed later, there is also a weak correlation between variables, indicating needs for investment or social spending, on the one hand, and specific categories of ODA on the other.

These developments have led to a change in the composition of total ODA at the expense of what could be referred to as "development aid" (i.e. ODA provided in support of economic and social infrastructure and the productive sectors), the share of which fell from 59 per cent in the late 1990s to 51 per cent in the period 2002–2006 (chart 5.5).

Chart 5.4

GDP AND ODA PER CAPITA, AVERAGE OF 2004–2006

(Current dollars)

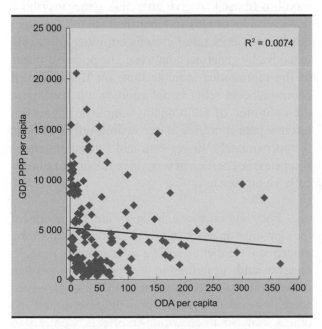

Source: UNCTAD secretariat calculations, based on OECD-IDS; United Nations Statistics Division (UNSD) database; and IMF, *World Economic Outlook* database.
Note: GDP is adjusted for purchasing power parity (PPP).

Chart 5.5

COMPOSITION OF TOTAL ODA BY MAIN SECTORS, 1990–2006

(Average in per cent)

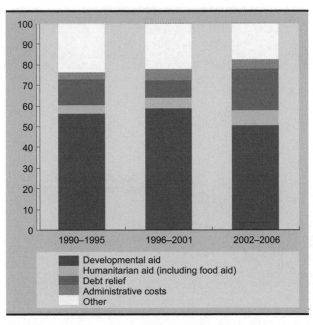

Source: UNCTAD secretariat calculations, based on OECD-IDS.
Note: The data, as reported by donors, are in current dollars and represent net disbursements. The component "other" includes: multisector/cross-cutting, support to NGOs, refugees in donor countries, commodity aid/general programme assistance and unallocated/unspecified sectors.

3. Additionality of debt relief and other forms of ODA

Although the HIPC Initiative for debt relief was conceived on the understanding that the debt relief provided would be a net addition to the total volume of ODA, the first five years following the launch of the HIPC Initiative saw a sharp fall in total net ODA transfers compared to previous trends. Aggregate ODA started to recover from 2002 onwards, with substantial increases in all categories of aid, but this is no proof that the debt relief was additional to other forms of aid.

According to Arslanalp and Henry (2006), debt relief under the HIPC Initiative has not been additional, while according to the World Bank (2006) it was not additional until 1999 but subsequently became

Chart 5.6

ODA DISBURSEMENTS AND ESTIMATED ODA PLEDGES, 2004–2010

(Billions of current dollars)

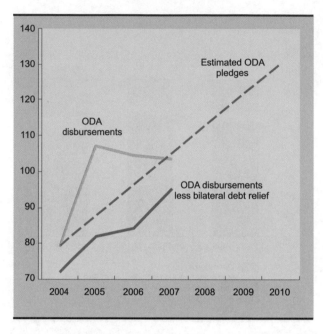

Source: UNCTAD secretariat calculations, based on OECD-IDS; and G-8 (2005) for OECD estimates of ODA pledges.
Note: The data, as reported by donors, are net disbursements.

additional. However, neither of these studies conducts a formal econometric analysis of the additionality of debt relief similar to that presented for the period 2000 to 2006 in the annex to this chapter.[9]

Assessing the additionality of the debt relief granted requires a comparison with a counterfactual scenario (i.e. the amount of ODA that would have been provided in the absence of debt relief). One way to construct such a scenario would be to consider the different pledges made by major donor countries to increase their ODA up to a certain level and within a certain time frame (G-8, 2005). In 2005, the OECD estimated that, on the basis of these donor commitments and other relevant factors, ODA from the G-8 and other donors to all developing countries would be higher by $50 billion in 2010 compared to its 2004 level. If this estimate is translated into annual increases along a trend line, and if these are compared to actual disbursements, total ODA excluding debt relief has been considerably lower than the assumed trend increase based on donor pledges (chart 5.6).

The econometric analysis of debt relief additionality undertaken for this *Report* is based on a narrower definition of additionality, one that is consistent with the Monterrey Consensus which stipulates that debt relief should be "fully financed through additional resources" (para. 49) and that donors need to ensure that "resources provided for debt relief do not detract from ODA resources" (para. 51).

Within this definition, additionality can be evaluated from the donors' or the recipients' side. From the donors' side debt relief is additional if it does not reduce total ODA net of debt relief extended by each donor. From the recipients' side it is additional if countries that receive more debt relief do not receive less ODA net of debt relief. The finding that debt relief is additional from the recipients' side and is not additional from the donors' side would suggest that, for any recipient of debt relief that receives constant (or increasing) ODA net of debt relief, there is a poor country that is not receiving debt relief and is also receiving less ODA.

The analysis of additionality contained in the annex to this chapter finds that, from the donors' side, an extra dollar of debt relief leads to a reduction of $0.22–$0.28 in other forms of ODA. Moreover, statistical analysis, which includes the period prior to the launch of the HIPC Initiative, shows that, if donor countries are split into three groups – parsimonious (those that give little aid), generous (those that give a lot of aid) and intermediate (all the other countries) – debt relief crowds out much of the aid extended by generous countries. The point estimates of the regressions indicate that, for this group of countries, debt relief is not additional according to the definition of additionality employed here. For intermediate countries, the crowding-out coefficient is approximately 40 per cent and for parsimonious countries the coefficient is positive (albeit not statistically significant).

Focusing on the recipients' side, the results of the statistical analysis suggest that there is no strong evidence for either crowding in or crowding out. In fact, the study described in the appendix shows that different statistical techniques yield different results: some find evidence of small crowding-out effects and others show small crowding-in effects. Contrary to the findings of the World Bank (2006), that debt relief through the HIPC Initiative has become additional in recent years, the test elaborated in the annex to this chapter does not find this to be the case. If the proposition is accepted that full additionality requires debt relief to be additional to other forms of ODA commitments on both the donors' and the recipients' side, then the results of the statistical exercise described in the annex lead to the conclusion that debt relief under the HIPC Initiative has not been fully additional.

The reasoning behind debt relief initiatives was that they free up fiscal space previously allocated to servicing debt, thus enabling reallocation of budgetary resources to social expenditures. This assumes that the forgiven debt will have been serviced, but in many cases the forgiven debt was non-performing at the time

> Debt cancellations have provided only a limited amount of new resources, if any.

of its cancellation (see also chapter VI, section C). Moreover, debt servicing *flows* that are purportedly liberated for use as social expenditures under the HIPC Initiative are well below the debt *stock* values that are reported as ODA in debt cancellations, resulting in inflated estimates of delivered assistance. Thus debt relief operations, while alleviating the future financial burden of servicing outstanding loans, have only provided a limited amount of new resources, if any, that could be used immediately for investment or social spending purposes. Accordingly, the discussion in the following sections shifts from a focus on the provision of *aggregate* ODA, to an analysis of ODA excluding debt relief.

D. Effectiveness of ODA

1. *The recent debate on aid effectiveness*

The role that ODA can play in supporting the development process depends not only on its level, but also on how effectively it is used. Indeed, along with the commitments made by donor and recipient countries at various international conferences, aid effectiveness has assumed a leading position on the international development cooperation agenda, as reflected in the Paris Declaration on Aid Effectiveness and the Accra Agenda for Action (OECD, 2005 and 2007; Accra High-Level Forum, 2008). The current debate on aid effectiveness is concerned mainly with issues related to the administration of ODA, such as ownership of ODA-financed projects and programmes, harmonization of aid delivery, mutual accountability, the untying of aid, and reporting and assessment frameworks (OECD, 2007).

With regard to ownership, it has been stipulated that, as a matter of principle, ODA should support development priorities identified by stakeholders in the beneficiary countries themselves rather than by donor countries. Similarly, technical cooperation activities are expected to achieve optimal results only when they are tailored to locally determined capacity-building needs. Moreover, the OECD also found that efforts by developing countries to strengthen national development strategies and budgets need to be complemented by efforts of donor countries to "make better use of partners' national budgets" and to "work aggressively to reduce the transaction costs of delivering and managing aid" (OECD, 2007: 52).

The Paris Declaration recognized that the stability of aid flows has a strong impact on aid effectiveness. Stability implies low volatility of net disbursements around the trend (which, following the commitments

Chart 5.7

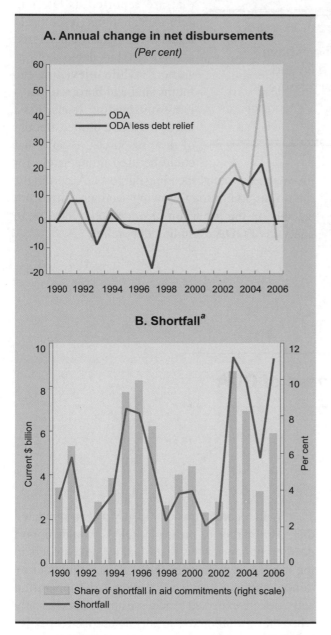

VARIABILITY OF BILATERAL ODA,
1990–2006

A. Annual change in net disbursements
(Per cent)

ODA
ODA less debt relief

B. Shortfall[a]

Current $ billion

Per cent

Share of shortfall in aid commitments (right scale)
Shortfall

Source: UNCTAD secretariat calculations, based on OECD-IDS.
  Note: The data, as reported by donors, are in current dollars.
      a Aid commitments less gross disbursements, excluding
        debt relief.

made in connection with the Monterrey Consensus,
should be a rising one). It can also be interpreted
to mean that aid flows should be reliable, and that
actual disbursements should not repeatedly and substantially fall short of aid commitments. Given that
ODA flows account for a substantial part of central

government expenditure in many recipient countries,
their instability can have immediate effects on the
provision of essential publicly provided goods in
those countries. It also impairs the effectiveness of
ODA in terms of contribution to per capita income
growth, as discussed in subsection 2 below. In reality, aid has been fairly volatile since the early 1990s,
including year-to-year reductions in absolute terms
in some years in the mid-1990s and again since
2005 (chart 5.7). Aid uncertainty, as measured by
the shortfall of gross disbursements against formal
commitments, excluding debt relief, has increased
since 2002.

A key question in the context of aid effectiveness relates to the variables against which it can be
measured. Traditionally, growth of per capita income
has been a key indicator for progress in development,
but with the Millennium Declaration, which does not
contain any explicit reference to growth, the focus
has been shifted to the MDGs. Obviously, depending on the objective, instruments and intermediate
targets tend to differ. If output growth is the objective,
enlarging productive capacity and productivity must
be intermediate targets, and financing of projects that
directly or indirectly contribute to these targets is an
indispensable instrument. By contrast, if short-term
or direct poverty reduction is the objective, direct
transfers and investment in and current spending on
health and education can be additional instruments
or intermediate targets, even if they have no measurable, or only a very long-term, impact on per capita
income growth. It is against this background that the
effectiveness of ODA in terms of generating faster
growth and achieving the MDGs is discussed next.

2. *Effectiveness of ODA with respect to growth*

Since the late 1960s, empirical research has
dealt with the aid-growth relationship in detail, but
the results have been inconclusive. Even the reverse
causality (i.e. growth leading to higher ODA flows)
cannot be ruled out, because some donors may tend
to reward improvements in economic performance.
However, earlier research has also pointed to the
necessity of decomposing aid flows in order to obtain
meaningful results for the ODA-growth relationship
(Cassen, 1986), and recent research following this

Box 5.1

RESEARCH ON THE RELATIONSHIP BETWEEN AID AND GROWTH

The assumption of aid having a positive impact on growth remained scientifically almost unchallenged during the 1950s and 1960s. It was Papanek (1972) who provided the first growth regressions on aid. He divided foreign capital flows into foreign aid, foreign investment and other capital inflows, and could thus isolate the particular effect of aid on growth. He found a positive correlation. Chenery and Carter (1973) developed the savings-gap model of the 1960s further and arrived at the conclusion that aid was well able to bridge the savings gap as well as the foreign-exchange gap. Following Rosenstein-Rodan, this additional foreign capital inflow was believed to provide a "big push" for poor economies.

This optimistic view was called into question at the beginning of the 1980s in light of the empirical evidence. Mosley (1980) introduced the "micro-macro" paradox of the aid-growth relationship. According to this, ODA may have positive effects when individual projects are evaluated at the micro level, but without evidence at the macro level to support the contention that aid has a significant impact on growth. Other researchers have sought explanations for the perceived weak impact of aid on growth in developing countries, and have criticized ODA from a number of angles: for generating false incentives, enhancing corruption or damaging private sector initiative, with negative effects on growth (see, for example, Bauer, 1982).

Until the mid-1990s, the common view on the impact of aid on growth was quite bleak. Boone (1996) found that, on average, aid had a neutral impact, given that poverty was not caused by capital shortages and aid flows in particular did not stimulate growth processes. He also pointed out that ODA flows did not have a significant effect on human development either. A new debate on the aid-growth relationship emerged from these results, with some authors highlighting the importance of the policy environment, in particular the quality of governance and institutions, for the growth effectiveness of ODA (Burnside and Dollar, 2000). The proposition that "good governance" was key to securing a positive effect from external aid soon entered into policy prescriptions of the international financial institutions, and many other donors started to base their lending decisions on these findings. However, the results of Burnside and Dollar (2000) were quickly refuted (for example, by Easterly, Levine and Roodman, 2004). For example, Hansen and Tarp (2000 and 2001) demonstrated that foreign aid may have a positive impact on growth even in a bad policy environment. Most researchers who advance this view would nonetheless agree that aid has diminishing returns, which can be explained by countries' limited absorptive capacities. Other researchers doubt that aid has positive effects on growth (e.g. Rajan and Subramanian, 2005 and 2007).

More recently, Roodman (2008) has checked the robustness of the main empirical results of the aid literature. He challenges previous techniques and concludes that the average effects of aid on growth are too small to be traced statistically. There is thus an inherent lack of robustness in aid-growth-regressions, for which no simple or definitive explanation may exist.

Another strand of the literature tries to establish causality between specific subcomponents of aid and growth, and studies the growth-enhancing effects of these subcomponents (e.g. Clements, Radelet and Bhavnani, 2004; Michaelowa and Weber, 2006; Dreher, Thiele and Nunnenkamp, 2007; and Mishra and Newhouse, 2007). While the results from this literature are still inconclusive, there is some evidence that sectoral aid is able to strengthen certain factors that are conducive to economic growth.

approach found that the short-term impact of aid on growth was considerably greater than what emanated from studies based on aggregate ODA data (see box 5.1 for details of the literature).

In pursuing this analytical approach further, an econometric test (described in greater detail in the annex to this chapter) is used to analyse ODA flows for various types of sectoral aid, programme

Chart 5.8

GROSS FIXED CAPITAL FORMATION (GFCF) AND ECONOMIC ODA PER CAPITA, AVERAGE OF 2004–2006

(Current dollars)

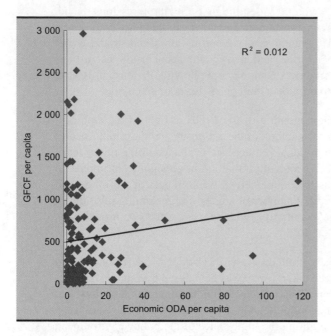

Source: UNCTAD secretariat calculations, based on OECD-IDS; and UNSD database.

Note: ODA data, as reported by donors, are gross disbursements. Economic ODA is ODA for economic infrastructure and production as defined by OECD/DAC.

and budget support, and debt relief for 162 developing countries, and their impact on growth during the period 1975–2006. This analysis also controls for a number of other factors, such as the quality of governance, degree of openness and level of educational attainment, which are generally believed to affect the aid-growth relationship.

The analysis shows that within the category of sectoral ODA, flows targeted at economic infrastructure contribute strongly to economic growth, whereas those earmarked for social infrastructure and services do not. These findings have important policy implications for financing of the MDGs and for development in general. While aid for social sectors is welcome, and should even be intensified in certain areas or regions, such disbursements should come in addition to sectoral ODA in support of capital formation in the productive sectors, which is a prerequisite for faster growth of value added and employment.

The analysis also shows that uncertainty with respect to aid disbursements has a significant negative impact on growth (see also Fielding and Mavrotas, 2005).

Another aspect that merits attention from the point of view of aid effectiveness is geographical distribution. In terms of actual need for foreign financing, it seems reasonable to expect that the share of ODA provided with the specific purpose of improving economic infrastructure and strengthening the productive sectors would flow primarily to those countries that have the lowest ratios of investment to GNI per capita. However, empirically the correlation is very weak and the actual distribution of "economic" ODA differs from what might be expected (chart 5.8).

Obviously, the effects of ODA, or specific categories of ODA, on per capita income growth discussed in this subsection can be expected to lead to, or at least facilitate the achievement of improvements in the different variables specified as indicators for development in the Millennium Declaration. Indeed, it is difficult to see how most of these indicators, in particular those related to poverty reduction, can be improved in the long term without higher investment in productive capacities that raise domestic value-added. Such investment would increase the level of income, and boost employment, which would improve income distribution in favour of the poorer parts of the population. However, independent of the growth effectiveness of ODA, or specific categories of ODA, in terms of higher investment and faster growth, the potential effects of ODA on social and human development indicators have received particular attention in connection with the efforts of the international community to support developing countries in achieving the MDGs. This aspect is examined in the next section.

3. Effectiveness of ODA with respect to the MDGs

In recent years, ODA is increasingly viewed as the contribution of the international community to the efforts of developing countries to achieve the MDGs, which reflect social and human development; growth is not explicitly mentioned as an objective or an intermediate target. This is a departure from the traditional premise that the purpose of external financing was primarily to raise the level of domestic investment in the productive sectors. The data reported by OECD-DAC on ODA for social infrastructure and services in the areas of education, health, and water supply and sanitation (referred to in what follows as "social aid") can be considered the most closely related to efforts aimed at achieving the MDGs. Social aid increased by 88 per cent from 1996–2001 to 2002–2006, and its share in total developmental aid rose from 52 to 65 per cent.

In particular, the share of social aid in total development aid has risen since the early 1990s, with a surge after the MDGs were agreed (chart 5.9). Since 2001, there has been an increase in all components of social aid. The steepest increase has taken place for government and civil society, which has become the single most important component of social aid (chart 5.10), in line with the international dialogue that emphasizes the importance of governance in the development process. In absolute terms, the smallest

Chart 5.10

COMPOSITION OF SOCIAL ODA BY MAIN SUB-CATEGORIES, 1990–2006

(Per cent)

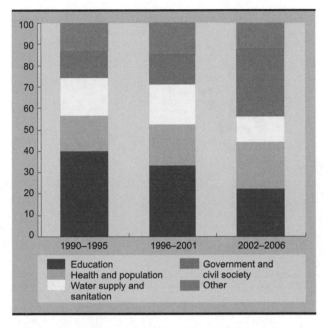

Source: UNCTAD secretariat calculations, based on OECD-IDS.
Note: The data, as reported by donors, are in current dollars and represent net disbursements.

Chart 5.9

COMPOSITION OF DEVELOPMENTAL ODA BY MAIN CATEGORIES, 1990–2006

(Per cent)

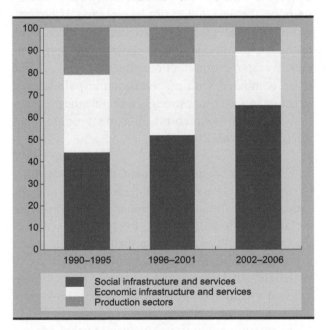

Source: UNCTAD secretariat calculations, based on OECD-IDS.
Note: The data, as reported by donors, are in current dollars and represent net disbursements.

increase has been registered for education, and the annual average ODA for water supply and sanitation even stagnated compared to the second half of the 1990s. Nevertheless, there is evidence that ODA has been successful in increasing educational attainment and health conditions (Michaelowa and Weber, 2006; Dreher, Nunnenkamp and Thiele, 2007; Mishra and Newhouse, 2007).

The 2008 *Global Monitoring Report* of the World Bank notes that progress towards achieving the MDGs has occurred across all regions, though the degree has been uneven. However, it also notes that despite incremental progress towards reducing poverty across all regions, many countries are off-track with regard to achieving the MDGs by 2015. It observes that in no country has aid been scaled up sufficiently to support a medium-term programme to achieve the MDGs (World Bank, 2008).

Looking at the geographical distribution of ODA for social infrastructure by comparing it with the

Chart 5.11

HUMAN DEVELOPMENT INDEX (HDI) SCORES AND SOCIAL ODA PER CAPITA

(Current dollars and index numbers)

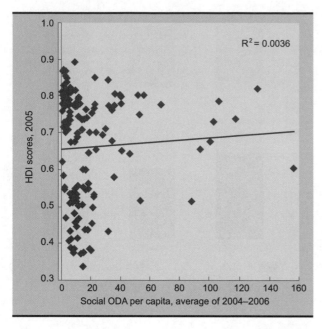

Source: UNCTAD secretariat calculations, based on OECD-IDS; and UNDP, *Human Development Report*, online.
Note: ODA data, as reported by donors, are gross disbursements. Social ODA is gross ODA disbursements for social infrastructure and services as defined by OECD/DAC.

score for countries in the UNDP's Human Development Index (HDI) (chart 5.11), reveals no correlation between the two variables. Despite the shift in the focus of ODA towards achieving the MDGs, and distinct from what might be expected, the geographical distribution of ODA for social purposes does not reflect the relative needs of countries as indicated by their HDI scores. This suggests that the effectiveness of ODA in helping countries attain the MDGs could be improved by taking better account of the relative needs of different countries, concentrating further increases in ODA grants on those countries that have the lowest level of social and human development.

Moreover, unless ODA is effective in helping growth, it is unlikely to be effective in reducing poverty in the long-term beyond 2015. Therefore, in order to achieve sustained poverty reduction, increases in ODA for social infrastructure and services must be accompanied by increases in ODA for economic infrastructure and productive sectors. Even

in these areas, there appears to be considerable room for improving aid effectiveness. One way could be to combine ODA in these areas with domestic financial reform, for example through the creation of institutions that would channel ODA into public and private investment projects financed jointly with domestic financial banks. This could help facilitate access of potential domestic investors to long-term financing and reduce the risks for domestic banks – and thus the spreads they charge – while at the same time helping to build a better functioning system of domestic financial intermediation.

4. ODA effectiveness, conditionality and governance

One way in which donors and creditors traditionally aimed at ensuring the effectiveness of their ODA grants and loans, and safeguarding the integrity of their financing, was by imposing different types of conditionality. These were shaped largely by the international financial institutions, but they also influenced bilateral donors and creditors. During the 1980s and 1990s, under structural adjustment programmes, conditionality became more far-reaching, including requiring commitments to reform macroeconomic, fiscal and trade policies. Since the mid-1990s, conditionality has focused more on the design and implementation of poverty reduction strategies, with greater attention given to the social implications of development policies. However, poverty reduction strategies typically are to be combined with macroeconomic policies and structural reforms that strongly resemble the prescriptions of previous structural adjustment programmes (UNCTAD, 2002).

There is broad agreement that new lending by the international financial institutions and the provision of official debt relief should be linked to certain conditions. However, the type and scope of the conditionality actually applied has come under growing criticism over the years, not only because of its deflationary bias, but also because of the proliferation and widening scope of the conditions (Goldstein, 2000; Kapur and Webb, 2000; and Buira, 2003). More recently, conditionality has extended beyond the economic sphere, entering into the broad area of domestic governance and institutions.

This recent trend reflects an increasingly influential strand of development thinking that emphasizes the role of good governance and institutions for enhancing growth and the effectiveness of ODA. While there is general agreement that improvements in governance and institutions are desirable in their own right, and are often positively correlated with economic development, there are different interpretations of the empirical evidence regarding this relationship, including the direction of causality (Khan, 2006; Mo, 2001). Moreover, views differ as to what constitutes good institutions and good governance, particularly when the large diversity of countries in terms of cultural, social, political, economic and natural heritage is taken into account.[10]

One major weakness is the lack of operational precision of the governance concept, the practical application of which frequently necessitates interpretation, which can be very subjective (Kapur and Webb, 2000). Moreover, a detailed analysis of developing countries, distinguishing between different groups of countries and different areas of governance, has shown that, although governance matters, "the very desirable goal of good governance may be neither necessary nor sufficient for accelerating and sustaining development" (Khan, 2006: vii).

The intellectual foundation for allocating aid on the basis of the quality of institutions and policies was elaborated in a well-known paper by Burnside and Dollar (2000). However, successive work has shown that, while the link between institutions and growth is undeniable in the very long run (Acemoglu, Johnson and Robinson, 2001), there is no robust evidence that aid produces better results in the presence of better policies or institutions (Easterly, Levine and Roodman, 2004).

Nevertheless, evaluations of countries according to their "scores" on different aspects of governance have become widely accepted, and seem to be increasingly influencing decisions by donors on the allocation of ODA. One important measure is provided by the Country Policy and Institutional Assessment (CPIA) of the World Bank, which strongly influences multilateral lending to countries. It is at the heart of the World Bank-IMF Debt Sustainability Framework, which is a determinant for debt relief under the HIPC Initiative and the Multilateral Debt Relief Initiative (MDRI) (see also chapter VI).

The CPIA measures the quality of 16 governance variables under the overall headings of economic management, structural policies, policies for social inclusion, and public sector management and institutions, and it consolidates the ratings on each of these variables into a single one. Obviously, the rating of policies requires certain value judgements and preferences for specific policy targets over others. For example, for macroeconomic management, countries receive the highest score if "... monetary/exchange rate policies have maintained price stability, and if public spending has not crowded out private investment" (World Bank, 2006: 6), although other possible criteria could be low and stable interest rates, increasing investment, faster GNI growth, or progress in structural change as measured by the expansion of the manufacturing sector. Similarly, fiscal policy is considered optimal when "the primary surplus has been managed to maintain a stable and low ratio [of] public debt to GDP ..." (World Bank 2006: 7), while its use for countercyclical macroeconomic management, or for the provision of certain public goods that are essential for the development of private productive activities, is not considered. With regard to trade policy, which is measured under the heading of structural policies, the best governance score can be achieved by countries that have an average tariff rate of less than 7 per cent and a maximum tariff rate of no more than 15 per cent on imported goods (World Bank 2006: 12). These examples suggest that, with respect to economic management and structural policies, good policies are interpreted subjectively as those that are in line with policy prescriptions under structural adjustment programmes; yet the performance of

> Conditionality has extended beyond the economic sphere, entering into the broad area of domestic governance and institutions.

> There appears to be a lack of coherence between the call for country ownership of ODA-financed projects and conditionalities.

Chart 5.12

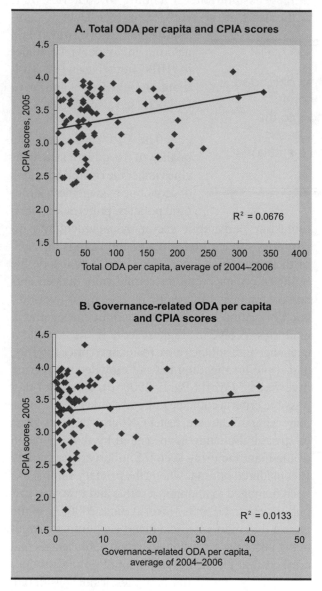

CPIA SCORES AND ODA PER CAPITA

A. Total ODA per capita and CPIA scores

$R^2 = 0.0676$

Total ODA per capita, average of 2004–2006

CPIA scores, 2005

B. Governance-related ODA per capita and CPIA scores

$R^2 = 0.0133$

CPIA scores, 2005

Governance-related ODA per capita, average of 2004–2006

Source: UNCTAD secretariat calculations, based on OECD-IDS; and World Bank CPIA data, online.

Note: The value of the consolidated CPIA rating varies between 1 and 6, with the latter indicating the best possible policies and institutions. Total ODA data, as reported by donors, are in current dollars and represent net disbursements. Governance-related ODA is gross disbursements of ODA for government and civil society as defined by OECD-IDS.

countries that followed these prescriptions in the past rarely met the high expectations (*TDR 2006*, chap. II). There also appears to be a lack of coherence between the call for country ownership of ODA-financed projects and programmes in the Paris Declaration on

Aid Effectiveness and conditionalities that impose restrictions on the orientation of economic policy and development strategy.

Under the heading of public sector management and institutions, the CPIA also measures country performance in terms of non-economic indicators, such as the quality of public administrations and transparency, accountability and corruption in the public sector. These are undoubtedly of great importance for the effectiveness and efficiency of public administration, but they cannot be measured objectively. Moreover, it appears that it is not the attained level or an improvement of an average measure of governance in these areas that makes a difference to growth and aid effectiveness; rather, it is the improvement of those governance capacities in countries that is critical for accelerating economic and social transformation (Khan, 2006). There has also been an intense debate on the design and function of the CPIA, particularly relating to its perceived policy biases and empirical flaws (see, for example, Alexander, 2004; van Waeyenberge, 2007; Herman 2007). Furthermore, proposals have been made to expand the CPIA index by introducing additional, outcome-oriented, variables (Kanbur, 2007; and Buiter 2007).[11]

Good governance indicators are not only a criterion for assistance at the multilateral level, but have also come to influence assistance at the bilateral level. For example, the Paris Declaration has set a target to significantly improve the performance of the CPIA indicator relating to public financial management in half of the recipient countries (OECD, 2005). In recent years, the promotion of good governance has thus become both a precondition for aid, as well as an intermediate target considered necessary for increasing the effectiveness of ODA.

Chart 5.12 shows the relationship between the CPIA scores of 75 countries and the amount of net ODA per capita they received in 2004–2006. It reveals a slight bias in favour of countries with higher scores (chart 5.12A). This reflects the importance of CPIA ratings for the allocation of IDA support. On the other hand, the distribution of governance-related ODA does not favour those countries that score low in the CPIA rating, and thus have a particular need for this support in their efforts to improve their governance and strengthen their public institutions (chart 5.12B).

In principle, linking ODA, especially in the form of grants, to certain conditions may be helpful for increasing its effectiveness. But in order for such conditionality to be coherent with other factors that determine the effectiveness of ODA, it might be useful to strengthen the dialogue between donors and recipients on the appropriateness of specific conditions. Their appropriateness should be determined by an evidence-based assessment of the relationship between the fulfilment of certain conditions and final development outcomes, taking into account governance and institutional weaknesses that hamper growth in the country-specific context.

It should also be recognized that compliance with conditionalities may require a front-loading of aid. The development of credible and capable institutions, for instance, is a formidable challenge, but many developing countries will require assistance in creating the necessary institutions and capabilities for fighting corruption and assuring good governance.

E. Remaining and new challenges

1. MDG financing and beyond

Since the adoption of the Millennium Declaration, securing sufficient financing to enable all developing countries to meet the MDGs has been an ongoing issue in the international development debate. In 2001, the Report of the High-level Panel on Financing for Development – the so-called *Zedillo Report* (United Nations, 2001) – estimated that an additional $50 billion per year would need to be added to net disbursements of ODA by DAC member States (which amounted to about $54 billion in 2000) in order to finance programmes designed to help countries reach the MDGs by 2015. Although DAC donors substantially increased their development assistance following the Monterrey Consensus, a large share of the recorded increase between 2000 and 2007 was on account of debt relief. Until 2007 total ODA disbursements net of debt relief remained below the level estimated as being needed by the *Zedillo Report*: the cumulative shortfall over this period

Until 2007, ODA disbursements remained below the level required for MDG financing.

amounted to $264 billion (chart 5.13). Furthermore, only a fraction of the increase in ODA was directed to MDG-related uses.

Estimates published in the report, *Investing in Development*, of the United Nations Millennium Project[12] (also known as the *Sachs Report*), which place a greater emphasis on the role of governments (UN Millennium Project, 2005), arrived at considerably higher figures on the ODA required for MDG financing. According to this report, ODA would need to increase gradually, from $121 billion in 2006 to $143 billion by 2010 and to $189 billion in 2015 (chart 5.13). Compared to the amounts suggested in the *Sachs Report* for ODA disbursements, those of the *Zedillo Report* would result in a cumulative shortfall of ODA for MDGs of $476 billion by 2015.

If ODA disbursements net of debt relief continued to follow their actual 2000–2007 trend until 2015, DAC donors would not reach their own aid target

Chart 5.13

**MDG FINANCING NEEDS, ODA
DISBURSEMENTS AND ESTIMATED
ODA PLEDGES, 2000–2015**

(Billions of current dollars)

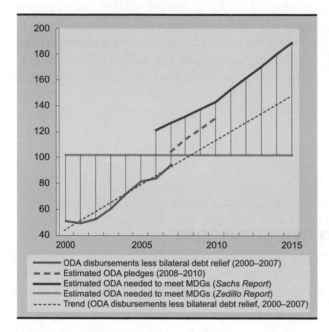

———— ODA disbursements less bilateral debt relief (2000–2007)
– – – Estimated ODA pledges (2008–2010)
———— Estimated ODA needed to meet MDGs (*Sachs Report*)
———— Estimated ODA needed to meet MDGs (*Zedillo Report*)
------- Trend (ODA disbursements less bilateral debt relief, 2000–2007)

Source: UNCTAD secretariat calculations, based on OECD-IDS;
G-8 (2005); *Zedillo Report* (United Nations, 2001); and
Sachs Report (UN Millennium Project, 2005).
Note: The data, as reported by donors, are in current dollars
and represent net disbursements.

(OECD, 2008). Moreover estimates in both reports assume that the suggested amounts, in their entirety, will take the form of additional financial resources – rather than debt relief – which the recipient governments can fully dispose of, and that they will be used entirely for the financing of MDG-related activities. However, it is highly unlikely that these assumptions will prove to be valid. In any case, despite the obvious efforts of donors to increase their ODA, actual aid disbursements are likely to fall short of the level required for reaching the MDGs (chart 5.13), let alone for longer term investment and growth objectives, especially if adjusted for population growth.

There is also the risk that a high concentration of ODA resources on projects that help achieve the MDGs by 2015 could divert financing away from other projects and programmes whose impact on growth and poverty reduction will only be felt in the long term. Yet many of those projects could be decisive for sustaining improvements in the indicators

of development contained in the MDGs. Higher and sustained rates of economic growth, which require concomitant levels of real investment, are essential for the creation of more productive employment opportunities, for raising household incomes and for achieving sustainable poverty reduction. It is therefore necessary to ensure that the increase in ODA for social and human development does not interfere with a necessary increase in ODA for economic infrastructure and production.[13]

2. New requirements and new financing instruments

The prospect of insufficient ODA, in its traditional forms, to finance the MDGs has energized efforts to design alternative or "innovative" financing mechanisms.[14] One set of proposals concerns the introduction of a global tax assessed on variables such as foreign currency transactions or the consumption of hydrocarbon fuels. Some of the proposals are not new, and their implementation is fraught with substantial practical and legal problems. Nonetheless, they merit further consideration in international forums, because of the need for additional financing, not only for the realization of the MDGs but also for addressing new issues of global concern that have gained prominence in recent years (see Kaul, 2008). These new issues include, in particular, measures for climate change mitigation, and the provision of global public goods such as international security, global communications and transportation infrastructures, and control of communicable diseases. However, given that the rationale for many national taxes is not restricted to their fiscal function but also includes the potential to influence the behaviour of consumers and investors, global taxes can also support the pursuit of non-fiscal objectives.

For example, the proposal for a tax on foreign currency transactions, which dates back to the early 1970s (and was discussed more intensely in the 1990s), was made initially not with a view to stepping up official development financing, but to reducing speculative capital flows and thereby increasing the stability of the international monetary and financial system after the collapse of the Bretton Woods arrangements.[15] The proposed tax would thus address two major problems in international financial governance at the same time and in a coherent manner. But although its attractiveness has become even more compelling in light of the exponential growth of financial markets and their increasing instability, since the proposal was first introduced in the 1970s, it continues to lack the required degree of international political support.

Heightened concerns over the global environment and the adverse effects of climate change have also strengthened the case for the introduction of some form of a global environmental tax. One of the most prominent proposals is for a global tax on fuel consumption, which would penalize the consumption of carbon dioxide emitting products while raising funds for development-related projects. A major obstacle to the introduction of such a tax would be the reluctance of many national governments to tax gasoline consumption above current levels. Furthermore, United States legislation prevents the Government of that country from participating in any global tax schemes and, as the United States is the single largest consumer of fuel, excluding it from such a scheme would reduce the potential global revenue of this tax by about 20 per cent.

The revenue potential of these proposals is very different: a tax of 0.01 per cent on foreign currency transactions would yield annual revenues of around $18 billion, whereas a uniform worldwide gasoline tax of $0.01 per litre could produce annual revenues of $180 billion (Reisen, 2004). Even if a gasoline tax were to be introduced only in high-income countries, the annual revenue potential is projected to be about $61 billion – an amount sufficiently large to cover the estimated needs for achieving the MDGs. Such an innovative approach to MDG financing therefore merits more serious political attention than it has received so far, the more so because it could also encourage a shift in energy consumption to more environmentally sound sources. Moreover, at current levels of consumption, a tax perceived on carbon dioxide emitting products would place the main burden on the richest countries, thereby also implying a compensation for industrial latecomers that will not be able to produce as much carbon dioxide as today's developed countries produced in the past.

> Insufficient ODA to finance the MDGs has energized efforts to design "innovative" financing mechanisms.

However, the administrative and political obstacles that are likely to emerge from the introduction of any form of a global tax, and the competition for funding between different development goals and global public goods, mean that the design, adoption and implementation of any of the above proposals probably would not be sufficiently rapid to meet the agreed targets by 2015. Alternative proposals, more modest in their financial impact, have been discussed following the Paris Conference on Innovative Financing Mechanisms in 2006.[16] The most notable, the Solidarity Levy on Air Travel, so far has demonstrated the greatest progress: 20 countries have committed to implementing the tax and 6 are already implementing it. This tax yielded revenues of approximately 200 million euros in 2007, which are earmarked for fighting diseases such as tuberculosis, malaria and HIV/AIDS.[17] Other mechanisms currently being discussed are advance market commitments for vaccines (AMCs) and private-public partnerships for microfinance. While these proposals have the merit of raising funding, including from possible non-official sources, and they represent encouraging add-ons to existing funding channels, they do not seem to have the potential to grow into programmes that could meet the remaining needs for MDG financing, even assuming that all the funds raised were directed to those goals. They certainly could not meet the additional financing needed to boost productive investment in the poorest countries to enable these countries to achieve the target of 7 per cent GDP growth, which would significantly narrow the gap in their per capita incomes with the more developed economies.

> The increasing importance of private aid flows raises the question of their effectiveness in terms of sectoral allocation, stability and predictability.

Nevertheless, the scope for channelling the increasing private aid towards developing countries seems promising. In six of the seven years between

1998 and 2005 private donations have grown faster than ODA excluding debt relief. Estimates based on OECD-DAC data suggest that private donations from DAC countries to developing countries in 2005 were $16.5 billion, equivalent to 20 per cent of total ODA excluding debt relief. For example, in the United States, private donations accounted for about 2 per cent of GNI, or around $250 billion, in 2005. Yet only $8.5 billion, or less than 4 per cent of this amount, was directed to developing countries through NGOs. In some European economies, private aid flows as a share of GNI are higher than in the United States, while they are less significant in others. This may partly be due to different tax treatments of private donations to international causes across OECD countries.[18] The increasing importance of private aid flows also gives rise to the question of their effectiveness in terms of sectoral allocation, stability and predictability. As private aid is distributed often through "vertical funds" (i.e. funds that support projects in specific areas such as environment or health), it will become ever more important to increase coordination between ODA and private aid flows.

Some observers consider non-DAC official donors to be promising alternative avenues for development cooperation and new sources of development finance for both MDGs and emerging issues of mutual global interest (Das, De Silva and Zhou, 2008). Attention is focused on development cooperation initiatives and contributions by capital-surplus middle-income countries in Asia and Latin America to lower-income developing countries, both in their respective regions and in sub-Saharan Africa. While sometimes labelled as "new" sources of lending to developing countries, a number of these countries, especially the oil-producers, first emerged on the development cooperation scene some 30 years ago, and have continued to play some role ever since (see, for example, UNCTAD, 1988).

The scale of ODA recently disbursed and pledged by other developing countries is especially significant for a number of recipient countries in Africa, and, as discussed in section B above, it has assumed a more important role overall since 2003. However, non-DAC aid could only make a marginal contribution to closing the official financing gap. Nevertheless, the fact that an increasing number of developing countries have become net exporters of capital indicates that they could provide additional loans, either bilaterally or multilaterally through regional financial institutions, to neighbouring or other developing countries.

As new sources and channels of official development financing gain importance, there is the risk of the aid delivery system becoming more fragmented, and oversight and coordination – both vital to aid effectiveness – more difficult. More comprehensive and consistent information on the concessional lending (and grant) activities of new donors from the South would certainly give greater coherence to the global ODA architecture, in addition to providing alternative criteria and benchmarks for evaluating aid effectiveness. But just as bilateral ODA serves a different function than that of multilateral aid and, as has been shown, some components of ODA are more effective for development than others, so too non-DAC aid can play a role that is additional to, and not a substitute for, scaled-up aid from traditional development partners.

F. Conclusions

In order to achieve the MDGs, it is understood that a larger proportion of ODA should be spent for health, education and other social purposes. This kind of ODA is essential and justified in its own right. However, poverty is a phenomenon closely, albeit not exclusively, related to the level of per capita income. Unless ODA helps boost growth, it is unlikely to be effective in reducing poverty in the long-term beyond the MDG target year of 2015. Sustained poverty reduction is not possible exclusively on the basis of income redistribution. It is therefore essential that, in addition to achieving the MDGs through increased ODA in social infrastructure and services, greater efforts be made to raise the level of investment in economic infrastructure and in the productive sectors with a view to increasing domestic value added. This is a necessary means to raising the level of income – and employment – in order to improve income distribution in favour of the poorer segments of the population. To the extent that such investment cannot be financed from domestic resources, because additional imports of capital require more foreign exchange than can be generated through exports, or because the domestic financial system does not provide long-term investment at a reasonable cost, ODA remains critical beyond what is needed for achieving the MDGs.

The composition of aid matters for its overall effectiveness. But it can only be measured meaningfully against clearly specified objectives. It is therefore useful to distinguish between social and human development objectives on the one hand, and growth objectives with appropriate intermediate targets – such as rates of productive investment – on the other. The first types of objectives can be pursued by increased ODA for projects in social infrastructure and services, whereas progress towards the growth objectives requires a concentration of project aid in economic infrastructure and the productive sectors. This in turn will also serve social and human development objectives in the medium and long term.

In order to achieve sustained poverty reduction, increases in ODA for social infrastructure and services must therefore not be at the expense of ODA for economic infrastructure and productive sectors, although even in these areas there appears to be considerable room for improving aid effectiveness. One way could be to leverage ODA with domestic financing, for example through the creation of institutions that would channel ODA into public and private investment projects financed jointly with domestic financial institutions. This could facilitate access of potential domestic investors to long-term financing and reduce the credit risk of domestic banks – and thus the spreads they charge – while at the same time helping to build a better functioning system of domestic financial intermediation.

The effectiveness of ODA with respect to growth or to the MDGs also depends on its distribution across countries. It could probably be improved by taking better account of the varying needs of countries and directing further increases in ODA grants to the poorest countries that have the greatest

> Unless ODA helps boost growth, it is unlikely to be effective in reducing poverty in the long-term, beyond the MDG target year of 2015.

difficulty in initiating a self-sustaining process of investment and growth. In the past, the geographical distribution of ODA had been governed mainly by criteria other than relative needs in terms of levels of per capita income and human development, or the degree of the fiscal or foreign-exchange gap. As the analysis in this chapter has shown, aid volatility and aid uncertainty may deter growth and could therefore seriously undermine other efforts to make aid more effective. Thus the promises made by donors through the Monterrey Consensus and the Paris Declaration for improving the stability and reliability of aid are more pertinent than ever.

Overall, a considerable financing gap appears to persist with respect not only to MDG-related activities, but also to investments that will be beneficial for growth and structural change beyond the MDGs, let alone for tackling new challenges for developing countries as a result of climate change. It is possible that in the medium term, a combination of innovative mechanisms and the continued growth of private aid flows may increasingly contribute to development finance. However, the only realistic chance of meeting the MDGs between now and 2015 is to dramatically scale up ODA flows and, to the extent possible through multilateral instruments, by an amount at least in the range of $50–$60 billion a year.

While greater efforts at increasing the effectiveness of ODA may contribute to narrowing the

> The only realistic chance of meeting the MDGs between now and 2015 is to dramatically scale up ODA flows.

financing gap, donors need to continue their efforts to provide more ODA. They need to meet the targets of 0.7 per cent of their GNI going as ODA to the developing countries as a whole, and 0.15–0.20 per cent of GNI going as ODA to the group of LDCs, as reaffirmed in the Monterrey Consensus. In addition, the international community would be well advised to mobilize the necessary solidarity and political will to utilize new and innovative sources of financing to help promote reforms in global economic governance and adjustments to global environmental challenges. At the same time, the developing countries need to redouble their efforts to finance investments out of domestic sources.

Debt relief has played an important role in ODA through the HIPC Initiative, and in particular since 2003. However, there is no clear evidence that it has been additional to other forms of aid, as called for in the Monterrey Consensus. Such additionality is indispensable, because while debt stock reduction can alleviate the debt-servicing burden in the future, it has a very limited effect on the capacity of governments to increase their expenditure in the period in which it is granted, although it is fully counted as ODA in that period. Full additionality would not only improve the chances of beneficiary countries to meet their growth and social objectives, including those set by the MDGs, it would also increase the possibility of these countries to achieve and maintain a level of debt that is sustainable, an issue taken up in greater detail in the next chapter. ∎

Notes

1 The following are examples of the financing commitments submitted by individual G-8 members: the EU will almost double its ODA between 2004 and 2010; both Germany and Italy have undertaken to reach 0.51 per cent ODA/GNI in 2010 and 0.7 per cent ODA/GNI in 2015; France announced its intention to raise its ODA/GNI to 0.5 per cent in 2007 and to 0.7 per cent in 2012, and the United Kingdom announced its aim to reach the 0.7 per cent target by 2013. Canada committed to double its international assistance between 2001 and 2010 and Japan to raise its ODA by $10 billion until 2010. Specific commitments were made for increasing aid to sub-Saharan Africa including by the United States, which proposed doubling its aid to that region between 2004 and 2010 (G-8, 2005).

2 For a survey, see Bacha, 1990.

3 Regrettably, data on real exchange rates is not available for all the developing and transition economies for which the changes in the current-account balance between 1992–1996 and 2002–2006 were examined. However, among 47 of the countries identified as experiencing a deterioration in their current account, only 8 saw an appreciation of their real exchange rate of more than 10 percentage points. In 15 of these countries the current account swing was negative despite a depreciation of the real exchange rate of more than 10 percentage points. The remaining 24 countries had movements in the real exchange rate of less then 10 percentage points. Looking at the LDCs for which the relevant data are available, 11 out of 19 saw a negative swing in their current account in spite of a real exchange rate depreciation.

4 As measured by different indicators, the MDGs seek to: (i) eradicate extreme poverty and hunger; (ii) achieve universal primary education; (iii) promote gender equality and empower women; (iv) reduce child mortality; (v) improve maternal health; (vi) combat HIV/AIDS, malaria and other diseases; and (vii) ensure environmental sustainability.

5 All ODA data in this chapter are ODA by DAC members, unless otherwise indicated. The 22 DAC countries are: Australia, Austria, Belgium, Canada, Denmark, Finland, France, Germany, Greece, Ireland, Italy, Japan, Luxembourg, the Netherlands, New Zealand, Norway, Portugal, Spain, Sweden, Switzerland, the United Kingdom and the United States.

6 See DAC Statistical Reporting Directives, DCD/DAC (2007) 34, April 2007: 12, para. 35.

7 If a transaction satisfies the condition of at least a 25 per cent grant element, which is calculated at a rate of discount of 10 per cent, the entire amount of the loan is reported as ODA. Within this broad definition, ODA transactions can take the form of, for example, goods in kind, services rendered, technical advice and training, emergency food aid, humanitarian assistance, financing for foreign exchange students, or contributions to multilateral development agencies.

8 Over the period 1996–2005, the top 10 non-DAC creditors, in order of magnitude of their total concessional lending, were: Kuwait, China, the Russian Federation, Saudi Arabia, the United Arab Emirates, the Republic of Korea, Turkey, the Bolivarian Republic of Venezuela, India and Poland.

9 Earlier econometric analyses of debt relief additionality in the period between the 1970s and 2001 have been inconclusive (see, for example, Ndikumana, 2004; Birdsall, Classens and Diwan, 2002; Powell, 2003; and Hepp, 2005).

10 Views on governance range from an instrumental view, which evaluates public administrations by the efficacy with which they achieve objectives that are in the societal interest, to a normative view, which evaluates public administrations by the way in which they pursue these objectives, as well as the objectives themselves. The latter view – which is reflected in the World Bank's indicators on governance – often equates good governance with the

democratic decision-making process and liberal economic objectives.

11   The principal proponents of the World Governance Indicators – the World Bank's broader framework for measuring the quality of governance and institutions around the world – have addressed some of its allegedly most persistent weaknesses, arguing that critiques have been either conceptually incorrect or empirically unsubstantiated (Kaufmann and Kraay, 2008).

12   The United Nations Millennium Project was established in 2002 as an independent advisory body to identify strategies to achieve the MDGs, particularly in those countries deemed to be far off-course in progress. The *Sachs Report* synthesizes the analyses prepared by the 10 task forces established under the project.

13   Based on this reasoning, the Third Programme of Action for the LDCs for the Decade 2001–2010 emphasized a series of infrastructure goals, as well as concrete economic goals, including a target growth rate of 7 per cent per annum and a targeted investment rate of 25 per cent of GDP.

14   A comprehensive assessment of various proposals for innovative financing instruments has been undertaken by the World Institute for Development Economics Research of the United Nations University (UNU/WIDER) in cooperation with the United Nations Department for Economic and Social Affairs (see http://www.wider.unu.edu/research/projects-by-theme/development-and-finance/en_GB/innovative-sources-for-development-finance/; and Atkinson, 2004).

15   This was discussed by UNCTAD already in 1996, when it was observed that "such a tax, which has also attracted interest as a potential source of revenue for various internationally agreed purposes, presents a series of difficult, though not necessarily insuperable, problems. Decisions would be necessary concerning the locations at which the tax would be imposed, the level of the tax and the coverage of instruments" (*TDR 1996*: 174–175).

16   In the aftermath of this ministerial meeting, the Leading Group on Solidarity Levies to Fund Development was established with the mandate to develop mechanisms for raising funds for MDG projects.

17   According to information obtained directly from Leading Group Secretariat.

18   Unlike most other EU countries, the two countries with the highest reported share of private aid flows in GNI, Ireland and the Netherlands, allow tax deductions for contributions to cross-border charities.

References

Accra High-Level Forum (2008). Accra Agenda for Action. Available at: http://www.accrahlf.net/.

Acemoglu D, Johnson S and Robinson J (2001). The colonial origins of comparative development: an empirical investigation. *American Economic Review,* 91: 1369–1401.

Alexander N (2004). The World Bank as "Judge and Jury": The Country Policy and Institutional Assessment (CPIA) rating system and the PRSP. Note for Dialogue on the CPIA and Aid Allocation. Task Force on Aid of Initiative for Policy Dialogue. New York, Columbia University, August.

Arslanalp S and Henry PB (2006). Debt relief. NBER Working Paper No. W12187. Cambridge, MA, National Bureau of Economic Research, May.

Atkinson AB ed. (2004). *New Sources of Development Finance*. Oxford, Oxford University Press.

Bacha EL (1990). A three-gap model of foreign transfers and the GDP growth rate in developing countries. *Journal of Development Economics*, 32: 279–296.

Bauer P (1982*). Economic Analysis and Policy in Underdeveloped Countries*. Westport, CT, Greenwood.

Birdsall N, Claessens S and Diwan I (2002). Will HIPC matter? The debt game and donor behavior in Africa. CEPR Discussion Paper No. 3297, April.

Boone P (1996). Politics and the effectiveness of foreign aid. *European Economic Review*, 40(2): 289–329.

Buira A (2003). An analysis of IMF conditionality. G-24 Discussion Paper No. 22. New York and Geneva, UNCTAD, August.

Buiter WH (2007). No bricks without straw: a critique of Ravi Kanbur's modest proposal for introducing development outcomes in IDA allocation procedures. Note for Dialogue on the CPIA and Aid Allocation,

Task Force on Aid of Initiative for Policy Dialogue. New York, Columbia University, 5 April.

Burnside C and Dollar D (2000). Aid, policies and growth. *American Economic Review*, 90(4): 847–868.

Cassen R and associates (1986). *Does Aid Work?* Oxford, Clarendon Press.

Chenery HB and Carter NG (1973). Foreign assistance and development performance, 1960–1979. *American Economic Review*, 63(2): 459–469.

Clements M, Radelet S and Bhavnani R (2004). Counting chickens when they hatch: the short-term effect of aid on growth. Working Paper No. 44. Washington, DC, Center for Global Development.

Das S, De Silva L and Zhou Y (2008). Background study for the 2008 Development Cooperation Forum on the South-South Triangular Development Cooperation. New York, United Nations, April.

Dreher A, Thiele R and Nunnenkamp P (2007). Do donors target aid in line with the MDGs? A sector perspective of aid allocation. *Review of World Economics*, 143(4): 596–630.

Easterly W, Levine R and Roodman D (2004). Aid, policies and growth: Comment. *American Economic Review*, 94(3): 774–780.

Fielding D and Mavrotas G (2005). The volatility of aid. WIDER Discussion Paper No. 2005/06. Helsinki, World Institute for Development Economics Research.

G-8 (2005). Gleneagles Summit Document: Africa. Available at: http://www.britishembassy.gov.uk/Files/kfile/PostG8_Gleneagles_Africa,0.pdf.

Goldstein M (2000). IMF structural programs. Paper prepared for the NBER Conference on Economic and Financial Crises in Emerging Market Economies. Woodstock, Vermont, 19–21 October. Available at: www.iie.com.

Hansen H and Tarp F (2000). On the empirics of foreign aid and growth. EPRU Working Paper Series. Copenhagen, University of Copenhagen, Department of Economics.

Hansen H and Tarp F (2001). Aid and growth regressions. *Journal of Development Economics*, 64: 547–570.

Hepp R (2005). Can debt relief buy growth? Mimeo. University of California, Davis.

Herman B (2007). Kill the CPIA! Note for Dialogue on the CPIA and Aid Allocation, Task Force on Aid of the Initiative for Policy Dialogue. New York, Columbia University, 5 April.

Kanbur R (2007). Reforming the formula: A modest proposal for introducing development outcomes in IDA allocation procedures. Note for the Dialogue on the CPIA and Aid Allocation, Task Force on Aid of the Initiative for Policy Dialogue. New York, Columbia University, 5 April.

Kapur D and Webb R (2000). Governance-related conditionalities of the international financial institutions. G-24 Discussion Paper No. 6. New York and Geneva, UNCTAD, August.

Kaufmann D and Kraay A (2008). Governance indicators: Where are we, where should we be going? *The World Bank Research Observer,* 23(1). Washington, DC, Spring.

Kaul I (2008). Beyond official development assistance: Towards a new international cooperation architecture. Mimeo.

Khan MH (2006). Governance and anti-corruption reforms in developing countries: Policies, evidence and ways forward. G-24 Discussion Paper No. 42. New York and Geneva, UNCTAD, November.

Michaelowa K and Weber A (2006). Aid effectivenes reconsidered: Panel data evidence for the education sector. HWWA Discussion Paper No. 264. Hamburg, Hamburgisches Welt-Wirtschafts-Archiv.

Mishra P and Newhouse DL (2007). Health aid and infant mortality. IMF Working Paper WP/07/100. Washington, DC, International Monetary Fund, April.

Mo PH (2001). Corruption and economic growth. *Journal of Comparative Economics*, 29(1): 66–79.

Mosley P (1980). Aid, savings and growth revisited. *Oxford Bulletin of Economics and Statistics*, 42(2): 79–95.

Ndikumana L (2004). Additionality of debt relief and debt forgiveness, and implications for future volumes of official assistance. *International Review of Economics and Finance*, 13(3) Elsevier: 325–340.

OECD (2005). Paris Declaration on Aid Effectiveness. OECD Development Co-operation Directorate, May; available at: http://www.oecd.org/dataoecd/11/41/34428351.pdf.

OECD (2007). Aid effectiveness: 2006 Survey on Monitoring the Paris Declaration, Overview of the results. Paris.

OECD (2008). We must do better. Trends in development assistance. Remarks by Angel Gurrioa, OECD Secretary-General. Tokyo, 4 April. Available at: http://www.oecd.org/document/7/0,3343,en_2649_34487_40385351_1_1_1_1,00.html.

Papanek GF (1972). Aid, foreign private investment, savings and growth in less developed countries. *Journal of Political Economy*, 81(1): 120–130.

Powell R (2003). Debt relief, additionality and aid allocation in low-income countries. IMF Working Paper WP/03/175. Washington, DC, International Monetary Fund, September.

Rajan R and Subramanian A (2005). Aid and growth: What does the cross-country evidence really show? NBER Working Paper No. 11513. Cambridge, MA, National Bureau of Economic Research.

Rajan R and Subramanian A (2007). Does aid affect governance? *American Economic Review*, 97(2): 322–327.

Reisen H (2004). Innovative approaches to funding the millennium development goals. Policy Brief No. 24. OECD Development Centre, Paris.

Roodman D (2008). Through the looking glass and what OLS found there: On growth, foreign aid and reverse causality. Center for Global Development Working Paper No. 137. Washington, DC, January.

Rosenstein-Rodan PN (1961). International aid for underdeveloped countries. *Review of Economics and Statistics*, XLIII(2): 107–138.

UNCTAD (various issues). *Trade and Development Report*. United Nations publication, New York and Geneva.

UNCTAD (1988). *Financial Solidarity for Development: 1987 Review*. United Nations publication, sales no. 88.II.D.4, New York and Geneva.

UNCTAD (2000). *Capital flows and growth in Africa*. United Nations publication, New York and Geneva, June.

UNCTAD (2002). *Economic development in Africa – From adjustment to poverty reduction: what is new?* United Nations publication, New York and Geneva, August.

UNCTAD (2006). *Economic Development in Africa – Doubling aid: making the "big push" work*. United Nations publication, New York and Geneva, August.

United Nations (2001*). Report of the High-level Panel on Financing for Development (Zedillo Report)*. United Nations publication, New York and Geneva, June.

United Nations (2002). Report of the International Conference on Financing for Development. Monterrey, Mexico, 18–22 March.

UN Millennium Project (2005). *Investing in Development: A Practical Plan to Achieve the Millennium Development Goals (Sachs Report)*. London and Sterling, VA, Earthscan.

van Waeyenberge E (2007). The missing piece: Country policy and institutional assessments at the Bank. Note for Dialogue on the CPIA and Aid Allocation, Task Force on Aid of Initiative for Policy Dialogue. New York, Columbia University, 5 April.

World Bank (2006). Debt relief for the poorest: An evaluation update of the HIPC Initiative. The Independent Evaluation Group of the World Bank. Washington, DC, September.

World Bank (2008). *Global Monitoring Report*. Washington, DC.

DETAILS ON ECONOMETRIC STUDIES

---

1. Econometric analysis of the impact of ODA on growth

The econometric analysis for the aid-growth relationship discussed in the main text covers a large panel data set for 162 developing countries for the period 1975–2006. Using stationarity-transformed data and panel data methods, various specifications were employed, of which only one result is presented in this annex. Details on the exact data definitions and data sources are given further below.

For the analysis, disaggregated ODA is being used with the following regression:

$$\Delta GDP^{pc} = \alpha + \beta_1 Aid_1 + \beta_2 Aid_2 + \beta_3 Aid_3 + \beta_4 Aid_4$$
$$+ \beta_5 Aid_5 + \beta_6 AidVolatility + \beta_7 AidUncertainty$$
$$+ \beta_8 Population + \beta_9 PerCapitaIncome +$$
$$\beta_{10} PrimaryEducation + \beta_{11} Investment +$$
$$\beta_{12} FDI + \beta_{13} Openness + \beta_{14} Governance +$$
$$\beta_{15} Reform + \beta_{16} LDC + \beta_{17} War + \varepsilon$$

where ΔGDP^{pc} is per capita GDP growth, Aid_{1-3} is sectoral aid, Aid_4 is general budget support, and Aid_5 is debt relief. Aid_1 refers to aid in social infrastructure and services, Aid_2 is aid flowing into economic infrastructure, and Aid_3 is aid for productive sectors. A proxy for *Education* is the primary education completion rate, which is more suited than the often employed school enrolment rates. *Investment* is the gross investment to GDP ratio, while *FDI* is the ratio of foreign direct investment to GDP. *Openness* is the ratio of trade to GDP. As standard governance indicators such as the World Bank's CPIA are not available for an analysis for the period 1975–2006, *Governance* is measured by the index of democratic accountability of the *International Country Risk Guide* of the PRS Group. *Reform* measures the change in bureaucratic quality as well as corruption. As this is clearly only a partial measure of governance, its coefficient must be evaluated with care, especially when comparing with previous studies on this subject. *War* and *LDC* are dummy variables.

Estimators are derived using the generalized method of moments (GMM). Technically, GMM-based dynamic panel data estimators take into account the presence of unobserved fixed country-specific effects and an autoregressive dependent variable. While static estimators based on ordinary least squares (OLS) are biased in this setting, GMM has proven to be consistent and asymptotically efficient. System GMM is especially appropriate with small samples as well as highly persistent series. Economically, this technique deals with policy and structural changes in the data set. Estimated parameters are invariant to policy regimes and free of

Table 5.A1

THE IMPACT OF DISAGGREGATED ODA ON ECONOMIC GROWTH

Variable	Coefficient	Standard error
Constant	0.09	0.11
Aid 1: social infrastructure and services	0.15	0.37
Aid 2: economic infrastructure	0.40	0.01***
Aid 3: production sectors	0.54	0.42
Aid 4: general budget support	0.43	0.80
Aid 5: debt relief	0.09	0.03***
Aid volatility	-0.01	0.48
Aid uncertainty	-0.74	0.00***
Population	0.09	0.01***
Income per capita	0.26	0.42
Primary education	0.60	0.21***
Investment	0.02	0.59
FDI	-0.43	0.45
Openness	-0.40	0.59
Governance	0.36	0.24
Reform	0.20	0.75
LDC	0.10	0.00***
War	0.57	0.24**

Note: For definitions of variables and sources, see explanatory notes at the end of this annex.
   ** Significant at 5 per cent.
   *** Significant at 1 per cent.

endogenous expectational issues. Hence, the method is useful for focusing on an analysis of subsequent "aid regimes" (e.g. pre- and post-transition phase, pre- and post-MDG commitments).[1]

The results presented in table 5.A1 give a comprehensive insight into the growth-related effects of ODA. Most notably, there is a positive, large and significant correlation between aid for economic infrastructure and economic growth. By contrast, aid for social infrastructure and services has, as would be expected, a relatively small and insignificant immediate effect on economic growth. But, as highlighted in this chapter, it may actually be more appropriate to measure the effectiveness of social aid by its contribution to social development, rather than by its effects on economic growth. The effect of debt relief on economic growth is positive and statistically significant, but small, which is to be expected, as debt relief often does not come as "fresh", additional money but rather as write-offs of – partially unserviced – debt stocks.

The analysis also shows a large and statistically significant negative effect of aid uncertainty on economic growth. The obtained negative parameter emphasizes once again that implementation of the international agreements reached in the Paris and Rome Declarations on Aid Effectiveness and Harmonization is key.

Population growth has a small and significant effect on economic growth, whereas education has been found to have a large and statistically significant effect. The educational variable exhibits a comparatively large estimated coefficient when compared to earlier studies on the same subject, which is most likely due to the analysis being based on school completion rather than enrolment rates.

Governance, as defined here, has not been found to have a significant impact on growth. Furthermore, the table shows no correlation between growth and openness or growth and FDI. Other definitions of openness to trade, and a breakdown of FDI into its subcomponents may yield different results.

2. Econometric estimates of the additionality of debt relief

This annex section describes a statistical exercise aimed at testing whether debt relief brings additional resources or crowds out other forms of ODA. The statistical tests measure additionality from the point of view of both donors and recipients. Since declarations at various G-8 meetings have called for an increase in ODA, it is unlikely that the estimations presented in this annex here are biased against finding additionality. Indeed, if donor countries had delivered on their promises of increasing aid net of debt relief, the estimates would be biased towards finding additionality.

Additionality from the donors' perspective

In order to test whether donors that grant debt relief give less aid that is not related to debt relief, it is possible to estimate the following regression:

$$ODANET_{i,t} = \alpha DR_{i,t} + \beta X_{i,t} + \mu_i + \varepsilon_{i,t}$$

Where ODANET is official development assistance net of debt relief provided by country i in year t, DR is debt relief offered by country i in year t. Both ODANET and DR are measured as a share of GNI of the donor country. X is a matrix of control variables, and μ_i is a country fixed-effect that controls for all possible donor-specific, time-invariant country characteristics (the model is also estimated with random effects and time-fixed effects). The model is estimated using data for 21 countries that are members of OECD DAC.[2] ODA and debt relief are measured using DAC data.

The parameter of interest is α. This parameter measures the relationship between debt-relief and non-debt-relief ODA. A point estimate of α equal to zero would indicate that there is no relationship between debt relief and ODANET, and that debt relief is additional. A positive value of α indicates that debt relief crowds in aid. This result, in which debt relief is more than additional, would suggest that donors realize that some countries need both debt relief *and* more resources. A negative value of α indicates that debt relief crowds out aid and that it is not fully additional.

The results reported in table 5.A2 suggest that debt relief is not fully additional. In particular, columns 1–4 show that each dollar of debt relief crowds out between 22 and 28 cents of non-debt-relief-related ODA.[3]

Additionality from the recipients' perspective

Additionality from the recipients' perspective is estimated using an approach similar to the one described above. The model is exactly the same, but all variables are now measured from the recipients' side and the set of controls in the matrix X is different.[4] The results obtained by estimating the equation from the recipients' and from the donors' point of view may differ for two reasons: the unit of analysis is different and developing countries receive ODA from both non-DAC donors and from various multilateral institutions.[5]

Table 5.A2

REGRESSION RESULTS WITH DEPENDENT VARIABLE: DONOR's ODA NET OF DEBT RELIEF AS A SHARE OF DONOR's GNI

(Only HIPC years)

	(1)	(2)	(3)	(4)
DR/Y	-0.23	-0.28	-0.22	-0.28
	(1.88)*	(2.13)**	(1.77)*	(2.09)**
Ln(GNIPC)	1.55	2.08	1.42	1.30
	(3.50)***	(1.74)*	(3.20)***	(0.98)
RER	0.03	0.04	0.04	0.06
	(0.41)	(0.48)	(0.49)	(0.63)
GOVBAL	-0.01	-0.01	-0.01	-0.01
	(2.12)**	(2.57)**	(2.57)**	(2.94)***
Constant	-3.23	-4.44	-2.93	-2.64
	(3.12)***	(1.60)	(2.83)***	(0.86)
No. of observations	166	166	166	166
No. of countries	21	21	21	21
Estimation method	Random effects		Fixed effects	
Year fixed effects	No	Yes	No	Yes

Note: For definitions of variables and sources, see explanatory notes at the end of this annex.
Absolute values of t statistics in parentheses.
   * Significant at 10 per cent.
  ** Significant at 5 per cent.
 *** Significant at 1 per cent.

The results reported in the first five columns of table 5.A3 show that most of the coefficients are positive (the exceptions being column 2 and 3), but rarely statistically significant. This is consistent with full additionality but no crowding-in effect. However, when the model is estimated with a statistical technique that puts less weight on outliers (columns 6–10), most coefficients become negative (the exception being column 6) and, in some cases, are marginally significant. Thus, when outliers are controlled for, there is some weak evidence that debt relief crowds out other forms of ODA, even when additionality is measured from the recipient's point of view.

Table 5.A4 focuses on the post-2000 period, and again finds that ordinary least square regressions do not yield a statistically significant correlation between debt relief and other forms of ODA (columns 1–5). When outliers are controlled for (columns 6–10), the model yields mixed results. The regressions that include the face value of the stock of debt suggest that debt relief crowds out other forms of aid. The regressions that include the net present value of the stock of debt show a crowding-in effect of debt relief.

Taken together these results suggest that, when measured from the recipients' perspective, there is no clear indication that debt relief crowds in or crowds out other forms of aid. Moreover, there is no evidence that, as claimed by the World Bank (see section C.3 of this chapter), debt relief has become more additional in the post-2000 period.

Table 5.A3

REGRESSION RESULTS WITH DEPENDENT VARIABLE: ODA NET OF DEBT RELIEF RECEIVED BY HIPCs, 1996–2006

(Fixed-effect estimates)

	(1)	(2)	(3)	(4)	(5)	(6)	(7)	(8)	(9)	(10)
DR/Y	0.07	-0.01	-0.01	0.02	0.02	0.04	-0.06	-0.05	-0.02	-0.03
	(1.09)	(0.15)	(0.25)	(0.40)	(0.37)	(1.34)	(1.75)*	(1.77)*	(0.74)	(1.03)
PPG/Y t-1		0.08	0.08				0.06	0.05		
		(4.71)***	(4.50)***				(7.23)***	(5.97)***		
Ln(GNIPC)		-0.02	-0.02	-0.05	-0.05		-0.09	-0.08	-0.10	-0.09
		(0.46)	(0.44)	(0.97)	(0.99)		(3.41)***	(3.17)***	(3.68)***	(3.65)***
SEAT UN SC		0.03	0.03	0.03	0.03		-0.01	-0.01	-0.01	-0.01
		(1.17)	(1.16)	(1.27)	(1.32)		(0.83)	(0.66)	(0.80)	(0.57)
INST		0.01	0.01	0.01	0.01		0.00	0.00	0.00	0.00
		(2.56)**	(2.28)**	(2.38)**	(2.09)**		(1.61)	(0.84)	(1.35)	(0.49)
Ln(POP)		0.22	0.28	0.28	0.35		0.11	0.31	0.15	0.35
		(4.10)***	(2.00)**	(5.31)***	(2.51)**		(4.29)***	(4.88)***	(5.52)***	(5.42)***
NPVPPG/Y t-1				0.09	0.10				0.07	0.06
				(4.17)***	(4.10)***				(6.40)***	(5.78)***
ARR/Y t-1	-0.01	-0.04	-0.03	-0.07	-0.07	-0.04	-0.09	-0.08	-0.12	-0.11
	(0.44)	(1.66)*	(1.50)	(2.60)***	(2.52)**	(4.58)***	(7.84)***	(7.81)***	(7.85)***	(7.83)***
Constant	0.14	-1.76	-2.36	-2.12	-2.78	0.10	-0.38	-2.16	-0.59	-2.39
	(23.68)***	(3.66)***	(1.79)*	(4.22)***	(2.10)**	(10.36)***	(1.55)	(3.75)***	(2.34)**	(4.05)***
No. of observations	260	248	248	246	246	260	248	248	246	246
No. of countries	28	27	27	27	27	28	27	27	27	27
Year fixed effects	No	No	Yes	No	Yes	No	No	Yes	No	Yes
Controlling for outliers	No	No	No	No	No	Yes	Yes	Yes	Yes	Yes

Note: For definitions of variables and sources, see explanatory notes at the end of this annex.
Absolute values of t statistics in parentheses.
   * Significant at 10 per cent.
  ** Significant at 5 per cent.
 *** Significant at 1 per cent.

Table 5.A4

REGRESSION RESULTS WITH DEPENDENT VARIABLE: ODA NET OF DEBT RELIEF RECEIVED BY HIPCs, 2000–2006

(Fixed-effect estimates)

	(1)	(2)	(3)	(4)	(5)	(6)	(7)	(8)	(9)	(10)
DR/Y	0.02	-0.01	-0.03	0.03	0.03	-0.05	-0.06	-0.07	0.06	0.16
	(0.37)	(0.24)	(0.66)	(0.59)	(0.60)	(1.41)	(1.88)*	(1.98)*	(1.94)*	(4.77)***
PPG/Y t-1		0.08	0.10				0.06	0.07		
		(2.44)**	(3.02)***				(3.57)***	(3.39)***		
Ln(GNIPC)		-0.04	-0.13	-0.09	-0.20		0.07	-0.04	0.03	-0.23
		(0.32)	(0.93)	(0.70)	(1.55)		(1.05)	(0.63)	(0.57)	(3.73)***
SEAT UN SC		0.00	0.02	0.01	0.02		-0.00	-0.00	0.00	-0.00
		(0.07)	(0.47)	(0.25)	(0.73)		(0.10)	(0.08)	(0.06)	(0.18)
INST		0.01	0.01	0.01	0.01		-0.00	0.00	-0.00	0.01
		(0.82)	(1.58)	(0.96)	(1.97)*		(0.57)	(0.13)	(0.52)	(2.37)**
Ln(POP)		0.02	-0.94	0.24	-0.69		-0.01	-0.68	0.00	-0.72
		(0.10)	(2.55)**	(1.60)	(2.06)**		(0.17)	(3.36)***	(0.03)	(3.96)***
NPVPPG/Y t-1				0.10	0.16				0.06	0.11
				(2.80)***	(3.50)***				(3.14)***	(4.43)***
ARR/Y t-1	0.04	0.02	0.02	-0.02	-0.05	0.01	-0.08	-0.09	-0.10	-0.04
	(1.37)	(0.87)	(0.61)	(0.47)	(1.35)	(1.04)	(5.05)***	(5.26)***	(5.93)***	(2.18)**
Constant	0.15	0.20	9.46	-1.53	7.73	0.43	0.04	6.62	0.13	8.17
	(20.60)***	(0.17)	(2.75)***	(1.22)	(2.40)**	(39.33)***	(0.06)	(3.72)***	(0.24)	(4.98)***
No. of observations	132	104	104	104	104	132	104	104	104	104
No. of countries	28	27	27	27	27	28	27	27	27	27
Year fixed effects	No	No	Yes	No	Yes	No	No	Yes	No	Yes
Controlling for outliers	No	No	No	No	No	Yes	Yes	Yes	Yes	Yes

Note: For definitions of variables and sources, see explanatory notes at the end of this annex.
Absolute values of t statistics in parentheses.
  * Significant at 10 per cent.
 ** Significant at 5 per cent.
*** Significant at 1 per cent.

DEFINITIONS OF VARIABLES AND SOURCES FOR REGRESSION ON AID AND GROWTH

Variable	Definition	Source
GDP growth per capita	GDP growth per capita (constant 2006 $)	World Bank, *World Development Indicators* database
Aid 1: social infrastructure and services	Social infrastructure and services, series 450.100.I (constant 2005 $, gross disbursements)	OECD-IDS
Aid 2: economic infrastructure	Economic infrastructure, series 450.200.II (constant 2005 $, gross disbursements)	OECD-IDS
Aid 3: production sectors	Production sectors, series 450.300.III (constant 2005 $, gross disbursements)	OECD-IDS
Aid 4: general budget support	General budget support, series 510.VI.1 (constant 2005 $, gross disbursements)	OECD-IDS
Aid 5: debt relief	Action related to debt, series 600.VII (constant 2005 $, gross disbursements)	OECD-IDS
Aid volatility	Standard deviation of the total ODA/GDP ratio	UNCTAD secretariat estimates, based on OECD-IDS
Aid uncertainty	Standard deviation of the error of an first-order autoregressive forecasting equation of the difference between commitments and disbursements	UNCTAD secretariat estimates, based on OECD-IDS
Population	Log of total population	*UNCTAD Handbook of Statistics* database
Income per capita	GDP per capita (constant 2006 $)	World Bank, *World Development Indicators* database
Education	Primary education (completion rate)	UNESCO, *World Education Indicators*, online.
Investment	Gross capital formation (per cent GDP)	World Bank, *World Development Indicators* database
FDI	Net inflows of foreign direct investment (per cent GDP)	*UNCTAD Handbook of Statistics* database
Openness	Total trade (exports plus imports of goods and services, per cent GDP)	World Bank, *World Development Indicators* database
Governance	Measure of democratic accountability	PRS Group, International Country Risk Guide
Reform	Measure of bureaucratic quality and corruption	PRS Group, International Country Risk Guide
LDC	LDC dummy variable	UN classification
War	Dummy variable measuring internal and external conflict	UNCTAD secretariat estimate, based on PRS Group, International Country Risk Guide

Explanatory note on tables 5.A2, 5.A3 and 5.A4

DEFINITIONS OF VARIABLES AND SOURCES FOR REGRESSION ON DEBT RELIEF AND AID ADDITIONALITY

Variable		Definition	Source
Donors			
ODA	Official development assistance	Net ODA, including debt relief; current prices ($ million)	OECD-IDS
DR	Debt relief given by donors	Debt forgiveness total; current prices ($ million), net disbursements	OECD-IDS
GOVBAL	Fiscal balance	Budget balance as share of GNI	OECD
Ln(GNIPC)	Logarithm per capita GNI	Logarithm of per capita GNI ($)	OECD
RER	Real exchange rate variation	Deviation of the real exchange rate from its long-run average	IMF, *International Financial Statistics*; and JP Morgan
Recipients			
ODA	Official development assistance	Net official development assistance from all donors, including debt relief	OECD-IDS
DR	Net debt relief	Net debt relief from all donors	OECD-IDS
DR1	Debt relief received by recipients	Principal forgiven + interest forgiven ($)	World Bank, *Global Development Finance* database
Ln (GNIPC)	Logarithm per capita GNI	Logarithm per capita GNI; PPP (constant 2000 international $)	World Bank, *World Development Indicators* database
PPG	Public and publicly guaranteed external debt	Public and publicly guaranteed external debt, total	World Bank, *Global Development Finance* database
GNI	GNI	GNI (current $)	World Bank, *World Development Indicators* database
ARR	Arrears	Principal arrears on debt outstanding (LDOD) + interest arrears on LDOD	World Bank, *Global Development Finance* database
Ln(POP)	Logarithm population	Logarithm of total population	*UNCTAD Handbook of Statistics* database
INST	Freedom House Index	Freedom measure, measured on a scale of 0 to 12, with 0 representing the lowest degree of freedom, and 12 the highest	http://www.Freedomhouse.org
Seat UN SC	UN Security Council seat	UN Security Council seat, with 0 representing no security council seat, and 1 representing Security Council seat	http://www.un.org/sc/members.asp
HIPC	HIPC	HIPC countries, with 0 representing no HIPC, and 1 representing HIPC	World Bank classification

Notes

1 The analysis was repeated with a static panel analysis with fixed and random effects, which did not significantly change results.

2 The sample does not include Luxembourg (the 22nd DAC country) because some of the control variables are missing. The control variables include the log of GNI per capita of the donor (lnGNIPC), the real exchange rate of the donor (RER) and the budget deficit of the donor (GOVBAL).

3 Column 1 presents random-effect estimates without year fixed effects, column 2 reports random-effect estimates with year fixed effects, column 3 reports fixed-effect estimates without year fixed effects, and column 4 reports fixed-effect estimates with year fixed effects. The regressions of table 5.A2 are restricted to the HIPC period (i.e.1996–2006), if additional years are included, the crowding-out effect ranges between 27 and 30 per cent.

4 The control variables include: the initial level of debt as a share of GNI (both in nominal and present value terms: PPG/Y and NPVPPG/Y respectively), the log of GNI per capita (ln(GNIPC)), a dummy variable that takes value 1 when the country has a seat in the United Nations Security Council (SEAT UN SC), a variable that measures institutional quality (INST), the log of population (ln(POP)), and arrears as a share of GDP (ARR/Y). All regressions are estimated using a fixed-effects model. A random-effects model yields similar results.

5 Composition effects can play an important role in explaining different results when additionality is measured from the two sides. Consider the following example. In the world there is only one donor and there are ten recipients. In year t, the donor gives $1,000 million of aid net of debt relief and no debt relief; in year $t+1$ the donor gives $970 million of aid net of debt relief and $100 million of debt relief. When additionality is evaluated from the donor's point of view, $\alpha = -0.3$ (1 dollar of debt relief crowded out $0.3 of other forms of aid). Looking from the recipients' point of view, and assuming there is one large recipient and there are nine small recipients, in year t each of the small recipients receives $10 million of aid, the large recipient receives $910 million of aid, and nobody receives debt relief. In year $t+1$, each of the small recipients receives $10.1 million of aid net of debt relief and the large recipient receives $879.1 million ($879.1 = 970 − 90.9$) of aid net of debt relief. Moreover each small recipient receives $1 million of debt relief and the big recipient receives $91 million ($91 = 100 − 9$) of debt relief. Hence, the small recipients have $\alpha = 0.1$ and the big recipient has $\alpha = -0.34$ ($-0.34 = (879.1 − 910)/91$). Since there are nine small recipients and one big recipient, the average value of is 0.056.

Chapter VI

CURRENT ISSUES RELATED TO THE EXTERNAL DEBT OF DEVELOPING COUNTRIES

A. Introduction

Large capital inflows are often seen as a sign of economic strength of a receiving country, and are sometimes cited as evidence of good institutions and investment opportunities. By contrast, large external debts are usually viewed as a sign of weakness, and developing countries are concerned about the accumulation of such debt. There is a lack of coherence in these perceptions, since debt accumulation is the natural consequence of large capital inflows, unless they take the form of grants or equity flows.

In case of excessive external borrowing, servicing of the external debt may become unsustainable, resulting in a financial crisis and reduced economic growth. A large foreign debt also reduces a country's policy space, as it limits the ability of the government to conduct an independent monetary or fiscal policy.

It is usually during periods of economic boom, when external capital is plentiful and external borrowing easy, that developing countries sow the seeds of future crises. These considerations are particularly important at the current juncture, as a large number of developing countries have strengthened their current-account positions, enabling them to reduce their external debt ratios. This improvement is likely to be due in part to better macroeconomic policies and debt management in debtor countries. It is also

due to considerable efforts by official creditors to provide debt relief to countries with unsustainable external debt burdens, starting with the launch of the Heavily Indebted Poor Countries (HIPC) Initiative in 1996, and especially since the beginning of the new millennium. But the major factor contributing to lower external debt ratios has been a favourable external environment, characterized by high commodity prices and low interest rates. The slowdown in growth in the developed economies (discussed in chapter I of this *Report*) and possible spillovers from the subprime crisis could reverse this favourable situation leading to a new deterioration in the debt situation of developing countries.

This chapter addresses a number of issues that could result from such a situation. Section B reviews recent trends in the external debt of developing countries and the different factors that have contributed to an improvement in traditional debt indicators. It shows that the overall debt situation has improved markedly over the past seven years, but with considerable differences across regions and countries, and mainly as the result of a favourable external environment.

Section C discusses the record of official debt relief and its contribution to the improvement of the external debt situation of developing countries. In order to be effective, debt relief should not be a substitute for other forms of aid; rather, in most cases it should be accompanied by an increase in ODA in order to help countries accelerate growth and structural change, and to achieve the Millennium Development Goals (MDGs) set by the United Nations in 2000.

Although, as discussed in chapter V debt relief may not have been fully additional, it has helped a number of countries to attain more sustainable levels of external debt over the past few years. For these countries, but also for those that have not experienced serious debt crises in the recent past, the challenge is to build on recent improvements in economic indicators and accelerate the process of investment, growth and structural change while maintaining a sustainable debt situation. Against this background, section D examines in greater detail ways and means to maintain debt sustainability in the medium and long term. It attempts to clarify some of the concepts

and definitions linked to debt sustainability and points to some problems with the debt sustainability frameworks adopted by the Bretton Woods institutions. The main message of this section is that debt sustainability analysis has to include a detailed analysis of the reasons behind debt accumulation. Accordingly, it is necessary to go beyond simple exercises based on the analysis of a few, often poorly estimated, debt indicators and debt thresholds.

Recognizing that even with the best policies in place, debt crises cannot be entirely ruled out, and in most cases they are triggered by external financial shocks, section E revisits the discussion on the need for an international framework to address unsustainable debt situations in an orderly manner. It suggests that a statutory mechanism for the resolution of sovereign default is a key element that is missing from the international financial architecture. The chapter concludes with recommendations for policies at the national and international levels in support of sound external financing and debt strategies.

B. Recent trends in the external debt of developing countries

While there can be different definitions of external debt, the term as used in this chapter refers to debt owed by residents of a country to non-residents, independent of currency denomination. This is the definition officially adopted by the main compilers of statistical information on public debt.[1]

Over the past three decades developing countries have experienced several financial and economic crises that have been closely related to their external debt situation. In the early 1970s, the total external debt of developing countries was relatively low (about 11 per cent of their gross national income (GNI)) and stable (charts 6.1 and 6.2). After the oil shock of the

mid-1970s, their debt started to grow rapidly and their debt indicators deteriorated. This was mainly due to the rapidly rising debt owed to commercial banks and to short-term debt in the context of what came to be known as the "recycling of petro-dollars" (i.e. the financing of rising trade deficits in the oil-importing countries) in a liberalizing international financial environment. This trend was reinforced in the early 1980s after a sharp increase in interest rates in the developed economies following a shift in the monetary policy regime of the United States. Debt owed to commercial banks and other private institutional lenders rose rapidly, while output in most debtor countries stagnated or even declined. This

Chart 6.1

EVOLUTION OF EXTERNAL DEBT IN DEVELOPING COUNTRIES, 1970–2006

(Per cent of GNI)

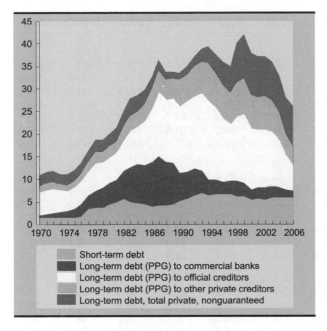

- Short-term debt
- Long-term debt (PPG) to commercial banks
- Long-term debt (PPG) to official creditors
- Long-term debt (PPG) to other private creditors
- Long-term debt, total private, nonguaranteed

Source: UNCTAD secretariat calculations, based on World Bank, *Global Development Finance* database.
Note: PPG is Public and Publicly Guaranteed debt.

triggered a deep economic crisis in many developing countries, especially in Latin America, that were indebted to international banking syndicates. Although there was little new lending (from this source), the accumulation of arrears by these countries led to an explosion of the external debt ratio, which reached 36 per cent of GNI in 1987.

Debt remained at high levels even after several emerging market countries started exchanging their defaulted syndicated bank loans with sovereign bonds issued under the aegis of the Brady Plan. The Brady Plan was effective in reducing developing-country debt owed to commercial creditors, but it did not affect debt with official creditors. As a result, the share of debt owed to commercial creditors fell from 43 per cent of total external debt in 1988 to 28 per cent in 1995. The subsequent increase in external debt was influenced by a series of financial crises that hit the developing world in the second half of the 1990s.

Following the Asian financial crisis in 1997, developing countries as a group suffered a marked slowdown in GNI growth, while their total debt rose rapidly, leading to a spike in the aggregate debt-to-GNI ratio (chart 6.2 and table 6.1). The reversal of

Chart 6.2

DECOMPOSITION OF CHANGES IN THE DEBT-TO-GNI RATIO IN DEVELOPING COUNTRIES, 1971–2006

(Per cent)

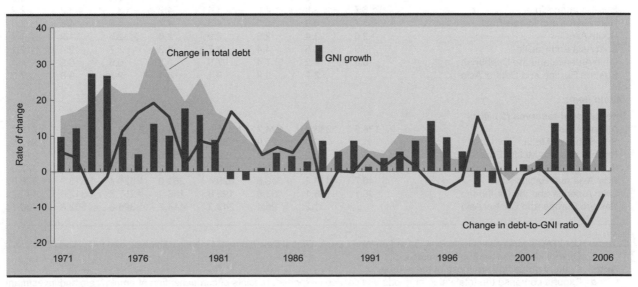

Source: See chart 6.1.

Table 6.1

DEBT INDICATORS FOR DEVELOPING COUNTRIES, 1980–2007

(Per cent, unless otherwise indicated)

	1980–1990	1991–1995	1996–2000	2001–2005	2000	2005	2006	2007
Total debt *($ billion)*								
All countries	892.3	1 627.4	2 192.2	2 538.9	2 256.6	2 739.9	2 983.7	3 357.2
Sub-Saharan Africa	111.0	202.1	221.7	220.5	211.9	216.2	173.5	193.8
North Africa and Middle East	106.1	152.9	155.2	154.2	145.2	148.9	141.3	151.3
South Asia	72.0	143.5	155.8	178.9	160.0	190.7	227.3	240.3
East Asia and Pacific	134.1	344.7	518.1	555.3	497.7	614.1	660.0	715.6
Latin America and the Caribbean	374.5	517.4	714.7	780.6	754.5	747.3	734.5	787.6
Eastern Europe and Central Asia	94.5	266.7	426.7	649.4	487.1	822.7	1 047.0	1 268.5
Total debt as percentage of GNI								
All countries	30.3	38.6	39.3	35.4	38.9	28.4	26.4	24.4
Sub-Saharan Africa	44.5	70.6	69.3	54.3	66.5	37.1	26.2	25.4
North Africa and Middle East	47.5	63.7	44.4	34.5	38.4	26.2	21.9	19.5
South Asia	22.9	37.1	28.3	23.4	26.7	18.8	19.8	17.1
East Asia and Pacific	26.8	37.0	34.2	24.3	29.6	20.2	18.4	16.3
Latin America and the Caribbean	50.3	37.6	37.6	41.0	38.9	30.7	25.8	23.7
Eastern Europe and Central Asia	..	28.0	46.6	48.1	54.9	40.7	43.2	40.9
Total debt as percentage of exports[a]								
All countries	173.6	172.0	141.9	103.2	122.6	73.6	65.8	62.0
Sub-Saharan Africa	180.7	250.2	213.3	143.9	178.9	88.8	59.8	57.8
North Africa and Middle East	165.8	159.0	134.4	86.0	103.7	59.8	49.1	45.9
South Asia	248.7	271.2	178.0	116.9	151.3	80.7	77.6	69.8
East Asia and Pacific	132.1	119.3	98.9	62.2	77.4	43.8	38.2	34.2
Latin America and the Caribbean	288.5	227.2	187.2	151.4	164.2	105.4	86.8	82.5
Eastern Europe and Central Asia	..	128.2	127.5	112.7	128.4	92.6	95.6	94.1
Debt service as percentage of exports[a]								
All countries	21.8	17.5	19.9	16.8	20.2	13.6	12.6	9.7
Sub-Saharan Africa	14.6	13.3	13.9	8.9	11.4	8.3	7.4	5.0
North Africa and Middle East	19.4	19.9	16.7	10.8	12.7	8.7	10.4	6.1
South Asia	22.1	24.8	18.4	14.6	14.6	11.9	7.5	6.9
East Asia and Pacific	19.1	14.5	12.7	9.6	11.4	5.9	5.0	4.3
Latin America and the Caribbean	37.6	25.4	36.1	29.1	38.9	22.8	23.0	15.3
Eastern Europe and Central Asia	..	12.0	15.9	21.3	19.0	21.7	20.0	16.7
Debt service as percentage of GNI								
All countries	4.1	4.0	5.5	5.8	6.4	5.2	5.1	3.8
Sub-Saharan Africa	3.7	3.8	4.5	3.4	4.2	3.5	3.2	2.2
North Africa and Middle East	5.7	8.0	5.5	4.3	4.7	3.8	4.6	2.6
South Asia	2.0	3.4	2.9	2.9	2.6	2.8	1.9	1.7
East Asia and Pacific	3.9	4.5	4.4	3.7	4.3	2.7	2.4	2.1
Latin America and the Caribbean	6.8	4.2	7.4	7.9	9.2	6.6	6.9	4.4
Eastern Europe and Central Asia	..	2.7	5.9	9.1	8.1	9.5	9.0	7.3
Memo item:								
International reserves *($ billion)*								
All countries	136.5	333.8	624.7	1 335.6	691.6	2 053.1	2 701.5	3 718.7
Sub-Saharan Africa	11.6	17.0	29.9	52.7	36.7	84.4	117.6	147.5
North Africa and Middle East	17.6	32.0	48.4	96.0	51.6	134.8	174.1	216.9
South Asia	11.8	22.5	38.6	114.4	47.2	156.7	198.5	277.3
East Asia and Pacific	40.7	116.2	248.6	629.4	283.0	1 020.4	1 315.7	1 856.8
Latin America and the Caribbean	46.1	108.1	163.8	199.8	158.4	257.3	312.8	444.7
Eastern Europe and Central Asia	..	51.2	95.4	243.3	114.7	399.6	582.8	786.1

Source: UNCTAD secretariat calculations, based on World Bank, *Global Development Finance* database; and IMF, *World Economic Outlook* database for 2007 estimates.

Note: Country groupings are those of the source.

a   Exports comprise the total value of goods and services exported, receipts of compensation of employees, and investment income.

this spike in 2000 is attributable to the rapid recovery of the East Asian economies. From 2000 onwards, debt levels fell, especially long-term public debt owed to official creditors. After a phase of relatively slow growth, recovery in developing countries since 2003 has resulted in a considerable decline in their debt-to-GNI and debt-to-exports ratios.

> Since 2003, the debt-to-GNI and debt-to-exports ratios of developing countries have declined considerably.

Nevertheless, the debt stock has continued to increase in absolute terms, albeit with important differences across countries and regions (table 6.1). Between 2000 and 2007 the amount of outstanding debt fell by more than 8 per cent in sub-Saharan Africa and remained almost constant in North Africa and Middle East, and in Latin America and the Caribbean. By contrast, it rose by more than 40 per cent in both South and East Asia and by more than 160 per cent in the Eastern Europe and Central Asia region, which in 2007 accounted for 37 per cent of the entire external debt of developing countries and economies in transition. Servicing of the external debt of the Eastern Europe and Central Asia region accounted for more than 7 per cent of GNI, a rate slightly higher than that registered for Latin America at the time of its debt crisis in the early 1980s. This development is all the more worrisome as the external environment has been much more favourable in terms of both interest rates and demand growth in the world economy.

The reduction in the external debt ratios of developing countries over the past few years has been accompanied by a sharp increase in their international reserves: by 440 per cent between 2000 and 2007 (table 6.1). This increase occurred not only in the regions where the stock of debt fell, but also in Eastern Europe and Central Asia, and in East and South Asia where the stock of debt rose. Such a situation reflects differences in the current-account performance of countries within these regions, as well as the fact that in some cases international reserves increased together with gross external debt. Indeed, Eastern Europe and Central Asia as a group saw the largest growth (in per cent terms) of

> The reduction in the external debt ratios has been accompanied by a sharp increase in international reserves.

international reserves between 2000 and 2007 (by 585 per cent), followed by East Asia (556 per cent, but this region had the highest absolute growth in international reserves) and South Asia (488 per cent).

Since 2006, total international reserves of all developing countries taken together have exceeded their total long-term debt. By the end of 2007, these reserves reached an estimated $3.7 trillion, equivalent to two thirds of the world's entire foreign exchange reserves (IMF, 2008). As most international reserves are held in assets issued by developed countries, developing countries, as a group, no longer have a net external debt.

In this context it is worth noting that the trends in the aggregate data in table 6.1 are heavily influenced by the performance of a few large countries and of a few countries which, in the mid-1990s, had extremely high debt ratios.[2] This is reflected in the alternative indicators contained in chart 6.3, which compares both the average and the median debt-to-GNI ratios with the ratio for the aggregate of all developing countries. It shows that in 2006, the average debt-to-GNI ratio for a developing country stood at around 55 per cent, and the median of that ratio for all developing countries was 37 per cent. Chart 6.3, which also shows the debt-to-GNI ratios for the countries in the 10th and 90th percentiles of the distribution of this variable, again reveals considerable differences. In 1990, the country at the 90th percentile of the distribution had a debt-to-GNI ratio of 198 per cent – almost seven times that of the country at the 10th percentile of the distribution, which had a debt-to-GNI ratio of 28 per cent. In 2006, debt levels were lower, but the variation in debt levels was still substantial. The country at the 90th percentile of the distribution still had a debt-to-GNI ratio six times higher than that of the country at the 10th percentile of the distribution (102 per cent versus 17 per cent).

These trends in indicators of external indebtedness of developing countries have been accompanied by considerable changes in the composition of

Chart 6.3

ALTERNATIVE MEASURES OF DEBT-TO-GNI RATIO OF DEVELOPING COUNTRIES, 1970–2006

(Per cent)

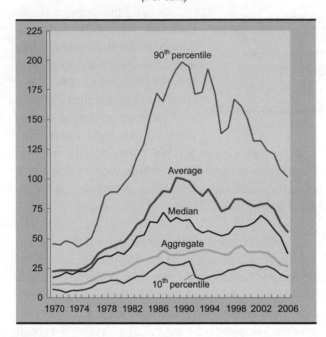

Source: UNCTAD secretariat calculations, based on World Bank, *Global Development Finance* database.
Note: The average refers to simple cross-country average and the aggregate is the weighted average of table 6.1.

external debt (table 6.2). In 1990, about 95 per cent of the long-term external debt of developing countries was owed by governments or public sector entities, or was guaranteed by such entities. By 2007, the share of this public and publicly guaranteed debt had fallen to approximately 52 per cent of developing countries' long-term external debt. The decline in the share of the external public debt has been due partly to an overall reduction in the total public debt of developing countries since the beginning of the new millennium and to a rapid growth in private external borrowing. It is also due to an explicit strategy to substitute external public debt with domestically issued debt. In 1994, about 30 per cent of developing countries' total public debt was issued domestically; by 2005 this share had increased to 40 per cent (Panizza, 2008a). While more recent data for all developing countries are not available, there is some evidence that this trend continued over the 2005–2007 period, especially in large emerging market countries. There has also been a change in the composition of lenders: the public sector's long-term external debt owed to official creditors was more than 70 per cent in the early 1970s and fell to about 50 per cent in 2007 (table 6.2). These changes in the composition of the external and public debt have important implications for debt sustainability, because different types of debt lead to different vulnerabilities.

Table 6.2

COMPOSITION OF EXTERNAL DEBT IN DEVELOPING COUNTRIES, 1980–2007

(Billions of dollars, unless otherwise indicated)

	1980–1990	1991–1995	1996–2000	2001–2005	2000	2005	2006	2007
Long-term debt	761.4	1 326.1	1 783.1	2 028.2	1 888.3	2 128.6	2 305.3	2 557.8
Public and publicly guaranteed debt	685.7	1 192.5	1 345.9	1 413.1	1 350.1	1 365.8	1 267.1	1 335.4
Private debt	75.7	133.5	437.1	615.0	538.2	762.7	1 038.2	1 222.4
Share of private debt in long-term debt *(per cent)*	9.9	10.1	24.5	30.3	28.5	35.8	45.0	47.8
Official creditors	318.7	695.7	774.4	780.6	779.3	726.5	649.6	646.8
Private creditors	442.7	630.4	1 008.7	1 247.6	1 109.1	1 402.1	1 655.7	1 911.1
Share of private creditors in long-term debt *(per cent)*	58.1	47.5	56.6	61.5	58.7	65.9	71.8	74.7

Source: See table 6.1.

The switch from external to domestic borrowing in developing countries was facilitated by improvements in their current-account balance, which reduced the need for external financing in many developing countries. It was also facilitated by relatively low international interest rates and abundant global liquidity, which encouraged investors to increase their holding of local instruments issued by developing countries.[3] However, it is not clear if this trend will continue in the current climate of tighter liquidity.[4]

Favourable external conditions, including relatively fast growth of the world economy and improved terms of trade for a large number of developing countries, have also driven the improvement in debt ratios over the past few years. A deep economic crisis in developed countries and a sudden rise in risk aversion among international investors could easily reverse the current positive trend. Thus,

> The external debt remains a major constraint on the implementation of development strategies in many countries.

while there can be no doubt that the debt situation of a large number of developing countries is more relaxed than it was a decade ago, external debt remains a major constraint on the implementation of development strategies of many countries, especially the low-income and least developed countries (LDCs). The launching of the HIPC Initiative in 1996, the Enhanced HIPC Initiative in 1999 and the Multilateral Debt Relief Initiative (MDRI) in 2005 were based on the recognition by the international community that debt overhang constitutes a significant impediment to growth and poverty reduction in these countries. These initiatives to alleviate the debt problem of developing countries, along with efforts within the broader framework of the Paris Club, have certainly contributed to the recent improvement of debt indicators. The following section takes a closer look at the results of these efforts.

C. Debt relief

One difficulty in measuring the actual benefits from debt relief is that, depending on the maturity structure, the net present value of the cancelled debt is considerably smaller than its face value (box 6.1). Moreover, a significant part of the forgiven debt was non-performing at the time of its cancellation, an aspect that is ignored by commonly used measures of debt relief. A recent study found that during 1990–2006, 6–7 per cent of debt relief represented recognition of arrears, and this share rose to about 15 per cent after the launch of the HIPC Initiative. For the HIPCs alone, arrears have represented up to 20 per cent of the debt relief received since 1996. Under the Enhanced HIPC Initiative, since 2000 this share has increased to 40 per cent (Panizza, 2008b). Thus, a considerable part of the debt relief granted under the

HIPC Initiative has been merely an accounting exercise, which may have had positive effects in terms of cleaning debtors' books but has not freed up any resources for public spending for other purposes.[5]

Until the second half of the 1990s, most of the debt relief and debt restructuring for low-income countries resulted from Paris Club rescheduling, and only covered bilateral debt.[6] This changed after the launch of the HIPC Initiative in 1996. The aim of this Initiative was to provide broad-based additional assistance to countries for which traditional debt relief mechanisms had proved insufficient, and to provide an exit for highly indebted poor countries from the repeated debt rescheduling process. The rationale for massive debt relief was that debt overhang had

Box 6.1

FACE VALUE AND NET PRESENT VALUE OF DEBT RELIEF

Both GDF and DAC data report the face value of debt forgiven, neglecting the fact that the present value of this debt might be much lower than its face value. The problem can be illustrated by the following example: country A has a debt of $100 million expiring in 2100, with an interest rate equal to the market rate; country B also has a debt of $100 million expiring in the year 2100, but this debt carries an interest rate which is only half the market rate. Assuming a market rate of 7 per cent to discount the flows of payments associated with these two debts, the present value of country A's debt is $100 million, while the present value of country B's debt is just over $50 million. Since debt relief data focus on the face value of cancelled debt, a debt relief initiative that cancels the debt of both countries would be recorded as cancelling $200 million worth of debt. But this overstates the amount of the actual debt relief.[a] Depetris Chauvin and Kraay (2005) have developed two measures (one based on creditor-reported data and the other on debtor-reported data) aimed at estimating actual debt relief. A comparison of GDF data on face-value debt relief using these authors' estimates for the present value of debtor-reported debt relief shows that the present value is always lower than the face value, with differences ranging between 15 and 65 per cent of the face value of debt relief

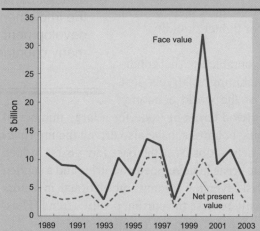

**DEBT RELIEF: FACE VALUE AND
NET PRESENT VALUE, 1989–2003**

Source: UNCTAD secretariat calculations, based on World Bank, *Global Development Finance* database; and Depetris Chauvin and Kraay, 2005.

(see chart). GDF data report that over the period 1989–2003 developing countries received debt relief amounting to about $137 billion. According to calculations by Depetris Chauvin and Kraay (2005), debtor-reported debt relief over the same period amounted to about $76 billion.

---

[a] This is not necessarily an issue relating to the calculation of debt relief as a proportion of total debt because both the denominator and the numerator may be affected by the same problem.

pushed the poor countries into a situation that prevented them not only from servicing their debt in an orderly manner, but also from achieving a growth path that would allow them to reduce poverty and narrow the income gap with the more developed countries.

Between 1996 and 2004, the HIPCs accounted for over two thirds of all debt relief granted by OECD countries and multilateral development banks. This share dropped to an average of less than 20 per cent in 2005 and 2006, when the bulk of debt relief was

granted to a few countries emerging from political and economic crises, in particular Afghanistan and Iraq, and one large middle-income debtor, Nigeria. The total amount of debt relief provided to developing countries, as a group, is fairly small compared to the total stock of developing-country debt. Thus, although debt relief has contributed significantly to improving the debt indicators of many countries individually (box 6.2), it explains only a small share of the improvement in aggregate debt indicators. The total debt relief provided to HIPCs and other countries between 1996 and 2006 amounted to $75 billion in

Box 6.2

DEBT REDUCTION UNDER THE HIPC INITIATIVE AND MDRI[a]

By December 2006, the HIPC Initiative and the MDRI had reduced by $96 billion the net present value of the external debt owed by countries that had reached the decision point under the Initiative, which qualifies them for interim relief. This is more than twice the net present value of the total external debt stock of post-decision-point countries at the end of 2005. According to IMF and IDA estimates, debt reduction under HIPC and MDRI will lead to a $1.3 billion reduction of debt service in 2007.

The initiatives were important in reducing the debt ratios of the participating countries. The average debt-service-to-export ratio fell from 18 per cent at decision point to 5.6 per cent in 2006, and is expected to reach 3.3 per cent in 2011. There are, however, large cross-country differences, and the reduction in debt service as per cent of GDP resulting from debt relief ranges between 0.3 per cent for Zambia and 1.8 per cent for Guyana.

The figure plots debt service as a share of exports for all post-decision-point countries at three points of time: at the decision point, at the end of 2006, and the projection for 2011. It shows that the Initiative drastically reduced debt service ratios in all participating countries, and that in most countries debt ratios are expected to keep declining in the near future (the exceptions being the Democratic Republic of the Congo, Mozambique, Niger, Rwanda, Sao Tome and Principe, Senegal and Sierra Leone). However, even though debt relief provided under the two initiatives improved the debt ratios of the receiving countries, more than half of the post-completion-point countries are still considered as having either a moderate or a high risk of debt distress, and only 10 out of 22 post-completion point countries have graduated to the low-risk category.

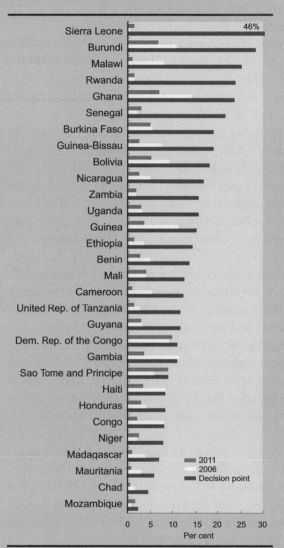

HIPC DEBT SERVICE AT DECISION POINT, IN 2006 AND 2011

(As a percentage of exports)

[a]   All the data reported in this box are based on IMF, 2007.

face value. This was equivalent to about 6 per cent of the 2006 stock of the long-term public external debt of developing countries, and accounted for 0.6 percentage points of the improvement in the aggregate debt-to-GNI ratio.[7]

Although the Monterrey Consensus urged the international community to pursue debt relief "vigorously and expeditiously", not everybody agrees on the desirability of debt relief. It has been argued, for instance, that debt relief may be beneficial for certain middle-income countries but not for HIPCs. According to this view, debt relief is considered beneficial for middle-income countries that suffer from debt overhang (i.e. a level of debt that is so high that creditors are unwilling to provide additional lending). This is not the case for HIPCs, where the main obstacle to investment is the lack of basic market institutions rather than debt overhang, as indicated by the fact that these countries have always had positive net transfers (Arslanalp and Henry, 2004; 2006). This view is consistent with the finding that debt relief provided to HIPCs does not lead to higher growth, whereas in other developing countries a debt cancellation equivalent to 1 per cent of GNI leads to an increase in the growth rate in the order of 0.2 percentage points (Hepp, 2005).[8] On the other hand, another study suggests that debt relief is the most effective form of aid because it supposedly reduces the transaction costs of conventional aid programmes (Birdsall and Deese, 2004). The study argues that, unlike aid programmes, government officials in the recipient countries do not need to satisfy the different interests and priorities of various donor agencies, and that the resources freed by debt relief are equivalent to flexible budget support, enabling recipient countries to use them in line with their own priorities. Debt relief is also considered as potentially more effective than other forms of aid because it cannot be tied to purchases from donor countries.

Another important question is whether debt relief will be sufficient to guarantee debt sustainability in the medium and long term. Easterly (2002) shows that before 1996 debt relief did not achieve this objective, and there is no clear evidence as yet that this has changed since the launch of the HIPC Initiative, although, since then, debt sustainability analysis has become a key element in the determination of debt relief. Some countries that received debt relief under the HIPC Initiative are again accumulating debt at a rapid pace, which may soon return to an unsustainable level (World Bank, 2006a; Birdsall and Deese, 2004). This trend is sometimes explained by policy failures: in the presence of voracious (and perhaps dishonest) politicians who borrow as much as they can, any attempt at solving debt problems through debt relief will cause a temporary boom and then precipitate the country into a new unsustainable situation (Easterly, 2002). An alternative explanation for the rapid re-accumulation of debt by countries that benefited from debt relief is the large extent of unsatisfied basic needs in these countries. Hence, when debt relief relaxes their budget constraint, governments borrow and spend as much as possible in order to meet those needs. This view is at the centre of Sachs' proposal (2005) for ending poverty and of the United Nations' report (2005) on how to achieve the MDGs. According to this view, debt relief is not wasted, but poor countries need both debt relief and more aid. This problem is accentuated by the fact that, under current initiatives, debt relief is conditional on increases in social expenditure, which, in some cases, may require a shift of public expenditure away from investment projects that are directly productive and would help the economy to grow out of its debt problems.

> **Poor countries need both debt relief and more aid.**

In July 2005, the Multilateral Debt Relief Initiative (MDRI) was launched with the objective of complementing the HIPC debt relief process by freeing additional resources to support countries' efforts to achieve the MDGs. Under the MDRI, countries that have graduated from the HIPC Initiative are granted 100 per cent cancellation of their debt owed to the participating multilateral financial institutions. While all the major regional development banks participate in the HIPC Initiative, MDRI only covers debt owed to the IMF, the International Development Association (IDA) of the World Bank, and the African Development Fund (AfDF). The Inter-American Development Bank (IDB) joined the initiative later, but did not receive any compensation for the debt relief it granted under the MDRI.[9]

> **All poor countries should be allowed to benefit from the MDRI.**

While the MDRI is an additional attempt to support efforts to combat poverty in highly indebted poor countries, it can lead to paradoxical outcomes, as it does not cover moderately indebted poor countries. To understand the problems with this approach, consider the case of two poor countries that have debt only with multilateral institutions.

Both have similarly low levels of income and similar needs to finance investment in social and physical infrastructure. The main difference is the level of their external debt. Country A has a net present value (NPV) of total external debt equivalent to 100 per cent of its gross domestic product (GDP). It is thus eligible for HIPC debt relief, and will also benefit from full debt cancellation under MDRI. Country B has an NPV of total external debt equivalent to 30 per cent of its GDP, and consequently does not qualify for HIPC debt relief, nor will it receive full debt cancellation under the MDRI. Following the granting of multilateral debt relief, the formerly highly indebted country A will have zero debt, while the moderately indebted country B will be left with its original debt. In order to prevent such discrimination against countries that were able to avoid unsustainable debt positions in the past, often at the cost of lower public investment and social spending, it would be more appropriate for participation in the MDRI not to be contingent on a country being highly indebted.

As discussed in chapter V, debt relief granted by official creditors is considered and accounted for as a form of ODA. Overall, the net benefits of debt write-offs depend on the extent to which such relief results in a slower increase in other forms of ODA. So far, evaluations of debt relief have not included an explicit measure of the additionality of debt relief. Indeed, in the absence of a straightforward counter-factual, it is difficult to assess whether the debt relief granted over the past few years, including under the HIPC Initiative, has been fully additional. Nevertheless, the analysis in chapter V gives the impression that this has not been the case.

This result also justifies doubts as to whether the main objective of the debt relief initiatives (i.e. to reduce the indebtedness of problem countries to a sustainable level) can be achieved. Under the current initiatives, the granting of debt relief has been conditional, *inter alia*, on the findings of a debt sustainability exercise. Thus, only countries found to have a level of debt that is deemed unsustainable are granted debt relief. While this seems to be a reasonable approach, there is substantial confusion surrounding the concept of debt sustainability, which is discussed in the next section.

D. Debt sustainability

Debt sustainability analysis has been developed in the context of the debt relief initiatives as an instrument to determine whether, and to what extent, a country is eligible for debt relief. But the scope of such an analysis goes far beyond this specific purpose. An appropriate framework for debt sustainability analysis can be an important tool for effective debt management and for the design of financing strategies that aim at accelerated growth and structural change in the medium to long term. It can help developing countries avoid debt crises in the future, and thus render the development process more stable, providing a better investment climate. It is from this perspective that this section discusses various aspects of debt sustainability analysis. The objective is to clarify some of the concepts and definitions linked to debt sustainability. In doing so, it also points to some weaknesses of the debt sustainability frameworks adopted by the Bretton Woods institutions.

1. Standard frameworks for debt sustainability analysis

There are two standard frameworks for assessing debt sustainability in developing countries. The first was developed by the IMF (2002a; 2003) and focuses on middle-income countries. The second was developed jointly by the IMF and the World Bank and focuses on low-income countries. Both frameworks define a policy stance as sustainable if "a borrower is expected to be able to continue servicing its debt without an unrealistically large future correction of the balance of income and expenditure" (IMF, 2002a: 4). Both frameworks formulate a baseline scenario based on long- and medium-term projections of the evolution of policies and macroeconomic variables, and evaluate the sustainability of the resulting debt ratios. As a second step, the frameworks stress-test the model by using different assumptions relating to the behaviour of policy variables, contingent liabilities, external factors and macroeconomic developments. This sensitivity analysis is then used to establish an upper bound for the evolution of the debt-to-GNI ratio under a worst-case scenario, and the projected evolution of the debt ratio can be used as a sort of early warning system of an unsustainable path that would require policy adjustments.[10]

The two frameworks differ mainly in their definition of debt thresholds.[11] In discussing its debt sustainability framework for middle-income countries, the IMF (2003) suggests that the probability of a debt "correction" increases significantly when the external debt exceeds 40 per cent of GDP, but it does not establish an explicit threshold above which debt is deemed to be unsustainable. By contrast, such explicit thresholds are a central element of the debt sustainability framework for low-income countries. These thresholds are also used to guide grant allocation by the IDA and some other donors. In practice, the debt sustainability framework for low-income countries compares long- and medium-term projections of various debt ratios with debt burden thresholds for countries grouped according to the perceived quality of their policies and institutions as measured by the World Bank's Country Policy and Institutional Assessment (CPIA) (see chapter IV, section D.3).

In this approach, the better the policies and institutions, the higher is the level of debt considered to be sustainable. On this basis, countries are classified into four groups: (i) low risk; (ii) moderate risk; (iii) high risk; and (iv) in debt distress.[12] High-risk IDA countries (also known as "red light" countries) receive 100 per cent grant financing from IDA at a

20 per cent volume discount (i.e. they receive less financing but entirely in the form of grants). Moderate-risk IDA countries ("yellow light" countries) receive 50 per cent grant financing at a 10 per cent volume discount. Low-risk countries ("green light" countries) receive 100 per cent loan financing without any volume discount.[13]

There has been much criticism of the use of the CPIA as the sole criterion for determining debt thresholds. Historical series for the CPIA index are not disclosed, and all analyses that link debt sustainability to the CPIA have been conducted by World Bank/IMF staff; no external researcher has been allowed to test the robustness of the links between these two variables. It is also questionable whether the quantitative impact of the CPIA on the probability of debt distress is large enough to formulate debt thresholds based only on the CPIA. Moreover, the CPIA tends to be an imperfect measure of policy and institutions (see chapter V).

There may be different judgements as to what constitutes "good policies and institutions", and even if there was unanimity in this regard, it would still be necessary to recognize that not all types of "bad policies and institutions" constrain economic development in the same way at all times or in all countries (Rodrik, 2008). Therefore, while it may be reasonable to use a measure of policies (perhaps a more transparent one) as *one* of the criteria used to define debt thresholds, it is harder to justify an approach that uses policies as the *only* criterion for defining debt thresholds.

A criticism that applies to both frameworks is that they do not sufficiently account for the interactions between external and fiscal sustainability. The framework for low-income countries is explicitly restricted to external sustainability, while the framework for middle-income countries covers, in principle, both external and public debt, though its focus remains on external sustainability. Another shortcoming of both frameworks is that the assessment of debt sustainability neglects the fact that debt can be accumulated for very different reasons: debt accumulated to finance consumption will be less sustainable than the same debt stock used to finance high-return investment projects.

> Debt sustainability analysis can be an important tool for effective debt management.

Debt sustainability analyses for developing countries normally concentrate on external debt, and the debt sustainability frameworks developed by the IMF and the World Bank are rooted in this tradition. The focus on external debt is due to the paramount importance of the transfer problem (Keynes, 1929), and to the perception that most of the external debt of developing countries is public and most of their public debt is external.[14] However, the debt crises of the 1990s and since the beginning of the new millennium have been characterized by the presence of either massive private external debt or a large stock of domestic public debt. In the current environment, about half of the long-term debt of developing countries is issued by private borrowers (see table 6.2) and about 40 per cent of their public debt is issued domestically (Panizza, 2008a). Domestic public debt is not a new phenomenon in developing countries, and it has been shown that the large accumulation of such debt has triggered several external debt crises (Reinhart and Rogoff, 2008a and b).

External debt sustainability refers to the ability of an economy as a whole to generate the foreign currency necessary to service the external debt, independent of the ability of each sector of the economy to generate the resources necessary to service its own debt. By contrast, public debt sustainability refers to the budgetary implications of the evolution of total public debt in relation to current public revenues, no matter to whom this debt is owed and in which currency it is denominated. Both concepts are important, but mixing them up adds confusion to the debt sustainability discussion.

2. *External debt sustainability*

Unless a country's external debt is issued in its own currency, its repayment on a net basis (i.e. without creating new foreign liabilities) requires a current-account surplus. As more than 98 per cent of the external debt of developing countries is denominated in a foreign currency (Eichengreen, Hausmann and Panizza, 2005), the foreign debt of developing countries always has to be repaid in terms of internationally tradable goods and services.[15] Since the

ability to generate the international currency necessary to service the debt is not necessarily related to a country's ability to grow or to broaden its tax base, debt-to-GNI or debt-to-public-revenue ratios do not reflect very well a country's ability to repay its external debt. Even the debt-to-exports ratio has its limitations as an indicator, because a large export sector is not sufficient to generate the needed resources if import growth outpaces export growth, or if additional exports have a high import content.

In order to evaluate whether a given amount of external debt is sustainable, it is necessary to understand how the mechanisms that drive the behaviour of the current account influence the external debt situation. The accumulation of net foreign liabilities is always the outcome of current-account deficits, while a net repayment of external debt requires a current-account surplus. Such a surplus can be generated either by a gain in international competitiveness of producers in the debtor countries or by a negative growth differential between the debtor country and the creditor countries. Thus, a real devaluation is necessary to repay the debt if a slowdown or even a recession in the debtor country is to be avoided. Such a devaluation may have an immediate negative effect in terms of a loss of confidence of foreign investors, and lead to a sharp increase in the debt-to-GDP ratio, but repayment of the debt will subsequently restore the country's credibility in the international capital markets.[16]

Debt sustainability cannot be analysed without considering how the borrowed funds are used: such funds could be used for productive or unproductive purposes, which have different effects on a country's ability to repay the debt.[17] External borrowing that increases the value of a country's stock of assets is more likely to be sustainable than external borrowing used to finance consumption or white elephant projects. Therefore, debt sustainability cannot be evaluated on the basis of macroeconomic ratios alone, but should also consider the relationship between liabilities and assets.[18]

As external debt needs to be repaid in foreign currency, it should be used to finance projects that can increase foreign currency revenues. Clearly,

> Debt sustainability cannot be analysed without considering how the borrowed funds are used.

foreign borrowing used to finance a consumption boom is likely to be unsustainable. However, there are conditions under which even debt used to finance investment projects can be unsustainable. For instance, if the debt is used to finance an investment project that has a return which is lower than the interest rate charged on the debt, but also if the debt is used to finance an investment project which has a high private or social return but no direct or indirect effect on a country's ability to increase its foreign exchange earnings. It is in this sense that proper debt management that is designed in a way to match debt structure with the flows of project funds plays a crucial role in guaranteeing debt sustainability.

3. Public debt sustainability

In assessments of public debt sustainability, the focus is not on the external transfer problem but on the internal transfer problem, which is related to a government's ability to raise enough tax revenues to service the public debt. In the presence of external public debt, the government will have both an internal transfer problem (raising tax revenues) and an external transfer problem (converting the tax revenues into foreign currency).

Unfortunately, most formal tests of fiscal sustainability are not applicable to developing countries because they tend to be too demanding in terms of data requirements.[19] Moreover, evaluating fiscal (and external) sustainability requires long-term projections on the behaviour of GDP growth, the government budget and the interest rate. Formulating such long-term projections is practically impossible in developing countries that are characterized by high levels of volatility and frequent structural breaks (Wyplosz, 2007). As a consequence, fiscal sustainability is often evaluated by using rule-of-thumb indicators such as the relationship between the primary budget balance[20] and the size of the public debt. The public-debt-to-GNI ratio either falls or remains stable if the primary budget deficit balance is smaller or equal to the stock of debt multiplied by the difference between the interest rate of the public debt and the economy's growth rate.

While simple and intuitive, this approach has several problems. The first problem is that, although it allows studying the conditions for stabilizing a given debt-to-GNI ratio, it does not say anything about the optimality of this particular ratio. The second problem is that analyses based on the above equation implicitly assume that its components are exogenous with respect to each other. This is a highly unrealistic assumption, since changes in the primary surplus are likely to have an effect on demand growth. Thus, if a fiscal adjustment has a negative effect on GNI growth, the ultimate effect of a policy aimed at restoring debt sustainability may result in an increasing, and even less sustainable, debt ratio.

Targets or limits for the primary budget deficit can help maintain or achieve debt sustainability from the fiscal perspective, but in determining such targets it would also be useful to consider that government borrowing for investment is likely to have a different impact on long-term growth than debt incurred to finance current expenditure. Country programmes designed by the main international financial institutions usually contain fiscal targets, and, as current expenditure tends to be more rigid, investment is the typical adjustment variable when the deficit exceeds the target. This makes public investment extremely volatile. It would therefore be reasonable to exclude investment expenditure from fiscal targets.[21] The rationale for this proposal is that the inclusion of investment expenditures in the fiscal target is equivalent to assuming that every increase in debt leads to a reduction in government wealth, implicitly assigning no value to investment expenditure. This suggests that an indicator aimed at stabilizing the debt-to-public-wealth ratio would be better than an indicator aimed at stabilizing the debt-to-GNI ratio.[22]

The third problem is that developing countries often have a volatile revenue base and a limited capacity to raise taxes. They are also subject to large external shocks that increase the volatility of GNI growth and debt service. Yet fiscal sustainability exercises are usually centred on an analysis of the budget deficit, even though it has been shown that the budget deficit only explains a small share of the variation of the debt-to-GNI ratio in developing countries (Campos, Jaimovich and Panizza, 2006).

> It would be reasonable to exclude investment expenditure from fiscal targets.

More than 90 per cent of this variance is explained by other factors, including external shocks and valuation effects linked to debt composition. This reinforces the argument for paying more attention to contingent liabilities and balance sheet effects associated with debt structure.

This discussion shows that there are no simple indicators of sustainability; any statement about a country's ability to meet its future debt obligations needs to be based on a careful analysis of several variables, including expectations on the future behaviour of a country's assets and liabilities. The fact that most shocks to the debt-to-GNI ratio depend on debt composition suggests that appropriate debt management can be as important as fiscal policy. The importance of debt composition is consistent with the recent findings that public debt levels are not closely related to the perception of default risk as indicated by sovereign credit ratings (IDB, 2006). It is also consistent with the absence of a robust correlation between the level of public debt and the probability that a debt crisis will actually occur (Manasse, Roubini and Schimmelpfennig, 2003).

> Appropriate debt management can be as important as a prudent fiscal policy.

4. Interactions between external and fiscal sustainability

The most obvious linkage between external and fiscal sustainability is that more than 50 per cent of the external debt of developing countries is public or publicly guaranteed and about 60 per cent of the public debt of developing countries is issued externally. But there are also less obvious linkages. In a country with a large external private debt, the inability of private borrowers to service this debt can lead to a currency and banking crisis, which can then have a negative impact on fiscal sustainability, as demonstrated by experiences during the Asian financial crisis that began in 1997. The opposite can also happen. A large domestic public debt has also often been at the root of several external debt crises

> In most developing countries, the capacity to issue long-term debt in domestic currency is limited.

(Reinhart and Rogoff, 2008a): the Mexican crisis of 1994–1995 and the Russian crisis of 1998, both of which originated in the market for short-term domestic currency instruments, are examples.

The most important interaction between fiscal and external sustainability has to do with the behaviour of the exchange rate. A real devaluation may be necessary for restoring external sustainability, but in the presence of a foreign-currency-denominated debt a large devaluation can lead to a sudden jump in the public-debt-to-GNI ratio; the opposite can result from a currency appreciation. However, as a real appreciation tends to lead to a deterioration of the current account, any improvement in fiscal conditions will only be temporary. This trade-off also implies that allowing for a depreciation of the real exchange rate in the presence of a foreign currency-denominated debt may lead to a debt crisis and, possibly, to a costly debt default. Such a trade-off does not exist for countries that can borrow abroad in their own currency. In this case, a depreciation of the real exchange rate will have an immediate positive effect on both fiscal and external sustainability, which creates an argument for switching from external to domestically issued debt, even if the latter may imply a higher *ex-ante* interest rate.[23] According to some commentators, this switch in debt composition will shield developing countries from future debt crises. However, it is also necessary to recognize that a switch from external to domestic borrowing may lead to a new vulnerability resulting from a maturity mismatch. This is because the possibilities for most developing countries to issue long-term debt in domestic currency are more limited. Therefore, one of the difficult tasks in debt management is that of having to choose the optimal debt structure by carefully evaluating these trade-offs.

The interactions between external and fiscal sustainability point to the need to include domestic debt in debt sustainability analyses. However, this would require more information than is currently available with regard to the level and composition of domestic debt. Clearly, different types of debt yield different vulnerabilities, and simply adding them up for the calculation of a single debt ratio hides these vulnerabilities. The vulnerabilities could be grasped by giving different weights to different types of debt according to their specific risk. This, in turn, would require more detailed information on the composition of the total debt.

E. Dealing with debt default

The main objective of debt sustainability analysis is to help policymakers avoid situations in which debt obligations cannot be met. However, even when countries adopt good policies such situations cannot be ruled out, not least because they can result from external shocks, the timing and strength of which are difficult to predict in a volatile international financial environment. Low-income countries tend to borrow from official creditors (governments or multilateral institutions), and when they cannot repay their debts, they renegotiate with these creditors, usually through the Paris Club. The situation of middle-income countries that have access to the international capital markets tends to be different. In this case, there are many, often anonymous, creditors and a large number of different debt instruments involved, and there is no appropriate institutional framework for renegotiations between sovereign debtors and private creditors. Consequently, sovereign defaults tend to be complicated, and often costly for debtors and creditors alike.[24]

If a private borrower does not repay its debts, creditors have a well-defined claim on the borrower's assets, and these legal rights are a necessary condition for the existence of a private debt market. In the case of sovereign debt, on the other hand, creditors' rights are either not well defined or non-enforceable. Theoretically, a sovereign debtor will repay its debts only if the cost of defaulting is higher than the cost of repaying. In this sense, costly defaults are a necessary condition for the existence of a sovereign debt market.

However, policymakers might believe that defaults are more costly than they actually are and, rather than defaulting too much and too early, they default too little and too late.[25] A recent survey of the costs of default (Borensztein and Panizza, 2008) found limited evidence that countries which default on their external debt obligations pay a high cost in terms of reputation that would reduce their access to credit or render it more expensive. With regard to the cost of default in terms of lost output growth, it has been found that a default episode is associated with a decrease in growth of between 0.5 and 2 percentage points (Sturzenegger, 2004), but the causal relationship is not clear. An attempt at establishing such a relationship by using higher frequency data indicates that it is the economic crisis that precedes the default and not the other way around. In particular, Levy Yeyati and Panizza (2005) have shown that a default episode often marks the end of an economic crisis and the beginning of recovery. This finding is consistent with the hypothesis of delayed defaults.

There are two possible explanations as to why defaults are delayed. The first relates to the fact that default episodes are often associated with political crises or, as a minimum, with the dismissal of the minister of finance of the defaulting country (for evidence, see Borensztein and Panizza, 2008).[26]

> Sovereign defaults tend to be costly for debtors and creditors alike.

As a consequence, self-interested politicians may choose to "gamble for redemption" and amplify the economic crisis by defaulting too late.[27]

The second reason relates to the idea that strategic defaults are extremely costly in terms of reputation (which is why they are rarely observed in practice), but "unavoidable" defaults carry only a limited cost (Grossman and Van Huyck, 1988). If this is the case, policymakers may decide to postpone a default in order to signal that the default is unavoidable and not strategic. According to this view, a well-intentioned politician chooses the lesser of the two evils, and is willing to pay the cost linked to delaying default in order to spare the country a much harsher punishment. In this case, there would be much value added in implementing an impartial mechanism for the resolution of sovereign default.

> A default episode often marks the end of an economic crisis and the beginning of recovery.

Not only may defaults come too late, but also, under the current system, the cost may be amplified by an often lengthy debt-restructuring process. One concern in this context is the so-called "holdout problem" (Sturzenegger and Zettelmeyer, 2007), caused by creditors that refuse to participate in a debt restructuring process with the hope of obtaining a better deal later. In most cases, holdouts are not the original creditors, but investors – often called "vulture" funds – that buy the defaulted debt with the explicit intention of litigating. If a "holdout" creditor can obtain better treatment with respect to the creditors who participate in the debt restructuring process, every creditor will have an incentive to be a holdout. This will stall the restructuring process, prolong the default state, and leave the debtor without access to new finance and the creditors without any payments. Distinct from public debt, there is no holdout problem in connection with debt owed by private creditors, because bankruptcy legislation guarantees equal treatment to all creditors that are in the same class.

> The number of emerging market issuers using CACs has grown continuously.

While tranquil periods are the best time to have a rational discussion about issues related to crisis resolution, attention to this topic tends to be cyclical and only picks up once a crisis has erupted. Thus, it was against the background of the crises experienced in the years preceding the International Conference for Financing for Development in 2002 that the Monterrey Consensus emphasized "the importance of putting in place a set of clear principles for the management and resolution of financial crises that provide for fair burden-sharing between public and private sectors and between debtors, creditors and investors." (United Nations, 2002: para. 51).

Specific proposals for the establishment of some form of international debt workout procedure had already been made in *TDR 1998* (Part One, chap. IV.B) and *TDR 2001* (Part Two, chap. VI.B). Indeed, the issue had been raised as early as 1986 in the context of the debt crisis of the 1980s. At the time, the absence of a clear and impartial framework for resolving international debt problems trapped many developing countries in situations where they suffered the stigma of being judged *de facto* bankrupt without a degree of protection and relief comparable to that resulting from the status of *de jure* insolvency (*TDR 1986*: annex to chap. IV). UNCTAD was the first international organization to call for orderly workout procedures for the international debt of developing countries, drawing on certain principles of national bankruptcy laws, notably chapters 9 and 11 of the United States bankruptcy law.[28] These proposals recognized that building on the principle of maintenance of open capital accounts and convertibility and guaranteed repayment to creditors may not always be successful in stabilizing the markets and avoiding costly crises.

The debate on the need for establishing such a mechanism regained momentum when the IMF put forward a proposal for a Sovereign Debt Restructuring Mechanism (SDRM) (Krueger, 2001), which was considered officially at a meeting in 2003 of the International Monetary and Financial Committee. However, many countries were concerned that the introduction of a statutory mechanism for debt restructuring would impair their access to international capital markets.[29] Another concern was that the proposal could result in a significant increase in the role of the IMF, as it would have the prerogative to decide about the sustainability of a country's external debt. As a result of these and other concerns, the SDRM proposal failed to elicit the required support.[30]

By contrast, a number of emerging market economies expressed their preference for voluntary approaches to debt restructuring, especially the incorporation of collective action clauses (CACs) in new bond issues.[31] However, while preferring this alternative, some issuers initially expressed concerns that the inclusion of CACs might be interpreted as an indication of limited ability or willingness to repay, and that investors would require larger spreads on such bonds. The experience with several bond issues by emerging market economies in the course of 2002 and 2003 alleviated these concerns, and the number of emerging market issuers using CACs has grown continuously.

In late 2007, about two thirds of the outstanding stock of emerging-market bonds included CACs, a share that it is expected to reach 80 per cent by 2010.[32]

In the absence of a fully-fledged statutory mechanism modelled on national bankruptcy legislation in developed countries, the inclusion of CACs in bond contracts can play a positive role in achieving orderly debt workouts in the long run. However, it would be more effective if it were to be complemented by a more general, formalized and internationally agreed framework. Such a framework might allow for a unilateral standstill on debt repayments that would be sanctioned by an international body while lending into arrears would continue (*TDR 2001,* chap. III, section D, and chap. IV). Moreover, the features of a statutory structure should give sufficient confidence to creditors that the system does not increase the incentive to default.

F. Conclusions: policy recommendations

Since the mid-1990s an unprecedented amount of official debt relief has been granted to developing countries. It has been intended not only to help the poorest countries raise per capita incomes and reduce poverty, but also to support some middle-income countries and countries emerging from political conflict to achieve sustainable debt positions, in order to place them in a better position to implement their development strategies. However, the large amount of debt relief delivered over the past few years appears to have partly crowded out non-debt relief aid flows. Evaluations of debt relief initiatives should therefore include an explicit measure of the additionality of debt relief.

Full additionality of debt relief, as called for in the Monterrey Consensus, is essential to enhance the

> Full additionality of debt relief is essential to enhance the ability of low-income countries to achieve the MDGs.

ability of low-income countries to achieve the MDGs while maintaining debt sustainability. It should also enable them to undertake the investments in economic infrastructure and in the productive sectors that are necessary for creating employment and increasing productivity. This is the only way they will be able to attain a level of per capita income that would allow sustained poverty reduction and lasting improvements in the other indicators contained in the MDGs.

Donors should also recognize that past debt relief efforts have neglected the considerable development needs of other low-income countries that have low debt levels, often as a result of more prudent external financing strategies. In order not to discriminate against such countries, it would be appropriate to allow all poor countries to benefit from the MDRI; thus, participation in the MDRI should not be contingent on being highly indebted. Moreover, it may also be necessary to consider providing debt relief for developing countries that are not eligible under the HIPC Initiative and the MDRI.

Recent empirical evidence on the relationship between net foreign borrowing and growth suggests that the accumulation of external debt is not necessary for all developing countries or at all times. For various reasons, including, in particular, higher export prices for primary commodities and macroeconomic policies aimed at preventing exchange-rate overvaluation, net capital imports of most developing countries have slowed down or even been reversed in recent years. This has resulted in their external debt growing more slowly than their GNI or exports. Several developing countries have even reduced their stock of debt or become net creditors to the rest of the world. However, many countries continue to rely on external resources, either because of structural current-account deficits or weak domestic financing mechanisms. Depending on the purpose for which external financing is used, the effects of such financing on the economy, including the sustainability of the external debt burden, can differ considerably.

A key challenge now is to stabilize the improved indicators and improve them further, while ensuring that external capital is put to uses that are the most productive in terms of growth, structural change and social development.

In a survey of 500 years of debt crises, Reinhart and Rogoff (2008a) have shown that booms in capital flows are almost always followed by default waves. This suggests that the first step towards achieving debt sustainability is to borrow for the right reason and not borrow too much during "good times". Borrowing for the right reason means that debt should be used only to finance projects that generate returns which are higher than the interest rate cost of the loan. Moreover, foreign currency borrowing should be limited to projects that can, either

> An accumulation of external debt is not necessary for all developing countries, or at all times.

> The first step towards achieving debt sustainability is to borrow for the right reason and not borrow too much during "good times".

directly or indirectly, generate the foreign currency necessary to service the debt.[33] In many cases, especially when the projects do not depend on imports, developing countries should seek to finance them with domestic resources. Debt strategies are therefore closely interrelated with renewed efforts to strengthen domestic financial systems, as discussed in chapter IV, and with macroeconomic and exchange-rate policies that aim at avoiding unnecessary current-account deficits.

Middle-income countries can reduce the probability of a debt crisis by using the current favourable external conditions to reduce their fiscal deficits, strengthen their domestic financial system and avoid an overvaluation of their exchange rate with a view to limiting the need for external borrowing. An important constraint for middle-income countries that have access to international financial markets is their vulnerability to the effects of the high volatility of these markets. Shocks that may lead to a liquidity crisis in the developing world often depend on external factors that may originate from policy decisions of developed countries. This is why developing countries must evince a particular interest in reform of the international monetary and financial system with a view to minimizing destabilizing speculative financial flows. They also need to push for the strengthening of institutions and mechanisms in support of macroeconomic policy coordination.

Implementing national policies to reduce the risk of a debt crisis is even more difficult for low-income countries. These countries have a very small domestic financial sector, and often depend on external resources to finance not only projects in the productive sectors of their economies and large infrastructure projects, but also the development of their health and education sectors. Although these social sectors yield high returns in the long run, they may not generate the cash flows necessary to service the debt in the short and medium term, and thus borrowing from external resources to finance these sectors could result in an unsustainable debt situation. This suggests that, since low-income countries cannot sustain high levels of debt, they should receive considerably greater external financial support in the form of grants.

In order to strengthen public and external debt management, a well-working mechanism for collecting and reporting data on the level and composition of sovereign debt, both external and domestic, is crucial.[34] This is a particularly difficult problem for countries with a federal structure and a large number of State-owned enterprises. Countries that issue debt instruments in the international capital markets and have a well-working domestic financial system should adopt a debt strategy that employs a comprehensive asset-liability management approach and takes into account differences in the cost and risk of the various debt instruments they issue. In particular the costs and benefits of issuing contingent and equity-like debt instruments should be evaluated carefully. Given that a large and increasing share of borrowing by emerging market countries originates from the private sector, these countries also need to carefully supervise the activities of private agents to ensure that private borrowing does not generate excessive vulnerabilities in the balance sheets of domestic banks and corporations.

> Because of their vulnerability to external shocks, developing countries must evince a particular interest in reform of the international financial system.

International support for efforts aimed at improving debt sustainability in low-income countries should start by recognizing that these countries have enormous needs for investment in social and physical infrastructure, but a limited ability to sustain the external debt necessary to finance these investments. According to the World Bank/IMF debt sustainability framework, these countries would have to forgo investment that brings high social returns in order to maintain external debt sustainability. Full debt cancellation and a large increase in aid are likely to be necessary in these cases.

The use of innovative debt instruments that reduce the vulnerability of developing countries to shocks or unfavourable developments in the international economic and financial environment could help maintain debt sustainability. The creation and dissemination of such instruments could be facilitated by support from the international community because of the required market size, externalities and the need for uniform standards. For instance, since few developing countries are able to issue external debt in their own currency, the international financial institutions could help create markets for local currency instruments by issuing their own bonds in the currencies of their borrowing countries.[35]

The launching of contingent debt instruments, in particular GNI-indexed bonds that provide for lower debt service payments when capacity to pay is low,[36] could also be supported by the international community through technical assistance and strengthening of the quality and reliability of the statistics necessary for pricing such new instruments. International financial institutions might even consider issuing such contingent debt instruments themselves. In order to accept debt instruments with a more variable return, international investors are likely to ask for a premium, which can be considered a cost of insurance against external financial shocks. In the case of GNI-indexed bonds, the necessary premium has been estimated to amount to approximately 100 basis points (Borensztein et al., 2004). The international financial institutions could promote this kind of insurance by creating a critical mass of such instruments and demonstrating their benefits.

Finally, it must be acknowledged that, even with improved debt management and better and safer debt instruments, debt crises are bound to occur. Thus, the international community should not abandon the idea of creating a mechanism aimed at providing speedy resolutions of debt crises and fair burden-sharing among creditors and debtors.[37] To this end, it would be desirable to create an independent international body, mandated by both debtors and creditors, to evaluate the debt situation of all countries facing an external debt problem and decide on the level and form of debt relief they would need (*TDR 2001*). ■

Notes

1 See *External Debt Statistics: Guide for Compilers and Users,* jointly published by the Bank for International Settlements (BIS), Eurostat, the International Monetary Fund (IMF), the Organisation for Economic Co-operation and Development (OECD), the Paris Club, UNCTAD and the World Bank. However, it should be pointed out that a strict application of this definition is not possible, since most of the external debt due to private creditors is held by investors who are, in principle, anonymous. Consequently, most countries report figures for external and domestic debt by using information on the place of issuance and jurisdiction that regulates the debt contract. This is problematic, because there is anecdotal evidence that more and more international investors are entering the domestic financial markets of developing countries, and that domestic investors often hold bonds issued in international markets. An alternative definition would focus on the currency in which the debt is issued, with external debt defined as foreign currency debt. But this definition does not seem appropriate because several countries issue foreign-currency-denominated debt in their domestic markets and have recently started to issue domestic-currency-denominated debt in international markets. Moreover, there is limited information on the currency composition of debt issued on the domestic market.

2 The five largest economies accounted for 50 per cent of the total GNI of the developing world in 2000. China accounted for 60 per cent of the total GNI of the East Asia-Pacific region. Brazil and Mexico for 60 per cent of the total GNI of the Latin America and the Caribbean region, and the Russian Federation for 30 per cent of the total GNI of the Eastern Europe and Central Asia region.

3 Foreign investors' holdings of locally issued instruments are supposed to be classified as external debt and not domestic debt, but this is rarely done (see note 1).

4 Conventional wisdom suggests that private and public borrowers from emerging market countries can now sell domestic-currency-denominated debt to foreign investors because these investors expect an appreciation of the local currency against the dollar. However, this view is only justified if the lenders expect a larger appreciation than the borrowers, and it is not clear why this should be the case. Caballero and Cowan (2008) suggest that domestic-currency-denominated borrowing is now in vogue because the expected appreciation allows prudent policymakers to hide the implicit insurance premium embedded in this form of borrowing.

5 Data on the amount of debt relief also differ depending on whether reference is made to debtor-reported data, such as that of the World Bank's Global Development Finance (GDF) database, or to creditor-reported data in the database of the OECD's Development Assistance Committee (DAC). The main advantage of the GDF database is that it indicates debt relief from all official creditors, including those that are not members of DAC. The main problem with this source is related to the fact that not all developing countries have strong debt recording capacities, and hence GDF data suffer from substantial measurement errors. Creditor-reported data from the DAC database tend to be "cleaner" than GDF data, but the coverage of non-DAC members is limited. As a consequence, the DAC figures tend to be smaller than the GDF figures, and GDF data tend to show greater volatility than DAC data.

6 For a discussion of the Paris Club and its procedures, see Rieffel, 2003.

7 Data for debt relief are from DAC (OECD-IDS) and for debt-to-GNI ratio from GDF.

8 Depetris Chauvin and Kraay (2005) tested the relationship between debt relief, growth and the composition of public expenditure. They found a positive, but not statistically significant, correlation between debt relief and GDP growth, and a positive, statistically significant, but not very robust, correlation between debt relief and government spending on health and education.

9 The modalities of eligibility and delivery of debt relief under the MDRI vary among the multilateral institutions. Each institution is separately responsible for deciding the implementation and coverage of the debt relief. While the majority of HIPCs are fully covered by the participation of the African Development Bank (AfDB) and IDB, Afghanistan, Kyrgyzstan and Nepal are not, because the Asian Development Bank (ADB) does not participate in the MDRI.

10 The frameworks would provide an extremely early warning, as some debt sustainability analyses are based on 20-year projections.

11 A minor difference has to do with the stress-testing exercises. Stress-testing is more important in the framework for middle-income countries for at least two reasons. The first relates to data availability, as some low-income countries lack sufficient data. The second has to do with the fact that middle-income countries have a more complex debt structure and are more susceptible to large shocks to their financing costs.

12 Countries are classified as low risk if all debt indicators are below the debt burden threshold and will remain below this threshold even if these countries suffer a relatively large negative shock. Countries are classified as moderate risk if their debt indicators are below the debt burden threshold but they risk breaching the threshold in case of a negative shock. Countries are classified as high risk if the baseline projections indicate that the countries will breach the threshold. Countries are classified in debt distress if their debt ratios are in breach of the thresholds (for more details, see World Bank, 2006b).

13 While not receiving grants, low-risk countries benefit from the concessional element that is part of all IDA loans.

14 It is sometimes argued that there is no transfer problem associated with the presence of external private debt, and that the only problem comes from external public debt. This view is often referred to as the "Lawson doctrine", following a 1988 speech of the then British Chancellor of the Exchequer, Nigel Lawson, who, while commenting on the current-account deficit of the United Kingdom, stated that the position of his country was strong because the current-account deficit was driven by private sector and not public sector borrowing. The Asian crisis, which occurred in a context of low public debt and deficits and was driven by private borrowing, discredited the Lawson doctrine. Indeed, even the United Kingdom entered into a deep recession soon after Mr. Lawson delivered his famous speech.

15 In theory, this is also true when external debt is denominated in a country's own currency, but countries that can issue the currency in which their debt is denominated have the option to debase their debt by printing more money.

16 As a counterpart to the swing of the debtor country's current-account balance into surplus, creditors need to accept a worsening of their current-account balance, and debt sustainability exercises also need to take into account a potential unwillingness of creditors to accept this.

17 In the United States, the 2004 Economic Report of the President emphasized this point by stating: "The desirability of positive net capital flows and a current account deficit depend on what the capital inflows are used for. Household borrowing – an excess of household spending or investment over saving – provides a useful analogy. Household debt could reflect borrowing to finance an extravagant vacation, a mortgage to buy a home, or a loan to finance education. Without knowing its purpose, the appropriateness of the borrowing cannot be judged. Similarly, for countries borrowing from abroad can be productive or unproductive" (United States, 2004: 256).

18 Although the value of assets for which there is no secondary market can only be estimated by making several assumptions, in some countries figures for both public debt and public assets are published. One example is New Zealand, where figures for all government-owned financial and physical assets, including roads, bridges and schools, are reported. This approach is likely to be problematic for assessing external sustainability in developing countries, because assets such as public libraries, hospitals and schools have limited liquidity and are unlikely to generate the foreign currency necessary to repay external debt.

19 Some tests developed for the United States use more than 100 years of data (Hamilton and Flavin, 1986). See Izquierdo and Panizza (2006) for a recent survey.

20 The primary budget balance is the budget balance net of interest payments on the public debt.

21 Governors representing 11 borrowing members of the IDB acknowledged this problem, and in 2004 they signed an open letter, which became known as Carta de Lima, asking for the exclusion of investment spending from fiscal targets (see http://www.iadb.org/exr/am/2004/carta_lima.pdf; an English translation of relevant sections of the letter is available at: http://www.iadb.org/exr/am/2004/index.cfm?op=press&pg=15).

22 Buiter (1985) suggests such an indicator of sustainability, defined as:

$$SUS = ps - (g - r)\frac{W}{GDP},$$

where W is public sector net worth, ps is the primary surplus, r is the real interest rate, and g is the economy's growth rate.

23 Besides local currency bonds, developing countries could issue other types of financial instruments with

an embedded insurance component. Such instruments include instruments with payments indexed to commodity prices, terms of trade, or the GNI growth rate. Alternatively, countries could obtain contingent coverage through the use of derivative contracts. However, many futures and options markets lack depth and liquidity, and therefore offer only limited scope for insurance (IDB, 2006). Some countries are starting to issue catastrophe (CAT) bonds. For a discussion of the benefits of country catastrophe insurance, see Borensztein, Cavallo and Valenzuela, 2007.

24   A sovereign default is usually defined as a situation in which a sovereign debtor fails to fully repay its debt obligations and reschedules those obligations on terms that are less favourable (with respect to the original debt contract) for the creditors (see Panizza, Sturzenegger and Zettlemeyer, 2008, for a survey of the law and economics of sovereign debt and default).

25   A memo prepared jointly by the central banks of the United Kingdom and of Canada states that: "The problem historically has not been that countries have been too eager to renege on their financial obligations, but often too reluctant" (Blustein, 2005: 102).

26   In some cases the opposite is true, and the decision to default is welcomed by the public. But this usually happens when the decision to default is made by a new government.

27   A policy that delays a necessary default might be costly because it may lead to restrictive fiscal and monetary policies and, by prolonging the climate of uncertainty, may have negative effects on investment decisions.

28   Similar to *TDR 2001*, Pettifor (2002) and Raffer (1990) have suggested adapting for the international debt market some features of chapter 9 of the United States bankruptcy code, which deals with municipal bankruptcies. According to their proposal, the adapted chapter 9 procedures would be chaired by neutral, ad hoc entities established by creditors and the debtor, as is traditional practice in international law.

29   For a more detailed discussion of the SDRM proposal, see Akyüz, 2003: 6–7.

30   For SDRM to become operational, the IMF's Articles of Agreement would have had to be amended, which would have required the support of three fifths of the members of the Fund and 85 per cent of the total votes. The amendment of the Articles of Agreement is de facto impossible without the support of the United States, which holds 17.1 per cent of the votes.

31   A CAC allows a supermajority of bondholders (usually between 75 and 90 per cent) to agree on a debt restructuring that is legally binding for all holders of the bond, including those who vote against the restructuring. CACs are regularly attached to bonds issued under British and Japanese laws. On the other hand, until 2003, bonds issued under New York law did not have CACs attached to them, making the restructuring of such bonds difficult, as it required the acceptance of the restructuring terms by all bondholders.

32   Keynote speech by the President of the European Central Bank, J.C. Trichet at the 25th Anniversary IIF Annual Membership Meeting, Washington DC, 20 October 2007, and IMF (2002b).

33   Since money is fungible, this does not need to be applied literally. However, whenever a country borrows abroad it needs to ensure that the economy can generate the external resources necessary to service the debt.

34   Data problems could be solved if there were political will to do so. In fact, lack of data on domestic debt is a fairly recent phenomenon. Reinhart and Rogoff (2008b) report that the League of Nations used to collect detailed data on the amount and composition of domestic public debt for both developed and developing economies, and that the United Nations continued to collect and publish such data until the early 1980s. It is not clear why it no longer does so.

35   Eichengreen and Hausmann (2005) have proposed that the multilateral development banks should issue bonds denominated in an index that pools currency risk from a diversified group of emerging economies.

36   For discussions of GNI-Indexed Bonds, see Borensztein and Mauro (2004) and Griffith-Jones and Sharma (2006).

37   The international community should also start thinking seriously about odious and illegitimate debt issues. These are controversial concepts on which there is a multiplicity of views. Some argue that odiousness should be defined *ex-post* (EURODAD, 2007), while others argue that declaring odiousness *ex-post* may generate some problems that could be solved by declaring odiousness *ex-ante* (Jayachandran and Kremer, 2006). Still others claim that, given the current state of knowledge, having an explicit odious debt policy, either *ex-post* or *ex-ante*, may do more harm than good (Rajan, 2004).

References

Akyüz Y (2003). New sovereign debt restructuring mechanisms: Challenges and opportunities, *WIDER Angle, 1*.

Arslanalp S and Henry PB (2004). Helping the poor to help themselves: Debt relief or aid. In: Jochnick C and Preston F, eds. *Sovereign Debt at the Cross*roads: Challenges and Proposals for Resolving the Third World Debt Crisis. Oxford, Oxford University Press.

Arslanalp S and Henry PB (2006). Debt relief. *Journal of Economic Perspectives*, 20(1): 207–220.

Birdsall N, Claessens S and Diwan I (2001). Will HIPC matter? The debt game and donor behavior in Africa (mimeo). Washington, DC, Carnegie Endowment for International Peace.

Birdsall N and Deese B (2004). Beyond HIPC: Secure sustainable debt relief for poor countries. Working Paper No. 46, Center for Global Development, Washington, DC.

Blustein P (2005). *And the Money Kept Rolling In (and Out): The World Bank, Wall Street, the IMF and the Bankrupting of Argentina*. New York, Public Affairs.

Borensztein E, Cavallo E and Valenzuela P (2007). Debt sustainability under catastrophic risk: the case of government budget insurance. IDB Research Department Working Paper 607. Washington, DC, Inter-American Development Bank.

Borensztein E and Mauro P (2004). The Case for GDP-indexed bonds. *Economic Policy*, 38: 165–216.

Borensztein E and Panizza U (2008). The costs of default (unpublished). Washington, DC, International Monetary Fund.

Borensztein E et al. (2004). Sovereign Debt Structure for Crisis Prevention. IMF Occasional Paper No. 237. Washington, DC, International Monetary Fund.

Buiter W (1985). Guide to public sector debt and deficits. *Economic Policy: A European Forum*, 1: 949–963.

Caballero RJ and Cowan K (2008). Financial integration without the volatility. MIT Department of Economics Working Paper No. 08-04. Cambridge, MA, Massachusetts Institute of Technology.

Campos C, Jaimovich D and Panizza U (2006). The unexplained part of public debt. *Emerging Markets Review*, 7(3): 228–243.

Cowan K et al. (2006). Sovereign debt in the Americas: new data and stylized facts. IDB Research Department Working Paper 57. Washington, DC, Inter-American Development Bank.

Depetris Chauvin N and Kraay A (2005). What has 100 billion dollar worth of debt relief done for low-income countries? (Mimeo). Washington, DC, Inter-American Development Bank.

Easterly W (2002). How did heavily indebted poor countries become heavily indebted? Reviewing two decades of debt relief. *World Development*, 30(10): 1677–1696.

Eichengreen B and Hausmann R (2005). The road to redemption. In: Eichengreen B and Hausmann R, eds. *Other People's Money: Debt Denomination and Financial Instability in Emerging-Market Economies*. Chicago, University of Chicago Press: 267–288.

Eichengreen B, Hausmann R and Panizza U (2005). The pain of original sin. In: Eichengreen B and Hausmann R, eds. *Other People's Money: Debt Denomination and Financial Instability in Emerging-Market Economies*. Chicago, University of Chicago Press: 13–47.

EURODAD (2007). Skeletons in the cupboard: Illegitimate debt claims of the G7; at: http://www.eurodad.org/uploadedFiles/Whats_New/Reports/Eurodad%20SkeletonsCupboardG7Report.pdf.

Griffith-Jones S and Sharma K (2006). GDP-indexed bonds: Making it happen. Working Paper 21, United Nations, Department of Economics and Social Affairs, New York.

Grossman HI and Van Huyck JB (1988). Sovereign debt as a contingent claim: Excusable default, repudiation and reputation. *American Economic Review*, 78(5): 1088–1097.

Hamilton J and Flavin M (1986). On the limitations of government borrowing: A framework for empirical testing. *American Economic Review*, 76: 809–819.

Hepp R (2005). Can debt relief buy growth? (Mimeo). University of California, Davis.

IDB (2006). *Living with Debt.* Cambridge, MA, Harvard University Press.

IMF (2002a). Assessing sustainability. Policy Paper prepared by the Policy Review and Development Department. Washington, DC, International Monetary Fund, 28 May.

IMF (2002b). Collective action clauses in sovereign bond contracts: Encouraging greater use. Washington, DC.

IMF (2003). Sustainability assessments: Review of application and methodological refinements. Policy paper prepared by the Policy Review and Development Department, 10 June. Washington, DC, International Monetary Fund.

IMF (2007). Heavily Indebted Poor Countries (HIPC) Initiative and Multilateral Debt Relief Initiative (MDRI): Status of implementation assembled by the staff of the IMF and IDA. Washington, DC, September; available at: http://siteresources.worldbank.org/INTDEBTDEPT/ProgressReports/21656521/HIPCProgressReport20070927.pdf

IMF (2008). *World Economic Outlook.* Washington, DC, International Monetary Fund, April.

Izquierdo A and Panizza U (2006). Fiscal sustainability: Issues for emerging market countries. In: Galal A and Ul Haque N, eds. *Fiscal Sustainability in Emerging Markets: International Experience and Implications for Egypt.* Cairo, American University in Cairo Press: 67–104.

Jaimovich D and Panizza U (forthcoming). Public debt around the world. *Applied Economics Letters.*

Jayachandran S and Kremer M (2006). Odious debt. *American Economic Review*, 96(1): 82–92.

Jeanne O and Guscina A (2006). Government debt in emerging market countries: A new data set. IMF Working Paper No. 06/98. Washington, DC, International Monetary Fund.

Keynes JM (1929). The German transfer problem; The reparation problem: A discussion; II. A rejoinder: Views on the transfer problem. III. A reply. *Economic Journal,* 39, March: 1–7; June: 172–178; September: 404–408.

Krueger A (2001). International financial architecture for 2002: A new approach to sovereign debt restructuring. Address given at the National Economists Club Annual Member's Dinner, American Enterprise Institute, Washington, DC, 26 November.

Levy Yeyati E and Panizza U (2005). The elusive costs of sovereign defaults. Washington, DC, Inter-American Development Bank.

Manasse P, Roubini N and Schimmelpfennig A (2003). Predicting sovereign debt crises. IMF Working Paper 03/221. Washington, DC, International Monetary Fund.

Ndikumana L (2004). Additionality of debt relief and debt forgiveness and implications for future volumes of official assistance. *International Review of Economics & Finance*, 13(3): 325–340.

Panizza U (2008a). Domestic and external public debt in developing countries. UNCTAD Discussion Paper No. 188. Geneva, UNCTAD.

Panizza U (2008b). The external debt contentious six years after the Monterrey Consensus. Paper presented at the review session on Chapter V (External debt) of the Preparatory Process on the Follow-up International Conference on Financing for Development to Review the Implementation of the Monterrey Consensus, New York, United Nations, 11 March.

Panizza U, Sturzenegger F and Zettelmeyer J (2008). The law and economics of sovereign debt and default (unpublished). Washington, DC, IMF.

Pettifor A (2002). Resolving international debt crises: The jubilee framework for international insolvency. NEF report. January.

Powell R (2003). Debt relief, additionality and aid allocation in low-income countries. IMF Working Paper No. 03/175. Washington, DC, International Monetary Fund.

Raffer K (1990). Applying Chapter 9 Insolvency to International Debts: An Economically Efficient Solution with a Human Face. World Development 18(2): 30.

Rajan R (2004). Odious or just malodorous? *Finance and Development*, December.

Reinhart C and Rogoff K (2008a). This time is different: a panoramic view of eight centuries of financial crises. NBER Working Paper No. 13882. Cambridge, MA, National Bureau of Economic Research.

Reinhart C and Rogoff K (2008b). The forgotten history of domestic debt. NBER Working Paper No. 13946. Cambridge, MA, National Bureau of Economic Research.

Rieffel L (2003). Restructuring sovereign debt: the case for ad hoc machinery. Washington, DC, Brookings Institution Press.

Rodrik D (2008). Second best institutions (mimeo). Cambridge, MA, Harvard University.

Sachs J (2005). *The End of Poverty: Economic Possibilities for Our Time.* New York, The Penguin Press.

Sturzenegger F (2004). Toolkit for the analysis of debt problems. Journal of Restructuring Finance, 1(1): 201–203.

Sturzenegger F and Zettelmeyer J (2007). *Debt Defaults and Lessons from a Decade of Crises.* Cambridge, MA, MIT Press.

UNCTAD (various issues). *Trade and Development Report.* United Nations publications, New York and Geneva.

United Nations (2002). Report of the International Conference on Financing for Development. Monterrey, Mexico, 18–22 March.

United Nations (2005). A practical plan to achieve the Millennium Development Goals. New York.

United States (2004). Economic Report of the President to the 108th Congress, 2nd Session, H. Doc. 108-145.

Washington, DC: United States Government Printing Office; available at: http://www.gpoaccess.gov/usbudget/fy05/pdf/2004_erp.pdf.

World Bank (2006a). Debt relief for the poorest. Washington, DC, Independent Evaluation Group, World Bank.

World Bank (2006b). How to do a debt sustainability analysis for low-income countries; available at: http://siteresources.worldbank.org/INTDEBTDEPT/Resources/DSAGUIDE_EXT200610.pdf.

Wyplosz C (2007). Debt sustainability assessment: The IMF approach and alternatives. HEI Working Paper No: 03/2007. Geneva, Institut de Hautes Etudes Internationales et du Développement.

**UNITED NATIONS CONFERENCE
ON TRADE AND DEVELOPMENT**

Palais des Nations
CH-1211 GENEVA 10
Switzerland
(www.unctad.org)

Selected UNCTAD Publications

Trade and Development Report, 2007

United Nations publication, sales no. E.07.II.D.11
ISBN 978-92-1-112721-8

Chapter   I   Current Issues in the World Economy
                Statistical annex to chapter I

Chapter   II   Globalization, Regionalization and the Development Challenge

Chapter III The "New Regionalism" and North-South Trade Agreements

Chapter IV Regional Cooperation and Trade Integration Among Developing Countries

Chapter V   Regional Financial and Monetary Cooperation
                Annex 1   The Southern African Development Community
                Annex 2   The Gulf Cooperation Council

Chapter VI Regional Cooperation in Trade Logistics, Energy and Industrial Policy

Trade and Development Report, 2006

United Nations publication, sales no. E.06.II.D.6
ISBN 92-1-112698-3

Chapter I   Global Imbalances as a Systemic Problem
              Annex 1: Commodity Prices and Terms of Trade
              Annex 2: The Theoretical Background to the Saving/Investment Debate

Chapter II   Evolving Development Strategies – Beyond the Monterrey Consensus

Chapter III   Changes and Trends in the External Environment for Development
              Annex tables to chapter III

Chapter IV   Macroeconomic Policy under Globalization

Chapter V   National Policies in Support of Productive Dynamism

Chapter VI   Institutional and Governance Arrangements Supportive of Economic Development

Trade and Development Report, 2005

United Nations publication, sales no. E.05.II.D.13

ISBN 92-1-112673-8

Trade and Development Report, 2004

United Nations publication, sales no. E.04.II.D.29

ISBN 92-1-112635-5

Trade and Development Report, 2003

United Nations publication, sales no. E.03.II.D.7

ISBN 92-1-112579-0

Trade and Development Report, 2002
United Nations publication, sales no. E.02.II.D.2
ISBN 92-1-112549-9

Trade and Development Report, 2001
United Nations publication, sales no. E.01.II.D.10
ISBN 92-1-112520-0

* * * * * *

These publications may be obtained from bookstores and distributors throughout the world. Consult your bookstore or write to United Nations Publications/Sales and Marketing Section, Bureau E-4, Palais des Nations, CH-1211 Geneva 10, Switzerland (Fax: +41-22-917.0027; Tel.: +41-22-917-2614/2615/2600; E-mail: unpubli@unog.ch; Internet: https://unp.un.org); or United Nations Publications, Two UN Plaza, Room DC2-853, New York, NY 10017, USA (Tel.: +1-212-963.8302 or +1-800-253.9646; Fax: +1-212-963.3489; E-mail: publications@un.org).

G-24 Discussion Paper Series

Research papers for the Intergovernmental Group of Twenty-Four
on International Monetary Affairs and Development

No. 48	November 2007	Sam LAIRD	Aid for Trade: Cool Aid or Kool-Aid?
No. 47	October 2007	Jan KREGEL	IMF Contingency Financing for Middle-income Countries with Access to Private Capital Markets: An Assessment of the Proposal to Create a Reserve Augmentation Line
No. 46	September 2007	José María FANELLI	Regional Arrangements to Support Growth and Macro-Policy Coordination in MERCOSUR
No. 45	April 2007	Sheila PAGE	The Potential Impact of the Aid for Trade Initiative
No. 44	March 2007	Injoo SOHN	East Asia's Counterweight Strategy: Asian Financial Cooperation and Evolving International Monetary Order
No. 43	February 2007	Devesh KAPUR and Richard WEBB	Beyond the IMF
No. 42	November 2006	Mushtaq H. KHAN	Governance and Anti-Corruption Reforms in Developing Countries: Policies, Evidence and Ways Forward
No. 41	October 2006	Fernando LORENZO and Nelson NOYA	IMF Policies for Financial Crises Prevention in Emerging Markets
No. 40	May 2006	Lucio SIMPSON	The Role of the IMF in Debt Restructurings: Lending Into Arrears, Moral Hazard and Sustainability Concerns
No. 39	February 2006	Ricardo GOTTSCHALK and Daniela PRATES	East Asia's Growing Demand for Primary Commodities – Macroeconomic Challenges for Latin America
No. 38	November 2005	Yilmaz AKYÜZ	Reforming the IMF: Back to the Drawing Board
No. 37	April 2005	Colin I. BRADFORD, Jr.	Prioritizing Economic Growth: Enhancing Macroeconomic Policy Choice
No. 36	March 2005	JOMO K.S.	Malaysia's September 1998 Controls: Background, Context, Impacts, Comparisons, Implications, Lessons
No. 35	January 2005	Omotunde E.G. JOHNSON	Country Ownership of Reform Programmes and the Implications for Conditionality
No. 34	January 2005	Randall DODD and Shari SPIEGEL	Up From Sin: A Portfolio Approach to Financial Salvation
No. 33	November 2004	Ilene GRABEL	Trip Wires and Speed Bumps: Managing Financial Risks and Reducing the Potential for Financial Crises in Developing Economies
No. 32	October 2004	Jan KREGEL	External Financing for Development and International Financial Instability
No. 31	October 2004	Tim KESSLER and Nancy ALEXANDER	Assessing the Risks in the Private Provision of Essential Services
No. 30	June 2004	Andrew CORNFORD	Enron and Internationally Agreed Principles for Corporate Governance and the Financial Sector
No. 29	April 2004	Devesh KAPUR	Remittances: The New Development Mantra?
No. 28	April 2004	Sanjaya LALL	Reinventing Industrial Strategy: The Role of Government Policy in Building Industrial Competitiveness

G-24 Discussion Paper Series
Research papers for the Intergovernmental Group of Twenty-Four
on International Monetary Affairs and Development

No. 27	March 2004	Gerald EPSTEIN, Ilene GRABEL and JOMO, K.S.	Capital Management Techniques in Developing Countries: An Assessment of Experiences from the 1990s and Lessons for the Future
No. 26	March 2004	Claudio M. LOSER	External Debt Sustainability: Guidelines for Low- and Middle-income Countries
No. 25	January 2004	Irfan ul HAQUE	Commodities under Neoliberalism: The Case of Cocoa
No. 24	December 2003	Aziz Ali MOHAMMED	Burden Sharing at the IMF
No. 23	November 2003	Mari PANGESTU	The Indonesian Bank Crisis and Restructuring: Lessons and Implications for other Developing Countries
No. 22	August 2003	Ariel BUIRA	An Analysis of IMF Conditionality
No. 21	April 2003	Jim LEVINSOHN	The World Bank's Poverty Reduction Strategy Paper Approach: Good Marketing or Good Policy?
No. 20	February 2003	Devesh KAPUR	Do As I Say Not As I Do: A Critique of G-7 Proposals on Reforming the Multilateral Development Banks
No. 19	December 2002	Ravi KANBUR	International Financial Institutions and International Public Goods: Operational Implications for the World Bank
No. 18	September 2002	Ajit SINGH	Competition and Competition Policy in Emerging Markets: International and Developmental Dimensions
No. 17	April 2002	F. LÓPEZ-DE-SILANES	The Politics of Legal Reform
No. 16	January 2002	Gerardo ESQUIVEL and Felipe LARRAÍN B.	The Impact of G-3 Exchange Rate Volatility on Developing Countries
No. 15	December 2001	Peter EVANS and Martha FINNEMORE	Organizational Reform and the Expansion of the South's Voice at the Fund
No. 14	September 2001	Charles WYPLOSZ	How Risky is Financial Liberalization in the Developing Countries?
No. 13	July 2001	José Antonio OCAMPO	Recasting the International Financial Agenda
No. 12	July 2001	Yung Chul PARK and Yunjong WANG	Reform of the International Financial System and Institutions in Light of the Asian Financial Crisis
No. 11	April 2001	Aziz Ali MOHAMMED	The Future Role of the International Monetary Fund
No. 10	March 2001	JOMO K.S.	Growth After the Asian Crisis: What Remains of the East Asian Model?
No. 9	February 2001	Gordon H. HANSON	Should Countries Promote Foreign Direct Investment?
No. 8	January 2001	Ilan GOLDFAJN and Gino OLIVARES	Can Flexible Exchange Rates Still "Work" in Financially Open Economies?

* * * * * *

G-24 Discussion Paper Series are available on the website at: www.unctad.org. Copies of *G-24 Discussion Paper Series* may be obtained from the Publications Assistant, Macroeconomic and Development Policies Branch, Division on Globalization and Development Strategies, United Nations Conference on Trade and Development (UNCTAD), Palais des Nations, CH-1211 Geneva 10, Switzerland; Fax (+41-22) 917.0274.

UNCTAD Discussion Papers

No. 188	March 2008	Ugo PANIZZA	Domestic and external public debt in developing countries
No. 187	Feb. 2008	Michael GEIGER	Instruments of monetary policy in China and their effectiveness: 1994–2006
No. 186	Jan. 2008	Marwan ELKHOURY	Credit rating agencies and their potential impact on developing countries
No. 185	July 2007	Robert HOWSE	The concept of odious debt in public international law
No. 184	May 2007	André NASSIF	National innovation system and macroeconomic policies: Brazil and India in comparative perspective
No. 183	April 2007	Irfan ul HAQUE	Rethinking industrial policy
No. 182	Oct. 2006	Robert ROWTHORN	The renaissance of China and India: implications for the advanced economies
No. 181	Oct. 2005	Michael SAKBANI	A re-examination of the architecture of the international economic system in a global setting: issues and proposals
No. 180	Oct. 2005	Jörg MAYER and Pilar FAJARNES	Tripling Africa's primary exports: What? How? Where?
No. 179	April 2005	S.M. SHAFAEDDIN	Trade liberalization and economic reform in developing countries: structural change or de-industrialization
No. 178	April 2005	Andrew CORNFORD	Basel II: the revised framework of June 2004
No. 177	April 2005	Benu SCHNEIDER	Do global standards and codes prevent financial crises? Some proposals on modifying the standards-based approach
No. 176	Dec. 2004	Jörg MAYER	Not totally naked: textiles and clothing trade in a quota free environment
No. 175	Aug. 2004	S.M. SHAFAEDDIN	Who is the master? Who is the servant? Market or Government?
No. 174	Aug. 2004	Jörg MAYER	Industrialization in developing countries: some evidence from a new economic geography perspective
No. 173	June 2004	Irfan ul HAQUE	Globalization, neoliberalism and labour
No. 172	June 2004	Andrew CORNFORD	The WTO negotiations on financial services: current issues and future directions
No. 171	May 2004	Andrew CORNFORD	Variable geometry for the WTO: concepts and precedents
No. 170	May 2004	Robert ROWTHORN and Ken COUTTS	De-industrialization and the balance of payments in advanced economies
No. 169	April 2004	Shigehisa KASAHARA	The flying geese paradigm: a critical study of its application to East Asian regional development
No. 168	Feb. 2004	Alberto GABRIELE	Policy alternatives in reforming power utilities in developing countries: a critical survey
No. 167	Jan. 2004	R. KOZUL-WRIGHT and P. RAYMENT	Globalization reloaded: an UNCTAD perspective

UNCTAD Discussion Papers

* * * * * *

UNCTAD Discussion Papers are available on the website at: www.unctad.org. Copies of *UNCTAD Discussion Papers* may be obtained from the Publications Assistant, Macroeconomic and Development Policies Branch, Division on Globalization and Development Strategies, United Nations Conference on Trade and Development (UNCTAD), Palais des Nations, CH-1211 Geneva 10, Switzerland; Fax (+41-22) 917.0274.

QUESTIONNAIRE

Trade and Development Report, 2008

In order to improve the quality and relevance of the Trade and Development Report, the UNCTAD secretariat would greatly appreciate your views on this publication. Please complete the following questionnaire and return it to:

Readership Survey
Division on Globalization and Development Strategies
UNCTAD
Palais des Nations, Room E.10009
CH-1211 Geneva 10, Switzerland
Fax: (+41) (0)22 917 0274
E-mail: tdr@unctad.org

Thank you very much for your kind cooperation.

1. What is your assessment of this publication?

	Excellent	*Good*	*Adequate*	*Poor*
Overall	☐	☐	☐	☐
Relevance of issues	☐	☐	☐	☐
Analytical quality	☐	☐	☐	☐
Policy conclusions	☐	☐	☐	☐
Presentation	☐	☐	☐	☐

2. What do you consider the strong points of this publication?

_____
_____
_____

3. What do you consider the weak points of this publication?

_____
_____
_____

4. For what main purposes do you use this publication?

Analysis and research	☐	Education and training	☐
Policy formulation and management	☐	Other (*specify*) _____	

5. Which of the following best describes your area of work?

Government	☐	Public enterprise	☐
Non-governmental organization	☐	Academic or research	☐
International organization	☐	Media	☐
Private enterprise institution	☐	Other (*specify*) _____	

6. Name and address of respondent (*optional*):

_____
_____
_____

7. Do you have any further comments?

_____
_____
_____